Creating
Investor Demand
for
Company Stock

Recent Titles from Quroum Books

Choosing Effective Development Programs: An Appraisal Guide for Human Resources and Training Managers
James Gardner

Investing in Japanese Real Estate
M. A. Hines

Planning, Implementing, and Evaluating Targeted Communication Programs: A Manual for Business Communicators
Gary W. Selnow and William D. Crano

The United States Trade Deficit of the 1980s: Origins, Meanings, and Policy Responses
Chris C. Carvounis

The Legal Handbook of Business Transactions: A Guide for Managers and Entrepreneurs
E. C. Lashbrooke, Jr., and Michael I. Swygert

Federal Statutes on Environmental Protection: Regulation in the Public Interest
Warren Freedman

The Marketer's Guide to Media Vehicles, Methods, and Options: A Sourcebook in Advertising and Promotion
Ann Grossman

Corporate Asset Management: A Guide for Financial and Accounting Professionals
Clark E. Chastain

The Control of Municipal Budgets: Toward the Effective Design of Tax and Expenditure Limitations
David Merriman

Business Strategy and Public Policy: Perspectives from Industry and Academia
Alfred A. Marcus, Allen M. Kaufman, and David R. Beam, editors

Professional Sports and Antitrust
Warren Freedman

Office Systems Integration: A Decision-Maker's Guide to Systems Planning and Implementation
Barbara S. Fischer

Entrepreneurial Science: New Links Between Corporations, Universities, and Government
Robert F. Johnston and Christopher G. Edwards

CREATING INVESTOR DEMAND FOR FOR COMPANY STOCK

A Guide for Financial Managers

RICHARD M. ALTMAN

QUORUM BOOKS
Westport, Connecticut • London

Library of Congress Cataloging-in-Publication Data

Altman, Richard M.
  Creating investor demand for company stock.

  Bibliography: p.
  Includes index.
  1. Stocks—Marketing. 2. Going public (Securities)
3. Corporations—Investor relations. I. Title.
HG4661.A57 1988   332.6'42   86-25566
ISBN 0-89930-173-8 (lib. bdg. : alk. paper)

British Library Cataloguing in Publication Data is available.

Library of Congress Catalog Card Number: 86-25566
ISBN: 0-89930-173-8

First published in 1988 by Quorum Books

Greenwood Press, Inc.
88 Post Road West, Westport, Connecticut 06881

Printed in the United States of America

The paper used in this book complies with the
Permanent Paper Standard issued by the National
Information Standards Organization (Z39.48-1984).

10 9 8 7 6 5 4 3

Copyright Acknowledgment

The author and publisher wish to acknowledge *The National Law Journal* for
granting permission to use extracts from James H. Fogelson, "Securities Laws
Retain Teeth Despite Recent Court Limitations," *The National Law Journal*
(February 22, 1982). Copyright © 1982, *The National Law Journal*, reprinted
with permission.

To GMA, who always helped.
To RCA, who always hoped.
To DAL, who always knew.
To SSA, in memory.

Victory Goes to Those Who Anticipate

Contents

Preface

The aftermarket. It conjures images of the afterlife. But it is really the beginning of "public" life for emerging companies. It is the world of public equity valuation in which managements' objective is to create economic value and to translate it into market value for shareholders.

Success in the aftermarket depends on lead investors and dominant sponsors. The first lead management to the second and the second lead management to popularity flow. Together, they lead to information and pricing efficiency and to fair market value of a company's equity securities. This demand-creating chain forms a company's critical connection to long-term investment capital at reasonable cost. It is through this link that managements finance future growth and create real economic value and wealth for shareholders.

Public companies aggressively compete with one another every trading day for Wall Street sponsorship. They battle to secure their fair share and more of investors' minds and money. Gaining that share heightens the likelihood that the future earning power of long-duration corporate assets may be priced fairly in the present.

But market sponsorship is an enormous obstacle for many emerging companies because size is the big advantage in capital markets. More than 26,000 U.S. public companies are available for investment. Only about 1,000 of them carry market capitalizations greater than $300 million. Emerging, small capitalization companies dominate the investment world in terms of numbers but large capitalization companies dominate it in terms of dollar value of equity investment.

Finance literature focuses on portfolio risk and expected returns. It concludes, in general, that competition for potential excess returns (above market returns) in the shares of "big cap" companies usually results in a pricing of their securities which is in line with their expected returns. It also demonstrates, but cannot fully explain, that over time risk-adjusted returns available in the shares of "small cap" companies usually exceed those available in big capitalization companies.

Why, then, don't sponsors rush to represent emerging companies and why don't investors rush to earn abnormal positive returns in their shares? Some do. Who are they? Where are they? Why do they? When do they? How do they? What can management do with them? How can management influence them? And ultimately, how can management use them to their and to shareholders' advantage? This book concerns what managements of emerging companies can do to identify these lead investors and dominant sponsors and to use them to create investor demand.

The challenge to achieve fair securities valuation is greater for the managements of emerging companies. More responsibilities are spread over less human and capital resources. Executives' familiarity with Wall Street is low, but Wall Street's demands upon them are high.

Creating Investor Demand for Company Stock responds to the competitive needs of emerging companies in today's capital markets. Its objective is to correct the following sort of management concern: "The 18 months or so after going public is a mushy and curiously unsatisfactory period for many chief executives. Between personnel and Wall Street problems compounded by new surprises, the entrepreneur may remember it as sort of a shapeless and spongy time of limited real accomplishment."[1]

Quite the contrary. Managements should remember that period of time and beyond in relation to Wall Street and to the equity valuation process as one of clarity and understanding. They should understand clearly and simply that when it comes to translating economic value created in capital and business strategies into market value and shareholders' realized returns on Wall Street, "the key to value is profitability. If you've got it, flaunt it. If you haven't got it, try to get it. If you can't get it, get out [of those capital and business strategies]."[2] Unrealized economic value is the key that starts the investor demand-creating engine. Stability of returns on equity is the lubrication that keeps it running smoothly for long periods.

After reading this book, executives will know how Wall Street works, who on Wall Street works for them, why they work for them, where on Wall Street they work and how to use Wall Street to their advantage. Use of this book will be their direct route to market sponsorship, information and pricing efficiency, liquidity and market value. The book could be subtitled, "The Financial Manager's Guide To Communicating Value To Wall Street."

The book is essentially divided into three parts. The first part deals with the equity valuation process: what investors value and how they value it. Chapter 1 defines the book's relevant terms, profiles equity ownership by stage of corporate lifecycle, and specifies the risks of weak investor demand. Chapter 2 considers the spectrum of valuation tools and measurements used in the equity valuation process, and chapter 3 builds market sponsorship into the going-public process.

The second part prepares management for sponsorship. It stresses the importance of shaping investors' perceptions of future cash flows and management decisions which affect those flows. Chapter 4 positions a company's equity product. Chapter 5 highlights what management must communicate when communicating value to Wall Street, and Chapter 6 spotlights the returns signals management sends to Wall Street.

The third part deals with market sponsorship. Chapter 7 highlights lead investors and tiers into which they fit. It discusses how to use them to get to dominant sponsors, the relationship between institutional ownership and expected returns and the barriers to institutional ownership caused by illiquidity. Chapter 8 highlights dominant sponsors and brackets into which they fit. It discusses how to use them to start a "popularity flow," the relationship between research coverage and expected returns, and the methodologies of securities analysts. Chapter 9 shows which sponsors influence which investors, how sponsorship changes with market value, and how ownership changes with sponsorship. Chapter 10 stresses the preservation of personal and corporate credibility.

Throughout the book I refer to the results of empirical studies of market efficiency. They highlight many of the book's central themes. Most important, they help management to anticipate capital markets reactions and the equity valuation process. They offer a glimpse of what executives can expect from investors, securities analysts, and money managers in terms of stock price reaction to their investment, financing, and operating decisions.

A long check in a university library of the journals mentioned in the bibliography will reveal a focus on core themes of concern to those who study the efficiency of capital markets around which a valued body of knowledge has developed. I support management goals and shareholder interests in this book and believe that both can best be served through a full understanding of how to use Wall Street. Ultimately, the translation of economic value created by managements into market value realized by shareholders breeds mutual prosperity.

Acknowledgments

My thanks to friends who inquired about my progress and who, in the course of conversation, challenged my perspectives. They helped to shape the content of the book. Any sins of omission or commission are mine alone. In particular I thank Howard L. Bilow, Frederic H. Clark, Louis M. Guenin, and Kevin J. Moynihan.

I appreciate the willingness of professionals at Technimetrics, Inc. and Business Research Corporation to share their time and database resources with me. In addition I thank Lynch, Jones & Ryan for providing access to its Institutional Brokers Estimate System (I/B/E/S) to highlight the information deficiency problem for emerging companies. Finally, I pay tribute to librarians everywhere. They saved me much time and effort in my research quest.

1

Share of Market, Share of Mind

One can create demand in two ways: superior performance (such as designer label fashions) or low price (such as airfares). Demand is driven either by product differentiation or cost. Each shapes a perception of short-term or long-term value, relative to alternatives. Success in creating demand depends upon spreading perception of that value. In consumer markets, the objective is to gain share of market. In capital markets, the objective is to gain share of mind.

This is a book about communicating value to Wall Street. It concerns the equity valuation process and how managements of public companies can affect the stock market's pricing mechanism. It is also a book about popularity, neglect, risk, and expected returns. The book concerns the managements of emerging companies and how they can use Wall Street's lead investors and dominant sponsors to their advantage in translating the economic value they create into market value their shareholders realize.

The book puts the equity valuation process into context and discusses how executives can influence the market's pricing of their companies' equity. In that sense, it focuses on market sponsorship for and pricing efficiency in the shares of emerging companies. It identifies Wall Street's players, prioritizes their importance, reveals their behavior, and shows managements how to use them to the economic benefit of their shareholders.

This book is about creating investor demand for the shares of emerging public companies. It is written from the perspective of the corporate financial manager and therefore concerns less what the investment community needs from emerging companies and more how managements can use Wall Street.

Managements of public corporations have two goals (see the second Treynor article in the bibliography). Maximizing the economic value of a company's

1

growth and growth opportunities is first. Maximizing shareholder wealth by translating that economic value into market value is second.

Achievement of the first goal depends upon management's investment, operating, and financing decisions. Investment decisions focus on the selection of capital strategies in which to invest harvest or sell in order to generate returns on investment of capital in excess of the costs of that capital. Financing decisions focus on supporting investment decisions with the lowest possible average cost of capital. And operating decisions focus on the selection of business strategies by which to compete in chosen markets at operating margins which generate profit in excess of the cost of capital.

Of the three, capital strategy is of initial greatest importance because it establishes minimum levels of returns required to create economic value. Of financing decisions, one adage states that bad financing will not kill a good investment but good financing cannot rescue a bad investment. And on an operating basis, a bad business strategy (operating profit below the cost of capital) can kill the economic value that can be created in a good capital strategy. But a good business strategy cannot rescue the economic value that will be destroyed in a bad capital strategy.

Achievement of the second goal depends upon management's ability to communicate the impact of its decisions on its company's future cash flows. It is also a function of management's ability to attract/develop what Professor Avner Arbel of Cornell University calls a "popularity flow" into its shares. That requires first, recognition and use of lead investors; second, identification and use of dominant sponsors; and third, that management think as buyers and owners of its shares. Executives must shape investors' perceptions of their company's growth/returns profile, growth/share relationships and competitive advantages in its product/markets. They must cultivate an understanding of their company's excess returns potential and returns stability relative to alternative investments of equal risk.

This book deals primarily with the second goal. The process of creating investor demand capitalizes on familiarity with the equity valuation process. It is a marketing function and an extension of a company's capital budgeting and strategic planning effort. But it goes beyond capital budgeting to capital gains. Managements are already responsible for creating economic value for shareholders. Now they can claim credit for translating that economic value into fair market value. Now they can effectively communicate value to Wall Street.

Customer demand for a company's products/services is often shaped by trends in social attitudes, demographics changes, new product introductions and government affairs. Consumer spending is also directly affected by trends in leading economic indicators. Shifts in consumption patterns, both positive and negative, give rise to growth opportunities or loss leaders.

Demand for company stock or lack thereof results from investors' perceptions of superior performance (earnings momentum) or low price (asset value relative to market value) arising from these shifts. They give rise to expectations of superior returns relative to alternative investments of equal risk. Creating investor demand aims to inform and to shape clear perception of a company's future growth (performance) or value (price) relative to alternatives. And it strives to spread that perception to those whose perceived influence sets share prices.

The management of every public company communicates with Wall Street whether it intends to or not. Some report only past performance, others issue only present results. Still others send signals about future returns potential and there are those that send no signals. But the market cares most about the future. It cares about the past as a benchmark against which to judge the present and to forecast the future. The market cares about the present insofar as it sends information signals about future cash flows and investors' expectations. But it values cash-generating ability in the future and translates it to share prices in the present. Current prices are assigned to securities in line with levels of expected future returns.

In this regard, managements of public companies often cannot understand why investors capitalize their company's future earning power at different (lesser) rates than other companies, especially peer competitors. They cannot comprehend why their company's stock sells at different (lower) multiples of price-to-earnings or market-to-book than the shares of other companies with similar fundamentals, or than industry or market multiples. The valuation differential is a major source of consternation.

The February 1984 *Business Week*/Louis Harris & Associates poll reported that top executives at more than 600 public companies believed that the financial marketplace seriously undervalued their companies. Sixty percent thought that the economic value of their company exceeded its market value. About 30 percent were satisfied with the market's valuation. Only 2 percent thought the market overvalued their company. Although the overall market was in the midst of a protracted bull phase which began in August 1982, the poll was conducted in the midst of an intermediate market decline. It began on October 10, 1983 (172.65 on the S & P 500) and bottomed on July 24, 1984 (147.82 on the S & P 500), a 16.8 percent market decline and a two-year low.

Senior executives of seasoned corporations know that their companies' stock price reflects investors' perceptions of expected returns on investment in their company's shares relative to alternative investments of equal risk. But they also know that investors' perceptions of the future can be unclear at times. That can lead to inefficient pricing of their company's common stock and unfair valuation of their company's equity. Market value can become detached from economic reality.

Management dissatisfaction with the market's pricing mechanism suggests one of two conclusions. Either the market does not know how much economic value management can potentially create (management may, in fact, possess information about the growth in the present value of future operating cash flows that the market does not have), or management does not understand what the market values or how to influence the market's pricing of what it values.

Executives usually react to this perceived unfairness in one of two ways: opportunism or frustration. Which reaction they show depends upon how well they understand the equity valuation process: how the market perceives and values their company and what their company's stock price implies about investors' expectations for the company's future returns. Opportunistic managements create value for their shareholders by correcting market misperceptions and mispricings. They shape rational expectations of their company's economic returns through lead investors and dominant sponsors. In the case of overvalued securities, they transfer value to shareholders by capitalizing on market mispricings. Frustrated managements chalk up market mispricings to investors' irrational behavior. They do nothing.

Hamish Maxwell, chairman and chief executive officer of the Philip Morris Companies, summarized the point about investors' perceptions and their impact on equity valuation. Management had completed an intense capital expenditure program to enhance the company's competitive position and future cash-generating ability. But the company's stock price implied that investors apparently did not clearly perceive the extent to which that incremental investment would contribute to incremental returns. Maxwell took action to correct an undervalued situation.

One objective was to raise the price of Philip Morris's stock, which he said did not reflect the company's earnings. "A significant factor in depressing the price," he said, "was perception by investors that the cigarette business, though highly profitable, did not have a bright future because of declining cigarette consumption in the United States."[1]

Maxwell's strategy to reshape investors' perceptions of the company's future growth and returns potential was to diversify through acquisition, rather than to buy back stock. Management tendered for and acquired the General Foods Corporation for about $5.8 billion cash.

The ability to create investor demand is a management opportunity. If accepted and achieved, efficient pricing and fair valuation satisfy a host of corporate needs from capital formation to employee morale. If foresaken, inefficient pricing and undervaluation highlight a host of corporate risks from the cost of future corporate growth, to potential vulnerability to takeover, to executives' job tenure.

Some managements ignore the opportunity. They merely satisfy their legal obligation to disclose (not inform). They prefer to exert no influence on the market's pricing mechanism and the equity valuation process. They believe that operating results should do the talking. Operating results do speak, but to the past, not to the future. Other managements try to "reach" the investment community. They try to guarantee pricing efficiency in their company's shares by sending company data to as many persons as possible as often as is necessary, usually a minimum of four times per year. They take a shotgun approach to a problem that requires a rifle.

Finally, some astute managements seize the marketing opportunity to systematically create investor demand for their company's shares. They visualize the equity valuation process. They talk to their stock and learn what price implies about future profit expectations. They understand how Wall Street values companies in their industry and perceives their company in particular. They can explain valuation differentials and steps required to correct them. They differentiate and position their company's equity product and think as buyers of stock. In the sole context of material public information, they shape perceptions of their company's future in buyers' language.

These managements recognize lead investors in their company's shares. They understand what attracts them and, through one-to-one relationships, they use them to get to potential dominant sponsors of their shares. They then use these sponsors to attract a flow of investment capital to their company's equity. The result is a carefully constructed valuation network through which they achieve information and pricing efficiency, liquidity and fair market value.

Every party benefits in the demand-creating process. Shareholders benefit because they build total return on their investment. Executives benefit because their net worth builds in the form of stock ownership and cash compensation. They build reputations as value-creators and attract new investment capital. Lead investors benefit because they generate portfolio total returns superior to that of preselected market indices. They build reputations for market timing and stock selection and attract new equity assets to manage. And dominant sponsors benefit because they generate fees and commissions for their firms and bonuses for themselves. They build reputations as stock-pickers and attract new sources of both fee and commission business.

Throughout this book, I refer to pricing efficiency. I define it in terms of expected returns. Theoretically, a company's yield plus dividend growth rate over a forecast period should equal its expected return at the end of that forecast period (discussed more in Chapter 2). In a perfect world in which earnings growth rates and dividend payout ratios are known with certainty, share price change over a forecast period would equal expected return over that period. The extent to which realized returns from holding a security over a forecast period vary from expected returns for the same period equals a security's risk.

Investment in inefficiently priced securities should enable an investor to earn positive abnormal returns in excess of market expected returns. If those excess returns persist, rational investors will compete for them (investor demand). They will bid up the price of a company's shares and eliminate the excess. Competition for returns results in pricing efficiency.

Market sponsorship and pricing efficiency are often real problems for emerging companies which are small in size (market value), often underresearched by analysts, and underowned by investing institutions. They suffer from neglect. Little information about their returns potential may be available. Their shareholder base may be narrow, their shares may be thinly (inactively) traded and volatile and the costs of sponsorship and ownership may be high.

The neglect problem, in and of itself, does not immediately mean that a company's securities are inefficiently priced or undervalued. Academic studies (discussed later), however, associate abnormal returns with neglect. The real problem for small capitalization companies is that neglect and pricing inefficiency may persist over time because managements of these companies may not know how to trigger the demand-creating process (discussed in Chapter 7).

Wall Street sponsorship is primarily an information processing function in the form of research coverage from brokerage firm securities analysts. It is an oligopoly, the focus of which is share volume potential in the trading of a company's shares. Research coverage (the flow of information) is concentrated in the hands of relatively few dominant sponsors and focused on the prospects of relatively few public companies (Chapter 8). And broad institutional ownership (the flow of investment funds) is concentrated in the shares of relatively few public companies (Chapter 7). Together they combine to skewer market sponsorship toward those companies which offer high commission-generating potential to analysts and low liquidity costs to institutional investors.

A 1980 "Capital Markets Survey" conducted by the American Stock Exchange and Drexel Burnham Lambert, Inc., made clear that managements were concerned about the potential impact of this oligopoly: low market sponsorship and high pricing inefficiency in their company's shares. More than 3,000 companies listed on the New York and American Stock Exchanges and the national list of the National Association of Securities Dealers were polled. About 56 percent of all chief financial officers (more than 60 percent from unlisted companies, 62 percent from mid-sized companies and more than 60 percent from small capitalization companies) were dissatisfied with the amount of brokerage firm research coverage provided to their companies.

There are lead investors, dominant sponsors and an equity valuation network for every public company. But all may lie dormant unless and until management uses them. Most executives of emerging companies do not know how to recognize and to use lead investors in their company's shares or how to identify and use dominant sponsors of their company's stock. As a result, they exert no influence on the market's pricing of their company's equity. Rather, many suffer from little research coverage, narrow ownership and low liquidity. The result is often reflected in inefficiently priced securities.

The managements of emerging public companies must use Wall Street to their competitive advantage. They must actively create investor demand, not just passively react to indications of investor interest. Executives must harness the power of lead investors and dominant sponsors in the equity valuation process. The benefits of translating economic value into market value accrue to both shareholders and executives.

I contend that a company's growth/returns profile has an important impact on market efficiency and market value. I claim that high growth/high returns companies attract the widest sponsorship, achieve the highest pricing efficiency and are usually able to raise the most capital at the least average cost to finance future investment opportunities. And I stress that stable returns on equity and predictable earnings growth have an important impact on market value and share ownership. Investing institutions "pay up" (earnings multiples in excess of earnings growth rates) for the shares of companies with low perceived earnings variance. And shareholders tend to be loyal long-term investors who support management rather than opportunistic short-term traders who capitalize on changes in price.

Creating investor demand for a company's shares is inextricably linked to capital budgeting and strategic planning. The first process identifies the risks and investment requirements of capital strategies that yield the highest returns on capital in excess of the costs of that capital. Those capital strategies create potential economic value. The second process identifies the competitive strengths and advantages of business strategies which yield the widest operating margins on sales in excess of the cost of capital. Those business strategies realize actual economic value.

The demand-creating process translates the results of capital budgeting and strategy analysis into real market value. The process is tied directly to marketing but differs markedly from creating consumer demand for a company's products or services. Creating investor demand seeks to increase unit price (stock price) independent of volume. Creating consumer demand strives to increase unit volume through price.

Market sponsorship and pricing efficiency are not just abstract concepts over which managements have no control, and investors' appreciation of the shares of certain companies is not just lucky or haphazard. Managements can create demand for their company's stock. Their words and actions send signals about, and shape investors' perceptions of, future cash flows. Executives' ability to communicate value to Wall Street determines the strength and clarity of those signals and the extent to which they have a desired impact on a company's market valuation.

Creating Investor Demand for Company Stock is intended for the financial managers of emerging public companies. It is written from their perspective, with an eye toward modern portfolio theory. Many corporate finance and "going public" seminars deal with what Wall Street wants and needs from corporate managers, but this book turns the tables. It deals with how corporate managers can use Wall Street to their own and to their shareholders' advantage. It makes Wall Street work for them.

EFFICIENT MARKET HYPOTHESIS

Scientists have studied the speed of light and the speed of sound. Modern portfolio theorists and academicians have researched the extent to which share prices reflect all publicly available information and the speed with which share prices adjust to the availability of new information.

The research resulted in a theory about share prices called the "efficient market hypothesis." The theory contends that a market is efficient when market participants agree completely on the significance of all available information to both current and future share prices. That agreement is reflected in rapid share price adjustment to that information. The theory assumes that information is released quickly and without cost to all participants, and it does not consider transactions costs. It has its critics as stock market performance anomalies have been uncovered. For example, persistence of excess returns has been associated with company size, degree of neglect, level of price/earnings ratios and time of year (seasonality).

Efficient market theory claims the market comprises two segments: an information market and a pricing mechanism. It distinguishes between information and data. The hypothesis argues that an information market may be inefficient both across stocks and over time. For example, it is reflected in superior risk-adjusted excess returns which have historically been available in the shares of small capitalization companies since 1926. It is also reflected in superior risk-adjusted excess returns which have historically been registered in the month of January in 21 of the last 23 years. Supporters of the theory argue that the fact that no one believes the market is efficient actually makes the market efficient.

Modern finance theorists define the information market as the abyss between those who release information and those who process information. It is that area through which information travels after it has been released but before it has been processed. Corporations are examples of information releasers. Investment information services, investment advisory services, brokerage firm securities analysts and the financial press are examples of information processors.

Academics define the market's pricing mechanism as the combination of the collective actions of every sort of information processor. From brokerage firms to investing institutions, it is they who interpret the impact of information on security returns. They also explain it in terms of the collective decisions of every manager of an actively managed diversified portfolio who acts on the information. Together, they compete aggressively for information which, on the margin, can improve total returns and eliminate excess returns. Ultimately, they set share prices in line with expected returns.

The theory also separates data from information. It states that data become information when, processed by the market's pricing mechanism, they affect share price. Data affect share price when they alter market-wide returns expectations. For a given level of risk, if the release of data leads investors in general to expect higher returns for one company (or group of companies) than for another, then the first's share price will rise. If, on the other hand, the release of data leads investors in general to expect lower returns for one company (or group of companies) than for another, then the first's share price will fall. Data remain only data if, after processing, they fail to affect expectations on a market-wide level. In that case data may affect share volume but not share price.

The efficient market hypothesis suggests that market efficiency occurs in strong, semi-strong, or weak forms. A strong form is idealistic but not necessarily realistic. It suggests that no market participant, inside or outside of a company, possesses any competitive information advantage. Share prices fully reflect all known information at all times.

Companies subject to merger terms or acquisition proposals are considered to operate in reasonably strong, efficient environments. They are closely scrutinized by information processors, money managers and arbitrageurs who compete intensely for and maintain a continuous flow of information. All developments are known by all competitors virtually as soon as they become available and are immediately reflected in share price.

Most large capitalization companies compete in a semi-strong form of efficient market. A competitive information advantage exists until all information becomes available. At that time, it is immediately impounded into share prices, thus eliminating the possibility of achieving any risk-adjusted excess returns by trading in those shares.

Small capitalization companies often compete in a weak form of efficient market. Their share prices tend to reflect only what is already known. Since little new information may be available, the predictive power of those share prices is essentially nonexistent.

Information availability is defined in various ways. Academicians use the period of a stock's exchange listing as one tool with which to build databases for empirical studies of the effect of differential information on security returns. Others use event studies to measure the magnitude of company announcements on the share prices of companies of differing market values. Others turn to the number of security returns observations which are available for a company. Still others use consensus estimates of earnings, the extent to which securities analysts agree or disagree about the future earnings prospects for a company.

Research coverage by brokerage firm securities analysts and share ownership by investing institutions are also often used as measures of information efficiency, or deficiency. In this regard, professors Avner Arbel and Steven Carvell of Cornell University studied 1986 percentage price changes for 2,000 companies listed on the New York and American Stock Exchanges and traded over-the-counter. They found an inverse relationship between research coverage and stock price performance, and institutional ownership and stock price performance. Neglected stocks outperformed popular stocks in both instances. For example, of companies with market capitalizations greater than $1 billion, they found that those followed by 10 analysts or less gained 34.8 percent in price in 1986, about double the increase for stocks followed by 10 analysts or more. And the 25 issues which gained 100 percent or more in market value in 1986 were followed by an average of only eight securities analysts, versus an average of 28 analysts for the companies in the Standard & Poor's 400-industrial stock index.[2] In addition, an average of only 14 investing institutions held positions in the 10 best stock price performers on the New York Stock Exchange, versus an average of 38 for the 10 worst performers. Neglect, more than popularity, seemed to offer opportunities for higher returns.

Avner Arbel offers a list of selected sources by which to identify companies that exist in a relatively weak form of efficient market (i.e., neglected).[3] First, he advises a check of the number of financial institutions that hold a company's shares and the number of shares they hold (source: Standard & Poor's *Stock Guide*, Moody's *Handbook of Common Stocks*, the *Value Line Investment Survey*). He found that a company whose shares are held by fewer than 10 financial institutions experienced market inefficiency and that the smaller the institutional holding, the greater the inefficiency (neglect). The trend in institutional holdings ("popularity flow") also indicates increases or decreases in relative efficiency (Chapter 7).

Second, the number of shares held by banks and mutual funds indicates relative efficiency (source: Standard & Poor's *Stock Guide* and Media General Financial Services's *Industriscope*, in hard copy and on-line). *Industriscope* allows easy comparisons of share holdings of companies within an industry because data is presented by industry subgroup.

Third, the number of major securities analysts who follow and publish earnings estimates on a company is a clear signal of relative efficiency and popularity (Chapter 8). There are three sources: Standard & Poor's *Earnings Forecaster* (published weekly on about 1600 companies), Lynch, Jones & Ryan's *Institutional Brokers Estimate System* (monthly summary on about 3000 companies), and Zacks Investment Research, *The Icarus Service* (on-line on about 1800 companies).

Arbel suggests that the smaller the number of forecasters listed, the more neglected the company. Failure to appear on the list means low levels of institutional interest. Since many emerging companies do not make any of these lists, by definition, they are neglected. Consequently perhaps, their shares may be inefficiently priced.

Fourth, the percentage of float (shares available for public trading) owned by banks or mutual funds rather than the absolute number of institutions implies a relative level of efficiency (source: William O'Neil & Co.'s *Daily Graphs* on about 200 banks). Fifth, abnormal trading volume implies institutional interest (same source). It may suggest improving market efficiency, if share price rises, or it may suggest looming inefficiency and neglect, if share price falls.

Sixth, media coverage of a company by major financial magazines is a signal of efficiency (source: *Daily Graphs*). Arbel suggests the less the coverage, the greater the neglect (inefficiency). Seventh, mention of a company either in announcements about shareholder or analyst meetings or in analyst reports or industry roundtables is a clue about visibility (source: *Wall Street Transcript*). Clearly, a lack of mention suggests a lack of interest.

Arbel advises that inefficiency (neglect) can be double-checked. An examination of several of the above-mentioned sources should confirm a company's status. And supplementary sources can also verify a company's relative level of popularity. For example, a company's investor relations officer should tell whether any securities analysts have written any research reports on the company in the recent past or whether any analysts or money managers have visited the company recently. No reports or no visits suggest low sponsorship and weak efficiency.

Professor Richard Brealey of London Business School offers six lessons of market efficiency.[4] First, capital markets have no memory. In other words, the past does not predict the future. Past share prices have no predictive ability concerning future share prices. Second, management should trust market prices. In an efficient market, share prices reflect their fair (true) value. Proving share price unfair is management's challenge.

Third, there are no financial illusions in an efficient market. In other words, investors focus on cash flows. They disregard those actions, such as stock splits, stock dividends and accounting changes which affect reported earnings but which have no effect on underlying cash flows.

Fourth, the do-it-yourself alternative suggests that investors will not pay managements to do for them that which they can do for themselves. In an efficient market, investors can regulate their risk exposure more cheaply and more easily than corporate financial managers. They can diversify or leverage their personal assets themselves. They will not pay managers to do it for them.

Fifth, in an efficient market, seen one stock, seen them all means that securities that offer similar expected returns for similar levels of perceived risk are reasonable substitutes for one another. But investors search for securities with superior risk-adjusted returns potential for given levels of risk. It is these for which substitutes are not easily available. And, sixth, reading the entrails means understanding the information signals about the future contained in leading economic indicators.

Over time, pricing inefficiency tends to reward patient investors. Those willing to assume more risk achieve higher returns. Academic research into the market anomalies mentioned earlier offers evidence. For example, small capitalization companies generate greater returns over time (12.1 percent between 1926 and 1981) than big capitalization companies (9.1 percent over the same period). Stocks with low price/earnings ratios tend to register larger risk-adjusted returns than stocks with high price/earnings ratios, and neglected companies deliver better returns than popular stocks.

Unfortunately, in the meantime, high inefficiency and low sponsorship may penalize corporate managements. Why? Because they keep stock prices low, jeopardize the affordability of investment opportunities which can create economic value, make equity financing of those opportunities difficult, and minimize shareholders' and executives' wealth.

PROFILES OF INVESTOR DEMAND

The profile of investor demand for a company's shares is a function of the growth/returns profile of the company. Companies move through the four stages of corporate growth and profitability: start-up (investment), growth (high growth/high returns), maturity (low growth/low returns) and aging (disinvestment). Investors move from venturesome (high price/earnings ratio, low yield, small capitalization companies) to aggressive, to defensive, to cautious (low price/earnings ratio, high yield, large capitalization companies).

William E. Fruhan, Jr., professor of business administration at the Harvard Business School, offers more perspective.[5] He studied the average rate of profitability and reinvestment (dollar annual growth in common stock equity divided by dollar annual profit after tax) of more than 1,400 U.S. industrial companies between 1966 and 1975. The study assumed a cost of equity capital of 20 percent expected to last for 10 years.

No start-up (pioneer) companies appear in Fruhan's study. These companies are high investment/high returns speculations. They are financed with venture capital and are cash consumers. They generate gradually increasing average returns on equity and reinvest at rates often 100 percent to 200 percent of their earnings. Their future is unpredictable. Their ability to develop a competitive advantage, to identify and penetrate a market, to develop, test and bring a product to market within a reasonable period and to establish market share, is highly uncertain.

EnMasse Computer (Acton, MA) is an example. After three rounds of financings and more than $18 million in venture capital, the three-year-old low-cost producer of fault-tolerant computers closed in late January 1987. The company's product development cycle was too long, its delivery to market was too late, its marketing strategy was unclear, its competition was too intense and its management was too unsettled (three presidents in three years).

Some start-ups are able to go public, especially in the Unlisted Securities Market in London. They have small market capitalizations. Their shares are relatively closely held. Buyers of their shares have long-term time horizons, high tolerance for risk and seek capital appreciation.

Companies with a competitive cost or pricing advantage usually emerge from the start-up stage. They are high reinvestment/high returns companies (reinvestment in working capital, fixed investment, distribution and marketing). In Fruhan's study, 1.2 percent of the 1,448 companies appeared to fit this category. These companies generated average returns on equity in excess of 25 percent. Of these, none reinvested more than 120 percent of earnings. About 0.1 percent reinvested between 80 and 119 percent of earnings and 0.2 percent between 60 and 79 percent. About 0.5 percent reinvested between 40 and 59 percent of earnings and traded at 460 percent of book value. About 0.3 percent reinvested between 20 and 39 percent of earnings and traded at 370 percent of book value, and about 0.1 percent of the companies reinvested 19 percent or less of earnings.

The biggest priority for these emerging growth companies is to increase market share. Their biggest challenge is to preserve profitability through strict internal controls. Transition from entrepreneurial to traditional management style is desirable. At this stage, these companies create enormous value and are classic growth investments. Their cash-generating ability and earnings power accelerate dramatically. Their share prices trade at very high percentages (multiples) of book value. Their price-to-earnings ratios expand quickly. Their equity expands rapidly. As their market value builds, ownership and research coverage expand, liquidity in their shares improves and volatility tends to decrease. Buyers of their shares are aggressive. They buy performance, not yield. They pick the stocks of these companies independent of prevailing market conditions.

Reebok International Limited (Avon, MA) is an example. The company (mentioned also in Chapter 2) designs and markets high quality athletic footwear. From 1982 to 1984, its return on equity averaged 142.83 while its operating margins virtually doubled from 1982 to 1985. In 1985, operating income and after-tax net income sextupled and its 1985 reinvestment rate was 192 percent (growth in common stock equity of $74.84 million divided by after-tax net income of $39 million). Its stock was offered in August 1985 at about 312 percent of book value. By March 31, 1986 it traded at 930 percent of book with a P/E of 16.

The only certainty about the high growth/high returns profile of these companies is that it will change. Growth will slow at some point in the future and returns will revert to mean industry levels. The question is how soon. As growth slows, management credibility hinges on its ability to preserve profitability and to identify new earnings opportunities.

In Fruhan's study, 6.6 percent of the 1,448 industrial companies seemed to fit this category. They earned average returns on equity between 18.0 and 24.9 percent. Of these, none reinvested more than 160 percent of earnings. About 0.5 percent reinvested between 120 and 159 percent of earnings and traded at 300 percent of book value. About 2.0 percent reinvested between 80 and 119 percent of earnings and traded at 210 percent of book value, 2.4 percent reinvested between 60 and 79 percent of earnings and traded at 190 percent of book value, and 1.2 percent reinvested between 40 and 59 percent and traded at 220 percent of book value. Finally, about 0.2 percent reinvested between 20 and 39 percent of earnings (price/book ratios were not meaningful), and 0.3 percent of the companies reinvested 19 percent or less of their earnings and traded at 140 percent of book value.

A total of 30.1 percent of the companies earned average returns on equity between 12.0 and 17.9 percent. Those that reinvested over 160 percent of earnings (0.4 percent) traded at 190 percent of book value, between 120 and 159 percent of earnings (2.8 percent) traded at 150 percent of book value, between 80 and 119 percent of earnings (10.6 percent) and between 60 and 79 percent of earnings (9.2 percent) traded at book value, between 40 and 59 percent of earnings (5.2 percent) traded at 110 percent of book value, between 20 and 39 percent of earnings (1.3 percent) traded at book value and 19 percent or less of earnings (0.5 percent) traded at 120 percent of book value. Research coverage of these companies usually remains broad. Institutional ownership of their shares usually remains high. Investors in these companies want growth and income, i.e., earnings and dividend growth.

Mature companies face different obstacles. They are high growth/low returns or low growth/low returns companies. In Fruhan's study, 32.7 percent of the 1,448 companies seemed to fit this category. They earned average rates of return on equity between 8.0 and 11.9 percent. Of the total, those that reinvested over 160 percent of earnings (0.9 percent) traded at 60 percent of book value. Those that reinvested between 120 and 159 percent of earnings (4.8 percent), between 80 and 119 percent of earnings (9.9 percent), between 60 and 79 percent of earnings (8.2 percent), between 40 and 59 percent of earnings (6.4) and between 20 and 39 percent of earnings (1.9 percent) traded at 70 percent of book value. Those which reinvested 19 percent or less of earnings (0.6 percent) traded at 40 percent of book value.

For companies in this stage, erosion of market share is expected. Minimizing investment and harvesting cash is strategic. Earnings retention rates usually outpace reinvestment requirements. Share prices trade at or below book value. Market capitalizations are usually large. Shares are widely held by investing institutions. Research coverage is broad. Liquidity is high and volatility is relatively low. Investors buy for preservation of capital, i.e., stability of share price and dividend income.

Companies in a period of aging usually face disinvestment. They may, however, expand their equity base through exchanges of stock in acquisitions perceived to offer new growth opportunities. They may reinvest to modernize, to improve cost structure and profitability. Or they may liquidate. In Fruhan's study 29.4 percent of 1,448 companies appeared to fit this category. They earned average rates of return on equity equal to or less than 7.9 percent. Of the total, those that reinvested over 160 percent of earnings (6.5 percent), between 120 and 159 percent of earnings (4.4 percent), between 80 and 119 percent of earnings (4.7 percent), between 60 and 79 percent of earnings (3.3 percent) and between 40 and 59 percent of earnings (3.1 percent) traded at 40 percent of book value. Those that reinvested between 20 and 39 percent of earnings (2.3 percent) traded at 30 percent of book value and those that reinvested 19 percent or less of earnings (5.1 percent) traded at 40 percent of book.

For companies in this stage, internal high growth/high returns investment opportunities are few or nonexistent. Returns on equity decrease. Payout ratios increase. Share prices trade at book value, at discounts to book value or at liquidation value per share. Institutional ownership erodes. Research coverage is adequate. Liquidity is high and volatility low. Passive investors buy for income (dividend potential). Aggressive investors buy on price, in anticipation of gains from organizational restructuring (asset sales, spin-offs, sell-offs, liquidating dividends, tax-free trusts or management shifts), or ownership restructuring (leveraged buyouts or cashouts or takeover attempts) or both.

RISKS OF WEAK INVESTOR DEMAND

Investor demand is inextricably connected to information availability. Given two companies with similar fundamentals and similar records of profitability, any difference in stock price and relative valuation (visible on a graph as in Chapter 4) will correlate directly with information quantity and quality. Both tend to lead to greater confidence with which investors are able to perceive and to predict future earning power. The consequences of information differentials are valuation differentials.

Simply put, weak investor demand and limited market sponsorship amount to neglect. They do the following:

1. Lower stock prices.
2. Raise earnings estimation risk and investors' expected returns.
3. Stifle investment decisons which involve exchanges of stock.
4. Toughen financing decisions by denying access to adequate equity capital at reasonable cost. They make capital formation more difficult and more dilutive.

5. Lessen the impact of strategy decisions on stock price.

6. Shorten senior executives' careers. Lower a company's ability to attract talented managers and to retain employees.

7. Lower executives' and employees' morale.

8. Prevent management from maximizing shareholders' and personal wealth. This attracts corporate raiders.

9. Erode shareholders' loyalty. This leads to shareholder resolutions.

10. Confuse and complicate efforts to translate economic value into market value.

Professor Arbel has shown[6] that information deficiency and neglect can be measured by number of shares and percent of outstanding equity held by institutions. He claims that this, more than company size or price/earnings ratios, generates higher returns to investors. Information efficiency and institutional popularity raise stock prices and lower returns.

Arbel has also found that there is a high correlation between company size and degree of neglect. Neglected companies tend to have lower price/earnings ratios than small capitalization companies. Consequently, neglected low P/E companies, as opposed to small low P/E companies, tend to generate higher returns. Arbel has also shown that the confidence with which consensus earnings estimates are forecasted decreases with neglect and that low levels of consensus generate higher returns in the form of capital gains versus dividends. These issues are discussed further at the start of both Chapters 7 and 8.

High capital costs directly impede the formulation of capital strategy and the execution of investment decisions. They raise asset managers' hurdle rates which are investors' minimum required returns on their equity capital. And they lower the number of investment opportunities or merger and acquisition candidates that can be considered viable in terms of their ability to generate returns in excess of the cost of capital.

A high cost of capital raises the discount rate used for capital budgeting purposes. It narrows, eliminates, or turns negative the capital spread between estimated returns on capital and costs of capital. It makes capital strategies less affordable. On a discounted cash flow basis, it lowers the cash premium over current share price a buyer can pay to a seller in any taxable stock-for-cash acquisition while still enabling the buyer to achieve minimum required returns.

Low stock prices also directly impede the execution of business strategy. Especially as it pertains to stock-for-stock deals (tax-free until stock is sold) in mergers and acquisitions, they increase the amount of stock that must be exchanged in any transaction. At a set price, more of a buyer's low-priced shares must be offered to satisfy the shareholders of an acquired company. Executives who believe their shares are undervalued will be reluctant to make acquisitions for stock. And an exchange ratio acceptable to a seller may be unacceptable to a buyer because it may jeopardize a buyer's target capital structure.

The combination of rising stock prices and the Tax Reform Act of 1986 has stirred renewed interest in stock-for-stock deals. For example, according to *Mergers and Acquisitions* magazine, 239 stock swaps valued at $8.5 billion, or 6 percent of the dollar value of all mergers, took place in 1985. The number rose in 1986 to 308, valued at $18.2 billion, or 9 percent of the dollar value of all mergers. In the first half of 1987, 122 stock swaps valued at $7.39 billion, or 10 percent of the dollar value of all mergers, were transacted.

A low stock price complicates equity financing decisions. They may be intended to reduce debt associated with cash-for-stock deals or to finance corporate growth. Chapter 6 shows that investor reaction to virtually every type of new offering by seasoned issuers tends to be negative, due more to information signalling than to price pressure (dilution). These offerings infer lower management expectations for net operating cash flows with which to reduce leverage or internally finance growth. Raising capital by selling low priced equity may also be perceived as a crisis move intended to avoid capital hemorrhages or to lessen perilous financial risk (low interest coverage).

Neglect dulls the impact of capital strategy on stock price. It weakens the connection between the two, slows the translation of economic value into market value and lowers executives' compensation. I mentioned in the preface of the book that I would refer to studies of market efficiency in order to help managements anticipate market reactions to management decisions. I now refer to academic studies to support these points.

Executives can expect their compensation to be sensitive to shareholders' realized returns. One study[7] examined executive compensation data for 461 executives from the proxy statements of 72 manufacturing companies between 1964 and 1981 (representing 4,500 executive years). It found a positive correlation between executive compensation, salary plus bonus, and current year performance, measured by shareholders' realized returns.

In a 943-executive-year subsample, chief executive officers received average annual increases in salary plus bonus of 3.9 percent. But when shareholders' returns dropped by 30 percent or more, chief executive officers received average pay decreases of 1.2 percent. When returns rose by 30 percent or more, chief executives' average compensation increased by 8.7 percent. There was no direct relation between compensation level and performance. According to Towers, Perrin, Forster & Crosby, 38 percent of U.S. chief executives' pay (usually stock options and bonuses) depends on individual or company performance. That figure is about 19 percent in Germany and about 15 percent in Japan (usually bonuses only).

A low stock price fails to recognize or reward management talent. It can neutralize incentive and can render incentive stock options worthless. Personal net worth may remain totally unrealized. In addition, it can wipe out all annual bonuses, perquisites, incentive compensation and job security. Executives should expect that poor performance may cost them their jobs.

One study[8] hypothesized that corporate boards control executives' behavior. By tying compensation and termination decisions to stock price performance, they establish managerial incentives that benefit shareholders. In that sense, the study found a negative correlation between stock price performance and executive turnover. It used data from *Forbes* compensation surveys to examine 249 companies (597 observations) between 1978 and 1980. It predicted percentage changes in compensation for executives less than 64 years old in various percentiles of distribution of abnormal shareholders' returns.

For example, the predicted percentage change in compensation for an executive whose company ranked in the top 1 percent of the study's distribution of abnormal returns (0.655 cumulative residual) was 10.17 percent. The probability of a turnover in chief executive officers was 3.1 percent. The predicted percentage change in compensation for an executive whose company ranked at the bottom 1 percent (−0.807 cumulative residual) was −9.86 percent. The probability of a turnover was 21.3 percent, seven times greater.

A further comparison of companies in the twentieth percentile (−0.377 cumulative residual) and eightieth (0.209 cumulative residual) percentile revealed differences in predicted percentage changes in compensation of −1.96 percent versus 4.06 percent. It also showed that the probability of executive turnover would be twice as likely, 10.5 percent versus 5.8 percent.

Historically, stock options have been an important performance incentive component of executives' and directors' compensation packages. Management contracts usually include stock options, outright stock ownership, or low interest loans with which to purchase company shares. The February 1984 *Business Week*/Louis Harris & Associates poll made clear executives' beliefs that market valuation of incentive stock options was still the primary route to personal wealth.

The study mentioned in Footnote 7 found that positive and negative changes in the value of executives' shareholdings are often three to five times greater than their salaries and bonuses. Another study[9] examined gains and losses to senior corporate managers and shareholders in 29 large conglomerates between 1970 and 1975. It found that in years when shareholders' realized returns dropped between 10 percent and 30 percent, the average top manager of a conglomerate lost 2.22 times his remuneration (stock total divided by remuneration). When realized returns ranged from 10 percent to 30 percent, average top managers made 1.44 times their remuneration. Above 30 percent, they made 5.17 times their remuneration.

In the past, executives' incentive compensation has usually been tied to accounting-based calculations of earnings per share. Critics argue that the link tends to favor decisions to grow earnings regardless of the effect on share price. But plan structures seem to be changing. They are gradually becoming more closely tied to economics and changes in economics. Compensation now depends more on target capital spreads (returns minus costs) times average capital employed. It increases with levels of operating cash flows above target capital spreads (operating spreads). The formulas apply at both operating unit and corporate levels.

Created economic value, especially when translated into market value for shareholders' benefit, is considered a more meaningful measure of executives' success than earnings per share. The belief is that reward for economic performance, not financial performance, more tightly ties managements' (and employees') interests to shareholders' interests. Either both prosper or neither prosper.

On average, stock prices rise at the announcement of adoption of or changes in executive compensation plans. Adopting companies tend to exhibit abnormal positive returns prior to plan announcements. One study[10] examined the proxies of 175 New York Stock Exchange companies voting on incentive plans between 1979 and 1982. It included announcements of adoptions of long-term executive compensation plans such as stock options, stock appreciation rights, restricted stock, phantom stock, performance plans or dividend units. It reported abnormal positive returns of 2.4 percent over a period of about 60 trading days from board meeting date through the day after Securities and Exchange Commission receipt of the proxy statement.

Another study reviewed 61 "golden parachute" contracts between 1975 and 1982.[11] It reported a statistically significant 3.4 percent average abnormal positive return from five days before through 10 days after the day on which the Securities and Exchange Commission received first proxy statement disclosure of the existence of a contract.

Finally, one study[12] perused short-term executive compensation plans tied to net income for 42 companies that adopted or proposed the adoption of short-term bonus plans between 1970 and 1980. These companies also had at least one long-term compensation plan in the form of stock option and/or performance shares. It found abnormal positive returns of 11.3 percent over a period three months before and the month of the proxy statement date, and an 11 percent abnormal positive return over a period seven months through four months before the proxy statement date.

Finance literature offers several theories to account for positive stock market reaction to adoption of executive compensation plans: management incentives (binding of management and shareholders' interests such that management will strive to maximize the economic benefit of any takeover bids); information content (signals concerning positive expectations of future net operating cash flows); and taxes (reductions of a company's and its executives' tax liabilities).

Empirical results seem to support the incentives hypothesis and the information hypothesis. Of the companies that announced adoption of short-term compensation plans in the above study, 90 percent registered unexpectedly high earnings and average abnormal positive stock price increases of about 8 percent over the 11 months after plan adoption.

Chronic undervaluation may harm a company's ability to retain capable asset managers and to attract new management talent. Incentive compensation is a major element in corporate recruiting campaigns. Stock options, in lieu of cash, are a key means by which to attract executive talent to emerging companies. As a cash substitute, they help management to tightly control such discretionary expenses as staffing and overhead.

A low stock price sends one clear signal to new recruits: the company's future may be uncertain. Its ability to grow and be profitable may be questionable such that the risk of management's not being able to afford and to reward the recruit may be high. Candidates react in different ways to this sort of situation. One job candidate's contrarian perception of potential opportunity from chaos may be another's sense of career checkmate due to managerial impotence. The effect of the latter perspective on management's recruiting ability may be stultifying, until changes are made.

In times of both good and poor performance, investors react positively to management appointments and dismissals by corporate boards of directors. Management attrition sends signals about changes in company policy. Internal executive promotions infer strong performance of existing managers (external recruiting does not). Internal promotions are more frequent than external appointments but become less meaningful for smaller companies. Dismissal, though suggestive of managerial underperformance, also results in positive investor response.

One study reviewed 323 appointments of chairmen, vice-chairmen, chief executive officer and president for large and small companies between 1975 and 1982.[13] It found that two-day average announcement period abnormal returns were 0.51 percent for 95 internal appointments by large companies (-1.22 percent for 29 external appointments) and 1.46 percent for 125 internal appointments by small companies (1.48 percent for 74 external appointments). In addition, average two-day announcement period abnormal returns for 62 dismissals were 0.26 percent for 33 dismissals with internal replacements, 0.72 percent for 11 dismissals with continued affiliation with the company and 3.17 percent for 11 dismissals under pressure.

The morale of executives and employees of many public companies is not only tied to the esprit associated with positive corporate performance (teamwork) but is also closely allied to the potential economic benefits of share ownership. Both may participate in employee stock option plans and dividend reinvestment plans. And, just as outside investors, they also watch daily share price performance. Their pride is often on the line. For example, as a reflection of her excitement and pride of association with her company, an employee of Apollo Computer Inc. (Chelmsford, MA) carried the final prospectus of the company's initial public offering in her purse. When asked where she worked, her response was quick, eager, and proud. But a low stock price can break that morale. When the perceived economic benefit of employees' share ownership dissipates, the corporate spirit of employees and executives withers.

Ideally, investors are to corporate officials what voters are to government officials. While the practice of one share one vote still prevails in the corporate world, both investors and voters function in a democracy. Each is squired by candidates and each is presented slates of and platforms from officials seeking their vote. Each closely watches the progress of those platform issues and demands the fulfillment of campaign promises. Each voices confidence or no-confidence in their respective leaders' ability to represent their interests. Each is the final arbiter of officials' performance and has the final power to retain or evict the current slate by casting ballots for or against incumbents.

Management must never forget that when a company goes public, shareholders own the company. Shareholders may comprise executives, employees, individuals or institutions. Financial managers work for the owners and are responsible for building economic value and wealth for them. In other words, they are the guardians of the owners' cash.

Executives are responsible for building the value of owners' cash investment. They have an obligation to earn a competitive return on investment of owners' cash in positive net present value opportunities. Otherwise, they must return that cash so that owners may make alternative investment decisions. Failure to do either reflects poorly on management. It suggests that executives are doing one or more of four things with owners' cash:

1. They are continuing to invest it in capital strategies which yield less than their capital costs. In other words, they waste owners' resources by investing in value-destroying strategies.

2. They are unwilling to shift a company's assets. They will not unlock the earning power associated with competitive advantages in units' high growth/high returns product/markets.

3. They are doing no more than passively compounding interest on retained earnings and claiming increases in shareholders' net worth. This warrants close scrutiny. Managers should only be rewarded for active asset management, not passive compounding.

4. They are hoarding owners' cash to perpetuate perception of their trusteeship role.

The quickest way for the management of any public company to create demand for its stock in this day and age is to manage underperforming assets (narrow margins on perceived high returns businesses) and to build passive cash on balance sheets. These actions invite takeover attempts, sometimes regardless of state legislative attempts to entrench management by one share/no vote legislation as discussed in Chapter 6. Takeovers clearly benefit shareholders (as Chapter 6 also shows). Corporate raiders buy on price. They are value investors who buy stock at fractions of replacement cost per share or at discounts to net current asset value per share. They also buy idle cash on corporate balance sheets. Then they restructure.

From an operating perspective, raiders usually believe they can enhance a company's competitiveness by cutting costs (usually through lay-offs). From an investment perspective, they believe they can lift returns by reducing capital intensity. In the latter case, they may sell off existing assets operating at or below break-even margins. Or they may unload "crown jewel" assets (so-called asset stripping) at multiples of asset values. Ultimately, wider margins on the same or lesser sales creates greater economic value than previously realized. These decisions benefit shareholders at the expense of current managers.

Managers may fail in their mission to build shareholders' wealth. In such cases, beware shareholders, either as a group or as lone raiders. They will not stand long for uneconomic use of their capital and of the company's assets. A low stock price has critical negative implications for shareholder loyalty. It pits shareholders against managers, capitalism against populism, and short-term trading opportunities against long-term corporate strategies.

A low stock price is similar to an immune deficiency and is the worst defense against dissatisfied shareholders. The corporate body loses its natural defense mechanism and becomes vulnerable to attack. Shareholders may initiate shareholder resolutions which contradict management desires. They may cast proxy ballots against management resolutions or submit slates of dissidents to replace current board members. They may initiate class-action lawsuits against management or file Schedules 13D or 13G with the Securities and Exchange Commission (indicating five or more percent ownership of a company's outstanding equity securities) with an intent to acquire the company.

Shareholder activism initiates shifts in the balance of power over corporate assets. It moves corporate control away from current management. Shareholders can be an unruly bunch that can strike fear into the hearts of even the strongest management personalities. They are the most powerful of any union with which management may have to bargain. When shareholders exercise their vote, they can be humorless employers. Shareholders wield voting power.

As might be expected, besieged managers do not take kindly to being voted out of office or relieved of their management duties. But managers of acquired companies are expendable (see footnote 8). For example, when Wells Fargo & Co. (San Francisco, CA) bought Crocker National Corp. (San Francisco, CA), the former took only three of the latter's 22 executive vice presidents. Leveraged buyouts are the only example of takeovers in which current management usually remains.

The lesson for corporate executives seems obvious, and the message is quite clear. Management of a public company is in place to serve as guardian of shareholders' interests, to translate economic value into market value for them, and to maximize their wealth. Managers are entrusted with the responsibility either to reinvest cash for shareholders or to return their cash to them, depending on the net present value characteristics of available reinvestment opportunities.

A landmark legal case made a major point about management accountability to shareholders. It concerned management decisions about asset restructuring, income reinvestment, or cash distribution. In July 1985, the Delaware Supreme Court upheld a shareholder suit against the management and board of directors of Trans Union Corporation (Chicago, IL). The suit contended that management, with board approval, had sold part of the company's business, without first consulting the owners of the company (shareholders). The suit charged that the board failed to serve shareholders' interests by allowing the sale of the company's assets at prices less than their market value. Shareholders won the suit. The company's directors were held personally liable for $13.5 million more than the company was insured for.

The court ruled that the long-established "business judgment" rule is not an automatic escape from financial liability if directors do not fully consider merger terms. The decision in favor of the company's shareholders has subsequently had a profound effect on corporate accountability. Liability insurance rates for board members have skyrocketed and the willingness of respected officials to sit on corporate boards has decreased significantly. Gone are the days of passive boards that just came to lunch and collected a fee while executives served themselves first and shareholders second.

Ultimately, information deficiency and institutional neglect, especially in light of positive company fundamentals, is a real threat to management. No reasonable observer would minimize management's challenge to create economic value, but one would not applaud management's success unless that economic value is translated into market value (shareholders' realized returns).

One conclusion is clear. Management cannot translate economic value into market value without first creating investor demand. It is the key to affecting the equity valuation process.

2

Risk, Expected Returns, and Share Prices

An adage states that of all the operating numbers a company generates, the only number the president looks at four times a day is the the company's stock price.

Why is a company's stock price so important? In isolation, share price is virtually meaningless. It reveals nothing about a company's future potential or past success. It indicates nothing about a company's being cheap or expensive as an investment. But to the president of a public company, to a company's board of directors and to its senior corporate officers, stock price tells all. It reflects investors' perceptions of the company's future cash-generating ability and competitive advantage and it implies minimum levels of returns which investors expect. Share price is a public vote of confidence, or no-confidence, in management.

Stock price is important to many parties besides management. William Beaver, Thomas D. Dee II professor of finance and accounting at Stanford University's Graduate School of Business, cites five major constituencies of public companies: investors, securities analysts, management, regulators, and auditors. For the purposes of this book, the first three are the most important.

Investors are first. They rely on a company's data in order to make informed investment decisions. They may be either individuals or institutions, professional or amateur, active or passive investors, buy performance or price, and hold diversified or concentrated portfolios. Securities analysts ("information intermediaries") are second in importance. They analyze and process financial data. The group comprises securities analysts at brokerage firms or institutions, investment advisory services, stock-rating agencies and bond-rating agencies.

Shareholders pay attention to stock prices for personal reasons. Variations in share prices affect individuals' financial security and economic well-being. Beaver claims that corporate financial reporting has seven economic consequences: wealth distribution, aggregate risk incurred and risk allocation, aggregate consumption and aggregate production, resource allocation, resources devoted to publicly available information, resources devoted to regulation, and resources devoted to private search for information.

Beaver relates these consequences to investors. He writes: "For example changes in prices alter the market value of an investor's wealth. This change in wealth can change the opportunity set for the investor. Therefore, prices will be associated with alterations in the investor's consumption-investment behavior, although the nature of the alteration will depend upon many factors, such as the nature of an investor's preferences."[1]

Professionals and amateurs invest in common stocks to improve their opportunity set. They want to be worth more tomorrow than today. They measure wealth in terms of cash flow from dividends or the sale of stock during a holding period. Wealth, expressed in percentage terms, is defined as total return, percentage changes in share price plus cash dividends at the end of a period divided by the purchase price of a stock at the start of that period. The result can obviously be positive and add to personal wealth or be negative and reduce one's net worth. Total return grows annually in one of two ways. Either both share price and dividends rise (only share price for emerging companies), or dividend yield exceeds percentage declines in stock price (capital losses).

Within the context of economic opportunity set, investors usually define their investment objectives in line with their risk tolerance and required level of returns. Depending on the array of these parameters, they seek to either enhance total return or to preserve cash flow and capital. The first is relatively high-risk oriented and geared to (rapid) changes in share prices. Emerging companies fit into this category. The second is relatively low-risk oriented and is geared to share price stability and income potential. Each adjusts to variations in portfolio strategy and style.

Shareholders judge corporate managements on their ability to create or to transfer economic value (wealth). They judge them in stock market (total return) terms, not earnings-per-share terms. For example, does management's capital strategy translate to positive capital spreads for each business unit and for the company as a whole? Does management's business strategy translate to larger market share? Does larger market share translate to wider operating margins above the cost of capital? Do wider operating margins translate to increases in economic value? Do increases in economic value translate to stock price? Does management actively create wealth (value) or passively increase the company's net worth? Does management hoard wealth, reinvest it in positive capital strategies, or is it distributed to shareholders, the company's owners?

For investors, corporate financial managers are their money managers—guardians of their wealth. They believe corporate executives' management of portfolios of economic (capital) assets is analogous to money managers' management of portfolios of financial assets. Accordingly, investors give corporate managers free rein to decide which investment, financing, and operating decisions will increase the value of their overall portfolio. They want capital assets to grow in both size and value, not just in size. Shareholders measure the performance of corporate managers in the same way as that of money managers: total return relative to peer competitors, industry composites and broad market indices.

Investors often look for companies with high growth/high returns product/market opportunities. They want managements which can create maximum potential economic value by investing in strategies that beat the cost of capital. And they want those that can realize maximum market value by operating at margins which generate profit in excess of their company's cost of capital. These managers know how to build growth, profitability, and the value of shareholders' equity.

Stockholders do a little arithmetic every year to calculate annual total return, how well their moneys' managers have done. They look at the effect of management's decisions on their money. By how much is stock price up? Has current income from dividends, if applicable, increased? Is their portfolio worth more? Are they more or less wealthy? Has management added to or subtracted from the value of their investment? Does management deserve to manage more of their money or does their money deserve better trusteeship?

Stock price is the first place they start. They may even calculate a few profitability, productivity, and relative ratios to determine the success of corporate strategy: return on equity (after-tax operating profit, before noncash charges, divided by shareholders' equity), return on assets (after-tax operating profit as a percentage of assets), pre-tax return on sales, price-to-earnings, price-to-book value and price/book-to-return on equity. But calculation of share price appreciation is their first move. It is their first signal whether to invest more or to invest elsewhere.

Much research has been done on securities prices as a proxy for wealth creation: what they are, why they move, when they move, what moves them, and who moves them. Evidence suggests that shifts in investors' perceptions of risk and expected returns move share prices. More specifically, shifts in perception of expected returns on an investment relative to alternative investments of equal risk, or shifts in perception of the risk of an investment relative to alternative investments of equal expected returns, move share prices up or down.

The world's capital markets are open arenas in which collective assessments of risk and expected returns are made every day. These markets are perception-driven. Information drives perception and perception drives share prices.

Within that context, bull equity markets usually reflect investors' perceptions of rising corporate profitability and higher expected returns on common stocks relative to alternative investments of equal risk. Bear equity markets usually reflect investors' perceptions of falling corporate profitability and higher risk (earnings variance) relative to alternative investments of equal expected returns.

Bull markets may be economy-driven, fueled by perceptions of higher expected returns from real growth in unit volume, increases in corporate earning power, and decreases in business risk. They may also be inflation and interest rate-driven, sparked by perceptions of lower financial risk, higher interest coverage, and resulting higher corporate profitability. In some cases, capital markets may be tax-driven, moved by expectations of higher net after-tax returns on investment. And, finally, they may also be liquidity-driven, fueled by too much institutional cash chasing too few equities. This can create a two-tier market for equity investments.

In the last case, Salomon Brothers, Inc., estimated that in 1986 about $161 billion in cash was returned to investors in exchange for their shares through mergers, acquisitions, share repurchase plans and leveraged buyouts. The firm claims that the resulting liquidity had an important impact on pushing up share prices.

Capital markets have been interest rate-driven since 1981 but became (earnings) economy-driven in 1986 and 1987. In mid-1986, they were also tax-driven, in anticipation of changes in federal tax laws. And at the start of 1987, considering the great divergence between "real" economic performance and "symbolic" performance represented by capital markets, they were also liquidity-driven. Institutional investors perceived greater risk to portfolio performance by not being invested in equities.

STRATEGIES AND SPREADS

Managing any business in a competitive environment requires that executives get involved in capital strategy and business strategy. Taken together, these two elements of business success have become known as "value-based planning." On these topics, I refer to the works of William Fruhan (Harvard University) and Alfred Rappaport (Northwestern University). Their research is prominent and thorough in its analysis of the processes in which management decisions create value. In contrast, this book concerns management actions that translate that economic value to market value.

Capital strategy concerns management decisions about markets in which to invest (or harvest or sell), how much to invest, and the cost of investing to create economic value. Business strategy concerns management decisions about how to compete in those markets to realize the most total economic value. Together they require calculation of economic income and returns over forecast periods on both corporate and business unit levels.

Capital strategy assesses every investment in new earning assets on the basis of net present values (NPV) and capital spreads. NPV reflects an investment's contribution to changes in today's value. It is the present value of future operating cash flows minus the present value of cash investment cost. It can only be positive and add to today's value if returns on capital exceed costs of capital. The size of equity capital spread determines how much the market value of a company's common equity exceeds the book value of its common equity.

A company's definition of "value-added" is similar to investors' definition of wealth (mentioned earlier). Recall that calculation of total return is cash flow from dividends or stock sales plus changes in price divided by beginning price. Management's calculation of economic return is cash flow from operations plus changes in the present value of residual values divided by beginning present value.

Rappaport defines cash flow as "after-tax operating profit plus noncash charges minus incremental fixed and working capital investment." Present value of future cash flows over any forecast period of even or uneven cash flows is [(cash flow per year) divided by (1 plus the cost of capital) compounded per year]. One year economic income is [(cash flow)] plus changes in the present value of residuals: [(cash flow before new investment at the end of the year divided by the cost of capital divided by the first year discount factor of 1 plus the cost of capital) minus (cash flow before new investment at the beginning of the year divided by the cost of capital)]. Change in present value over a forecast period is [(the cumulative present value of cash flows plus the present value of the ending residual) minus (the present value of the beginning residual)].

Business strategy examines competitive opportunities on the basis of operating margins in relation to capital spreads. Assuming positive spreads, economic value is realized when operating profit exceeds minimum required returns (cost of capital) set in capital strategy. Formulae which equate operating margins to zero net present value (present value of cash flows and cash costs is equal) are in footnote 3.

In capital strategy, calculation of the cost of equity capital (discussed at length in the next section) is a cornerstone of value-based planning. It establishes minimum levels of returns investors require (expect) on equity capital investment. Minimum returns are those available in alternative investments of identical risk. Most companies incorporate debt into their optimal (minimum average cost) capital structures. The appropriate rate at which they discount future cash flows to present values is the weighted (proportion of capital structure) average cost of equity capital and after-tax debt capital. It should be estimated at both the corporate and business unit level. This calculation is the essence of risk for corporate managers. It establishes minimum returns and hurdle rates which capital strategies must surpass in order to create economic value.

Research indicates that those companies that can invest the most equity capital at the widest positive capital spreads for the longest periods potentially (depending upon operating margins) create the greatest economic value. In contrast, those that continue to invest the most equity capital at the widest negative capital spreads for the longest periods (depending on operating margins) destroy the most economic value.

The extent to which a company's capital strategy creates economic value (based on discounted cash flow techniques) in excess of book value of common equity can be seen in an economic value/book value ratio matrix[2] established by Professor Fruhan. It shows the multiples to book values at which equity securities with different investment profiles can be expected to trade (Fruhan's calculation of the above ratio appears in the footnotes). The matrix is bounded by equity capital spread on top, estimated duration of that spread on the left, and the size of investment opportunity on the right (measured by $ annual growth in common stock equity/$ annual profit after-tax). The cost of equity capital is assumed to be 10 percent.

Moving from economic destruction to economic creation, the matrix shows that the equity securities of companies with 30 percent reinvestment rates at −0.5 percent (negative) equity capital spreads estimated to last for five years can be expected to trade at 80 percent of their book value. That ratio will tend to remain at 80 percent even as the rate of reinvestment rises to 200 percent as long as the negative spread is expected to last for only five years.

The equity securities of companies with 30 percent reinvestment rates at −0.5 percent (negative) equity capital spreads expected to last for 30 years can be expected to trade at 50 percent of book value. It falls to 40 percent if reinvestment rises to 70 percent and to 20 percent if reinvestment rises to 100 percent.

In contrast, equity securities of companies with 30 percent reinvestment rates at 0.5 percent (positive) equity capital spreads estimated to last for five years can be expected to trade at 120 percent of their book value (130 percent if reinvestment rises to 200 percent). If that positive spread is expected to last for 30 years, then a 30 percent reinvestment rate results in equity securities priced at 170 percent of book value (580 percent if reinvestment rises to 70 percent and 1,350 percent if reinvestment rises to 100 percent).

In further contrast, equity securities of companies with 30 percent reinvestment rates at 20 percent (positive) equity capital spreads estimated to last for five years can be expected to trade at 190 percent of their book value (320 percent if reinvestment rises to 200 percent). If that positive spread is expected to last for 30 years, then a 30 percent reinvestment rate results in equity securities priced at 580 percent of book value (3,080 percent if reinvestment rises to 70 percent and 16,160 percent if reinvestment rises to 100 percent).

Turning to business strategy, the calculation of minimum operating margins (pretax) at which operating profit equals investors' minimum required returns (the company's cost of capital) is the cornerstone of strategic planning. It establishes the operating thresholds at which different business strategies create or destroy economic value (the formulae appear in the footnotes).[3] Assuming a positive equity capital spread, those companies that operate at the widest spreads between their cost of capital and their operating profit margins for the longest periods and generate the highest sales growth rates for the longest periods at those spreads create the most actual economic value. This is discussed further in Chapter 4.

The calculation is a company's best measure by which to compare the real value-creating potential of different business strategy choices. It reveals the operating margins and operating spreads at which each generates the greatest internal (discounted cash flow) rates of return. Operating spread is defined in terms of cost of capital minus operating margin. The result is either positive and creates value, neutral and creates no value, or is negative and destroys value. The parameters in a company's business strategy considerations to which the creation of economic value is most sensitive are its operating margin, sales growth rate, incremental fixed and working capital investment, and income tax rate (I consider cost of capital part of capital strategy).

Positive operating spreads usually decay over time to the cost of capital as competition in a market intensifies and competitive advantage erodes. The rate of decay varies with barriers to entry into a market such as technology, production lead time, capital intensity, economies of scale, cost advantage and more. Professor Rappaport suggests that business strategies based on new product introductions using R & D intense technologies which require long lead times (i.e., biotechnology) tend to maintain long-term competitive advantages. Their capital intensity bars market entry and results in a pricing advantage that can last up to 10 to 15 years. In contrast, strategies based on broadened product lines in existing mature markets tend to have short-term competitive advantages. They may last only three and five years.

The relationship between capital strategy (cost of capital) and business strategy (operating margins) in creating economic value is such that there are two ways by which to increase economic value: first, reduce the cost of capital (assuming positive operating spreads remain constant) through optimal capital structure or new financing techniques, or second, expand operating margins (assuming positive capital spreads remain constant) as low cost producer or price/performance leader.

The following research results are important to corporate managements. They suggest that executives should be prepared to discuss how they invest and how they compete so that investors can judge how they perform relative to alternatives. They should be ready to discuss their investment decisions and planning systems by which they quantify the risk of and estimate the returns on their capital strategies. And they should be prepared to talk about their operating decisions and strategy analysis in which they assess the value-creating potential of their business strategies. This includes market characteristics, industry competition, product protection, prices, costs, and earnings sensitivity to unexpected changes in macroeconomic variables.

Executives should consider their company's equity securities as buyers think of them, in terms of competitive advantages and excess returns potential. They should also consider them as owners, in terms of growth in the present value of future operating cash flows. Their understanding of the returns-generating process and their ability to shape investors' perceptions of risk and expected returns enables them to clearly communicate value to Wall Street in terms buyers and owners can appreciate.

MANAGEMENT PERSPECTIVES ON RISK AND EXPECTED RETURNS

The job of capital strategy is to quantify risk. In the world of business, risk is defined in several ways. Business risk is usually defined in terms of the variance in a company's operating cash flows. It is attributable to several factors, such as demand variability, sales price variability, input price variability, the fixity of costs, and the ability to adjust output prices to changes in input prices. Chapter 5 discusses this further.

Financial risk is usually defined in terms of the variance in a company's net income. It is expressed as percent change in net income divided by percent change in sales, which equals the degree of operating leverage times the degree of financial leverage. Portfolio risk is usually defined as the variance in a company's expected returns. It is the extent to which realized return from holding a security varies from the expected return from holding it.

One survey examined cost of capital techniques used by Fortune 1000 financial managers.[4] It found that corporate financial managers measure the risks of capital projects individually or they group projects into classes of risks. It also learned that their adjustment of risk varies with their capital budgeting technique: payback, average return on book value, internal rate of return, or profitability index. Those who used net present value risk-adjusted the cash flows of each capital project. Those who used internal rate of return risk-adjusted the cost of capital which applies to each capital project. Managers' risk assessments depended mostly on the dollar size of a capital project, the project's estimated payback period and its level of estimated returns relative to alternative projects.

The survey also found that a large gap seemed to exist between theory and practice in cost of capital calculations and capital budgeting (see Pruitt/Gitman in the bibliography). Most managers seemed familiar with financial theory but few seemed to use it. Among a variety of techniques used in capital budgeting, some managers used sensitivity analysis, risk-adjusted discount methods, formal risk analysis and the capital asset pricing model. (See Brick/Weaver in the bibliography for a discussion of which technique best identified profitable or unprofitable investments: after-tax weighted average cost of capital, before-tax weighted average cost of capital, equity residual method, or adjusted present value method). But most seemed to rely on other methods to determine costs of capital, usually calculated as an average cost weighted by target capital structure rather than market value.

Portfolio theory has contributed to a greater understanding of capital strategy by offering one widely used method by which to calculate a company's cost of equity capital for capital budgeting purposes. Portfolio theory quantifies the risk of equity ownership. It correlates that risk with estimates of expected returns and identifies those equities with superior expected returns at equal levels of risk.

Research into the methods by which investors identify the relative attractiveness of equity investment opportunities led to the development of modern portfolio theory (MPT). In his pioneering March 1952 article, "Portfolio Selection" (*Journal of Finance*), Harry Markowitz (of the RAND Corporation) isolated risk and expected return as the two most important considerations in the construction of any investment portfolio. He also specified that achievement of the highest risk-adjusted returns on investment was the most important objective of an efficient portfolio.

Two general approaches to assessing risk prevail in finance theory: factor models and equilibrium theories. Factor models try to identify the value of security "attributes" to which significant numbers of securities' returns are sensitive (discussed in the next section). Single-factor models were first introduced in 1959. Multi-factor models were proposed in the 1960s.

Equilibrium theories of security prices were introduced in the 1960s. They attempted to provide insight into the behavior of stock prices, the measurement of risk and the expected relationship between risk and return. Two major theories emerged: the Capital Asset Pricing Model (CAPM) and the Arbitrage Pricing Theory (APT). Each facilitates estimates of the costs of equity capital. The first has gained widespread use in capital strategy and in capital markets.

The Capital Asset Pricing Model was introduced in 1964 by William Sharpe (Stanford University)[5] and in 1965 by John Lintner (Harvard University).[6] The theory is based on the assumptions that investors are primarily risk-averse, that they structure portfolios on the basis of perceived risk (variance in expected returns), that they perceive identical risk in all securities, that their investment time horizons are the same, that they can be expected to diversify their holdings to reduce risk, and that risk-free assets exist. It does not consider taxes or transactions costs.

The model quantifies the risk of individual equity securities in relation to a single-index (single factor) model of the overall stock market. Via linear regression between past returns for a security and past returns for the Standard &

Poor's 500-stock index, CAPM describes risk as the slope coefficient of the regression line. It expresses it as a figure less than, equal to, or greater than 1.0 (market risk) and calls it "beta."

Security-specific risk (investors' minimum required returns on equity) is thus proportional to market risk. Managements must adjust this market risk by a proportional factor of beta to arrive at an estimate of investors' minimum required returns.

Calculation of the cost of equity capital equals the risk-free rate of return (i.e., Treasury bills) plus an equity risk premium. The latter is calculated by multiplying a "beta" coefficient (of historic volatility relative to the overall market) for a particular security times a market risk premium above the risk-free rate. This market premium equals market expected return minus the risk-free rate of return. This spread has historically averaged between 5 and 5.5 percent. If beta is known, the calculation of the discount rate is easy. One study found, as might be expected, that between 1955 and 1969 the beta coefficient on a portfolio of national over-the-counter stocks was greater (1.12) than that on a portfolio of New York Stock Exchange stocks.[7] In other words, small companies were riskier than large capitalization companies.

Academicians try to associate a company's beta (systematic risk) with the characteristics of its real assets. They break down the real determinants of beta (risk decomposition) into previously mentioned operating leverage and financial leverage. One study[8] reported that financial leverage (percent change in net income divided by percent change in pretax operating profit), which may lead to variances in net income, explained about one-quarter of a common stock's systematic risk. Another[9] found that operating leverage, the ratio of fixed to variable operating costs, may lead to variances in operating margins (percent change in operating profit divided by percent change in sales). Systematic risk will increase with operating leverage.

David W. Mullins, Jr., associate professor of business administration at the Harvard Business School used the capital asset pricing model to offer 1982 perspective on the pricing of equity capital as a function of risk.[10] He calculated estimates of expected returns for a variety of industries. For example, high-risk stocks carry high estimates of expected returns and high average beta coefficients. The estimated cost of equity in the air transport industry in 1982, for example, was 26.20 percent (beta of 1.80); 24.20 percent (beta of 1.60) in the electronics industry; 23.05 percent (beta of 1.45) in the consumer durables industries; 21.70 percent (beta of 1.30) in the producer goods, aerospace, business services, apparel, construction, and motor vehicles industries; 20.80 percent (beta of 1.20) in the railroad shipping and forest products industries, and 20.25 percent (beta of 1.15) in the conglomerate, drugs/medicine, and domestic oil industries.

In contrast, medium-risk stocks carry lower estimates of expected returns on equity capital and lower average beta coefficients. The estimated cost of equity capital in the nonferrous metals and agriculture/foods industries in 1982 was 19.00 percent (beta of 1.00) and it was 17.65 percent (beta of .85) in the international oil and banking industries.

Low-risk stocks carry low estimates of expected returns and low average beta coefficients. The estimated cost of equity capital in the telephone industry in 1982, for example, was 16.75 percent (beta of 0.75); 15.40 percent (beta of .60) in the energy/utilities industry; and 13.15 percent (beta of .35) for gold.

The difference (positive or negative) between estimates of company-specific expected returns and market expected returns is called "alpha." Viewed in terms of stock price, this valuation differential is a relative strength measure of how much a company's share price moves independent of market (S & P 500 index) moves.

For perspective on beta and alpha, management should find a monthly statistical report published by Merrill Lynch titled, "Security Risk Evaluation" (the Beta book). It ranks about 5,000 stocks by these two attributes, and may be found at the leading business school libraries (call number HG4915. M48a).

The previously mentioned survey of cost of capital techniques found that most financial managers calculate their company's cost of equity capital (discount rate or hurdle rate on capital strategies) in terms of minimum returns investors require. In deriving estimates of those expected returns, they frequently rely on dividend growth models, such as that developed by John B. Williams in 1938 and rediscovered by Myron Gordon and Eli Shapiro (then of the School of Industrial Management at M.I.T.) in 1956. The model states that expected returns equal a company's next year dividend yield plus an estimated annual growth rate in dividends, assumed to be a company's earnings retention rate. A rearrangement of the model indicates that share price equals next year's cash dividend divided by expected return minus an estimated annual growth rate in dividends. Managers also rely on calculations of risk-adjusted (by beta) market returns.

In the survey, 65 percent of the executives estimated that their companies' overall cost of capital (as of October 1980 when risk-free government bonds yielded 12.4 percent) ranged from 11 to 17 percent with a mean value of 14.3 percent. Over 50 percent of polled executives also claimed that their companies' overall costs of capital had not varied by more than 2 to 4 percent during the prior two-year period, seemingly in line with variations in yields on risk-free government bonds over the same period.

Models that assume constant annual growth in dividends are considered most useful in estimating the expected returns on companies with predictable streams of future income. But they are not applicable to companies which pay small dividends, no dividends, or unpredictable dividends (emerging companies). They also do not reflect inflation.

It was mentioned earlier that the capital asset pricing model is used widely in capital strategy to estimate expected returns. The main drawback in this estimation approach is that beta is historical, not predictive. Some studies mentioned in the bibliography suggest that predictive betas can be calculated based on company fundamentals (see Rosenberg/Guy) or analysts' forecasts (see Carvell/Strebel). And beta must be estimated for emerging companies and company business units.

In addition to Merrill Lynch's Beta Book, Value Line's *Investment Survey* (New York, NY), and *Daily Graphs* (William O'Neil & Co., Los Angeles, CA) give the beta coefficient for many publicly traded issues. Standard & Poor's has recently begun to include the figure on the top of its *Stock Reports*. (For a discussion of whose beta estimates are best see Harrington in the bibliography.)

Wall Street assigns risk to individual securities in three ways: beta, sigma and dispersion. Much of Wall Street's securities analysis makes use of beta. Responding to its extensive use, the New York Stock Exchange introduced a beta index option by which to hedge a portfolio of volatile stocks in May 1986. It comprised 100 NYSE-listed issues with high relative beta coefficients. Since 1983, the beta coefficient of the index has been 1.7. That suggests that the equity risk premium of the index on average has been 170 percent of market risk and that, on average, the index can be expected to move 70 percent more up or down than the overall market.

The second measure of security-specific risk is sigma, total business/financial risk versus systematic risk. It is the standard deviation in monthly total return of a stock relative to its past returns.

The third measure is dispersion. It is the variation from consensus (average) expectations in analysts' estimates of earnings per share. The coefficient of variation (cross-sectional variance) is the standard deviation of individual analysts' forecasts. The average coefficient is the standard deviation divided by the mean earnings forecast. Variation in this "expectational data" is considered "estimation risk." Much academic study has found this to be the single best measure of security-specific risk, that institutional investors perceive estimation risk to be their greatest risk in security selection (and portfolio returns), and that dispersion is directly associated with information availability.

Average variation from consensus by which two-thirds of analysts' estimates of 1986 earnings for *Business Week's* 1000 companies with greatest market values was 15.3 percent. Variation percentages ranged from less than 2 percent for companies in the drug, utility, beverages, food, services, and banking industries to 50 percent or more for companies in the natural resource, metals, and oil service industries. In general, those companies with depressed earnings demonstrated the lowest consensus and the highest perceived estimation risk. This correlates with results of studies mentioned in Chapter 8.

Data from Lynch, Jones & Ryan's *Institutional Brokers Estimate System* (I/B/E/S) show that dispersion lowers share prices. For example, as reported in *Business Week* on January 21, 1985, only 8 percent of analysts' estimates for Anchor Hocking was significantly below the average consensus estimate in 1984. That percentage rose to 31 percent in 1985 and the company's stock price dropped 65 percent from its 52-week high. For Nike, only 6 percent of analysts' estimates varied significantly from consensus in 1984. But that percentage rose to 39 percent in 1985 and the company's stock price fell 50 percent from its 52-week high.

Bethlehem Steel went from 58 percent dispersion in 1984 to 71 percent in 1985 and its shares fell 38 percent. PaineWebber went from 5 percent to 45 percent and its shares fell 28 percent. General Instrument went from 18 percent to 25 percent and its shares fell 54 percent. And dispersion from consensus in analysts' estimates of Ryan Homes rose from 14 percent in 1984 to 35 percent in 1985. The company's shares fell 29 percent from their 52-week high.

PORTFOLIO PERSPECTIVE ON RISK AND EXPECTED RETURNS

Academic research into the portfolio selection and diversification process has tried to isolate and to estimate the magnitude of those risk factors which affect variations in returns on specific securities, but also those factors which influence the covariance of expected returns among securities in a portfolio. To how many factors can variance in security returns (risk) be attributed?

Expanding the realm of equilibrium theory beyond the Capital Asset Pricing Model, a single factor returns generating model, the Arbitrage Pricing Theory was introduced in 1976 by Stephen Ross (Yale University).[11] It interpreted stock price behavior (variance in expected returns) in terms of a multi-factor returns generating model. The theory asserts that managers of large stock portfolios can diversify away "idiosyncratic" risk, that specific to a company, industry, or group of stocks. In that way, a portfolio's expected returns are only sensitive to a few macroeconomic risks inherent in the overall market.

The theory claims that a portfolio's average long-term return is directly sensitive to unexpected changes in four macroeconomic factors: inflation, the anticipated level of industrial production, unforeseen shifts in spreads between low-grade and high-grade bonds, and surprise changes in spreads between long- and short-term interest rates.

The APT diverges from the CAPM. It claims that portfolios of financial assets with the same historic risk profile (beta) relative to the overall market may show different levels of sensitivities to unexpected changes in these macroeconomic variables. One study examined 127 stocks between 1970 and 1979.[12] It found that the APT outperformed CAPM in terms of providing estimates of expected returns which were closer to real average actual realized returns. For example, for 17 of these stocks, estimates of expected returns using CAPM averaged 23 percent whereas estimates for the same group using APT averaged 18.8 percent.

In contrast to equilibrium theories, factor models offer insight into the sources to which variances in portfolio expected returns can be attributed. They examine historic variances in security expected returns among stocks (time series analysis over stocks) and over time (cross-section analysis over months). Assuming the stability of factors and of their magnitudes of influence over time, cluster analysis, principal components analysis, and factor analysis help to quantify portfolio risk in terms of security "attributes" to which significant numbers of securities' returns are sensitive.

Factor models suggest that portfolio risk, the variance in expected returns on a portfolio of common stocks, may be explained by four broad factors: (1) a market factor which affects all stocks, (2) an industry factor which affects stocks within a particular industry, (3) a group factor which affects stocks with similar earnings sensitivities, and (4) a firm-unique factor particular to an individual company.

One academic study estimated the magnitude of influence of each factor above. It reviewed share price changes for 316 New York Stock Exchange companies listed continuously from May 1927 through December 1960.[13] It found price shifts in groups of stocks could be explained by: 31 percent market factors, 12 percent industry effects, 37 percent group effects and 20 percent company-specific factors. Assuming unsystematic, security-specific risk can be diversified away (shown later), then market-related effects on risk are of most concern to portfolio managers because they are undiversifiable.

The market factor which affects all stocks might be described as overall market sensitivity to unexpected changes in those macroeconomic variables described by the Arbitrage Pricing Theory: inflation, production, shifts in spreads between long-term and short-term interest rates, and shifts in spreads between high-grade and low-grade bonds.

Industry factors measure covariation of returns across companies within an industry. The flow of institutional money into or out of entire industries and groups of industries suggests investors' belief that company returns and share prices move together within an industry. One study examined 43 industry groups between 1972 and 1984.[14] It found that rankings of the best and worst performing industries varied considerably, but industry-specific stock price movements tended to persist for at least two quarters. In recognition of the importance of this factor, major brokerage firms designate research responsibility to analysts exclusively by industry.

Group factors are a "broader-than-industry method of classifying past price movements in stocks." Covariation of returns within industries is used as a proxy for covariation across industries. For example, money managers rotate into and out of groups of stocks across entire industries because they assume a positive correlation exists between companies and share price movements within industries.

Academic research suggests many group factors may exist. This book refers to one widely-used group classification system. For example, analysis of 100 common stocks in one study found that "in a sense the groups can be thought of as representing four different equity markets: 1) a growth stock market, 2) a cyclical stock market, 3) a stable stock market, and 4) an oil stock market."[15]

Growth stocks are "represented by companies expected to show an above average rate of secular growth."[16] A company with a historic five-year annual compound earnings growth rate between 10 and 15 percent, returns on equity more than 20 percent, price more than several times book value, and a price/earnings ratio greater than earnings growth (i.e., 20) classifies as a growth stock.

Cyclical stocks "are defined as those of companies that have an above average exposure to the vagaries of the economic environment. Earnings of these companies are expected to decline more on average in a recession and to increase more on average during an expansion phase of the business cycle."[17]

Stable stocks "are those of companies whose earning power is less affected than the average firm by the economic cycle. Earnings of these firms are expected to show a below average decline in a recession and less than average increase during the expansion phase of the business cycle."[18]

Past research has relied on the use of a stability index of earnings to distinguish between cyclical and stable stocks. For example, in one study the index was "based on the variability about a least-squares trend line in a firm's past 5-year quarterly earnings per share, i.e., a stability factor of 0.05 indicates that two-thirds of all 12-month earnings fall within a 5 percent band around the earnings trend line."[19] Cyclical stocks were identified as those with "an earnings-stability index of 0.25 or greater." Stable stocks were those with "an earnings-stability index of 0.10 or less plus earnings growth of less than 10 percent."[20]

Companies in a group of stable stocks usually manifest a consistent earnings growth rate of about 10 percent or less compounded annually over the previous five years. Those in a growth group usually manifest an estimated rate of sustainable future earnings growth, out several years, close to 15 percent. Emerging companies are viewed as having aggressive growth. They exhibit potential compound annual rates of future earnings growth, estimated to be sustainable over periods of about two to five years, approaching or in excess of 30 percent per year.

Firm-unique factors apply to security-specific risk, variance in security-specific (versus portfolio) expected returns. One study[21] estimated that the magnitude of influence on security-specific returns was: about 45 percent market-related factors, about 12 percent industry factors, and about 43 percent firm-unique factors. Other factors to which after-the-fact differences in returns among individual securities are attributed are discussed in the next section.

Professional managers of diversified portfolios do not expect to get rewarded for bearing security-specific risk. Research into MPT has provided evidence that portfolio managers can diversify away the risk associated with investment in specific companies. They can thus lower portfolio risk associated with a given level of expected returns. They should not expect to be rewarded with higher portfolio returns for bearing higher company-specific "unsystematic" risk. Rather, they should only expect to be rewarded for bearing market-related risk because it is "systematic" and non-diversifiable. Portfolio strategy, group rotation, industry switching, and stock selection reflect money managers' attempts to cope with systematic risk and to achieve the highest possible risk-adjusted returns.

Several academic studies have shown how diversification reduces portfolio risk. One study[22] demonstrated not only that additions of stocks to a portfolio reduced variance in portfolio returns but also that only a relatively few additions were required to achieve the fairly full benefits of diversification. For example, the variance (risk) in returns of a one-stock portfolio was 40 percent, a two-stock portfolio was 32.4 percent, an eight-stock portfolio was 25.6 percent, a 16-stock portfolio was 24 percent, a 32-stock portfolio was 23.6 percent, and a 128-stock portfolio was 22.8 percent. Variance on an index fund was 22 percent.

To explain differences in actual security-specific returns among companies, models of the returns-generating process attribute returns to several factors. For example, firm-unique factors pertain to financial attributes such as: growth in shareholders' equity, cash flow yield, dividends plus share repurchases net of newly issued shares and valuation changes (changes in price/book ratio). One study[23] examined actual 1985 returns and their components for the Dow Jones Industrial 30 stocks. It found that after-the-fact return estimates using a model based on these three sources of returns closely approximated actual returns. It explained more than 90 percent of the differences in returns among those 30 securities.

The study also determined that growth in shareholders' equity was the largest source of long-term returns and was more stable than expected. Cash flow yield (return on equity minus growth in equity divided by price/book ratio) was the smallest source of returns and was relatively stable. Valuation change (change in price/book ratio divided by price/book ratio times 1 plus growth in equity) was the largest component of returns in the short-term (one to two years) but was highly unpredictable. Finally, the study found that the sum of the first two factors was the source of real, repeatable, actual returns and that money managers with good recent portfolio performance records tended to have derived most of their returns from shifts in valuation.

It was mentioned earlier that firm-unique factors are company-specific and occur among stocks and over time. They pertain to statistical attributes such as: alpha (the excess of security-specific expected returns over market expected returns, i.e., the intercept on the regression calculation of beta), beta (historic security-specific volatility relative to the volatility of a market index), bond beta (historic security-specific volatility relative to the volatility of the long-term government bond market), yield and size (market capitalization). Recall that Merrill Lynch's Beta Book provides a monthly rundown on the first two attributes.

Another academic study[24] found systematic influences for these five firm-unique attributes were factors in New York Stock Exchange security returns between 1931 and 1979. It found that after-the-fact return estimates using a statistical model based on these attributes may explain about 10 percent of the variation in actual returns on individual stocks in a typical month (though none by itself explained as much as 4 percent) and about 40 percent of the variations in returns on a typical stock over time.

At this point, historical perspective on risk and returns is important.[25] Between 1925 and 1985, the risk-free rate of return on U.S. Treasury bills ran at an annual compound rate of 3.4 percent and the average annual rate of inflation, measured by the Consumer Price Index, ran at 3.1 percent. Annual compound rates of return on long-term U.S. government bonds were 4.2 percent and 4.8 percent on long-term corporate bonds. Returns on common stocks have run at an annual compound rate of 9.8 percent per year, up from 9.1 percent for a 50-year period ended in 1975. During these same years, the equity risk premium for the overall market, above the risk-free rate of return, (historically between about 5 percent and 5.5 percent) averaged an annual compound rate of 6.4 percent. Equity investors turn aggressive when the equity risk premium rises above 9 percent. They are neutral between 5.5 and 6 percent and defensive when it falls below 3 percent.

Between 1926 and 1981, returns on the quintile of smallest capitalization stocks listed on the New York Stock Exchange ran at an annual compound rate of 12.1 percent. Investors' inflation-adjusted, mean annual real pretax rates of return earned on various kinds of financial assets from 1926 to 1981 were 5.9 percent on common stock, 8.8 percent on small capitalization stocks, 0.0 percent on U.S. Treasury bills, −0.1 percent on long-term government bonds, and 0.5 percent on long-term corporate bonds.

BUSINESS STRATEGY: MARKET SHARE AND CASH FLOWS

This book deals primarily with company-specific influences on the returns-generating process (and share prices) of emerging companies: capital costs (capital spreads), operating margins (operating spreads), the duration over which each is expected to last, the rate at which cash flows are expected to grow, the profile of reinvestment opportunities, and the capital structure required to support the lowest average cost of capital.

Assuming similar capital structures and costs of capital, firm-unique strategy analysis explains variations in cash-generating abilities, operating margins and security-specific returns among companies within industries. They also make clear why share prices of some companies trade at different premiums or discounts to book values and earnings from other companies in the same industry.

In business strategy, cash is generated either by introducing new products, penetrating new industrial or geographic markets, broadening lines in existing products, or establishing new distribution channels in existing markets. Amounts of future cash will vary with two parameters: prices charged for end-products or costs of goods sold and/or costs of sales. Future returns will vary with these and capital intensity (investment/sales, revenue/assets and average capital employed).

In terms of sales growth and market share (strategic analysis is discussed further in Chapter 5), public companies in general tend to find themselves in one of four market environments: (1) large share of a rapid growth emerging market; (2) small share, perhaps in a fragmented industry, of a rapid growth market; (3) large share of a mature no-growth, slow-growth, or negative growth industry; or (4) small, but growing, share of a no-growth, slow-growth, or negative-growth market. Successful emerging companies usually find themselves in categories one or four and are usually accorded high economic value/book ratios as a result.

Venture capitalists prefer emerging companies in category one. They believe high growth/high returns companies in rapid growth markets allow for management mistakes in growing a business. Those with large market shares also have pricing flexibility and can protect margins. Investors, on the other hand, prefer the safety of category four. They believe high growth/high returns companies in no-growth, slow-growth or negative-growth markets do not invite competition. They insulate market competitors, thus sheltering them to a certain extent from rapid erosion of market share.

The Strategic Planning Institute (Cambridge, MA) offers perspective on the growth/cash flow character and strategy/cash connection of companies in categories two and three. Using its "profit impact of market strategy" database of more than 1700 product and service businesses, the Institute drew three conclusions.[26]

First, growth measured by real market growth rate and rate of increase in selling prices drains cash. Second, a high relative market share generates cash. Small-share businesses with high cash reinvestment rates in rapid-growth markets generated the least cash, a negative cash flow of 3 percent. Large-share businesses with low cash reinvestment rates in slow-growth markets generated the most cash, a positive cash flow of 9 percent. Finally, aggressive asset management is critical to reduce capital intensity to assure adequate cash flow.

The Institute found that a model of growth/share relationships explained only about 10 percent of dispersion in cash flow rates across business units. Another model focused on cash-generating ability and cash uses. It addressed cash sources such as market share and capital intensity in the long run and new product introduction rates and marketing expense growth in the short run. It also examined cash uses such as real market growth, selling price growth, percentage change in market share and changes in investment/sales ratios. This sources/uses model accounted for about 67 percent of the dispersion in cash flow rates.

In terms of profitability and operating margins (discussed more fully in Chapter 5), Professor Fruhan offers perspective on the characteristics of companies in categories one and four which enable them to earn high rates of return on equity and carry high economic value/book value ratios.[27] First, they benefit from barriers to market entry in one of four areas. Each protects them from competition. Differentiated products (patents, trademarks, advertising) provide a pricing advantage. Scale economies (production, marketing, product maintenance) support a cost advantage. Absolute cost advantages (scarce resources) give a cost advantage. And capital requirements (high initial investment) offer a pricing advantage.

Second, the product lines of these companies are highly focused. More than 70 percent of total sales is concentrated in one line of business. In addition, they tend to dominate. They carve the largest national market share in the industries in which they compete. As a result, they enjoy the potential economies of scale which arise from such a competitive advantage.

Third, earnings retention rates of these companies exceed their reinvestment rates. They generate cash faster than working capital or debt service consumes it. In effect, they operate debt-free with no financial risk and negative operating leverage. These passive assets reduce reported returns on equity. In a Fruhan study, 38.3 percent of 72 companies with returns on equity greater than 15 percent for the years 1966–1975 generated more cash than they could use in every year of the decade.

Finally, high growth/high returns companies are often overvalued by the market. Their share prices and market value-to-book value ratios imply a level of future expected returns greater than management can reasonably achieve (see the formula, Footnote 2).

Reebok International Limited (Avon, MA) is an example of a company in category one. The company is a low cost producer (75 percent production from South Korea) and market share leader (80 to 90 percent share), in the $260 million emerging aerobic and fitness shoe industry. That combination plus the company's ability to broaden its product lines to running, basketball and walking shoes and widen its distribution channels drove its profitability.

Reebok exhibited great earnings visibility. It earned $.05 cents per share in 1983, $.47 per share in 1984, $2.72 per share in 1985 and $1.56 against $.35 per share in the first quarter of 1986. The visibility of its projected earnings growth rate seemed clear out two years. Earnings estimates were about $5.50 per share in 1986 and $6.50 per share in 1987. As a reflection of the perceived duration of its growth and profitability, Reebok registered dynamic stock price performance between August 1985 and May 1986. Reebok came public at $17 per share in July 1985. It traded to a high of $80 per share by May 1986.

In an April 1986 *Business Week* survey of the top 1000 public companies, in terms of market value, Reebok ranked 611, with a $685 million market capitalization. For 1985, the company ranked second overall in sales growth, up 365 percent to $307 million, and fourth overall in earnings growth, up 534 percent to $39 million. Reebok also placed fourth in return on equity, at 52.9 percent on 13 times more equity outstanding (versus a weighted three-year average return on equity of 142.8 percent according to Standard & Poor's *Stock Reports*). The company commanded a price per share which was 930 percent of its book value per share. Every percentage point improvement in its return on equity made the company worth 17.6 percent more than the amount of equity capital stockholders put into it. Its price-to-earnings ratio was 16.

In contrast, *Business Week* reported that trailing 12-months sales of Nike, Inc. (Beaverton, OR) rose 10 percent in 1985 and earnings rose 115 percent. Return on equity was 13 percent (versus a weighted four-year average return on equity of 34.2 percent). The company's shares traded at 211 percent of book value. A one percentage point increase in return on equity added about 16.2 percentage points to share price (as a percent of book value). Its price/earnings ratio was 11 and its market value was $629 million.

Compaq Computer (Houston, TX), a maker of personal computers, is an example of a price/performance leader in category four. In 1985, the company tripled its share in the microcomputer segment of the $9 billion business computer market to 15 percent, increased sales by more than 50 percent, and doubled earnings. Sales in 1985 were $503 million, up 53 percent. Earnings were $26.6 million ($.90 cents per share), up 107 percent. Return on equity was 21.1 percent (the company was too young to demonstrate a multi-year return on equity track record) and its price per share was 308 percent of book value per share (as of March 31, 1986). Every point improvement in its profitability made the company worth 14.6 percent more than the amount of equity capital stockholders put into it. Its price/earnings ratio was 15. Its market value was $388 million.

Broadened product lines and higher performance machines drove the company's profitability. In the first fiscal quarter of 1986, Compaq's sales rose another 48 percent, to $144 million, and net income increased 80 percent, to $8.3 million, or $.30 cents per share. During this time, the more mature mainframe segment of the computer industry experienced virtually no growth. For example, IBM's profits in the first quarter of 1986 grew 3.1 percent and Digital Equipment's sales grew about 14 percent, almost half of its historical rate of revenue growth. For fiscal 1986, Compaq's sales rose 24 percent, to $625.2 million, and fully diluted net income increased 61 percent, to $42.9 million, or $1.33 per share.

In contrast to Compaq, *Business Week* reported that sales of IBM rose 9 percent in 1985, earnings were unchanged, return on equity was 20.5 percent (versus a weighted five-year average return on equity of 23.2 percent according to S & P) and share price was 287 percent of book value per share. A one percentage point increase in IBM's return on equity added 14 percentage points to its share price (as a percent of book value per share). Its price/earnings ratio was 14. Its market capitalization was almost $92 billion.

And (per *Business Week*) trailing 12-month sales for Digital Equipment rose 13 percent in 1985, earnings fell 18 percent, return on equity was 8.6 percent (versus a weighted five-year average return on equity of 12.64 percent according to S & P), and share price (as a percent of book value per share) was 197 percent. A one percentage point increase in the company's return on equity added 22.9 percentage points to share price (as a percent of book value per share). Its price/earnings ratio was 21. Its market capitalization was about $9 billion.

CASH FLOW VERSUS EARNINGS

Of most fundamental importance to the shareholders of every company are corporate financial managers, who do one of three things to economic value. Independent of earnings per share, they either create economic value, do nothing to it, or destroy it.

Economic value can only be created if rates of return on equity capital exceed costs of equity capital (investors' minimum required returns), or if rates of return on total invested capital exceed weighted average costs of equity and after-tax debt capital. But economic value can only be realized if operating margins on incremental sales and on total sales exceed investors' minimum required returns. The combination helps to distinguish between growth and growth opportunities.

Controversy surrounds the assessment of value. It concerns differences of opinion about the effects of accrual accounting versus cash accounting (they diverge with growth) in the evaluation of corporate profitability, health and wealth: the timing, amounts and (un)certainty of a company's future cash flows. Debate centers on the most reliable methods by which to gauge changes in the present value of a company's future operating cash flows and amounts of that cash assignable to a company's equity capital.

Discussion focuses on differences between discounted cash flow-based economic income and accounting-based book income. Economic income and economic return were defined earlier solely in terms of cash flows: (cash flow plus changes in present value over a forecast period) and (cash flow plus changes in present value over a forecast period divided by present value at the beginning of a forecast period).

In contrast, Professor Rappaport defines accounting-based book income as (operating cash flow minus book depreciation and other noncash charges plus new fixed and working capital investment). Accounting-based book return is calculated as (cash flow minus book depreciation and other noncash charges over a forecast period divided by the average book value of assets over that forecast period). If changes in present value differ from book depreciation, then economic income will differ from book income.

The difference between economic income and book income becomes particularly critical in light of differences between reported growth in earnings per share and actual growth in total return to shareholders. Growth in earnings may not necessarily create value for shareholders. Growth in book value may not necessarily translate to growth in market value.

The conflict began in the early 1970s. Professor Rappaport, Leonard Spacek Professor of Accounting and Information Systems at Northwestern University, found that during the 1973–1978 period, expectations of increasing inflation and interest rates factored into share prices but not earnings.[28] Results showed that earnings per share for the Standard & Poor's 500 grew at a rate of 8.6 percent per year. But total returns to shareholders (percentage changes in share price plus dividends) grew at a rate of less than one percent per year.

For example, earnings per share for the S & P 500 grew 27.1 percent in 1973 but total return declined 14.7 percent. In 1974, earnings grew 9 percent while total return fell 26.4 percent. In 1975, earnings fell 10.5 percent while total return rose 37.2 percent. They both rose in 1976. Earnings rose but total return fell in 1977, and they both rose in 1978.

In 1982, expectations of decreasing inflation and interest rates, not earnings growth, lifted stock prices. For example, earnings fell 17.7 percent but total return rose 21.4 percent. They both rose in 1983 and 1984. But in 1985, earnings fell 12.5 percent while total return grew 32.2 percent.

Rappaport conducted another study of the performance of Standard & Poor's 400-industrial companies in the 1970s. He found that 172 of the 400 companies registered compound growth in earnings per share (primary earnings from continuing operations) of 15 percent or more per year during the 1974–1979 period. But over the same time frame, 27 of these companies (16 percent) delivered negative rates of total return (dividends plus capital losses) to shareholders. Another 60 companies (35 percent) delivered rates of total return less than the 8.0 percent rate of inflation (measured by the consumer price index) during the 1974–1979 period.

Finally, Rappaport found similar results over a 10-year time frame. He found that 48 of *Fortune* magazine's Fortune 500 in 1980 had registered positive annual growth per year in earnings per share between 1969–1979 but, over the same period, had delivered negative rates of total return to shareholders. He cited names such as Anheuser Busch, Coca Cola, Corning Glass, Honeywell, Eli Lilly, Schering-Plough and Xerox as examples of companies that have demonstrated this pattern more recently.

Even the stock price performance of the 36 publicly-traded "In Search of Excellence" companies warranted his scrutiny.[29] Total return to shareholders in these companies between 1960 and 1980 was not consistently superior. Rappaport found their stock market performance was superior to the average New York Stock Exchange-listed issue in only 12 of 20 years. And they failed to consistently outperform their industry or their peers. (See Clayman in the bibliography for further discussion of the market performance of these companies, especially in contrast to "in search of disaster" companies.)

As a result of this dichotomy, cash flow (and discounted cash flow techniques) has emerged as perhaps the most meaningful means by which to judge corporate health, financial risk and economic value. Analysis of funds flow statements has become as important as analysis of balance sheets and income statements. And the cash flow effect of operating, investment, and financing decisions is perceived as a truer signal than earnings of the creation or the destruction of economic value.

Securities analysts flinch a bit when underwriters market public offerings on the basis of operating cash flow instead of reported earnings. But cash flow adherents contend that such an approach is justified. They argue that calculations of sustainable cash flows (and profitability ratios) in terms of net operating profit before depreciation and interest and after taxes exclude distortions to reported earnings caused by historical depreciation rates, and include income tax investment incentives.

Cash flow proponents also claim that accounting policies and treatments that affect reported earnings are discretionary. They do not affect underlying cash flows, and they do not reflect actual cash outlays needed to support growth in working and fixed capital investment, the effect of leverage on the cost of capital, or the time value of money.

I believe earnings are a proxy for cash flow and stock price (market/book) is a proxy for economic value (see the formula in footnote 2). As evidence, Professor Fruhan found a "general congruence" of economic value and actual market value data for companies with similar historic investment opportunity profiles, reflected in their historic returns on equity and historic equity expansion rates.

Throughout this book, I rely on historic intraindustry market value-to-book value ratios as measures of investors' perceptions of corporate cash-generating abilities among companies with similar capital and business strategy fundamentals. The ratio and its derivatives reflect the effects of management decisions on the creation of economic value. It also indicates the success with which managements translate economic value they create into market value shareholders realize. And distortion to reported returns on equity through leverage or inflation is mitigated through use of weighted averages of ROE over many years. Attention is paid to after-tax operating margins (as a percent of sales, assets and equity) to be certain that profitability is truly a function of real business growth and effective asset management.

I also contend that share prices are tied to investors' perceptions of the size and duration of a company's competitive advantage in its positive capital strategies. As a result, those companies with long-term sustainable competitive advantages in high growth/high returns product/markets will create and command the greatest economic value (as a percentage of book value).

I believe further that investors reward most in the present those managers who consistently anticipate value-creating or value-transferring opportunities. I claim that investors commit long-term capital to companies with managements that, they perceive, can consistently generate stable returns in excess of investors' minimum required returns for longer periods than their competitors.

And I emphasize that the clarity of investors' perceptions depends fully on the extent to which executives communicate value to Wall Street. There are economic rewards for those who successfully shape investors' perceptions of the magnitude and duration of their companies' future growth opportunities (positive net present value investments) and spread that perception to those few investors who set share prices. Those executives who successfully translate economic value into market value not only achieve market sponsorship, pricing efficiency, and fair securities valuation, they and their shareholders realize personal wealth.

SHARE PRICES: THE EQUITY VALUATION PROCESS

Efforts to value financial assets so that they could be bought and sold gave significance to Wall Street and birth to the securities industry. Earliest attempts to determine fair value were made in 1792 when the Buttonwood Agreement was signed under a buttonwood tree on the southern tip of Manhattan. In modern times, thousands of securities analysts compete against one another every day to be first to identify value in the securities of thousands of public companies.

Definitions of economic income, returns and value were offered earlier. The relevant questions for this book are: how does economic value manifest itself in stock prices, and how do Wall Street professionals identify it. The Strategic Planning Institute studied 600 industrial companies between 1974 and 1981. It found that four factors explained about 70 percent of the dispersion observed in stock prices (economic value as measured by price-to-book multiples) across companies: profitability, growth, risk, and stock market outlook.[30]

Growth was defined as investment growth and research and development as a percent of sales. It represented reinvestment opportunities relative to capital spreads. Profitability was defined as return on equity. It represented competitive advantages reflected in operating margins. Risk was defined as interest coverage and payout ratio and the stock market's outlook for corporate profits, interest rates, inflation, etc. It represented potential variances in operating cash flows and net income.

The study also found that market outlook alone explained only 5 percent of the dispersion. Market outlook and profitability (43 percent) explained 48 percent. Market outlook, profitability and growth (18 percent) explained 66 percent of the dispersion. Profitability was clearly the major key to value but not the only key.

Investors' perceptions of these four factors help to explain movements in stock prices. More appropriate, share prices tend to rise (fall) as a direct consequence of shifts in investors' perceptions of risk and expected returns (the cause), not because there are more buyers than sellers (the effect).

There is one reason for analysis but two reasons for trading on Wall Street (see first Treynor article in the bibliography). Identification of value is the reason for securities analysis. In the context of the stock market, value is described as the perceived spread between the estimated worth and the actual market value of equity securities. This "value spread" is the basis on which investors buy either performance or price. The balance of this chapter shows that securities analysts use a variety of models and methods to identify value.

Value or expectations are the reasons to trade. Ultimately, all trading on Wall Street is information-driven. But it is either value-driven or expectations-driven. The first is a disciplined approach that relies on publicly available information and numbers-crunching to estimate value. The second is an entrepreneurial approach that relies on information discovery to alter investors' expectations. Both rely on changing prices to generate expected returns. Value traders care about absolute price and less about time, until the spread between estimated value and market value narrows or closes. Information traders care about time in terms of the speed of adjustment in share prices to the arrival of new information, but less about the absolute price which results from that adjustment.

In the search for economic value, Wall Street professionals use one or a combination of three equity valuation methods: present value analysis, relative ratio analysis, and asset value analysis.[31] Each requires assessment of the present and assumptions about the future. Each views equities in terms of risk and expected returns and tries to discover those which offer higher expected returns relative to alternatives of equal risk. And, by definition, the results of each vary from consensus expectations. Management will find that large brokerage firms with highly structured research departments combine the first and second methods. However, executives will most likely encounter more firms which combine the second and third methods.

Implicit in each of these techniques is the economic notion of average values, that over time the performance of competitors in any sort of market reverts to mean levels of that overall market. It occurs because of the dynamic nature of competition. The profit potential in high growth/high returns businesses attracts increasing numbers of competitors who drive high returns to lower average levels. The lack of potential in low growth/low returns businesses leads to decreasing numbers of competitors who lift returns to higher average levels.

The implication for the equity valuation process is that lead investors discover companies for which performance expectations are too far below average values or too high above average values. In the first case, consensus expectations underestimate and undervalue equities, thus creating a spread between estimated values and market values. Lead investors buy those stocks. In the second case, consensus expectations overestimate and overvalue equities, thus also creating a spread between estimated value and market values. Lead investors sell or sell short those stocks. Their discovery attracts dominant sponsors who stimulate a popularity flow or outflow which drives returns up to, or down to, mean market levels.

Ideally, over time there should be no spread between market value and estimated value. The implication for management, and the central theme of this book, is that communicating value to Wall Street narrows spreads and facilitates the fair valuation of the company's equity securities. The extent to which a spread exists and persists varies with information availability and quality. In effect, executives stand guard over the equity valuation process. They have the power to reduce the size and the duration of any valuation differential.

PRESENT VALUE ANALYSIS

Academicians and investment professionals agree that, from an investor's perspective, the rational economic valuation of an investment in a company's equity securities depends upon both the amounts of future cash that flow from investment in existing assets and the amounts of incremental cash that flow from incremental investment in new earning assets. In other words, growth plus growth opportunities create economic value. The issues they may not necessarily agree on are how large those cash flows may grow in the future, how long they may last, and how much they may be worth today (intrinsic value).

In 1961, Professors Franco Modigliani and Merton Miller (then professor and associate professor of economics at the Graduate School of Industrial Administration at the Carnegie Institute of Technology) outlined four theoretical approaches to the intrinsic valuation of equities[32] using present value analysis.

Discounted cash flow (DCF) was first. It is ordinarily used in a capital budgeting context to determine the internal (economic) rate of return on investment in earning assets. Investment opportunities was second. It is an earnings and earnings opportunities approach which is often applied to acquisition analysis. Stream of dividends was third and is the most popular valuation approach in use today. Stream of earnings generated versus dividends distributed to shareholders was fourth.

Stream of dividends is the most popular approach because cash from dividends is considered more important than cash from sales of stock. Present value analysis is based on the theory that investors buy stocks for growth in prospective cash flows either from cash dividends or the sale of shares for cash, regardless of whether a company pays dividends. But the theory argues that the further into the future an investors' time horizon stretches the greater the present value of dividends and the lesser the present value of a stock's residual value.

For example, Professor Rappaport used Value Line dividend projections to estimate the proportion of current stock prices assignable to dividends beyond five years in the future.[33] The proportion, called the "long-term value index," is a proxy of investors' confidence in management's ability to create sustainable, long-term, economic value.

Rappaport calculated the index for over 1,200 companies and a broad cross-section of industries. He found a large clustering of companies around an 80 percent proportion. In other words, the present value of estimated dividends over the next five years amounted to only about 20 percent of current stock price. About 80 percent was assignable to dividends beyond five years. Defensive issues, such as major public utilities, registered the lowest proportion, in the range of 60 to 70 percent. The highest proportions were in growth industries, such as electronic components (93 percent), medical instruments (89 percent), retail drug stores (89 percent), radio-TV transmitting equipment (88 percent), and electronic computers (86 percent).

The interrelation of growth, duration of growth, and risk form the foundation for value-oriented dividend discount models on which present value analysis relies. They are a disciplined ranking system by which to judge the relative attractiveness of equities. They require forecasts of earnings growth, dividend payout ratios and the cost of capital. They are helpful in discerning valuation differences between companies with varying growth/returns profiles. However, they do not adjust costs of capital for inflation, and applicable growth rates in dividends per share are those expected by the market, not the company.

Many large brokerage firms with structured research departments use conventional dividend discount models to calculate the present value of streams of future dividends. Kidder, Peabody & Co., Duff & Phelps, Salomon Brothers, Inc., Prudential-Bache Securities, Sanford C. Bernstein & Co. and Drexel Burnham Lambert are a few examples. The First Boston Corporation, on the other hand, relies on a stream-of-future-earnings approach.

Conventional dividend discount models are used to calculate: (1) theoretically appropriate share prices from projected future dividend streams and estimated discount rates, (2) security-specific expected returns from estimated future dividend streams and current share prices (present value minus market value divided by market value), and (3) implied earnings/dividend growth rates from current share prices and estimated market discount rates.

Estimates from these models are very sensitive to growth, duration, and risk assumptions (as evidenced at the end of this chapter). But to the extent that managements can affect investors' assumptions and perceptions of rates of growth in future cash flows (higher), durations of that growth (longer), or risk (lower), independently of one another, they can affect equity valuation and share price (higher).

The theoretical results of these models do not fully explain fluctuations in share prices. For example, unexpected shifts in stock prices have been about five times greater than fluctuations in the present value of predictable dividend streams since 1870 (see Grossman/Shiller in the bibliography). But results should prompt management to seek reasonable answers to three questions raised by David Hawkins,[34] professor of accounting at the Harvard Business School. He suggests that executives learn:

1. Why their company's actual stock price may differ from its theoretical value.
2. Why investors assume that the company's cash flows will grow at the rate implied by theoretical models.
3. Why investors require a higher than market return.

Dividend discount models ascend in complexity as the predictability of growth rates in dividends over the stages of a company's life descend. Four types are most common: a P/E model, a constant growth rate model, a two-period growth rate model, or a three-period growth rate model.

One academic study[35] found that as these models became more complex, both portfolio returns and the ability to distinguish between underperformance and overperformance of equities improved appreciably. For example, over a short two-year period, the top-ranked portfolio, using a three-phase dividend discount model, had an annual return 3.5 percent greater than that of the top-ranked portfolio using a constant growth (in perpetuity) model. The study also found that the spread between returns on the best and worst portfolios ranked by the constant growth model was 22.26 percent, versus 35.63 percent for the three-phase model.

The Gordon-Shapiro formulation of constant dividend growth is the dividend discount model most widely used to arrive at theoretically appropriate stock prices. Similar to the NPV formula for economic income (mentioned earlier), the dividend capitalization model states that current share prices equal future dividend streams discounted to present values by investors' minimum required returns. It is expressed as: [(dividends) increased by a constant percentage each year of a forecast period] divided by [(1 plus the cost of capital) compounded in each year of a forecast period].

Assuming earnings grow at a constant rate and payout ratio is fixed, then dividends grow at a constant rate. Those who buy stocks on the basis of required returns believe that the present value of a stream of dividends is a company's [(current cash dividend per share) divided by its (cost of equity capital minus its estimated constant percentage growth rate in dividends per share)]. For complex models, the discount rate must be estimated by trial and error or computer program. In its simplest form, expected return is earnings yield, (earnings divided by share price), the cost of a dollar of equity.

Constant dividend growth models are most useful with companies that pay predictable streams of future dividends. Standard & Poor's monitors more than 300 dividend-paying companies. National Medical Enterprises is an example of a company with dividend predictability. It has the highest annual dividend growth rate, 38.8 percent per year for 13 years. Winn-Dixie is another. It has the longest record of annual dividend growth, 10.7 percent per year for 42 years, and Bank of Boston has paid dividends for the longest period, since 1784. For further statistical perspective, the annual growth rate in dividends for Standard & Poor's 500 companies peaked at slightly more than 11.5 percent in late 1982, according to Merrill Lynch data, and was about 4 percent in the third quarter of 1986.

The applicability of the constant growth model to emerging companies is limited. Their earnings growth rates, equal to their rates of growth in return on equity, are usually so fast that their growth rate in dividends, if paid out at a constant rate forever, would be greater than their cost of capital. That would negate use of the Gordon-Shapiro model.

Multi-phase dividend discount models are used most often to calculate theoretically appropriate share prices for companies which pay no, little, or unpredictable dividends. They incorporate consideration of the various stages of corporate growth, usually in line with a company's product/market lifecycle. The models make clear that those companies with the greatest competitive advantages in their chosen markets carry the highest estimates of earnings growth rates, which are expected to last for the longest periods. They command the highest theoretical share prices.

In a two-phase dividend discount model[36] (the formula for which appears in the footnotes), a first phase is associated with a forecast period of above-average growth, expected to last two to seven years. Growth in a second period equals market growth. In a three-phase model,[37] a second phase is usually associated with straight-line (same rate per year) decelerating growth rates over about a five-year period. A third phase equates a company's earnings growth rate to market growth rates. These calculations of discounted dividends over periods (multi-phases) of uneven growth plus the present value of the shares at the end of those periods (residuals), are the same as calculations of internal rates of return on projects with uneven cash flows.

Professor Rappaport's research highlights weaknesses in the use of conventional multi-phase dividend discount models. Conventional models focus only on earnings and dividends. They do not consider the cash consequences of changes in a company's sales growth, operating (cash) margins, investment requirements per dollar of sales growth, and financial leverage on its ability to pay dividends. In shifts from periods of above-average growth to periods of normal growth, conventional models will tend to understate a company's first-year dividend in the latter period due to the models' failure to associate reduced reinvestment with slower sales growth. Rappaport argues that this may lead to consistent understatement of the relative attractiveness of stocks. Security-specific expected returns may exceed market expected returns and have positive alphas.

In contrast, he claims that a company's "affordable" dividend payout rate may rise immediately after transition to periods of normal growth. It is a function of two elements: the difference in sales growth rates between period one and period two, and the difference in investment requirements between the two periods. Recognition of this potential payout increase after transition to normal growth periods leads to higher estimates of security-specific expected returns than conventional models. When compared to market expected rates, this leads to higher alphas and higher equity valuations.

Rappaport offers a matrix of affordable dividend payout rates.[38] For example, a company with a 14 percent sales growth rate, a debt/equity ratio of 25 percent, and 24 percent cash margins can afford a payout rate of only 33 percent at a high 90 percent investment rate. The rate rises to 41.6 percent and 50.4 percent as sales growth falls to 12 percent and 10 percent respectively. At an 80 percent investment rate, a company with 14 percent sales growth can afford a 40.5 percent payout rate. It rises to 48.1 percent and 55.9 percent as sales growth falls to 12 percent and 10 percent respectively. At a 70 percent investment rate, a company can afford a 47.9 payout rate. It rises to 54.5 percent and 61.4 percent as sales growth falls to 12 percent and 10 percent respectively. All numbers are lower as debt/equity ratios fall and/or operating margins narrow.

For cyclical companies, conventional calculations of discounted dividends require use of normalized earnings growth estimates which smooth the cyclical effects of economic cycles. For growth companies three-phase dividend discount models are often used (discussed later in this chapter).

Two formulations of price/earnings ratios arise from the dividend discount model. The first views earnings growth in terms of expansion in earnings and assets. The second views growth and growth opportunities in terms of expansion in positive net present values.

First, in the Gordon-Shapiro formulation, a company's price/earnings ratio equals its [(dividend payout ratio) divided by its (cost of capital minus its annual dividend growth rate)]. According to this formulation, a company's P/E ratio expands if its dividend payout rises, its growth rate in dividends rises, or its cost of equity capital falls.

This is not to suggest that management can affect the price of a company's shares by altering its dividend policy (discussed in Chapter 5). Earnings and dividends have the same present values because they come from the same stream of operating cash discounted at the same cost of capital. Cash dividends are considered only a way to package and distribute those present values. Rates and amounts of cash dividends depend on the success of investment and operating decisions, not the reverse. And, as Chapter 6 shows, changes in investors' expectations about future net operating cash flows associated with changes in dividends, not changes in dividends themselves, affect share prices.

Based on this formulation, Professors Fruhan and Thomas Piper (Harvard University) constructed a matrix of theoretically appropriate P/E ratios. They based them on profitability over time, ability to reinvest, and a cost of equity capital of 15 percent.[39] For example, companies with earnings reinvestment rates of 30 percent at −0.5 percent negative equity capital spreads (i.e., returns on book equity of 10 percent) expected to last for 5 years, traded at 8.2 multiples of earnings. They traded at 8.1 when earnings reinvestment rates rose to 70 percent and 8 multiples with earnings reinvestment rates of 100 percent.

In contrast, companies with earnings reinvestment rates of 30 percent at −0.5 negative equity capital spreads expected to last for 30 years, traded at 6 times earnings. They traded at 4.5 multiples when earnings reinvestment rates rose to 70 percent and 2.6 multiples with earnings reinvestment rates of 100 percent.

In further contrast, companies with earnings reinvestment rates of 30 percent at 0.5 percent positive equity capital spreads (i.e., returns on book equity of 20 percent) expected to last for 5 years, traded at 5.9 times earnings. They traded at 6.1 multiples when earnings reinvestment rates rose to 70 percent and 6.2 multiples with earnings reinvestment rates of 100 percent. Companies with earnings reinvestment rates of 30 percent at 0.5 percent positive equity capital spreads expected to last for 30 years, traded at 7.5 times earnings. They traded at 10.8 multiples when earnings reinvestment rates rose to 70 percent and 17.9 multiples with earnings reinvestment rates of 100 percent.

Companies with earnings reinvestment rates of 30 percent at 15 percent positive equity capital spreads (i.e., returns on book equity of 30 percent) expected to last for 5 years, traded at 5.3 times earnings. They traded at 5.7 multiples when earnings reinvestment rates rose to 70 percent and 6.2 multiples with earnings reinvestment rates of 100 percent. Finally, companies with earnings reinvestment rates of 30 percent at 15 percent positive equity capital spreads expected to last for 30 years, traded at 10 multiples of earnings. They traded at 33.3 multiples when earnings reinvestment rates rose to 70 percent and 132 multiples with earnings reinvestment rates of 100 percent.

Results clearly indicate that investors' perceptions of the future contribute meaningfully to differences in earnings capitalization rates. But they are also surprising in that they show higher P/E multiples in the short-term (five years) on companies with lower returns on book equity. There seem to be two reasons. First, a theoretical price (calculated with the constant growth dividend discount model) divided by low current earnings equals a high multiple. And, second, investors may expect an increase in earnings and dividend growth and in dividend payouts after five years.

The second formulation of price/earnings ratios from the dividend discount model arises from Miller-Modigliani's perspectives on growth and growth opportunities. It stresses the investment opportunities approach: growth in sustainable cash flows from investment in existing assets plus growth in cash flows from new investment in positive net present value earnings opportunities.

The calculation of a company's current P/E ratio has two parts. First, a company's P/E ratio on existing assets before new investment is: 1 divided by the cost of capital. It is the same as a company's [(after-tax operating profit divided by its cost of capital) divided by (its after-tax operating profit)].

Second, a company's P/E ratio on cash flows from new investment in growth opportunities has three terms: [(incremental fixed and working capital cash investment) divided by (sustainable operating cash flow from existing operations) times (average capital spread divided by the cost of capital) times (1 divided by 1 plus the cost of capital) compounded over the duration of the forecast period of the growth opportunity]. This second factor is added to the first to equal a company's total P/E ratio.

The significance of this calculation is that it reveals the extent to which a company's current share price is assignable to constant growth and future growth. If a company's internal rate of return equals its cost of capital, then the second portion of the equation will equal 0. The market will not capitalize cash flows from new investments because those investments will create no economic value. A company's P/E will only be that on constant cash flows from investment in existing assets. Therefore, according to this formulation, companies can expand their price/earnings ratios by investing in growth opportunities (positive net present value investments) at wide positive capital spreads for long periods. This formulation is also applicable to Professor Rappaport's research discussed in Chapter 5.

One academic study[40] found that neither the Gordon-Shapiro nor the Miller-Modigliani formulations explained more than 22 percent of the total variation of P/E ratios across companies. The second, however, explained more of the differences and more of the persistence of those differences over time. Other studies have concluded that a number of factors may influence P/E ratios: growth in earnings and dividends, risk, accounting policies, levels of corporate debt, corporate profit margins. and inflation.

RELATIVE RATIOS

Relative ratio analysis is a very popular Wall Street valuation approach. It measures the cost of profitability and the price of growth of issues in the same industry, of the industry itself and of the broad market. Those stocks whose costs are less (more) than alternatives of equal profitability and which are priced less (more) than those alternatives are considered attractive (unattractive).

This sort of analysis is fundamental and value-oriented. It uses price "descriptors" such as price-to-earnings, book value, cash flow, or yield to highlight these relative values. In and of themselves, these ratios are meaningless. They must be considered in light of company fundamentals. Comparisons reveal relative under-, fair, or over-valuation.

Price-to-earnings (P/E) is the most common relative ratio. It reflects how much investors are willing to pay for a company's earnings. It is usually calculated over trailing 12-months and over horizon 12-months earnings. A company's current P/E ratio is also calculated as a percentage of the S & P 500's P/E ratio (or S & P 400's P/E ratio for industrial companies). It is then usually compared to a five-year average of the same ratio. And a company's five-year average P/E divided by its current P/E ratio reveals how a company is priced relative to its past. A company selling for less than its past average has a ratio greater than 1 and is attractive to value buyers. A company selling for more than its past average has a ratio greater than 1 and is unattractive. Earnings/price ratios (E/P), mentioned earlier, measure a company's earnings yield, earnings per dollar of stock price. Value buyers search for low P/E, or high E/P, stocks.

The InvesTech Market Letter (Kalispell, MT) claims that price/earnings ratios have averaged 13.5-to-1 over the past 80 years but averaged 24-to-1 in early 1987. Since 1972, P/E multiples on the S & P 500 have ranged from a high of 18.6 times earnings in 1972 to a low of 6.5 times in 1979. Its historic high was 22.8 times trailing 12-month earnings in 1961. On the S & P 400, they have ranged from a high of 19.5 times earnings in 1972 to a low of 6.6 times in 1979.

P/E-to-estimated earnings growth rate ratios (PEG) show the price of forecast earnings growth. They are a company's current P/E ratio (based on normalized trailing 12-month earnings) or horizon price/earnings ratio (based on estimates of normalized forward-running 12-month earnings) divided by its forecast normalized five-year forecast earnings growth rate. High earnings growth companies command ratios less than 1 (growth rates exceed P/E ratios) and are attractive. Low earnings growth companies command ratios more than 1 (P/E ratios exceed growth rates). They are measured against a benchmark of PEG ratios for a company's industry or a company's history. Companies with PEG ratios less than 0.5 are considered undervalued and attractive.

P/E-to-expected return ratios indicate the price today of expected returns tomorrow. They are a company's horizon P/E ratio divided by its (five-year average internal earnings growth rate plus current dividend yield). Companies with high expected returns command ratios less than 1 (expected rates of return exceed P/E ratios) and are attractive. Those with low expected returns command ratios greater than 1 (P/E ratios exceed expected returns). Measured against a benchmark of ratios for a company's industry or a company's history, the ratio also suggests over-, under-, or fair relative valuation. P/E-to-reinvestment rate ratios (internal rate of equity growth) can also be calculated.

P/E-to-return on equity ratios may be formulated to measure the cost of profitability. Relative to a company's fundamentals, a company with a P/E ratio greater than its return on equity (ratio more than 1) is considered overvalued, i.e., too costly. One with a P/E ratio greater than the S & P 500 (or 400) but with a return on equity less than the S & P 500 (or 400) would be considered overpriced. A company with a P/E ratio less than its return on equity (ratio less than 1) is considered undervalued. One with a P/E ratio less than the S & P 500 but with a return on equity greater than the S & P 500 measure would be considered underpriced.

Price-to-book (or market-to-book) value per share (mentioned earlier) is an important relative ratio. It measures how much more a company's equity is worth than the book value of the common equity owners have invested in it. Share price change equals percentage growth in book value plus percentage change in the multiple of price-to-book. The inverse book-to-price ratio, (B/P) is used to measure a company's book value of common equity per dollar of share price. Value buyers search for low P/B, or high B/P, companies.

High investment/high returns businesses usually return to investors a dollar amount in market value greater than a dollar of invested equity capital. Their share prices trade at multiples of their book value. High investment/low returns businesses usually return to shareholders a dollar amount in market value less than a dollar of invested equity capital. Their prices per share are likely to trade at a discount to their book values per share.

Differences in price/book ratios among companies in the same industry may be explained by differences in profitability and growth of book equity. Price/book-to-return on equity ratios used in Chapter 4 are considered a more consistent means than P/E ratios to make this relationship more clear. Differences in ratios among companies across industries may be explained by differences in industry fundamentals, dividend policy, accounting policies, inflation and other macroeconomic variables which affect the growth/returns profiles of companies.

As of July 1986, stock prices, measured by the S & P 400-industrial index, traded close to 2 times book value. It was the highest level since 1973 and well above past peaks in bull markets in November 1980 or in September 1976. At its 1972 high, the S & P 400-industrial stock index traded at 2.28 times book. The ratio was 2.14 in 1973 but fell to 1.26 in 1979. InvesTech Market letter statistics indicate that price/book ratios have averaged 1.45-to-1 over the past 80 years but averaged 1.97-to-1 in early 1987.

Price (per share)-to-free cash flow (per share) ratios are also considered a more consistent means than price-to-earnings ratios by which to compare companies. They reflect how much investors are willing to pay for a company's cash-generating ability. Equity (per share)-to-cash flow (per share) is a measure of a company's average cash-generating ability. It indicates the length of time in years required to build shareholders' equity at a company's current rate of cash flow.

Analysts also look at relative yields in their assessment of relative values. Analysts examine:

1. Dividend yields.
2. Earnings yields.
3. Cash flow yields.
4. Earnings retention yields (earnings per share—dividends per share divided by share price).
5. Yield-to-book (dividend yield divided by book value).
6. Yield-to-three-month Treasury bills (dividend yield divided by three-month Treasury bill yield).
7. Earnings yield-to-double/triple A rated corporate bond yields (stocks are considered fairly priced when the two are equal).

By March 1987, the average dividend yield on stocks in the Dow Jones Industrial Average had fallen to about 3 percent (previously approached at market tops in 1966, 1968 and 1973) from 6.9 percent in July 1982. Treasury bill yields were more than 1.9 times average dividend yields. InvesTech Market Letter statistics suggest that price/dividend ratios have averaged 22.5-to-1 over the past 80 years but averaged 29-to-1 in early 1987.

Analysts also use momentum models to gauge improving fundamentals and to judge the relative attractiveness of securities. Earnings momentum models measure changes in the rate of earnings growth. For example, the inverse of the PEG ratio is an earnings momentum model: [(five year actual earnings growth rate) times (1 plus next year's estimated earnings growth)] divided by horizon P/E.

High growth companies with strong earnings momentum have ratios greater than 1 and are attractive. Low growth companies with weak earnings momentum have ratios less than 1.

Profit momentum models measure changes in rates of return. For example, they measure the slope of a regression line through a company's previous five year returns on equity. For sales growth momentum models, they measure the slope on the regression line through the last five year annual sales per share. Profit momentum models also compare a company's [(1 plus latest return on invested capital) divided by (1 plus its five-year average return)] divided by horizon P/E ratio. High growth companies with strong profit momentum have ratios greater than 1 and are attractive. Low growth companies with weak profit momentum have ratios less than 1.

Relative strength returns models examine a company's total return for the last month and last quarter relative to last year, to market returns, and to returns on other stocks over the same period. They reveal a company's stock market performance strength. Regressing a stock's returns over market returns over 30 months reveals a company's excess price volatility. Relative price strength models compare the past 30-day moving average of a stock's price to the moving average of the overall market. A higher than market average is attractive.

Earnings surprise models translate unexpected earnings results to relative price strength or weakness. Chapter 6 also deals at length with market reaction to announcements of both positive and negative unexpected earnings. The ratio is the difference between (actual earnings and consensus estimates of earnings) divided by (the standard deviation in the consensus). Positive surprises are obviously attractive.

Relative valuation measures have pluses and minuses. The advantage, for mature companies, is that data are available with which to compare seasoned companies within and between industries. The disadvantages are that they do not reflect, and may have no bearing on, the future. Neither the time value of money nor the cost of capital factors into the arithmetic. Accounting policies may also affect results. And, most important, there may be no valid basis for comparison of relative values of emerging companies with those of mature companies.

ASSET VALUATION

Asset valuation is a third approach to equity valuation. It is also a disciplined ranking technique by which to grade the attractiveness of equities. It is fundamentals-oriented and was emphasized by Benjamin Graham and David Dodd, co-authors of *Security Analysis*, considered the bible of fundamental analysis. This technique looks for divergence between current market values and current asset values.

In assessing this divergence, Graham used 10 stock selection criteria. The first five correlate with risk. The second five correlate with reward. The criteria are:

1. An earnings-to-price yield at least twice the AAA bond yield.
2. A price/earnings ratio less than 40 percent of the highest P/E ratio the stock had over the past five years.
3. A dividend yield at less than two-thirds of the AAA bond yield.
4. Stock price below two-thirds of tangible book value per share.
5. Stock price below two-thirds "net current asset value."
6. Total debt less than book value.
7. Current ratio greater than two.
8. Total debt less than twice "net current asset value."
9. Earnings growth of prior ten years at least at a 7 percent annual (compound) rate.
10. Stability of growth of earnings in that no more than two declines of 5 percent or more in year-end earnings in the prior year are permissible.

Other benchmarks used by these value buyers include "Q" ratios of share price to the replacement cost of corporate assets or of market value of debt and equity to current cost net book value of assets. Takeover targets usually have low Q ratios. Low ratios of share price to liquidated cash (break-up) value, restructured value or takeover value per share also attract value buyers.

One study examined the performance of portfolios comprising New York and American Stock Exchange companies which met Graham's criteria between 1974 and 1981.[41] It found that stocks selected on the basis of numbers one and six above achieved a mean annual return of 38 percent versus 14 percent mean annual return on the Center for Research in Securities Prices (University of Chicago) index of NYSE/AMEX companies. Another study reviewed the performance of portfolios formed on the basis of the net asset value criterion above (number five). These portfolios achieved higher mean returns than market benchmarks between 1970 and 1983 (see also Oppenheimer, 1986 and Rea in the bibliography).

Asset valuation is a conservative approach. It usually involves scrutiny of five to ten years of historic operating data in order to adequately assess historic ranges of cash-generating ability. Future growth and profit potential can then be forecasted within reasonable margins of safety. It examines operations in terms of after-tax returns on equity, capital, assets, and pre-tax return on sales. It views financial condition in terms of current ratios, low debt as a percent of total capital, interest coverage, etc. It pays close attention to yields and payout ratios in terms of growing dividend yields but falling payouts. And it considers relative ratios and earnings growth rates relative to the S & P 500 ratios and rates. To the extent that managements can shape investors' assumptions and perceptions of operations (stronger), financial condition (sounder) and future cash-generating ability (greater), they can affect share prices.

Those who espouse modern portfolio theory and use of dividend discount models contend that there is a big caveat in asset valuation. They claim that past rates of growth and profitability evidenced in financial statistics or guiding corporate philosophies are no guarantee of future rates, as evidenced in the performance of the "In Search of Excellence" companies (see Clayman in the bibliography). They argue that assessment of past corporate performance must be considered in light of current company fundamentals. And they advise that specific estimates of future growth and profitability should be used to make specific estimates of expected returns.

Ultimately, there is no right or wrong approach to the identification of value. Stock selection strategies incorporate considerations of value, yield, momentum, growth, risk, and liquidity. Each has been shown to produce average annual returns that exceed market returns by 1.3 percent to 9.3 percent over time. But some have worked better than others.

Goldman, Sachs examined the performance of strategies based on present value analysis, relative ratio analysis, and asset value analysis.[42] It measured the returns (as of June 30, 1987) on several strategies against the S & P 500 over two decades and over a one-year period (total return of 21.19 percent), and against stocks ranked in the bottom 20 percent by each valuation model. The firm found:

	Returns (Percent)		
Strategy	Two Decades vs. S & P 500	For The Year vs. S & P 500	For The Year vs. Bottom 20 Percent
Small Capitalization	9.3	−1.7	−2.4
Price Momentum	7.6	−5.0	−6.7
Low Analyst Coverage	7.0	−1.0	−3.8
Dividend Discount	7.0	−6.8	−16.3
Earnings Momentum	5.8	−0.89	−11.8
Implied Growth	5.7	−5.19	−16.8
Returns Momentum	5.1	2.82	3.0
Low P/E Ratio	4.7	−8.6	−19.8
Historical EPS Growth	4.7	−12.0	−29.3
Price/Cash Flow	4.6	7.31	1.65
P/E to Market P/E	3.6	−7.79	−20.4
Low EPS Uncertainty	1.3	−6.4	−20.5

Only stock selection strategies based on cash flow yield and returns momentum produced positive results over the 1986–1987 period. And selection of overvalued, high P/E, low growth, low yield, high analyst coverage, large capitalization companies surpassed the performance of other strategies above over the 12-month period ending June 30, 1987. It was the first time in 19 years, according to Goldman, Sachs. Those results were attributed to liquidity, speculation, and unexpected acceleration in earnings from cyclical sectors of the economy. And results of equity valuation analysis is as individual as the person performing the calculation. There is no right or wrong answer to questions of perception but differing assessments of value among many analysts can spread confusing perception. One brokerage firm analyst's initiation of research coverage or recommendation to purchase a company's shares on the basis of relative value may be another's termination of research coverage or recommendation to sell those same securities.

For example, Nucor Corporation (Charlotte, NC) experienced the phenomenon first-hand. In the first half of calendar year 1985, the company's shares were recommended for purchase and sale virtually at the same time by four different brokerage firm analysts. In February, PaineWebber recommended sale. In March, Oppenheimer recommended purchase. In April, Merrill Lynch recommended sale, and in May, Tucker Anthony recommended purchase. Whose perception was accurate? The company's shares subsequently rose about 30 percent in market value.

VALUATION OF EMERGING COMPANIES

Equity valuation of emerging growth companies, especially new issues, is particularly problematic. Intra-industry comparisons may be difficult because emerging companies may either dominate their industry or have a small but rapidly growing share in a fragmented industry. Ultimately, a lack of adequate data may invalidate any attempted comparisons.

Relative ratio analysis may also not work as growth slows. Ratios based on past growth rates may differ significantly from those based on estimated future growth rates. P/E-to-earnings growth rate ratios (PEG) may be used but may fall short because they mechanically equate companies with similar ratios to one another without considering the effect of different rates of compounding on growth. And asset value analysis may be difficult because operating track records may span too few years. Data from which to draw conclusions about the sustainability of competitive advantages may also be unreliable. And consensus expectations of normal period growth and profitability may have yet to form. Estimation risk may run high such that shifts in expectations result in volatile share price movements (as seen in the share price swings of Home Shopping Network Inc., in 1987).

Securities analysts do examine several relative ratios in their assessments of the relative value of emerging companies. They usually compare a company's price/earnings and price/sales (per share) ratios to those of competitors, the industry, and for a broad market index (S & P 500) in current and past markets. And they look at an industry's price strength relative to the S & P 500 (or S & P 400, if an industrial issue).

Performance buyers, who may be opportunistic short-term traders, will buy new issues in industries with relative price strength in expectation of strong underlying investor demand and rising prices in the short-term. A buyer on price will buy issues in industries with low relative ratios (i.e. price/earnings ratios below market multiples and low price/sales ratios) and improving relative price strength and hold for the long-term.

Analysts also examine market capitalization-to-sales ratios in new issues markets. These ratios offer perspective on investors' relative willingness to pay for rapid growth. In 1983, the average market capitalization-to-sales ratio for new issue companies was 4.1. It was highest in the first quarter of 1983, at 6 times sales. Market capitalization rates dropped to an average of 2.73 times sales in 1984. It was highest in the first and second quarters of 1984 at 3.3 times sales. In 1985, the ratio dropped to 2.05. It was highest in the second quarter of 1985 at 3.7 times sales. Investors were obviously more cautious and less willing to pay as much for future growth in 1985 as they had been in 1983.

Investors sometimes pay handsomely for perceived future growth. At the end of 1985, *Business Week* classified 10 companies as "The Little Giants," in terms of their market capitalization-to-sales ratios. Each had annual sales below $100 million, but each also had relatively high market values. They ranged from annual sales of $97 million (Forum Group) to $22 million (Tejon Ranch). Market capitalizations ranged from $2.2 billion (Genentech) to $331 million (Forum Group). Multiples of market capitalization-to-sales ranged from 27.72 (Tejon Ranch) to 3.4 (Forum Group). The average multiple was 8.97.

Theoretical present value models may also be questionable in determining the economic value of emerging companies. They require uncertain assumptions about growth rates of future operating cash flows, duration of that growth and risk. Three-phase, or more complex, dividend discount models, however, may still be used to calculate theoretical share prices and expected returns.

Analysts try to skirt the theoretical pitfalls of these stock price models. They explore company-specific/market relationships of growth and duration discounted by market rates of risk which eliminate the need to estimate security-specific risk. For example, one academic study[43] developed a growth and duration model by which to determine the extent to which a growth stock's higher earnings growth rate supported a higher price/earnings multiple. The model's formula was: [(growth stock price/earnings ratio divided by market P/E) equals (1 plus the total return growth rate of a growth stock divided by 1 plus the total return growth rate of the market) compounded over a forecast period].

The equation can be solved logarithmically for duration. Results show how long it may take for a company's higher earnings growth rate to compensate for the higher price (P/E) of its growth. If a forecast period is assumed, the term to the right of "equals" above can also be solved for target relative ratios of company P/E to market P/E at the end of the forecast period. The ratio of target to actual relative ratios reveals whether higher earnings growth is fairly valued.

A high ratio (percentage) suggests a large value spread. A low ratio infers full value. Results must consider company fundamentals.

Dean Witter Reynolds Inc. used the second term above in a three-stage formulation to estimate target P/E ratios for high growth emerging companies in terms of market growth. Results in its February 1985 "Emerging Growth Stock Monthly" showed the sensitivity of its calculations to changes in estimated earnings growth rates or assumed growth durations.

For example, the firm's model assumed a market discount rate (market expected returns) of 11 percent for the S & P 500-stock index. An emerging company with an estimated 20 percent earnings growth rate assumed to last three years (discounted by the market rate of return) carried a relative P/E of 1.51 times the market multiple. This rose to 1.76 if growth was assumed to last for five years, 2.06 if expected to last for seven years. One with an estimated 30 percent earnings growth rate assumed to last three years carried a relative P/E multiple to the market of 2.24. This rose to 3.07 if growth was assumed to last for five years, 4.21 if expected to last for seven years.

An emerging company with an estimated 40 percent earnings growth rate assumed to last three years carried a relative P/E multiple of 3.19 times the market. This rose to 5.07 if growth was assumed to last for five years, 8.07 if expected to last for seven years. And one with an estimated 50 percent earnings growth rate assumed to last three years carried a relative P/E multiple to the market of 4.41. This rose to 8.05 if growth was assumed to last for five years, 14.71 if expected to last for seven years.

Analysts also monitor the T. Rowe Price New Horizons Fund (Baltimore, MD) for signals concerning the relative cheapness or expense of emerging growth issues in general. They track the total return performance of the Fund and the Fund's P/E ratio relative to that of the S & P 500. "It's [the fund] called every major market top in small growth stocks for 25 years, without failure and without exception—1983, 1981, 1972, 1968 and 1961."[44]

Founded in 1960, the New Horizons Fund is the oldest equity mutual fund that specializes in emerging growth companies. Its first investment was in the shares of a company which had changed its name from Haloid Corporation to Xerox Corporation. And it is the largest such fund, with about $1.3 billion in equity assets.

The New Horizons Fund has ridden through 10 market cycles of total return performance. Five were periods in which total return on emerging growth companies declined. But only four were periods in which total return for the Fund and the broad market index declined simultaneously. Five were periods in which total return increased for both emerging companies and the S & P 500.

The Fund's shortest cycle, a downward turn, lasted about six months, from December 1961 to June 1962. Total return decreased 38.6 percent while that for the S & P 500 declined 22.3 percent. The two longest cycles each lasted about six and one-half years. The first, an upward turn, occurred from June 1962 to December 1968. Total return on the Fund increased 391.5 percent while that for the broad market increased 133.9 percent. The second, also an upward turn, occurred from September 1974 through March 1981. Total return on the Fund increased 387.4 percent while that for the market rose 193.2 percent.

In the most recent bull market beginning in August 1982, total return for the Fund increased 98.4 percent from June 1982 through June 1983 while that for the S & P 500 increased 61.2 percent. But from June 1983 through November 1984, the Fund's performance dropped 24.4 percent at the same time as the general market rose 3.9 percent. The Fund's performance during this cycle was the worst ever relative to the S & P 500 and the only one of 10 cycles in which the Fund's performance ran contrary to market performance.

Over this period, the fund's price/earnings ratio, relative to the S & P 500, has spanned a range from a low of 0.95 in the first quarter of 1977, the middle of an upward market cycle, to a high of 2.16 in the second quarter of 1983, at the top of an upward market cycle. Market tops have occurred five times when the fund's relative P/E approached 2 times that of the S & P 500. Market bottoms have occurred three out of four times when the fund's relative P/E ratio was in a general range of 1 to 1.3 times that of the S & P 500.

Use of the Holt growth duration model (footnote 43) in comparing the Fund's target relative P/E ratios to actual relative P/E ratios further improves the ability to anticipate cycle tops and bottoms. The results are a gauge of the relatively narrow or wide appreciation potential of emerging companies relative to the S & P 500.

Management's challenge is clear. Executives must understand how, by which models and which methods, analysts and investors value their company's equity securities. It is the only way they can affect the assumptions on which those valuations are based. And they must know what those models say about the value of their company's equity securities. It is the only way they can identify differences between market values and intrinsic or asset values. It is the only way they can shape investors' perceptions of the future and affect the market's pricing mechanism. Familiarity with the equity valuation process is essential to effectively communicating value to Wall Street.

3

Creating Investor Demand Begins Before an Initial Public Offering

The history of new issues markets reflects periods of general price/earnings ratio expansion.[1] Inflation tends to be manageable, real corporate profitability rises (operating margins expand), real corporate financial risk falls (financial leverage falls, debt ratios improve), and business risk falls (operating leverage falls, operating ratios improve). Stock prices move up and new issues are saleable. Over the past 25 years, the combination of the price/earnings ratio on trailing 12-months earnings of the S & P 500-stock index plus the underlying rate of inflation (measured by the Consumer Price Index) has tended to equal 20. It is called the 20 Rule. When inflation runs high, market price/earnings ratios tend to run low and vice versa.

History's hottest new issues market, in terms of dollar value and number of new issues (academicians define it differently as will be shown later), was in 1986: 717 initial public offerings valued at $22.4 billion. History's second hottest new issues market was in 1983. Emerging companies raised about $12.5 billion in 687 initial public offerings of stock. The underwriting figures for 1983 stand in stark contrast to prior years. In 1981, a total of 355 companies raised about $3.155 billion, an increase from 152 companies that raised about $1.4 billion in 1980. In 1982, a total of 124 companies raised about $1.4 billion.

The groundwork for 1983 was set throughout the 1970s. The price/earnings ratio on the Standard & Poor's 400-industrial stock index peaked in 1973 at 19.5. It subsequently fell continuously through the decade, reaching a low of 6.6 in 1979. The decline coincided with a rise in the rate of inflation from a low of 3.4 percent in 1972 to a high of 13.3 percent in 1979.

Earnings per share for the S & P 400 index grew at a 7.5 percent annual rate between 1966 and 1981. That rate was above the annual 6.9 percent rise in the Consumer Price Index over the same period, but less than the 8 percent CPI rate

67

of growth between 1974 and 1979. The inflation-adjusted value of the S & P 400 fell by about 50 percent between 1966 and 1981. Inflation started to moderate in 1979 (3.9 percent by 1982) and industrial P/Es started to improve (12.1 percent by 1982). A bull market began in August 1982.

After capitalizing on a fast-paced new issues market in 1983, emerging high technology companies committed unforgivable mistakes and disappointed investors. They failed to meet investors' earnings expectations. Their earnings failed to materialize and their stock prices plummeted. The roster of losers is long. Between January 1983 and October 1984, 20 new issue companies lost more than 70 percent of their total market value.

Victor Technologies was a disaster. It lost 99.3 percent of its market value. Fortune Systems lost 86.4 percent. Televideo Systems lost 80.6 percent, Kaypro 73.7 percent, Micro D 73.4 percent, and Select Information lost 70 percent of its total market capitalization. In 1985, the Pizza Transit Authority, a fast-food company, lost the most market value of any new issue. It surrendered 64 percent of its market capitalization.

New issues of emerging companies in high technology industries in 1985 suffered the consequences of 1983's disappointments. Equity capital for high technology companies was only 3.8 percent of the total amount of new capital raised in 1985, down from 18.8 percent in 1983.

As a percent of total new equity capital raised in 1985, new equity capital for computer software companies fell from 6.7 percent to 2 percent. It fell from 4.1 percent to 0.8 percent for instrumentation companies. Financial services companies, retailers, biotechnology companies and investment funds were 1985's most saleable issues.

Valuations in 1983 were technology-driven. In 1985 and 1986, valuations were market-driven. But investors seemed less willing to pay high prices for uncertain growth opportunities in high technology in 1986. As a result relative equity valuations were more modest.

Earlier mention was made that price/earnings multiples contracted in the decade of the 1970s. At the time, investors paid 10 to 12 times earnings for shares in high quality companies growing predictably at a 25 to 30 percent rate per year. They paid a price roughly half to a third of a company's future earnings growth rate. Those companies were undervalued as multiples lagged growth rates.

But by 1983, investors were overpaying for unpredictable future earnings growth. In March 1983, companies went public at average price/earnings multiples of 29.7 times trailing 12-months earnings, versus an average P/E ratio of about 12 for the S & P 500. Prices for some issues were 50 to 60 times trailing 12-months earnings.

Diasonics, for example, went public at $22 per share, a multiple more than 70 times its trailing 12-months earnings. At their high, the company's shares traded at $27.25. By 1984, its shares traded at $2.50 per share. And three-year-old

Fortune Systems Corp. offered five million shares at \$22 per share in March 1983, a market capitalization of \$500 million. But the company had annual sales of only \$26 million and had never operated at a profit. Its shares subsequently fell to \$2.125 per share. The company ultimately changed its name to Tigera Group.

By 1985, ranges of price/earnings multiples had fallen to 15 and 30 times trailing earnings. In 1986, average P/E multiples on new issues were in the low 20s, versus an average P/E of about 17 on the S & P 500. It reflected a return to the general pricing rules of the 1970s. At that time, the prevailing belief was that an emerging company's P/E ratio should be equal to about half of its anticipated earnings growth rate.

Market capitalization-to-sales ratios were relatively more modest in 1985. The average ratio for a new issue in 1983 was 4.1. On the high end, LSI Logic Corp. and Seeq Technology, Inc. sold stock at more than 20 times their annual revenues. But in 1985, new issues were capitalized at an average rate of about 2.05 times their annual revenues. Cypress Semiconductor Corp. sold shares at about eight times its annual sales. Corporate longevity also became more important. The average age of new issue companies rose to approximately seven years in 1985 from five years in 1984 and three years in 1983.

Investment bankers had to work hard to earn their fees in 1985, especially on the heels of such major new issue disappointments as in 1983. Corporate finance departments of major underwriters (managers of 10 or more initial public offerings) generally underwrote the securities of companies that were leaders in their markets, were supported by strong and reputable venture investors, demonstrated superior cash-generating abilities (operating margins), and had strong management teams in place.

Academicians define hot or cold stock markets by the returns behavior of new equity issues on their offering day. They measure the percentage change from offering price to aftermarket price to determine one-day initial returns. A stock is bought at the offering price and then sold, on the same day, at the stock's closing bid price. The percentage difference reflects investors' perceptions of expected value relative to alternative investments of equal risk and investment bankers' perceptions of investor demand.

One study[2] summarized the results of many academic studies on the topic. It found that one-day initial returns on 120 new issues averaged 11.4 percent from 1960 to 1969, 16.8 percent on 2,650 new issues from 1960 to 1970, 18.8 percent on 5,162 new issues from 1960 to 1982, 13.8 percent on 440 new issues between 1974 and 1982, 26.5 percent on 1,028 new issues from 1977 to 1982 and 48.4 percent on 325 new issues between 1980 and 1981.

Scrutiny of these results suggests that the market for new issues was relatively cold from 1977 to 1982. Average initial returns were 16.3 percent. The market was particularly hot from 1980 to 1981 due to a clear industry effect for natural resource companies. Average initial returns were 48.4 percent. For the calendar year of 1985, about 70 percent of all new issues rose in price in the aftermarket. But only about 50 percent rose more than the 26.33 percent rise in the S & P 500.

In 1986, the hottest new issue was Home Shopping Network, Inc. (Clearwater, FL). The company came public in May 1986 at $18 per share. The stock opened immediately at $42 per share and closed its first day of trading at $42.625 per share, for an unannualized one-day initial return on share price appreciation of 136.8 percent. Its one-month initial return was 99.7 percent, closing price per share at the end of May was $95.375 per share. And its one-year initial return was almost 520 percent at a closing price per share at the end of the year of $37.50, adjusted for a 3-for-1 split.

In 1987, the hottest new issue (as of this writing) was that of Aldus Corporation (Seattle, WA). Priced at $20 per share (up from a target range of $14-$16 per share) on June 16, 1987, the company's one-day initial return was 78.75 percent (closing bid per share of $35.75). Its one-month initial return was 62.5 percent at a closing bid per share of $32.50 on June 29, 1987.

In terms of this definition of hot and cold markets, one of four conditions (measured by initial realized returns) prevails during an initial public offering. Either the market is hot and the company is hot, the market is hot and the company is cold, the market is cold and the company is hot or the market is cold and the company is cold. The implications of these conditions for the pricing of new issues is discussed later in this chapter.

Condition one maximizes investors' initial realized returns on investment in a company's shares. Condition two neutralizes shareholders' initial realized returns. Condition three optimizes initial realized returns, and condition four minimizes or eliminates initial realized returns. Academicians argue that the best quality of earning assets comes to market in cold markets.

Hot companies in a hot market or hot companies in a cold market benefit most from public offerings. They tend to be able to raise the most capital and surrender the least equity. They excite the market and fuel investors' returns expectations. They satisfy those investors who capitalize on short-term price changes and trading opportunities and appeal to those whose attitude and time horizons are geared to long-term loyalty.

The initial public offering of Morgan Stanley Group, Inc. (New York, NY) in early 1986 epitomized condition one. It was a hot company in a hot market. The preliminary prospectus, or "red herring," dated February 14, 1986, quoted a tentative offering price of $42 to $46 per share. At that time the Dow Jones Industrial Average stood in the low 1600s.

A successful offering of securities in another firm a week earlier had primed the market for this offering. The earlier initial offering of the shares of L.F. Rothschild & Co. (New York, NY) had been increased both in size and price from its initial filing with the Securities and Exchange Commission. The original six million shares had been increased to 7,676,325. Pricing tentatively set at $16 to $19 per share had been raised to $20.50 per share. Upon being offered, Rothschild's stock immediately traded to an interday high of $24. The stock closed its first trading day at $23 per share, a 12 percent one-day initial return. One-month initial return (March 28, 1986 close of $23.875) was 16.5 percent and 1986 initial capital loss was 36.6 percent at a $13 per share close for the year.

In response to strong investor demand, the tentative pricing of the shares of Morgan Stanley Group was raised to $54 to $57 per share from the initial indication of $42 to $46 per share during the week before the offering. By the time of the offering, on March 21, 1986, the Dow Jones Industrial Average had closed the previous day's trading session above 1800 for the first time in history.

Morgan's offering of 5.18 million shares was co-managed by a stable of prestigious national institutional brokerage firms: Morgan Stanley Group, Inc., Bear Stearns & Co., Inc., The First Boston Corporation, Goldman, Sachs & Co., Merrill Lynch Capital Markets, Salomon Brothers, Inc., and Shearson Lehman Brothers, Inc. It came to market at $56.50 per share, a $292-million new issue.

At the offering, Morgan's market capitalization was about $1.39 billion. The deal was priced at about two times book value and between eight and nine times trailing 12-months earnings. Brokerage stocks had not commanded price/book multiples of this magnitude since 1973. Both figures were below industry averages at the time.

The new issue traded immediately, on the first sale, at $70 per share on a 500,000 block. It traded at an interday high of $74.25 and an interday low of 69.25 per share. The stock closed its first trading day at $71.25 per share, a 26.1 percent one-day initial return (unannualized) on volume of 1.93 million shares. Its one-month initial return was unchanged from its one-day initial return. Its 1986 inital return was 14.8 percent at a closing price per share for the year of $64.875.

Sun Microsystems, Inc. (Mountain View, CA), and Teknowledge, Inc. (Palo Alto, CA) were examples of cold companies in a relatively hot market. The S & P 500 index had risen 26.33 percent in 1985 and was on its way to a 14.62 percent rise in 1986. Investors had high expectations for Sun Microsystems. The company was considered one of the fastest growing and most profitable start-ups in the engineering work-station industry. After only three years of operations, it was second in market share to the industry leader, Apollo Computer, a company with a history of a successful initial public offering. It had offered 4 million shares at $22 on March 3, 1983. Its initial one-day return was 20.5 percent; one-month return was 34.1 percent.

Sun planned to offer 4.6 million shares at a tentative price of $16 to $18 per share through Alex. Brown & Sons, a retail/institutional brokerage firm, and Robertson Colman & Stephens, a major regional firm. The company offered four million shares at $16, a $64-million issue. It was aggressively priced at about 20 times anticipated 1987 earnings. It was capitalized at a market value 2.9 times its estimated 1986 revenues. With 26.3 million total shares outstanding, the company's market capitalization was about $420.8 million.

Offered on March 4, 1986, its one-day initial capital loss was 1.5 percent (closing bid price per share on the first trading day was $15.75). Sun Microsystems' one-month initial capital loss was 9.4 percent (closing bid per share at the end of March was $14.50). Its 1986 initial return, however, was 33.3 percent as its shares closed for the year at $24 per share.

Teknowledge, Inc., a leader in applied artificial intelligence, also carried high investors' expectations. The company went public on March 5, 1986 at $13 per share. Its market capitalization was 7.2 times its annual revenues at the time of its offering.

But the new issue was a disappointment. Its one-day initial return was 0 percent (closing bid price per share on the first trading day was unchanged from offering price). Its one-month initial capital loss was 4.8 percent (closing bid price per share at the end of March was $12.375). The company's 1986 initial capital loss was 27.9 percent as its shares closed for the year at $9.375 per share. Rumors, after the offering, of overly aggressive pricing of the issue laid blame on Eastman Kodak whose cost basis on its recent purchase of Sun's shares was estimated at about $13.33 per share. Kodak apparently believed a pricing of $14 to $14.50 per share, instead of $16 per share, was unsatisfactory.

In cold markets, premiums in the aftermarket disappear to a large extent. Both one-day and one-month initial returns tend to be low, nonexistent or even negative. It happened in 1984. Inflation crept up from 3.8 percent in 1983 to 4.64 percent. Price/earnings ratios for industrials, represented by the S & P 400-industrial stock index, fell from a high of 13.2 in October 1983 to a low of 10.2 in July 1984. The S & P 500-stock index fell about 16 percent from an October 1983 high to a July 24, 1984 low. Only twelve new common stock issues of industrial companies came to market during the month of July 1984. In a hot new issues market, several emerging industrial companies may make their initial public offerings of common shares in a day.

Transtector Systems, Inc. (Hayden Lake, ID), a manufacturer of circuit protectors, was the only example of a hot company in that cold market of July 1984, the month in which the market reached an intermediate two-year bottom. The company made its initial public offering on July 12, 1984 at $5.50 per share. On its first day of trading, the company's shares closed at $7.50 bid per share, a one-day initial realized return of 36.4 percent. Its one-month initial return was 4.5 percent (closing bid price on July 31 was $5.75 per share). Its one-year initial capital loss was 20.4 percent at a closing bid price on July 31, 1985 of $4.375 per share.

Investors in most of the companies that made their initial public offerings during July 1984 realized minimal or no initial returns. For example:

1. Display Components, Inc.: offered at $4 per share on July 2, 1984, closed at $4.125 bid per share for a one-day initial return of 3.1 percent.

2. American Shared Hospital Services: offered at $5 per share on July 3, 1984, closed at $5.75 bid per share for a one-day initial return of 15 percent.

3. Kappa Networks, Inc.: offered at $6 per share on July 12, 1984, closed at $6.25 bid per share for a one-day initial return of 4.2 percent.

4. Computer Depot, Inc.: offered at $9 per share on July 12, 1984, closed at $9 bid per share for a one-day initial return of 0 percent.

5. Shoppers World Stores: offered at $3.25 per share on July 16, 1984, closed unchanged for a 0 percent one-day initial return.

6. Audio Video Affiliates: offered at $11 per share on July 17, 1984, closed at $11.125 bid per share for a 1.1 percent one-day initial return.

7. Ceradyne, Inc.: offered at $7.50 per share on July 18, 1984, closed unchanged for a 0 percent initial return.

Cold companies in the cold market of July 1984 realized one-day initial capital losses of about 5 percent:

1. Edudata Corp.: offered at $5 per share on July 20, 1984, closed at $4.75 bid per share for a 5 percent one-day initial capital loss.

2. MMI Medical, Inc.: offered stock at $8 per share on July 24, 1984, closed at $7.625 bid per share for a one-day initial capital loss of 4.7 percent. Its one-month initial capital loss was 1.6 percent ($7.875 bid per share on August 31, 1984). Its one-year initial capital loss was 26.6 percent ($5.875 bid per share on July 31, 1985).

3. Hooper Holmes, Inc.: offered stock at $10 per share on July 26, 1984 and closed at $9.50 bid for a one-day initial capital loss of 5 percent. Its one-month initial capital loss was the same. Its one-year initial return was 25 percent ($12.50 bid per share on July 31, 1985).

Any decision to go public should be based on one fundamental premise. It is the expectation that management will report positive near-term earnings in line with, or better than, analysts' consensus earnings estimates.

Microsoft Corp. (Bellevue, WA) ably demonstrated the premise. In its first quarterly report after going public in March 1986, the company reported a 24.1 percent increase in year-to-year sales from $40.7 million to $50.5 million. It disclosed earnings of $10.6 million, or $.42 per share, a 24.7 percent increase over the prior year's $8.5 million, or $.37 per share. For the year ended June 30, 1986, the company expected to report a revenue increase in excess of 35 percent, margins close to 20 percent, and profit of about $1.50 per share, about double that of 1985.

GOING PUBLIC

Going public is just one step in the equity valuation process. Fair equity valuation, the ongoing objective of the process, begins before any underwriter is chosen and proceeds continuously after an offering has been completed. In general, the size and duration of perceived earnings opportunities determine a company's need to raise money in public capital markets. And while market conditions determine the company's timing of its public offering, investor demand determines a company's ability to go public.

Managements of emerging companies in growing product/markets, with respectable cash-generating track records (high operating margins), self-financed growth through internally generated funds and above-average future earnings potential will usually find their companies the objects of much Wall Street attention. Underwriters court them, investment bankers woo them, corporate finance departments keep tabs on them, and new business representatives call on them. The activity is, at times, more reminiscent of marriage than finance, and perhaps with good reason.

Selection of an underwriter in the going public process (also discussed later) is a very sensitive management issue. Senior executives of emerging companies review the credentials of attentive investment banking firms with an eye toward an enduring future relationship. They debate the qualifications of each. They try to be objective, within the subjective context of what is good for the company.

Executives listen to the opinions of their venture capital investors, their accountants, their lawyers and their commercial lenders. They gauge a brokerage firm's ability to price and to distribute the company's securities. And they hope that the firm can strongly support the company in its new public life, the aftermarket of its initial public offering.

Managements of emerging companies often lose perspective on the initial public offering process. They focus more on the time-consuming process of going public than on the timeless process of being public. They get wrapped up in today's excitement but ignore the fact that public capital markets look to tomorrow. They may perform well on road shows but they fail to realize that the show has only just begun.

Senior executives of emerging companies usually congratulate themselves on successful public offerings, forgetting that they now face the ongoing challenge of successful public valuations. They may bask in the current attentiveness and support of their underwriter, expecting that shareholders will pay similar deference. But if their initial public offering is a cold deal, they will find that their underwriters neglect them and their institutional shareholders sell stock. Managements of these emerging companies get disappointed. Stock price falls, euphoria dampens and they are orphaned in the aftermarket. Wall Street reality sets in quickly.

Some executives learn earlier than others that harmony between management and shareholders cannot be taken for granted and that shareholder activism may be a real threat to management independence. Some may find themselves forced to take their companies public, the timing for which may be different than management had in mind.

For example, venture capitalists, occasionally called "vulture capitalists," may force the move within a specified number of years after their initial venture investment. They use the going public process as a "cash out" mechanism to satisfy their liquidity requirements. Or venture investors may apply pressure on management to find a merger partner, or to buy back their stock. Some managements may take action into their own hands and take their companies public to wrest control from venture capital investors.

Managements of emerging companies may easily misunderstand the role of venture capitalists. In an absolute sense the two share the common goal of creating value (total return) for shareholders. In a relative sense, however, their objectives differ. Management tries to build a business of capital assets. Venture capitalists try to build a portfolio of financial assets. The former are asset managers. The latter are money managers, not management consultants. Similar to an investing institution, they manage other people's money but invest only in private companies. The former build economic value. The latter build market value which requires portfolio turnover.

And executives may find that underwriters try to enslave them. Some underwriters force their new corporate finance clients to enter into three to five year "right of first refusal" contracts for future financings. They lock their firms in to emerging companies' future capital needs. If the client company prefers another investment banking firm in the future, it must buy out its contract.

Going public is truly a capital decision that requires a total reversal of management perspective. Attention turns completely from minimizing reported net income, for income tax purposes, to maximizing reported net income, for shareholders' purposes. The shift brings the company face-to-face with the world of government regulation in the form of the Securities and Exchange Commission. Management must disclose and abandon any previous third-party dealings or tax shelters designed to minimize net income. Senior executives must disclose their annual compensation. Strategic information from which competitors can deduce costs, margins and price structure becomes available.

Many entrepreneurs advocate any alternative to tapping public capital markets: private capital, creative financing from customers or suppliers, or leveraging every penny out of the business. They advise this because after a public offering, management becomes the agent of other owners. Corporate executives lose their autonomy. They face new rules of performance and disclosure, different from private investors, imposed by government sources and institutional investors, and they may not necessarily gain personal liquidity. Federal restrictions on sales of securities apply to corporate insiders. Much of their net worth may remain on paper.

Venture capitalists believe that a private company should, before going public, have manufactured and delivered its first product. It should know its prospective customers to the extent of being able to forecast its customer buying cycle. It should have as diversified a revenue base as possible, a predictable cash flow and operating margins at least at break-even.

In addition, they claim that an emerging company should be able to define the market share and market size of its product/market opportunity, and it should expect to report good operating numbers in the fiscal quarter immediately after the offering. A strong cash-flow-generating record is desirable. Benchmarks are $1 million or more in current earnings and a strong predictability of visible cash flow out 18 to 24 months.

Venture capitalists also desire liquidity in the aftermarket for their portfolio companies. They associate trading liquidity with market capitalization and think in terms of both raising capital in an offering and achieving liquidity after an offering. They believe, in general, that new-issue companies raising $10 million or more in public markets should achieve a market capitalization greater than $25 million. They believe that being a little bit public with shares which are publicly traded but are essentially illiquid is disastrous.

Managements take their companies public for a plethora of reasons. A public offering is usually the first independent valuation of a young company. It assigns a known value. Going public may also improve a company's access to capital and may reduce its cost of capital.

An aggressive growth strategy may require going public. It can lend corporate credibility and a competitive cash advantage to a company. And execution of growth strategy based on buying market share, which may demand an exchange of shares, is easier if a company's shares carry known public value and liquidity. Optimum combinations of cash and stock can more easily be determined. Also, management may want to establish an incentive plan to reward key employees. One method is to issue incentive options on stock with visible market value.

Managements have other purposes too. In the case of Microsoft, management wanted more visibility within the financial community. Senior executives wanted easier access to more capital to facilitate planned expansion or to negotiate prospective acquisitions.

Other companies, such as Genentech and Cetus Corp. (both in San Francisco, CA), capitalized on hot market conditions for new issues of biotechnology companies in 1982. Investors placed high value on biotechnology's perceived future earning power from potential new product introductions in a wide variety of potential markets. Managements used the proceeds to fund research and development, 10 percent or more of sales for some, and bankrolled the balance.

Finally, original investors in a company may want to diversify their personal portfolios. Selling shares enhances their liquidity. Insider sales of shares on the offering, though, send information signals which affect investors' perceptions. Would-be buyers see either owners' retention of interest in a company or their "bail-out." They prefer the former. They may avoid purchase of shares if insiders sell about 30 percent or more of the offered shares on the offering or if their personal proceeds from the offering exceed the company's cumulative historic earnings.

For example, the founder of Vestron, Inc. (Stamford, CT), publisher of prerecorded videocassettes, tried to realize maximum personal liquidity in the company's initial public offering in September 1985 . The preliminary prospectus indicated that the founder and the company were to sell equal amounts of stock in a proposed $205-million initial public offering. Afterward, the founder would still own 70 percent of the company's outstanding shares.

Investors balked. Their demand for the offering was weak. Institutional investors decided that personal liquidity in this case amounted to personal aggrandizement. The offering could not be sold and was therefore restructured. Share size was scaled back and offering price was reduced from the $16 to $19 per share range to $13 per share. The founder offered no shares.

Virtually any company of any quality can sell stock to the public at any time, but at a price. *Venture* magazine reported that 478 companies went public in 1985. Of that total, it claimed that 147 had annual revenues of $10,000 or less; 176 showed losses in net income and 62 were blind pools, investment firms without assets or business plans. Only 194 companies, 40.6 percent of the total, offered shares to the investing public at prices of $5 or more. The 10 largest offerings in 1985 amounted to $828.3 million, 23 percent of the year's total market value of new issues.

Administrative duties associated with making a public offering require a significant amount of management's time. The opportunity cost of that lost time can mount dramatically and the process is expensive. Besides underwriters' spreads, bills mount from lawyers, accountants and printers. Some companies, to reduce paperwork and cost, go public in the Unlisted Securities Market (USM) in London, where reporting requirements are less stringent. The initial public offering process may take less time, four months instead of six, and may save several hundreds of thousands of dollars.

In 1985, *Venture* magazine also studied the corporate costs of going public. It examined the prospectuses of every new issue offered in that year to determine the range of expenses associated with offering stock to the public. It found that the total cost, for underwriters, lawyers, printers, accountants and transfer agents ranged from a low of 6.4 percent of the dollar value of the offering proceeds for Alco Health Services Corp. (Valley Forge, PA), which raised $75.2 million, to a high of 41.4 percent, for Intercell Corp. (Cortez, CO) which raised $225,000.

A quality investment banking firm's gross underwriting spread, before legal, accounting, printing, and nonaccountable expenses runs, on average, from 6 to 9 percent of the total dollar value of an offering. In contrast, going public in London's USM may cost no more than 1.25 to 2 percent of a total, although smaller, offering.

The underwriting spread is usually divided three ways: a selling concession, about 60 percent of the spread, goes to the syndicate members who sell (distribute) the issue. The management fee, for the managing underwriters, is about 20 percent. The syndicate fee for the syndicate's bearing the expense and risk of a firm underwriting commitment to the company is about 20 percent. Companies with backgrounds of self-financed growth, perceived competitive advantages in high growth/high returns markets, cut the best deals with underwriters.

THE MARKET FOR PUBLIC EQUITY FINANCING

The securities industry, in general, can be broken down into a bracket structure of influence and prestige. Each bracket reflects the influence of member firms within the context of overall capital markets. Each has its share of prestigious and nonprestigious firms.

Bracketing is a historical Wall Street custom. The position of firms in underwriting syndicates and tombstone advertisements has historically followed a very strict pattern. Co-managers of a deal appear at the top. The major bracket of national institutional firms comes below. The mezzanine bracket of national wirehouse firms and retail/institutional firms follows. The sub-major bracket of major regional firms comes next and the regional bracket of small regional firms comes last. A firm's position in the bracket, decided by whichever firm manages the book on the deal, indicates its relative importance in and to the deal.

Customary bracket structure began to change in the late 1970s. Commissions went from fixed to negotiated in May 1975 and securities industry profit margins started to get squeezed. Competition for new business began to rob Wall Street's old boy network of its traditional stable of clients. Competition for fee income intensified.

The consequences seemed dramatic. Corporate finance clients decided that two firms could more efficiently distribute their equity securities at less cost than one firm. They demanded co-managed, instead of sole-managed, underwritings. Managers that traditionally had sole responsibility were forced to share top billing with co-managers. National institutional brokerage firms such as Morgan Stanley Group balked initially. But, since investment banking is a customer-driven business, managements' demands carried more weight than underwriters' preferences. For the sake of preserving their underwriting business, brokerage firms complied with corporate finance clients' specifications.

Competition between institutional and retail brokerage firms continued into the 1980s. Underwriters' spreads tightened while competition for brokerage commission revenue intensified. Discount brokers became aggressive competitors for agency orders from institutional investors. Global capital markets became more free. Investment banking required more capital to compete for worldwide financing business. Initiation of or participation in mergers and acquisitions necessitated stronger capital bases. Trading of new financial instruments, such as mortgage-backed securities, options, and index futures, required strengthened capital positions.

Erosion of market share in the traditional securities business loomed as a serious problem for brokerage firms. They faced the need to broaden their revenue base and product mix. Some were evolving into quasi-banks and banks were becoming quasi-securities firms. Distinctions between the two, mandated in the Glass Steagall Act, began to blur, but the need for more capital to remain competitive was crystal clear. As a result, private partnerships among Wall Street firms tended toward obsolescence in the mid-1980s. Many came public, others were acquired, and some received capital infusions.

For example, Morgan Stanley Group, a prestigious national institutional firm, had lost market share as lead managing underwriter of U.S. issues. The firm had slipped from first in 1980, a year in which it was lead manager of 19 percent of the total dollar value of underwritings, to sixth in 1985 with 7.5 percent market share. The firm gained ground in 1986 finishing third with 10.4 percent share.

The firm also suffered from comparatively weak institutional trading capability in the United States and abroad. It had experienced clearance and processing problems in its mortgage-backed securities trading operation and the firm was reportedly losing portions of major asset management accounts. The firm made its choice. It came public to raise fresh capital to compete more effectively.

Securities firms began to go public in 1985. A series of hot offerings of financial services companies was made in a hot market. Bear Stearns & Co., Alex. Brown & Sons, Inc., L.F. Rothschild & Co. and Morgan Stanley Group left the domain of private partnerships. In other major transactions, Kidder, Peabody & Co. agreed to be acquired by General Electric Financial Services and Goldman, Sachs & Co. sold 12.5 percent of non-voting stock to the Sumitomo Bank (Tokyo) for $500 million.

Bracketing, however, has never died. Securities firms still try to distinguish themselves from one another in terms of their prestige and influence. In 1985, for example, national institutional firms created a so-called "bulge" bracket to separate themselves from retail-oriented brokerage firms. It included firms such as First Boston Corp., Goldman, Sachs & Co., Merrill Lynch Capital Markets, Morgan Stanley, Salomon Brothers, Inc., and Shearson Lehman Brothers. Bulge firms dominated the new issues business while retail firms fought to preserve their past influence. The bracket wars were on again.

These battles for position had and have ramifications for the aftermarket support of emerging companies. For example, some brokerage firms, excluded from certain syndicates, threatened retaliation on syndicate managers. They warned they would reduce their selling efforts for and research coverage of new issues. Such conflict harms an emerging company's sponsorship and efficiency in the aftermarket of its initial public offering.

Brackets are similar to layers of a pyramid. In tombstone advertisements, which announce initial public offerings after-the-fact, brackets are separated alphabetically. Within those advertisements, a new bracket of lower firms follows directly after the end of a higher bracket, starting with the first letter of the alphabet.

National institutional brokerage firms, the smallest in number, are at the top of the pyramid. They are usually old-line firms with the strongest capital positions with which to compete most aggressively for fee and commission business. They command the greatest spheres of influence with investing institutions. Local and small regional firms are at the bottom, forming the foundation of the pyramid. Their network of influence is retail-oriented.

Emerging companies are fair game to underwriters. There are no hard and fast rules governing which firms underwrite which emerging companies. Competition for new underwriting business is intense, but, over time, underwriting patterns do emerge. They serve as useful, general benchmarks for consideration and selection of an investment banker.

Five types of brokerage firms (corresponding to five brackets) manage most initial public offerings of emerging companies. In descending order of corporate finance (and bracket) influence they are: (1) national institutional brokerage firms, (2) national wirehouse firms, (3) retail/institutional firms, (4) major regional firms, and (5) small regional brokerage firms. The first category underwrites the greatest dollar volume of equity financings.

According to Technimetrics, Inc. (New York, NY), a research and database management firm, 242 domestic brokerage firms fall into these five categories. This book divides the universe in this manner: 15 firms in the national institutional bracket, 10 firms in the national wirehouse category, and 10 firms in the retail/institutional sector. Technimetrics' findings suggest that there are 57 firms in the major regional division and 150 firms in the small regional category.

Every bracket has its target market or niche of investment banking clients. Targets may be based on industry sector, financial performance, or geography. But, in general, each tends to focus on underwritings of a certain share volume, share price and total dollar volume, and market capitalizations of certain size. *Money* reported that the average dollar value per offering of issues underwritten by active underwriters between 1980 and 1985 was $18 million.

Securities firms in the national institutional category command reputations of the greatest influence and most prestige among institutional investors. They also do business with "substantial" individual investors. Firms in the national wire-house category cater to both institutions and to the general public. In recent years they have adopted a "financial supermarket" approach to selling financial prod-ucts. Firms in the retail/institutional category tend to do business with investing institutions and wealthy individual investors. Beginning in 1983, they developed a reputation for specializing in emerging growth technologies. Firms in the major and small regional division often build their credibility on intimate knowledge of their regions' emerging companies.

Selection of a national institutional brokerage firm or a national wirehouse firm or a combination of the two for an initial public offering often sends the signal that investors should expect a new issue of relatively large dollar volume. Selection of retail/institutional firms or major regional firms signals an offering of medium dollar volume, and the services of small regional brokerage firms often suggest an offering of relatively small dollar volume. In some cases, companies raise money in public markets through obscure underwriters. The choice infers that the company may have a questionable operating record and, as a result, may have "shopped" its deal. Or it may suggest that it selected an underwriter on the basis of price, or that the underwriter was the only one willing to do the deal, perhaps only on a best-efforts basis.

National institutional firms tend to focus on corporate financings priced above $25 per share, raising more than $40 million and generally resulting in market capitalizations of hundreds of millions. Of the most active new issue underwri-ters with the best records of aftermarket performance in this bracket since 1980, Salomon Brothers, Inc. (New York, NY), has averaged $62 million per new issue (27); Bear Stearns & Co. (New York, NY) has averaged $22.96 million (26); Morgan Stanley Group (New York, NY) has averaged $56.47 million (30), its average figure in 1985 was $39.72 million (5). Drexel Burnham Lambert Inc. (New York, NY) has averaged $18.06 million (47); Merrill Lynch (New York, NY) has averaged $35.01 million (98); First Boston Corp. (New York, NY) has averaged $42.74 million per deal (19); Shearson Lehman Brothers (New York, NY) averaged $44.21 million (62); and Goldman, Sachs & Co. (New York, NY) has averaged $67.83 million (40).

Among national wirehouse firms, since 1980, PaineWebber, Inc. (New York, NY) averaged $18.47 million per new issue (38). The average figure on its 15 best-performing new issues since 1980 was $13.81 million. E.F. Hutton (New York, NY) averaged $25.14 million per deal (50), its 1985 average figure was $23.43 million (7). Dean Witter Reynolds, Inc. (New York, NY) averaged $19.35 million per new offering (40), and Prudential-Bache Securities (New York, NY) averaged $21.79 million per offering (48).

Retail/institutional firms and national wirehouse firms compete for deals pri-ced approximately from $15 to $25 per share, raising new capital roughly from $15 million to $40 million, generally resulting in market capitalizations in the high tens or low hundreds of millions. For example, of the most active new-issue underwriters with the best records of aftermarket performance in these two brackets since 1980, Alex. Brown & Sons, Inc. (Baltimore, MD) has averaged $19.52 million per initial public offering (44). For 1985, its average figure was $18.67 million (7). During the same period, L.F. Rothschild & Co. (New York, NY) averaged $28.36 million per new issue (69). Its 1985 average figure was $9.4 million (5), and Hambrecht & Quist (San Francisco, CA) averaged $13.93 million per deal (27).

Management may combine retail/institutional and national wirehouse firms and should balance co-managers' distribution and research strengths. If three co-managers are selected, two should be research choices. Firms with an industry research bias, more than a geographical bias, should be included in the syndicate. Offerings of large size may require greater distribution capability than major regional or small regional firms can harness.

Major regional brokerage firms tend to concentrate on deals priced between $7 and $15 per share, raising total capital from about $5 million to $15 million, generally resulting in market capitalizations in the middle to high tens of millions. For example, of the most active new issue underwriters with the best records of aftermarket performance in these two categories since 1980, Blunt Ellis & Loewi (Milwaukee, WI) has raised an average of $5.6 million per offering (of 10 total offerings) for its new issue clients, and William Blair & Co. (Chicago, IL) has averaged $12.86 million per offering (16).

Among other major regionals, J.C. Bradford & Co. (Nashville, TN) averaged $10 million per initial public offering (13). During the same period, Advest Incorporated (Hartford, CT) has averaged $5.13 million per initial public offering (23). Ladenburg, Thalmann & Co., Inc. (New York, NY) averaged $6.48 million (21), its average figure was $6.6 million per new issue underwriting in 1985 (7). Piper, Jaffray & Hopwood, Inc. (Minneapolis, MN) averaged $9.2 million per deal (10). Robinson Humphrey Co. (Atlanta, GA) averaged $11.29 million (17), and A.G. Edwards & Sons, Inc. (St. Louis, MO) averaged $10.6 million per new issue (10).

Small regional underwriters tend to do corporate financing deals priced at about $6 or less per share, raising total capital of approximately $10 million or less, generally resulting in market capitalizations in the low tens of millions. They, and small money managers who may lead an emerging company to them, may demand warrants on the stock, exercisable above public offering price, as part of an underwriting agreement. The warrant position is advantageous to the company. It gives the underwriter, the money manager, or both an obvious economic incentive to support and to sponsor the company in the aftermarket. Ideally, in a new issue managed by two or more small regionals, at least one co-manager should be from the company's headquarters region.

Management may choose two underwriters from the same bracket. It is advantageous to management that one co-manager come from the company's headquarters region or have a retail sales office in or near the company's headquarters city. For example, management of Norton Company (Worcester, MA), used the "speaker system" at the local securities sales office of E. F. Hutton (its investment banker), to broadcast an update on the company to the firm's national sales force. Called a "Profitline" broadcast, the 10-minute presentation enabled management to shape or reshape many brokers' perception of the company's operating progress.

Management may split brackets between small regional and major regional or between major regional and retail/institutional underwriters. If management chooses two major regional firms, one should be in or near the company's headquarters region. Once again, a network of research sponsorship made up of those firms with known research coverage of the industry or of peer competitors should be built into the syndicate. Attention should also be paid to including firms located in the same region as the company.

Aftermarket stock price performance of new issue clients is one key test of an underwriter's success. *Money* magazine studied the share price (total return) performance of initial public offerings from 1980 through 1985. The average price gain per year for new issues, unweighted for differences in market capitalization, was 9.8 percent.

The magazine also ranked the most active underwriters, lead managers of 10 or more issues, on the basis of their corporate finance clients' average share price gain per year. The range in unweighted average gain among the top 25 firms was 30.2 percent (PaineWebber) to 4.1 percent (Goldman, Sachs).

The range of unweighted average gain among the top 10 firms from 30.2 percent (PaineWebber) to 21.2 percent (Bear Stearns). Of the top 10 firms whose new issue clients had the best aftermarket share price performance, two were national institutional brokerage firms, Salomon Brothers, Inc.–25.5 percent, and Bear Stearns. One was a national wirehouse firm (PaineWebber). Two were retail/institutional firms (Alex. Brown–23.8 percent and Ladenburg, Thalmann–22.2 percent). And five were major regional firms, (Blunt Ellis & Loewi–29.6 percent, Advest–28.6 percent, William Blair–26.8 percent, Piper, Jaffray & Hopwood–22.4 percent, and Robinson Humphrey–21.7 percent).

Digressing for a moment to emerging companies in a start-up stage, going public in the Unlisted Securities Market (USM), the junior market of The Stock Exchange (London, UK) is a realistic financing alternative to U.S. capital markets. Total capitalization of the UK equities market was $419 billion, as of April 1986. It is the third largest equity capital market in the world, behind the U.S. and Japan. Of that total, USM market capitalization was estimated at about $5.4 billion. Since its beginning in November 1980, a total of 443 companies have obtained a quotation, about 340 of which were trading as of March 31, 1986.

Start-ups can raise more equity capital at less cost in the UK than in the U.S. Underwriting spreads run 2 to 4 percent of the dollar value of the underwriting versus 6 percent or more in the U.S. Financial reporting requirements are less stringent than those imposed by the Securities and Exchange Commission and disclosure requirements are fewer. Release of such sensitive information as overhead, general and administrative expenses, operating margins, or pricing structure is not required. Public offerings are priced in pence per share at an equivalent rate usually less than $2 per share (US).

Start-up companies may also carry a higher valuation in the UK than in the U.S. The Stock Exchange allows the managements of emerging companies to choose between pricing their company's new issue on the basis of trailing (historic) earnings or on horizon (estimated) earnings for the fiscal year in which the offering is being made. In contrast the SEC requires that new issues of stock offered to the public in the U.S. be priced only on the basis of trailing earnings. No profit projections are permitted.

In the UK, management's choice to price its new issue on the basis of its profit forecast (projected earnings) is tantamount to a bond of credibility with investors that earnings performance in the immediate future is virtually certain to meet forecast. As a result, price/earnings ratios on new issues, if calculated on horizon earnings, tend to be higher than they might ordinarily be in the U.S., if calculated on trailing earnings. Consequently, the capitalization of start-up companies in the UK tends to be higher than it might be on an equivalent basis in the U.S.

The USM system fuels high investors' expectations. A company's future earnings are expected to equal or exceed forecast. Shortfalls can be devastating and may damage the reputation of the company, the underwriter and the stockbroker, and unrewarded first investors do not soon forget. Subsequent financings may be more costly, even if able to be done.

"Flotation" in the USM, or a full listing on The Stock Exchange is usually a part of a larger business strategy to build market share overseas. It is usually done to enhance visibility and presence with potential international customers. It is important to relationship-building, contact-making, and gains in market share. It signals a management commitment and long-term business orientation to international markets.

In London, "reporting accountants" rather than attorneys, as in the U.S., serve as primary business advisers to corporate managements concerning public offerings of stock. They, for no fee, or financial intermediaries, for a fee, introduce prospective offerors to potential English "sponsors" or English "brokers" which may handle their future "flotation." Reporting accountants work closely with sponsors and/or brokers for quality control purposes throughout the public offering process. As of the end of the first calendar quarter of 1986, more than 72 English sponsors, more than 56 brokers and more than 39 reporting accountants had been involved in USM flotations.

However, English brokerage and underwriting traditions changed radically in October 1986. "Big Bang" occurred on The Stock Exchange. It was the equivalent of "Mayday," May 1, 1975, on the New York Stock Exchange because it deregulated Britain's financial markets. Fixed commissions were abolished, exclusive agency brokerage business was eliminated, competitive market-making in British stocks and government bonds proliferated. To gain market share, American, European, and Far Eastern financial services companies bought about 90 British brokers and merchant banks doing about 90 percent of The Stock Exchange's business. The implications for emerging American companies' "flotation" plans were important.

Strategy for "flotation" in the USM may be part of a long-term financing strategy which includes U.S. capital markets. Its execution usually begins with contact with an accounting firm. Management should establish a working relationship with a firm, probably one of America's big eight accounting firms, which has a branch office close to the company's U.S. headquarters. A local relationship with a firm which has a London presence is valuable. The firm's London office will introduce management to potential English sponsors. Financial intermediaries will, for a fee, also make the introductions. As the process progresses the sponsor will visit with management at the company's home office, and the accounting firm will devote much time to verifying the company's accounts. The effort will be reflected in the "Short Report" and "Long Report" in the company's prospectus.

Next, managements of emerging American companies should use the introduction process to make contact with an English sponsor owned by an American brokerage firm, an English sponsor with ties to an American firm or with presence in the U.S. or an American firm which makes markets in British securities on The Stock Exchange. A co-managed offering may take place in London but an avenue to future financing and known equity valuation in U.S. capital markets will be in place.

Ideally, the American firm involved in a USM flotation should be large enough to maintain a London-based corporate finance and securities sales presence. It underscores relationships with English investors. This probably limits underwriter selection to national institutional, national wirehouse or retail/institutional brackets. By definition, the firm should also have research presence in the U.S. In this manner, emerging companies can guarantee research sponsorship on one continent at the time of offering, a pipeline of information to a second continent as American investors develop interest, and a means by which to avoid the risks of being orphaned overseas.

Aftermarket support in America for American companies making flotations in the USM is difficult. The Stock Exchange (London) prohibits purchase of the shares of USM companies by North American residents for periods usually not less than six months after an initial flotation. As a result, shares of American USM companies will not be registered with the SEC for public trading in America by American investors.

This does not mean, however, that management of an American company trading in the USM should not sponsor itself in the aftermarket in America. Executives of companies with a USM flotation should plan to hold an annual meeting in the U.S. in addition to its annual general meeting in the UK, regardless of the percent of share ownership in the U.S. It is an opportunity to identify and to network with those American investors and analysts who may ultimately affect the company's market valuation and market sponsorship.

Managements of American USM companies can build their own valuation network. They can collaborate to attract UK investors and brokers to the U.S. A mutual desire for broader market sponsorship and institutional share ownership forms the common bond.

For example, about five U.S. companies which had made USM flotations, including CVD, Pacer Systems, and Colorgen (all in Massachusetts), organized the "London Connection". In June 1986, about 20 UK investment funds and stockbrokers visited with the management of each company at its headquarters. It was an obvious valuation network built around a relatively few lead investors and potential dominant sponsors who could affect the share prices of these companies in the USM.

UNDERWRITING AGREEMENTS

Strategy to create investor demand takes a global approach to the underwriting process. It focuses on pre-offering market preparation for and aftermarket support of an emerging company's securities. It concerns the fair valuation and efficient pricing of the shares of emerging companies. It stresses five important elements: selection of an underwriter(s), composition of the syndicate, pricing of an issue, distribution of an issue, and aftermarket support of an issue.

First, underwriter selection gives visibility, or invisibility, and high, or low, profile to a company. It shapes investors' perceptions of company quality and prestige. Second, syndicate composition creates patterns of demand among investors who either buy performance (earnings growth) or price (value). The pattern depends on how the issue is sold to investors. Third, pricing of new issues should reward first investors. Fourth, distribution of a company's shares should be to strong hands with minimal turnbacks to the syndicate. And, fifth, aftermarket support, at minimum, should include research coverage from an underwriter's securities analyst and market-making from an underwriter's trader.

Top bracket underwriters court new business prospects with a variety of enticements. From a corporate finance perspective, they claim knowledge and understanding of investors' perceptions of a company in the marketplace. Bankers state they know how to sell the company's securities just as the company knows how to market its products/services. They cite their underwriting track record and roster of past corporate finance clients.

Bankers discuss their syndicate departments. They think that syndicate operations form the critical juncture between a firm's promotional and selling efforts. They mention the strength of their syndicate department as a marketing manager of a fast-moving distribution system. They claim the structure of their syndicate reflects the pattern of investor demand. Their market intelligence, they suggest, enables them to target the right investors for an issue of the company's securities. They imply that targeting ability lends financial, perceptual, and image support to a company in the aftermarket of an offering.

At the same time they talk of securities sales and highlight their firm's research and trading capability. Investment bankers speak of the quality and size of their research department. They refer to the amount invested annually in information processing. At the same time, they talk of speed of information dissemination to their securities sales staffs and to their institutional investing clients. They boast of the commission production of their securities sales staff and observe that strong production makes their direct selling efforts more effective. They discuss their securities salespersons' access to institutional and individual portfolios.

They claim their business is building long-term service relationships with corporate finance client companies. They refer to their firms' continuous communications network that enables bankers to support investors by apprising them of the company's earnings momentum. And it enables bankers to support the company by posting management on investors' perceptions of the company's future. They suggest that the best measure of a firm's relationships is seen in portfolio treatment of client companies' securities. They say they watch investors' initial purchase of the company's securities, observe how long they maintain a portfolio position in the company's shares, and monitor how often they add to that existing position.

Investment bankers also talk about aftermarket support, although providing it is another matter. They discuss research coverage of the company. They cite the continuity of their sales staffs' daily contact with the company's current and prospective shareholders. They suggest such contact helps to stabilize the company's share ownership and to strengthen any future financing effort. They reveal their firms' market-making capability. They believe they can assure reasonable liquidity in the trading of the company's shares and maintain that such an inducement strengthens investor demand.

Selection of both an underwriter and an auditor sends signals to the investment community. They are important associations in a world of capital markets that values relationships. Just as investment bankers scrutinize a company's caliber of venture capital backers, investors cue on the quality and visibility of an emerging company's auditor and underwriter for signals about the company's prospective market value.

Academic studies have shown a positive correlation between market value and auditor choice for new-issue companies. One study[3] found that managements of companies with positive information about their company's expected market value retained higher quality public accounting firms (associated with greater disclosure) than managements of companies with less positive expectations. And one survey[4] found that underwriters not only associated the potential for higher pricing of a new issue with management's selection of a high quality auditor but that they advise new-issue corporate finance clients to switch to national auditing firms from local or regional firms to enhance that valuation potential.

This book deals with management's choice and use of its underwriter. Selection of an underwriter alone obviously implies a plan to offer stock to the public. The actual choice of an investment banker transmits three information signals: how large (shares and dollar volume) the offering will be, how it may be priced, and who will buy the deal.

Academic research into the behavior of investment banking firms suggests differences between and among them. Marketing strength and bargaining power are an underwriter's tools in trade and have a positive, neutral or negative effect on the type and character of new issues. They may also have a similar effect on the tenor of the market at the time of an initial public offering.

Research identifies firms as being "prestigious" and "nonprestigious."[5] One study examined 250 new issues between March 1965 and February 1969. It indicated that the former are more selective than the latter in the issues they underwrite, even in terms of specifying minimum dollar values of offerings. It also found that prestigious firms lose market share in hot new issues markets and that the performance of issues offered by nonprestigious firms is positively related to the number of other new issues offered in the same month.

Capital position and reputation are determining factors of prestige. Equity capital is the measure of an investment banking firm's size, its ability to commit capital to do deals and its ability to gain the confidence of corporate clients. In 1985, Merrill Lynch had the largest capital position, $2.647 billion. "Reputation capital" is a firm's measure of credibility and a key to its client retention rate. Studies hint that the prestige of an underwriter managing an offering substitutes for the prestige of the company making the offering.

Prestige firms, over time, seem able to expect more certain investor demand for their offerings. They are thus useful for distribution purposes. Many investors select new issues on the basis of the reputation of venture capital investors and underwriters. The perception of the issuer may be linked to perception of the underwriter, both of which affect participation of investing institutions. The pricing of a new issue also seems positively related to prestige of the underwriter. Nonprestigious firms, on the other hand, seem to experience less certain investor demand for their managed issues.

None of this, however, is to suggest that on all occasions prestigious firms do a better job for their corporate clients than non-prestigious firms. In fact, the reverse may be true. For example, prestigious underwriters may be more concerned with underwriting market share in an entire growing industry than the public offering of just one issuer in that market. They may therefore care more about the next deal than the last deal.

This is especially true when the underwriting fees from one new issue are considered relative to the fee potential from secondary offerings or underwritings of larger, more frequent, and more predictable corporate finance clients. And commission potential from researching and recommending the shares of large capitalization companies is simply greater than that associated with aftermarket support of small capitalization issues. As a result, management cannot casually expect sponsorship from its underwriter in the aftermarket, especially if its new issue is cold. Rather, management may have to fight for it from prestigious underwriters.

Corporate managements choose their underwriters for any number of reasons. In general, the most important are: firm reputation, personal relationships, pricing ability, distribution capability (sales force), underwriting cost structure, firm commitment to aftermarket client support (corporate finance, research coverage and market-making) and the breadth of an underwriting firm's professional capabilities.

Before considering a firm's record in pricing and distributing securities, an investment banker's understanding of a company's product/markets is the most important thing in a successful public offering. Firm commitment to support the company in the aftermarket is second (and depends on the first), and a banker's personality and ability to get along with management is the third most critical element.

In addition, the aftermarket stock price performance of the firm's past new issue clients (firm credibility) and the banker's personal credibility with management rank highly. The relevance of a banker's advice concerning the company's financing decisions and target capital structure is meaningful. And his or her ability to demonstrate the applicability of financing techniques, methods and trends in raising least average cost capital to finance the company's growth is valuable.

Some managements choose their underwriter on the basis of reputation and a desire to establish a relationship with a strong investment banking firm. Others select a firm because of its specialization in providing financing for, or research coverage of, certain industries. Others choose a firm primarily because of the reputation of its industry securities analyst. Still other managements decide about an underwriter on the basis of price. They want maximum net proceeds but wish only to pay the narrowest underwriting spread (smallest management fee) to raise capital.

And managements replace their underwriters for numerous reasons related to aftermarket service and sponsorship. A firm may relegate the company to junior members of the firm's corporate finance department. Bankers may offer minimal financial counsel after an offering, or analysts may provide irregular or no research coverage. For example, Genetics Institute (Cambridge, MA) fired Morgan Stanley for this reason. And finally, the underwriter's market making efforts may be unsatisfactory because share price seems too volatile, market-maker's spread too wide, and trading costs too high.

Companies, on the other hand, may also outgrow their underwriter and creep into higher underwriting brackets. Financing requirements to support earnings opportunities may require the services of larger firms or more firms. Management may add to its original co-management team or executives may substitute firms. Management may believe wider distribution is necessary. Corporate managers may desire additional research coverage from another firm's highly regarded securities analyst. Or competition for the company's financing business among underwriters may present management with the opportunity to purchase more services for less price.

Management must decide which type of firm is best suited to service the needs of an emerging company of its size and in its industry. Executives might consider both small, relatively less prestigious firms with industry specialization as well as large prestigious firms with capital clout and visibility. Nonprestigious firms stress close working relationships. Prestigious firms tout transactions capabilities.

It was mentioned earlier that the luxury of being squired by, and able to choose among, solicitous underwriters depends upon several factors: the growth/returns profile of a company's product/market opportunity, its growth/share relationship in these markets, its operating (cash-generating) track record, the size and perceived duration of its competitive advantage, its historic self-financing ability, and the quality/depth of its management. With these attributes, many investment bankers will come knocking. Competition for the company's underwriting business will be intense but selection of co-managing underwriters will be a buyer's market. Management will be in the driver's seat. It can write the company's underwriting ticket and make many demands upon its underwriters. For these companies, the probability of broad sponsorship and broad ownership in the aftermarket will be a virtual certainty.

Management must capitalize on this potential control position as buyer in a buyer's market. Executives must avoid being mesmerized by the going public process itself and focus on sponsorship and pricing efficiency in the aftermarket. The securities industry is a service business and management should be certain it gets the service it pays for during and after an initial public offering. Executives should make investment bankers earn their underwriting fee by providing research coverage and market-making in the aftermarket. Underwriters should retain their corporate finance clients only if they supply these services.

Microsoft Corp. (Bellevue, WA) was an example of a company in the driver's seat. In negotiating its underwriting agreement, management of the company was tough on price and costs. It dictated the pricing of its issue and the maximum underwriting spread it was willing to pay to its underwriters, about 6.2 percent of the value of the offering. The spread was slightly higher than the 6.13 percent spread negotiated by Teknowledge, Inc. in its initial public offering earlier in 1986. Microsoft was also tough on underwriter selection. Management chose two firms, a national institutional brokerage firm for distribution, Goldman, Sachs & Co., and a high technology-oriented, retail/institutional firm for research, Alex. Brown & Sons.

Management must take several steps before an initial public offering to reasonably assure market sponsorship, pricing efficiency, liquidity, and fair valuation in the aftermarket. First, executives should assume that their offering will be cold (explained later). Second, corporate executives should plan a co-managed initial public offering. Third, for distribution purposes, management should choose at least one high bracket, prestigious underwriter. Fourth, for research purposes, management should choose an underwriter with extensive knowledge and understanding of the company's product/market and high visibility with investing institutions in covering those product/markets.

Fifth, management should pack the underwriting syndicate with firms that form the core of a market sponsorship network. Sixth, management should identify those few lead investors and dominant sponsors perceived to be influential in affecting share prices in its industry, and should build a valuation network around them. Seventh, management should create demand for its shares in the secondary (trading) market in advance of its primary offering. And eighth, executives should manage their underwriter's merchandising efforts.

A sole managed underwriting is potentially dangerous to a company's health. From a banking perspective, if a sole manager were to merge, be acquired or liquidate, management might lose its investment banker. From a sponsorship perspective, it unnecessarily constrains a company's breadth of aftermarket sponsorship. Processing of the company's information becomes concentrated in one firm's hands. Depending upon the size of the firm and the importance of the company to it, if the analyst covering the company were to leave the firm, management could lose its base of research coverage. Worse, if no sponsorship is forthcoming from a company's underwriter after the company's initial public offering, the company effectively becomes orphaned.

Analysts' shifts to other firms can have its sponsorship benefits, however. First Union Corporation, Inc. (Charlotte, NC), a regional bank holding company, found that an analyst's departure can actually expand research coverage. An analyst's past firm might still follow the industry and the company and the departed analyst's new firm might also initiate coverage. Management must act as the catalyst to preserve and to broaden research coverage of the company.

Managements of emerging companies should select at least two firms to co-manage their initial public offering. To reemphasize the point, for distribution of securities to the highest tier of investing institutions, at least one firm should be prestigious, from the highest possible bracket. To keep stock in institutional hands and to broaden institutional ownership (research), at least one firm should have analyst(s) perceived to be deeply knowledgeable of the company's product/markets. Management may select from the same bracket or split brackets. If three firms are selected, at least two should be for purposes of continuous research coverage.

Information flows most widely from the top of the pyramid, the highest bracket of brokerage firms. It concentrates more narrowly at the bottom, the lowest bracket of brokerage firms. The firm chosen for its research capability should have an industry securities analyst recognized for his or her industry knowledge, insight and contacts, regardless of his or her firm's bracket position. Solid understanding of product/market fundamentals can transcend bracket structures.

The firm's securities analyst should preferably be an industry specialist. Otherwise, he or she can be a multi-industry generalist analyst who actively researches peer competitors within the industry or a multi-industry generalist analyst who follows the industry closely. An analyst's involvement with the company's industry in general is important because the analyst can serve management not only as a liaison to lead investors and money managers but also as an ongoing mechanism by which to monitor investors' perceptions of the company.

Several sources rate brokerage firms' research capabilities from the perspective of large investing institutions. Taken in their proper context, however, these ratings may be biased in favor of selling instead of analysis. The sources uncover opinions about analysts who are usually the most successful merchandisers of their ideas to major investing institutions and who provide the most extensive service to these same customers. These analysts generate the most volume of commission business. By definition, these sources may not represent the opinions of smaller institutions about those analysts who may be most adept at analysis of small capitalization companies.

Sources such as Greenwich Associates (Greenwich, CT), *Institutional Investor* magazine, *Pensions & Investment Age* and *Financial World* magazine annually poll professional money managers at major investing institutions for their opinions about which firms produce and merchandise the highest quality research product. Managements would also do well to check the reputation and visibility of an underwriter's securities analyst and the lineup of the industry's leading analysts with executives of publicly-held competitors within their company's industry.

It was mentioned earlier that management should plan its initial public offering as though the offering would be cold. The reason for this is to avoid surprises in the aftermarket. Sponsorship in the form of research coverage from an underwriter's securities analyst after an initial public offering is not at all automatic. Rather it is an issue of brokerage economics, i.e., size of a deal and whether it is hot. If the commission potential from trading and recommending a new issue of a company's securities is equal to or greater than the potential fee income from doing another deal, then underwriters will initiate research coverage. If the potential falls short, then underwriters and investing institutions will lose their incentive to be active in a stock and will turn their attention to new deals.

Underwriting firms usually commit to making a trading market in their corporate finance clients' shares for up to a year after an initial public offering as part of an underwriting agreement. But they do not necessarily commit to providing research coverage. As a result, managements may be more than a little disappointed and upset when research coverage from their investment banker is not forthcoming in the aftermarket.

For example, NEECO, Inc. (Canton, MA) went public on June 18, 1986, just about at that year's performance peak for small capitalization issues. Management offered 1.5 million shares through Moseley Securities at $6 per share, raising $9 million. With 3.2 million shares outstanding, the company's market capitalization at its offering was $19.2 million. The company's one-day initial return was 2.1 percent ($6.125 closing bid per share on June 18) and its one-month initial return was 4.2 percent ($6.25 closing bid per share on June 30). The offering was cold, the company's market capitalization was small and the market for small capitalization issues turned cold. The company received no sponsorship (research coverage) in the aftermarket.

During the balance of the calendar year, the company's shares continued to languish. They traded to a low of $4.875 bid on September 15, closed at $5.125 bid per share at the end of the third quarter and at $6.75 bid per share at the end of the year. The market for small capitalization issues was cold during this period relative to the market for large capitalization companies. For example, the 1986 high of 411.16 for the NASDAQ composite index occurred on July 3. The index closed at 323.01 for the year, up only 7.36 percent, versus a rise of 14.62 percent for the S & P 500-stock index and a rise of 22.58 percent for the Dow Jones Industrial Average.

In the meantime, management was on its way to increasing sales by more than 150 percent, from about $22 million to about $59 million, and to increasing reported net income by about 180 percent, from about $784,000 to about $2.2 million. And during the fourth quarter of 1986, management actively made contact and personally visited with potential lead investors and dominant sponsors to shape their perception of the company's future growth and profitability. As a result, the company's stock started to run on about January 12, 1987. It moved non-stop from $6.75 bid to $18.50 bid on February 18, 1987 (the high for the quarter). The company offered 1.7 million more shares at $18.25 per share in

March. With 4.4 million shares outstanding, the company's market capitalization rose to $80.3 million.

The combination of the company's profitability, its greater market capitalization and an improved market for small capitalization companies (the NASDAQ composite rose 12 percent in the first 10 trading days of 1987 alone) showed itself in increased sponsorship for NEECO. The company went from no sponsors after its initial public offering to three dominant sponsors by the time of its second public offering. All published research reports on the company: Moseley, Dillon, Read and Tucker Anthony.

Genetics Institute, Inc. (Cambridge, MA) is another example of a company which was denied sponsorship by one of its investment bankers after its initial public offering. The company split brackets. It offered 2.875 million shares at $29.75 per share on May 20, 1986 through Morgan Stanley and Robertson, Colman & Stephens. Initial market value was about $334 million. Its offering was a relatively cold issue. It registered one-day initial returns of 5.9 percent (closing bid per share of $31.50) and a one-month capital loss of 2.7 percent (closing bid per share of $29 on May 30, 1986). Its one-year initial return was 21 percent at $36 bid at the close on May 20, 1987.

In its first year as a public company, the company's shares traded in a wide range from a low of $17.25 bid per share to a high of $47.75 bid. During that time, only Robertson, Colman published research reports. For its second public offering on June 16, 1987 (2 million shares at $34.25 per share), the management of Genetics Institute fired Morgan Stanley and retained Goldman Sachs (another top bracket firm) and Robertson, Colman as co-managers.

The 70 New England-based thrift institutions that came public in 1985 and 1986 are another example. Low inflation, low interest rates and an impressive record of operating gains during the high interest rate environment of the early 1980s opened the financing window to many of these small community banks. Many prestigious underwriters competed for their underwriting business. These same firms provided market-making (liquidity) as part of their underwriting agreement. But they provided virtually no research coverage to support their own corporate finance clients in the aftermarket. Thrift managements never demanded it. Most of these thrifts suffered from clear cases of information deficiency.

Executives and underwriters usually negotiate several points before an underwriting agreement is signed. Terms and conditions of the offering must be agreed upon. Underwriting spread must be hammered out. Rights of first refusal on future financings must be discussed. "Lock-outs" (rights of corporate insiders to sell shares) must be clearly understood. But much bargaining remains.

Preparing for their new issue as though they expected it to be a cold deal enables executives of emerging companies to anticipate sponsorship problems in the aftermarket. It also prepares them to manage their underwriters' merchandising efforts. They must incorporate research coverage into their underwriting agreement, just as they incorporate market-making efforts. Managements must demand in the agreement published and merchandised research from their under- writers' industry securities analyst immediately after the 90-day cooling-off period following the initial offering, and at least four times (quarters) per year (subject to fundamentals remaining intact). They should demand continuity in market-making efforts. And they should insist upon inclusion in the syndicate of other firms which may sponsor the company on a research or market-making basis in the aftermarket.

Managements must prepare to monitor analysts' merchandising (or lack of it) of research products centered on the company. And they should avoid assign- ment of research coverage by analysts who only follow the underwriter's corpo- rate finance clients. These information processors tend to lack credibility with investing institutions. And some money managers think that their efforts are similar to "pimping" for the corporate finance department. Executives should not ask their underwriter if the firm's analyst will provide research coverage in the aftermarket. They should tell their underwriter they demand that coverage as part of the underwriting agreement.

PRICING, DISTRIBUTION AND SPONSORSHIP

Emerging companies face three major risks in the underwriting process: pric- ing, distribution, and aftermarket support. Each are of immediate concern. If not done well, they may damage investors' perception of the company. They may penalize its current market valuation and its future financing ability. From the perspectives of both banker and corporate executive, the pricing and aftermarket share price performance of a new issue are important indicators of an under- writing's success.

Investment bankers perceive success in a relative sense. They believe that the psychology of first investors is critical. They want to reward buyers on the deal. They want them to make money and to realize initial returns so that either future offerings of the issuer's securities or future deals which the underwriter manages will be in demand. They want to price a deal so that share price rises immediately in the aftermarket. Corporate managers, on the other hand, view success in an absolute sense. They want maximum net proceeds from an offering.

Pricing has its own strategy. Investment bankers tend to price offerings of new issues of corporate securities in line with their (un)certainty about investors' perceptions of the expected value of those securities (the market clearing price) in the aftermarket. They price new issues at levels less than their expected value (less than the price they think investors may pay) to reward first investors for assuming the risk of owning securities with previously unknown values. In this way they "leave something on the table" for first investors. Historic average underpricing of new issues, percentage post-offering price change in first day trading, i.e., one-day initial returns, has tended to exceed 15 percent, about 10 percent for new issues of established companies.

New issues markets are cyclical and move through stages of underpricing by investment bankers and of realized initial returns by shareholders. The first phase is usually conservative. Companies with respectable operating histories go public at relatively low valuations and are modestly underpriced. Investors realize modest one-day initial returns.

For example, Autodesk, Inc. (Sausalito, CA) went public on June 28, 1985 at $11 per share. Its one-day initial return was 9.1 percent (closing bid price per share at the end of the first trading day was $12). Its one-month initial return was 36.4 percent (closing bid price per share at the end of July was $15). The company's 1985 initial return was 125 percent at a year-end closing price per share of $24.75.

Positive unannualized initial returns for first investors in this early period set the stage for the second phase of the new issues cycle. Underpricing increases as investment bankers underestimate the certainty with which investors will place an expected value on new issues. Realized one-day initial returns build and post-offering equity valuations expand. Companies sell less equity to raise desired amounts of capital.

Microsoft Corp. is an example. The company came public on March 13, 1986 at $21 per share. In the aftermarket, it achieved a one-day initial return of 33.3 percent (closing bid price per share at the end of the first trading day was $28) and a one-month initial return of about 29.7 percent (closing bid price per share at the end of March was $27.25). Its 1986 initial return was about 130 percent at a year-end closing price per share of $48.25.

Investors' demonstrated ability to successfully exploit the excess returns available in new issues leads to a third stage of the cycle. It is a period in which underwriters significantly underestimate investors' perceptions, investors speculate wildly, and shareholders realize dramatic one-day initial returns. The aftermarket performance of Home Shopping Network in 1986 is an example. It was mentioned earlier that one-day initial return on investment in the company's shares was 136.8 percent, its one-month initial return was 99.7 percent and its one-year initial return was about 520 percent.

Though difficult to predict, it is immediately after this last stage in the cycle, of highest average initial one-day realized returns in hot new issues markets, that the timing for a new issue of an emerging company's stock is most opportune. At this time, companies can sell least equity, raise most capital, and achieve highest valuations.

One study examined 242 new issues of natural resource companies during the 1977-1982 underwriting period.[6] It found that in the 1977-1979 period prior to a hot new issues market, 28 new issuers on average raised relatively low average net proceeds ($2.853 million), surrendered relatively high amounts of equity (49 percent) and were relatively highly underpriced by their underwriters. Average postoffering market/book ratios were 2.13 at offering price versus 3.23 at the closing bid price on the first day of trading, a 51.6 percent difference.

In contrast, 99 new issuers in the 1980-1981 first quarter hot new issues market on average raised greater average net proceeds ($4.421 million) and surrendered less equity (45 percent). These companies were priced at slightly higher multiples. Average postoffering market/book ratios were 2.46 at offering price. Yet they were relatively more highly underpriced by their underwriters (i.e., investors would have paid much more). Average postoffering market/book ratios were 2.46 at offering price versus 4.69 at the closing bid price on the first day of trading, a 90.7 percent difference.

Finally, 115 new issuers in the relatively cold new issues market from 1981 second quarter-1982, on average raised about the same average net proceeds as in the prior hot market ($4.222 million). But they surrendered the least equity (39 percent). They were priced at the highest multiples. Average postoffering market/book ratios were 2.66 at offering price, and they were relatively fully priced by their underwriters. Average postoffering market/book ratios were 2.66 at offering price versus 2.84 at the closing bid price on the first day of trading, a 6.8 percent difference.

Another study reviewed new issue underpricing[7] between 1974 and 1982. It found that new issues underwritten on a firm commitment basis earned one-day initial returns of 10.6 percent versus 52 percent for those underwritten on a best efforts basis. Between 1977 and 1982, firm commitment underwritings earned one-day initial returns of 14.8 percent versus 47.8 percent for best efforts underwritings.

Offerings are considered successful if a company's shares trade to an approximate 10 percent premium to offering price ("something on the table") in the immediate aftermarket. Premiums for most new issues tend to peak within about two months after an offering and plateau, or shrink over the subsequent months.

For example, one study perused the first five days of trading in the aftermarket for 510 initial public offerings priced at $1 or more between 1982 and 1983[8]. It found that aftermarket premiums, excess returns to investors, were usually achieved on the first day of trading only. No significant returns occurred after that time.

The study also found that the one-day initial returns potential of a new issue was directly related to the (un)certainty of the expected value of the issue, measured in terms of price, volume, and bid-ask spreads. For example, average one-day initial net returns for the total sample were 9.87 percent. For 356 initial public offerings, positive initial one-day returns were 15.39 percent. For 154, one-day realized capital losses were −2.88 percent. The upper limit on the cost an investor should be willing to bear for perfect information concerning the expected value of the issues in this sample was 5.52 percent (15.39 minus 9.87.)

Finally, market efficiency prevented investors in the aftermarket from benefitting from the initial underpricing of these issues. One-month initial returns for the total sample were 12.95 percent, versus one-day initial returns of 9.87. One-month initial returns for the positive sample were 20.17 percent, versus one-day returns of 15.39 percent and −3.72 percent versus −2.88 percent for the negative sample.

But unforeseen problems can arise. An offering may "go out too soon," without a well developed business strategy and a well tested competitive position in its market. It may report unexpected low earnings and decline markedly in price. Or an issue may be overpriced, reflecting bankers' overestimation of investors' uncertainty about an issue's expected value. An issue may be too rich and too aggressively priced for investors. For example, Teknowledge, Inc. was priced at a 7.2 multiple to sales, about 1.5 times that of Microsoft. Investors marked the issue to a discount from its initial offering price. Recall that Teknowledge's one-month initial capital loss was 20.2 percent.

At the other end of the spectrum, pricing may grossly underestimate investors' certainty about an issue's expected value. Such was the case with the new issue of Home Shopping Network, Inc. (Clearwater, FL) mentioned earlier in the chapter. Recall that the company's stock was offered at $18 per share, immediately traded to a large premium and closed at $42.625 per share on the day of its offering, a one-day initial return of 136.8 percent. Within approximately one month, the shares traded close to $100 per share before being split 3-for-1.

Pricing can present an obvious conflict between managements and underwriters. In the case of Home Shopping Network, first investors were thoroughly rewarded in terms of one-day, one-month, and first year initial returns on investment in the company's shares. But management failed to maximize the net proceeds from the offering. The opportunity cost to the company of the underpricing of its new issue approached $55 million ($18 per share versus $42.625 first day close).

Finally, pricing of an issue may be full, reflecting an informed estimate of investors' certainty about an issue's expected value. For example, the Henley Group, Inc., a group of 35 companies in a spin-off from Allied-Signal Corp., sextupled the size of its initial public offering in May 1986. The company increased the number of shares for sale to 69 million and the dollar volume of the offering to $1.6 billion. The size set a new record for a U.S. company's initial public offering.

First investors in Henley, however, became concerned that the size of the deal had been increased too much and that pricing left nothing on the table. A preliminary prospectus estimated maximum pricing of Henley's shares at $23 per share. The offering was priced at $21.25 per share. The company's stock closed its first day of trading unchanged, at its offering price, on 6.2 million shares for a one-day initial return of 0 percent. It closed for the year at $22.625 per share, a 1986 initial return of 6.5 percent.

Investment bankers risk market share loss if they underprice too much because they lose corporate finance clients. They also risk it if they underprice too little because they lose institutional investors. For example, the previously mentioned study (footnote 7) reviewed 49 underwriters that managed or co-managed at least four new issues between 1977 and 1981 (246 managed or co-managed at least one new issue between 1977 and 1982). Market share for the 24 that deviated most from their estimated normal underpricing in their subsequent pricing of new issues between 1981 and 1982 fell from 46.6 percent to 24.5 percent (five of the 24 went out of business, i.e., did not merge). Market share for the remaining 25 that deviated least in their subsequent pricings fell from 27.2 percent to 21 percent (one went out of business).

Pricing is intended to stimulate trading, not selling, of shares in the immediate aftermarket of an offering. Postoffering share volume is an immediate indication of whether a deal is hot or cold and whether investors are certain or uncertain of an issue's value. And, relative to share price change, it reflects how well an underwriter created residual demand for the shares of a new issue. The study mentioned in footnote 8 found that average first day trading volume for the entire sample was 326,600 shares, equal to 22.1 percent of the share size of the average issue (1.48 million shares). That compared to average annual share turnover of about 30 to 40 percent for New York Stock Exchange issues between 1975 and 1985. Trading was greater for those issues which were more underpriced. Results also indicated that spreads between bid and ask prices for underpriced new issues were greater than overpriced issues.

A Shearson Lehman Brothers study also analyzed trading activity in the first three days in the aftermarket of 21 new issues raising at least $5 million and offered at P/E multiples of 10 or more in 1979. It measured total trading volume and share volume as a percent of total shares offered.

In the first day of trading in the aftermarket, the study found a high of 40.3 percent of shares offered and a low of 4.4 percent changed hands. An average of 116,500 shares were traded. Turnover represented an average of 17.8 percent of the new issues. In the second day, a high of 31.3 percent with a low of 2.6 percent changed hands. An average total of 72,400 shares were traded, an average turnover of 11 percent of total offerings. In the third day of trading activity, a high of 12.6 percent and a low of 1 percent of offered shares were traded.

The total number of traded shares averaged 41,500, an average of 6.3 percent of the new issues. Three-day totals showed that a high of 84.2 percent and a low of 8 percent of offered shares were traded. The average total number of shares sold was 230,400 and average share turnover was 35.1 percent of shares sold.

Small regional underwriters of small capitalization companies in particular think that aftermarket share volume is crucial. They think it is critical to retaining current investor interest and stimulating new investor interest, rather than losing investors to new deals. They advise their clients to stimulate share volume by paying attention to the information needs of investors. They link investor demand and equity valuation to information efficiency.

Distribution is another risk to the credibility and reputation of both the company and the underwriter. Traditionally, a company's shares are distributed through a syndicate of brokerage firms. In a firm underwriting, syndicate firms pool their capital to buy an entire issue of securities from a company. They guarantee a certain amount of net proceeds to the company and bear the risk of selling the securities. The issue is then marked up and sold to investors. If distributed poorly, some of the company's securities are turned back to the syndicate and go unsold.

Unconventional means of distribution have recently become popular for high quality, large capitalization industrial companies unconcerned about narrow distribution. Shares are now sold without use of syndicates, more than 31 percent of new common stock in 1985. They are also sold in block trades, about 3 percent of new common stock in 1985.

Generally, in any distribution, underwriters try to build the institutional "pot." They attempt to place 10-percent pieces of the issue with a few key lead institutional investors. Then they try to get a few more institutional buyers in for pieces ranging from 1 percent to 5 percent. Finally they spread the pot out. They target about 50 to 60 percent of the deal for roughly 15 to 25 institutions. The balance is sold to retail clients. In speculative markets, those figures often reverse. Institutional ownership narrows, retail ownership expands, liquidity lowers and volatility is high.

Distribution of a company's securities is a tension-filled exercise for an underwriter. Investment bankers contend with an inherent conflict. They serve two masters and are therefore caught in a credibility catch-22.

Underwriters have an allegiance to issuers of corporate shares on one hand, and institutional buyers of shares on the other. They offer shares in their hottest deals to their best commission clients, expecting that they will also participate in deals which are less hot. Sellers want maximum net proceeds from the offering. Buyers want maximum capital gains. In a perfect world, investment bankers satisfy the seller's pricing and distribution goals and the buyer's total return objectives. Bankers believe distribution is an art form. Underwriters must discern which institutional buyers of a corporate clients' shares are "real." They must strive to put stock into the portfolios of those who really want to buy and hold, not buy and sell or "circle" and "turnback" a company's shares to the syndicate on the offering. Other customers may only appear real. But they may be "flippers," institutions that flip the stock back to the syndicate or, in the case of international equity offerings, sell stock back to buyers in the offerer's homeland. In that sense, the underwriter's challenge is the same as that of any business person: know your customers and define your product in terms of your customers, not your customers in terms of your product.

Many underwriters contend with the potential "flippers" problem by imposing commission payout penalties. To encourage the sale of newly issued stock to customers who really want to own it, firms deny commissions to stockbrokers whose clients really want to sell it. Firms may pay no commission on the original sale of deal stock if the shares are sold before settlement date or within a specified period of weeks after the offering.

Prudential-Bache Securities went further for its participation in an $8 billion underwriting of British Gas in December 1986. The firm made two moves to try to guarantee distribution of its allotment of shares to real buyers (few sales and no short sales) and to try to motivate additional buying in the aftermarket.

First, the firm witheld commissions. If a broker's customer sold British Gas stock above its offering price, the firm paid commissions only on the resale of the stock, not on the original sale. If a customer sold stock at or below the deal's offering price, the firm paid no commissions on either sale. Second, the firm bought stock in the aftermarket for resale to the public. In effect, it made more stock available for distribution both to customers who could add to positions and to those who had not been able to buy stock on the deal.

Management's interests are at stake in the distribution of a company's securities. Attention must be paid to the composition of the underwriting syndicate through which the company's shares will be distributed. Management should try to "pack" the syndicate with firms partial to its perceived earnings opportunities and returns potential. Executives can offer a commission opportunity to them in exchange for research coverage and market-making. They can fill the selling group with firms that may provide sponsorship in the aftermarket.

Large firms with industry specialists or multi-industry generalist analysts known to follow the industry or competitors in the industry may already be included in the syndicate. But, depending upon the size of the issue, small or local firms in a company's home region, in regions in which the company maintains divisions, subsidiaries or major plants and in regions in which the company sells much of its goods or services, are important to a new issue.

Many syndicate firms may follow a company for only a short while after an offering, for the benefit of their brokerage customers who bought the stock on the deal. But management's packing of the syndicate can create a long-term sponsorship network in the aftermarket. It can lower information deficiency and raise pricing efficiency.

Considering underwriters' efforts to build the institutional "pot" and the belief that managers of actively managed diversified portfolios seem most responsible for setting share prices, one could debate the merits of road shows in the underwriting process. They are expensive selling efforts in terms of both actual dollars and the opportunity cost of lost management time.

Academicians argue that the process unnecessarily distorts a company's natural investor constituency. They contend that it forces a company's securities into a broader range of ownership than may be necessary. For example, during the thrift conversion process in 1985 and 1986, the public offerings of many thrift institutions were oversubscribed. Shares had to be allotted to depositors/ shareholders in the community according to the size of their deposit. But many thrifts still travelled far afield to sell their deal. As part of the road show process, they journeyed to major American money centers and even to London.

Investment bankers argue that, if road shows are not conducted, distribution may be too narrow. Underwriters claim that road shows motivate securities salesmen to sell an issue and create underlying demand for new issues. Without road shows they advise that brokers will sell other securities, investors will make alternative investments, and a company's deal will not get done.

Road shows and information meetings are valuable. They offer to management a built-in means by which to establish key relationships with those who may emerge as lead investors and dominant sponsors (discussed more fully in Chapter 4). It is also a time to expect service from investment bankers. Executives should ask their underwriters to introduce them to two kinds of Wall Street players. First, they should meet money managers perceived by their bankers to be (or to have been) lead investors in peers' stocks. These investors will have once owned, held over time, or recently established positions of size (percent of outstanding equity or number of shares) in the shares of peer competitors. It is they whose perceived influence can affect consensus expectations for the company and, ultimately, the company's share price.

Second, executives should meet with securities analysts (and big commission-generating stockbrokers) perceived to be dominant sponsors of peers' stocks. Their influence stems from the perceived quality and depth of their research coverage, the extent to which they put away researched stocks into institutional portfolios and the success of their research recommendations on institutions' portfolio returns.

In both cases above, each will already be familiar with the industry in which the company competes. Each will understand the company's fundamentals. Each will know how companies in the industry are valued and how investors perceive peers, and each will be able to appreciate a company's growth and profit potential. Both money managers and analysts can also cross-refer management to individuals in the other's group. A company's valuation network is under construction. Executives should plan to follow-up with these individuals after the 90-day cooling off period following completion of an offering.

The quality of shareholder is another indication of underwriting success. A familiarity with which bracket structure of underwriters influences which tier structure of investors (discussed in Chapter 7) enables management to generally anticipate the type of investors who may buy shares on their company's offering. And understanding how an issue is sold and the pattern of investor demand that that selling creates enables management to sculpt the profile of its institutional shareholder base. It also helps executives to interpret subsequent shifts in that base.

To understand how their underwriter sells their initial public offering to lead investors, executives should know how their banker sold their deal to the firm's securities sales force. And they should plan to sit with their underwriter's institutional and retail brokers while they make their sales calls to potential buyers (to get circles on the deal). Actually listening to these conversations as the sales staff pitches management's deal offers valuable insight into the distribution process. It also reveals the valuation considerations of lead investing institutions and their perceptions of the company's future growth and profit potential. It unveils patterns of investor demand.

For example, the 1986 deluge of new issues of thrift stocks showed clearly that institutional investors who bought stock on deals did so on the basis of both price and performance. Thrift shares traded at discounts to book values such that investors bought bank assets for as little as $.50 to $.80 cents on the dollar in many cases. And strong product/markets combined with expectations of low inflation and low interest rates boosted their earnings momentum. Initial institutional shareholders were aggressive growth and active value buyers, such as equity mutual funds and investment advisers. They tended to be venturesome opportunists in search of short-term price changes on low P/E, low yield securities.

But market conditions changed in July 1986. They prompted money managers to rotate portfolio positions from interest-sensitive to economy-sensitive issues. Early owners of thrift shares sold their positions to passive value investors in the secondary market. They bought thrift shares more on price than performance. For example, money center commercial banks, regional banks and other thrifts bought for price appreciation from expected takeover attempts of thrifts in the future. Growth and growth and income equity mutual funds bought unappreciated future earning power, perceived to be relatively insensitive to swings in short-term interest rates.

UNDERWRITER SELECTION

Before selecting an underwriter, management should check the firm's past success in pricing, distributing and supporting new issues, and in retaining corporate finance clients. Executives should ask for an unscreened list of a firm's corporate finance clients. The second section of the *Directory of Corporate Financing* (published by Dealers Digest, Inc.) lists underwriters and the issues they have underwritten. Management should make contact with and ask several questions of a firm's past corporate clients. In terms of service, management should ask:

1. Did the banker maximize the company's net proceeds from its initial public offering? Total gross proceeds from the offering were what percent of pre-offering assets? How did the figure compare to industry peers which had gone public?

2. Did the banker correctly assess market conditions at the time of the offering? How did the banker decide on the correct size of the offering? The offering was what percentage of postoffering shares outstanding? How senior was the firm's banker who worked on the deal with management?

3. Were managements satisfied with the banker's pricing of their shares? Were they underpriced? How much was left on the table? What was the aftermarket share price performance of the corporate finance client company? Answers should be in terms of: (a) one-day initial realized returns on share price change. (b) one-day initial change in postoffering market/book ratio.

4. How did the banker sell the issue to the firm's securities sales staff (so that brokers could sell the issue to their customers)?

5. Did the investment banker keep close touch with management after the deal? How often? For what purposes?

6. Did the banker alert management to prospective merger and acquisition ideas which might further enhance shareholder value, to financing windows or new financing techniques?

7. Was the manager of the firm's syndicate department accessible and helpful to management during the actual offering? Were managements of past corporate finance client companies satisfied with the syndicate department's handling of the distribution of the company's shares?

8. Were commission penalties imposed upon brokers whose clients sold stock back to the firm too quickly after the syndicate broke?

9. How much volume in the company's stock, as a percentage of shares offered, traded in the first few days in the aftermarket?

10. Was the investment banking firm also a venture capital firm which sold the company's shares in the aftermarket of the offering?

Investment banking is a transactions-oriented business. As such, as mentioned earlier, the economics of deal-making is a risk to emerging companies. If a deal is not hot, if the postoffering market capitalization of the issuer is too small or if the performance of small capitalization indices (issues) lags the general market, both underwriters and investing institutions may lose their incentive to support new issues in the aftermarket in favor of doing new deals. To gain perspective on what to expect, management must learn:

1. Did the brokerage firm sponsor the company on a trading basis? Did it commit to make a trading market in the company's shares in the aftermarket of the public offering?

2. Did the banker sponsor the company on a research basis in the aftermarket? Did the firm commit the firm's research department, its central information processing unit, to regularly scheduled published research coverage of the company? Or was coverage irregular due to attrition or understaffing in the firm's research department, or nonexistent?

3. To which analyst was the company assigned: industry specialist or corporate finance client analyst? How frequently were research reports published? How well were they merchandised? To how many investing institutions were they distributed? To how many of the firm's stockbrokers were hard copies of the research reports distributed?

4. Did the underwriter identify dominant sponsors of industry stocks? Which other firms had industry specialist securities analysts? Which analysts followed peer competitors? Did the banker furnish to the company a list of each? Did the banker know how often those analysts had published research reports on the industry? On peer competitors? Which analysts were considered best? By whom? Why? Had the banker furnished any past reports?

5. Did the banker know which brokerage firms in the syndicate already covered either the industry or peer competitors on a research basis? Which firms made a market in competitors' shares? Did the banker furnish their names or make an introduction?

6. Did the banker know how the shares of comparable companies traded in the open market? What was their trading pattern? Which brokerage firm traded the most volume of peer competitors' shares?

In terms of an aftermarket equity valuation network:

1. Did the banker identify lead investors? Which investing institutions currently owned, previously owned, recently added to or recently sold portfolio positions in the shares of peer competitors?

2. Did the banker furnish to the company a list of those institutions and the sizes of their positions in competitors' shares? Did those same institutions show an "indication of interest" in buying shares on the company's deal? Did they "circle" a certain number of shares on the offering?

Management should plan to visit the main facilities of underwriters under consideration. Several of the firm's personnel are pivotal to the company's prospective long-term relationship with its underwriters. Introductions and discussions should take place with the firm's securities analyst who will provide regularly scheduled research coverage of the company. Ask the analyst these questions (other questions appear in Chapter 8):

1. Does he or she already follow the industry and/or peer competitors? How closely? Reasons for not following them?

2. How often should management expect to hear from or see the analyst? Expect a written report from the analyst? How often on average does the analyst publish reports on companies in general? On companies in the industry? How often on the industry?

3. Can management expect that the analyst will call the company to update senior executives on industry trends and developments? On shifts in investors' perceptions of the industry or the company? On indications of buy or sell interest from lead investors and key money managers?

4. What models and what methods does the firm or the analyst use in its equity valuation efforts? For how long? Why?

The lead underwriter manages the "books" for the company's initial public offering. Familiarity with the lead underwriter's syndicate manager will be very important during the actual offering process. Executives should plan to maintain close contact. Ask the syndicate manager these questions: will the syndicate manager keep management current on whether the "book" (of the deal's buyers) is weak or strong as the deal becomes "effective?"

There are more questions to ask:

1. Will the syndicate manager confirm how stockbrokers will sell the deal to investing institutions?

2. Will the syndicate manager apprise management of the company's likely shareholder mix by types, sizes and tier resulting from the offering?

3. Will the manager be able to identify pockets of concentration of share ownership by type and location of investor?

4. Will the manager indicate which syndicate members did the best job of distributing the company's shares? Which could have sold more? This is a clue to future sponsorship.

Executives should see the firm's trading department and meet the over-the-counter trader who will make a market in the company's shares in the after-market. Find out answers to the following:

1. Does the trader currently make a market in the shares of competitors' companies? Which is most active? How does it trade? How many other securities firms also make a market in competitors' shares (visible on level 1 of the trader's National Association of Securities Dealers Automated Quotation—NASDAQ —machine)?

2. What does the trader expect will be a reasonable spread between bid and ask price in the future quote of the company's shares? This is a measure of trading cost. Does he or she expect the spread to be wider or narrower then the spread in the quotes of competitors' issues? What will determine the size of the spread that he or she makes in the company's quote? What will narrow that spread?

3. How firm will the trader's spread tend to be? For what size of trade, in terms of number of shares, will the spread be good for? How does that compare to similar issues?

4. What amount of average daily share volume will be reasonable to maintain a narrow spread in the company's quote? What behavior of the market-maker should management expect if volume is low, the stock is volatile, or the spread is wide?

5. What level of daily or monthly share volume will be reasonable for the company? What level of volume would be too low for the firm's market-making needs?

6. Does the trader know the trading pattern in competitors' shares? Have those patterns changed? What does the trader think will be the trading pattern in the company's shares? What level of liquidity and volatility does he expect for the company's shares?

7. Can management expect that the trader will apprise management of any trading programs or rumors which generate abnormal volume? Will the trader suggest who, which type of investor, may be behind it?

Information and pricing efficiency and fair valuation in the aftermarket are major goals of any strategy to go public. For example, Automatix, Inc. and Stratus Computer consciously incorporated these goals into their initial public offering strategies. When each decided to raise capital in public markets, each looked beyond the going public process to the equity valuation process. Each focused on sponsorship in the secondary market to help make the primary offering a success. Each split brackets and selected underwriters to fit their strategy. Each built aftermarket sponsorship and pricing efficiency into their public offering.

Automatix, Inc. (Chelmsford, MA) was a leader in the robotics industry. The founder, Phillipe Villers, selected two underwriters to co-manage his company's initial public offering. He chose Hambrecht & Quist, a retail/institutional brokerage firm, and Prudential-Bache Securities, a national wirehouse firm. He believed each brought complementary strengths to the offering.

Automatix viewed Hambrecht as a highly regarded and prestigious high-technology underwriter. The company's founder was comfortable that William Hambrecht, the brokerage firm's cofounder, understood his company's business. He thought the firm could successfully broaden the company's institutional share ownership.

For example, the brokerage firm's west coast headquarters balanced the company's east coast location. The founder also calculated that the firm's international connections might help to expand its end markets. Also, thinking that companies never get as much attention from the financial community as desired, he thought international exposure would potentially broaden the company's research sponsorship.

Automatix also guaranteed itself an active valuation network in the aftermarket. It built into its offering strategy regularly scheduled management presentations to investing institutions. Hambrecht & Quist annually hosts a highly respected high-technology conference in California. Corporate managements present themselves and their strategies to leading securities analysts and money managers. As a corporate finance client, the company was automatically invited to speak. It was a built-in opportunity to communicate value. In addition, management planned to make a presentation at one of several American Electronics Association conferences designated for emerging growth companies.

Management chose Prudential-Bache Securities to co-manage its initial public offering for entirely different reasons. The firm had Wall Street's most visible and best-known robotics industry securities analyst. The company's founder believed that the industry analyst would regularly process the company's information. After the initial public offering, the analyst did produce a lengthy 22 page research report. And the firm had a retail distribution network which spanned the country. Automatix believed individual investors were an important investor constituency and that the company's shares could be sold to them through this network.

The company offered 1.3 million shares in its initial public offering on March 1, 1983 at $19 per share, raising $22.8 million. Its one-day initial return was 5.3 percent (closing bid price per share was $20). Its one-month initial return was 35.5 percent at a closing bid price per share on March 31 of $24.75.

Stratus Computer (Maynard, MA) also guaranteed itself information and pricing efficiency in the aftermarket. The company manufactures fault-tolerant computer systems. In May 1980 the company attracted $1.7 million in venture capital financing. Three subsequent rounds of venture financing raised another $15 million. The company went public on August 26, 1983. The offering successfully raised $30 million. The company's founder and president, William Foster, believed there was never any question about whether the company would go public. The more pertinent question was when it would go public.

Stratus came public earlier than expected because of favorable market conditions. The founder saw that capital was readily available at a reasonable cost. He was certain the offering would minimally dilute the company's equity.

Many investment banking firms competed intensely for Stratus's underwriting business. The company was approached by New York-based underwriters and was courted by corporate finance boutique firms. Management narrowed the list of prospective underwriters to five firms which Foster interviewed, and Stratus's president and chief financial officer visited the facilities of each firm.

Stratus was very particular in its initial public offering strategy. The company wanted at least two underwriters to co-manage its new issue. It desired a New York-based prestigious, national institutional firm for distribution and a prestigious high-technology firm, known for the quality of its research. Management finally selected three co-managers to do the deal. Foster chose a national institutional firm, Morgan Stanley Group, as its lead underwriter and two retail/institutional firms, Alex Brown & Sons and Hambrecht & Quist. The latter two underwriters were closely allied with high-technology research capability.

Management believed these selections assured strong national and international distribution of its securities. In particular, management observed that Alex Brown had Wall Street's best staff of high-technology securities analysts. The firm appeared to be focused in its securities research efforts. Management discerned that four to five analysts, instead of one industry specialist, covered every particular area of high technology. And its securities sales force seemed to tap the market of high-net-worth individual investors. Management believed that specific retail sector was an important investor constituency for the company.

Finally, as a corporate finance client, the company's invitation to Hambrecht & Quist's annual high-technology conference was automatic. Invitation to Alex Brown's annual high-technology conference was also a given. Morgan Stanley's research efforts further strengthened Stratus's lock on a broad base of research sponsorship. Stratus built its valuation network into its offering.

The company offered 3 million shares in its initial public offering on August 26, 1983 at $12 per share, raising $36 million. Its one-day initial return was 12.5 percent (closing bid price per share on August 26 was $13.50). Its one-month initial return was 20.8 percent at a closing bid price per share on September 30 of $14.50.

Business Week magazine's April 1986 survey of the 1,000 largest public companies, in terms of market value, ranked Stratus Computer number 982 in market value but number 13 in 1985 sales growth. Sales grew 90 percent in 1985, to $80 million, earnings rose 105 percent, return on equity was 15.6 percent and share price (as a percent of book value) was 600 percent. A one percentage point increase in return on equity added about 38.5 percentage points to share price (as a percentage of book value per share). Its P/E ratio was 41.

"Wall Street" is a relationship business. Investment bankers cultivate relationships for new business purposes. Securities analysts build relationships with institutional securities analysts and portfolio managers for purposes of high research rankings and gross commissions allocation. Institutional securities salesmen wine and dine institutional traders to preserve an ongoing flow of orders and commissions. Retail representatives claim the credo in squiring new individual investors. And investing institutions develop relationships with corporate executives as owners of corporate equities.

Wall Street is a word of mouth business built on trust. One's word is one's bond. Verbal agreements made over telephone lines, worth millions of dollars, are honored. Strong relationships form the core of Wall Street's distribution networks. They preserve existing clients and attract new business.

Relationships are also critical to equity valuation. They help to attract dominant sponsors and to keep lead investors, to cement valuation networks and to affect the market's pricing mechanism. In the going public process, managements of emerging companies should start building relationships with Wall Street even before they begin the underwriting process. Pre-offering spadework lays the foundation for a valuation network and market sponsorship in the aftermarket. It greases Wall Street's pricing mechanism and information processing function.

An initial public offering is an ideal public relations opportunity. After selecting an underwriter, management should issue a press release. It should include details of the size of the planned offering, both in dollars and shares, the planned use of proceeds from the offering, the chosen underwriter and the expected date of the offering.

In addition, executives can build relationships on the retail level: employees, customers, suppliers, dealers, residents in communities local to the company's headquarters and operating facilities, trade journalists and local business media, relevant trade association members, local chambers of commerce, and friends and relatives of executives and employees. These individuals have far less influence than investing institutions in affecting share prices but together they can form a base of long-term shareholder loyalty and support.

4

Creating Investor Demand is a Marketing Function

Companies must, by law, abide by a so-called quiet period during registration of their securities for sale to the public. After an initial public offering, the Securities and Exchange Commission requires a 90-day cooling-off period in which to let the company's shares establish a normal trading level and range. During both periods, no predictions, forecasts, projections or opinions concerning the company's valuation can be made. But the period need not be totally devoid of information. Management may continue with regularly scheduled activities and may deal with unsolicited requests for factual, not predictive, information.

If planning is not already completed before an initial public offering, the cooling-off period is a time to plan marketing strategy to penetrate Wall Street. This chapter determines how equities in an industry are valued and identifies a company's problems and opportunities arising from this assessment of investors' perceptions. It also differentiates and positions equity products on the basis of both risk/expected returns and share price/profitability (Chapter 5 does so on the basis of capital strategy and business strategy). Finally, it establishes marketing objectives and equity valuation strategy. Chapter 5 discusses cash flow communications responsibility, and Chapter 6 examines the signals management sends to Wall Street.

SITUATION ANALYSIS

Management's first action before or after an initial public offering should be to view the relative value of the company in comparison to its peers and to the industry.

At this point, I take the liberty of referring to material that appears later in this chapter. The above comparisons can be made visually (see Figures 1 and 2 in the section titled "Differentiation and Positioning"). They should lead management to ponder: how are the industry's stocks valued relative to industry profitability and to the profitability of one another? How are they valued in terms of risk and expected returns relative to the market, to the industry and to one another?

Visual differences in relative equity valuations should raise several questions:

1. Why are the company's shares valued as they are (as opposed to why are competitors' shares priced as they are)?
2. Do investors fairly appreciate the company's profitability and growth potential relative to peers with similar fundamentals?
3. Why does the company trade at its P/E ratio, given its level of profitability?
4. Why does the company's stock carry its beta coefficient?
5. Why do investors require a higher than market return to own the company's shares?
6. What are investors' perceptions of the industry, of peers and of the company? Are they accurate? Do they explain relative values? Should they be changed or reinforced?

Rather than leading directly to answers, these questions lead naturally to other questions from which decisions about how to communicate value and what to communicate to Wall Street can reasonably be made.

Management must learn how the market values companies in its industry in general and how investors perceive companies in the industry in particular. It clarifies reasons for valuation differentials among companies in the same industry and actions to assure pricing efficiency and fair market value for the company. In this chapter, I use the converted thrift industry in Massachusetts to highlight the process of assessing investors' perceptions.

At the start of 1987, there were 45 publicly-held thrift institutions in Massachusetts, 32 of which converted from mutual to stock form of ownership in 1986. Virtually all of those which converted were small community savings banks which had served their communities over the years as dependable residential mortgage lenders. They had been managed conservatively and profitably as evidenced by the ability of many to weather the high interest rate environment of the late 1970s without suffering operating losses.

A combination of a robust economy, evidenced by rising loan volume and a track record of operating strength, evidenced by expanding operating margins and operating spreads, made the market very receptive to new issues of thrifts' shares in 1985 and 1986. The public offering of New Milford Savings Bank (New Milford, CT) in February 1986 was the first indication of a relatively hot market for new issues of thrift stocks. The bank offered stock at $16 per share and the first trade in its shares took place at about $26 per share. Its stock closed at $27.75 bid for a one-day initial return of 73.4 percent.

Going public presented some immediate problems for these thrifts. First, they became immediately overcapitalized. The ratios of equity capital to assets for most had already been satisfactory (at or in excess of a low limit of about eight percent by Massachusetts law). Public offerings raised those ratios to levels of 20-to-1 in some cases.

The effect of this abundant new capital was to depress returns on equity and put pressure on thrift managements to lever up the capital with earnings assets as soon as reasonably possible. In addition, by the middle of 1986, institutional funds began to rotate from interest-sensitive issues to economy sensitive issues, thus further depressing thrifts' market valuations.

Second, by Professor Arbel's measures of information deficiency mentioned in Chapter 1, most of these thrifts were neglected and underresearched by industry analysts. Even analysts at firms which underwrote new thrift issues did not immediately provide coverage of their firm's corporate finance clients at the end of the cooling-off period.

It became clear to thrift managements that the most direct route from the company to their underwriter's research department was through the underwriter's mergers and acquisitions department. The bankers wanted to earn more fee income by helping these thrifts to put their capital to work through acquisition strategy. The prospect tended to make them much more responsive to management's sponsorship needs.

Third, thrift stocks tended to be underowned. Depositors were given the first opportunity to subscribe to new offerings. As a result, many deals were significantly oversubscribed within their own communities, effectively creating a private market among local individuals. For some of these thrifts there was literally no public trading market for their shares.

The market value of the entire thrift industry, about $20 billion including California's large savings and loans, was only slightly more than the market value of American Express Company alone. Thrifts' capitalizations, by definition, were relatively small, sometimes less than $10 million, and trading in their shares was very illiquid and costly.

By mid-autumn of 1986, the supply of thrift stocks was abundant. Professional investors perceived returns opportunities eleswhere as market timers (asset allocators) shifted portfolio concentraion to more economy-sensitive issues. Thrifts' equity capital/asset ratios had risen, their price/book ratios had fallen, pressure on management for strategy decisions was mounting, depositors'/ shareholders' wealth was at stake and executives' net worth was at risk. Research coverage was low, ownership was narrow, and trading markets were thin.

By themselves, these factors do not equate to inefficient pricing of thrift shares. Thrift fundamentals must be considered. But, as will be seen in Chapter 6, thrift equities as a group were revalued by more than 10 percent at the beginning of 1987 and by as much as 34 percent within the first quarter of 1987. Considering valuation differentials among thrifts, the pressing issues for thrift managements were the questions of how Wall Street valued thrifts and how Wall Street perceived individual thrifts within the industry. The answers held the key to marketing and cash flow communications strategy.

In resolving this issue, it is tempting for the management of any company to believe it already knows how Wall Street values equities in its industry or to disagree with the results of survey research which point to investors' perceptions of a company which conflict with management's perceptions. But, in the business of equity valuation, outright dismissal or casual disregard of investors' perceptions is a mistake.

On Wall Street, investors' perceptions of risk and expected returns translates to market value. A real challenge for managements is to acknowledge and accept the existence of investors' current perceptions which drive their company's stock price up or down. At that point, management's option is to reshape perception, reinforce perception or do nothing. In the case of the first two, management cannot do either unless it knows what those perceptions are.

Too often managements talk about issues pertaining to their industry and company which they think are important to the valuation of their company's equity without having any idea what investors perceive to be important. Too frequently managements discuss management issues with investors without discussing investor issues with investors. They waste their own time and investors' time. In fact, they create investor supply (sellers) not investor demand for their company's shares.

Effective cash flow communications identifies those few variables critical to valuation of equities in an industry, and those investor perceptions which drive the valuation of the equity of individual companies.

There are three ways to determine how the market values companies in a particular industry and how it perceives a particular company in an industry. First, talking to a stock uncovers specific variables considered critical to valuation of equities in an industry and specific factors critical to perception of company-specific value.

Survey research is the most popular method used by public companies by which to talk to their stocks. A survey of brokerage firm and institutional securities analysts and money managers asks questions of a company, its industry, and its peer competitors. It asks "valuation" and perception questions concerning capital strategy, (planning systems), business strategy (competitive positioning), operating ability, management quality, and market reaction to management decisions/actions. In a survey sponsored by one company but initiated by an outside consultant, these questions are usually scattered among others so as not to reveal their relative importance and no indication of the sponsoring company is given.

In response, analysts cite the critical variables in their analysis of value in an industry. And they reveal their perception of a company and its peer competitors within the industry. Survey results show how the market values the company, identify investors' (mis)perceptions, and suggest courses of action to shape or reinforce perception of fundamentals.

Second, quantitative results of statistical analysis offer insight into the equity valuation process. Financial managers identify critical valuation variables. They take a large sample of data from companies in the same industry or in an industry with similar operating characteristics. They examine data spanning many years. Relationships between operating characteristics and market valuation emerge. A valuation model can be constructed.

Third, the case study method reveals precedents in the equity valuation process. Management has to find other companies comparable in growth, profitability, business risk and financial risk. Study leads to an understanding of how investors may value a company relative to peer competitors and the industry.

I use survey research in this chapter to demonstrate how to talk to stock. Management benefits in two ways from the exercise. First, important valuation themes become apparent and, second, a valuation network of potential lead investors and dominant sponsors emerges.

In constructing a survey, management or an independent organization should identify and make contact with portfolio managers at investing institutions who own or have owned shares of one or more peer industry competitors. And they should isolate those who have recently added to existing portfolio positions or those who have recently sold all or part of their positions at a profit. They should also make contact with sell-side brokerage firm securities analysts who provide research coverage of companies in the industry.

Vendors of computer-based screens and database services can facilitate the identification process, although management should put its underwriter to work at no charge to the company. Four vendors monitor the portfolio transactions of investing institutions which manage more than $100 million in equity assets and which must file quarterly position reports, Form 13F, with the Securities and Exchange Commission, within 45 days after the conclusion of every calendar quarter. The resulting information is called ownership data.

For example, a profile of investing institutions' transactions in the first quarter of 1986, ended March 31, takes shape in late May and early June. The filings only show positions held at the close of a quarter, not the actual transactions which took place during the quarter. Mutual fund companies are required to file semi-annual N–SAR reports.

The four vendors are CDA Investment Technologies, Inc. (Silver Spring, MD) in both hard copy and on-line, Vickers Stock Research Corporation (Huntington, NY) in both hard copy and on-line, H.L. Pearson & Co. (Huntington, NY), and Disclosure, Inc. (Bethesda, MD) in hard copy and on-line. They classify securities by which institutions hold them and institutional portfolios by which securities they hold.

Vickers Stock Research Corp., for example, monitors the portfolios of 3,600 investing institutions: banks, insurance companies, mutual funds, foundations, colleges, and closed-end investment companies. The service follows 75 industries and publishes a series of *Vickers' Guides* to the portfolios of a variety of types of institutional investors. CDA's *Spectrum Corporate Extracts* covers the 800 largest U.S. institutions, 550 U.S. investment company funds, and 430 largest European investment companies and tracks the quarterly total return performance of more than 300 investment advisers.

Brokerage firms subscribe to these services for trading purposes. They want execution speed and agency commissions. In the event of a block trade, they can quickly determine which investing institutions have positions in a stock and can quickly make contact with them. The institution might want to participate as a buyer or a seller in the transaction. Management should ask its underwriter to retrieve this ownership data from the Quotron stock quote machines used by the firm's stockbrokers.

Ownership data revealed that the data processing industry was the most heavily owned industry at the end of the first calendar quarter of 1986. Institutions held $97.5 billion worth of stock in the industry, up $28.3 billion or 40.9 percent from the previous reporting period. Holdings of IBM's shares, $68.3 billion, up $20.5 billion or 43 percent from the previous reporting period, comprised more than two-thirds of the total dollar value of institutional holdings in the industry.

Ownership data published by *Business Week* in April 1986 also showed that average institutional share ownership of the largest 1000 companies by market capitalization was 43 percent. The stock of CNA Financial was the most heavily owned, about 95 institutions held 94.1 percent of the company's 62 million share float. UAL Corp. (parent of United Airlines) was fiftieth most heavily owned, about 240 institutions held 71.3 percent of the company's 35 million share float.

Executives can find industry securities analysts either through the *Membership Directory* of the Financial Analysts Federation (New York, NY) or through the *Directory of Wall Street Research* (Port Chester, NY). They can find information about which analysts have written recent research reports about their industry or companies in the industry in a newsletter titled *New Research Reports* (Business Research Corp., Boston, MA).

Executives can obtain hard copies of research reports either directly from securities analysts who write them or indirectly through on-line access to financial information databases such as *Investext* (Business Research) or *Exchange* (Mead Data Central, Dayton, OH). Finally, the *Wall Street Transcript* (New York, NY) publishes comments about industries made by industry securities analysts during roundtable discussions.

Making contact with any of these individuals at institutions or firms is as easy as a telephone call. To find the address and telephone number of a money management firm, executives can examine one of several directories such as the

Directory of Pension Funds and Their Investment Managers: The Money Market published by Money Market Directories, Inc. (Charlottesville, VA) or *Pensions & Investment Age* annual special annual profile issue of money managers or *Institutional Investor*'s annual January issue. For the addresses and track records of mutual funds, managers can make contact with the Investment Company Institute (Washington, DC) or examine the Weisenberger Investment Company Service at any business library.

The money management firm's client contact can connect executives directly to either the firm's money manager(s) who holds portfolio positions in companies in the industry or to the buy-side analyst who follows the industry and companies in it. Making contact with brokerage firm securities analysts is more straightforward.

Management should ask these sorts of questions to each money manager or analyst:

1. How do you value a company in the industry?
2. How do you distinguish among and between companies in the industry?
3. What do you pay for in a company in the industry? What do you avoid?
4. What are the biggest perceived risks to industry operating margins? To individual company operating margins?
5. What constitutes a strong competitive position in a given market (discussed in Chapter 5)? Which companies are perceived to have the best competitive position in their markets? Why? Perceived to last for how long? The worst positions? Why? How might they improve?
6. How does the strength of that competitive position manifest itself in operating margins and operating spreads?
7. What are the most critical issues of quality?
8. How do you assess management capability and depth or the quality of corporate planning systems?
9. Which profitability performance measures are most important to valuation of equities in the industry?
10. What relative performance levels are most desirable for companies in the industry?
11. What would be your (money manager/analyst) response to management's acquisition of a new business or sale of an existing business line (change in organizational structure), declaration of an initial dividend or initiation of a share repurchase plan (signal concerning future operating cash flows)?
12. What constitutes an undervalued (overvalued) equity in the industry?
13. What valuation models do you use to determine intrinsic value and expected returns? What criteria do you use to identify asset values? What relative ratios do you use to measure the cost of profitability or the price of growth?
14. Why and when would you recommend purchase/sale of stock? Why and when would you initiate/terminate research coverage of a company in the industry?

15. What, and how often, do you want to hear from executives of companies in the industry?
16. What trading strategies have historically been applied to companies in the industry?
17. What types of investors have historically held portfolio positions in the industry?

PROBLEMS AND OPPORTUNITIES

In the wake of the surge in volume of new thrift issues in 1986, the author initiated a perception study for thrift executives to assess how Wall Street valued thrift equities. It was intended to identify critical valuation variables for and prevailing perceptions of the industry and its competitors.

There were four general conclusions:

1. Earnings momentum and takeover potential drove thrift share prices.
2. Wall Street valued thrifts' future earning power from business strategies which broadened lines in existing products or expanded distribution channels in existing markets.
3. Securities analysts perceived the thrift industry as a commodity business (lending with no pricing advantages). They had trouble differentiating among thrifts but did so initially on the basis of perceived competitive advantage: low cost processors in areas of rising loan volume.
4. Respondents valued individual thrifts more on the basis of their operating skill than their investment skill (i.e., earnings from continuing operations versus gains on sales of securities).

Specific findings included:

1. Future earning power and takeover potential drove thrift share prices.
2. Lending markets with rising employment, rising per capita income and rapid turnover of homes (unit volume) were most valued.
3. Thrift operating margins and earnings were interest-rate sensitive and vulnerable.
4. Low cost processors had the greatest competitive advantage.
5. Thrift fundamentals, not unique business strategies, were valued.
6. Earnings quality meant income from recurring sources, not gains from securities sales or from sales of assets.
7. Return on assets sufficed as a proxy of thrift profitability in the absence of return on equity.
8. Inflation or recession would weed out the best thrifts, by squeezing operating margins and reducing earnings.
9. The biggest risk was how management would lever its new capital: new products in new markets, broadened lines in existing products or expanded distribution channels in existing markets.
10. Analysts preferred thrift managements with commercial banking background. They perceived lower risk in new product diversification.

11. Commercial bank products were perceived as relatively low risk sources of new volume.

12. Most thrift managements did not communicate well.

13. Analysts could not distinguish among most thrifts.

14. Research coverage was a function of market capitalization.

15. Investing in takeover candidates seemed to be the best strategy.

16. Investors buying performance wanted earnings and were less interested in dividends.

17. The dollar value of executives' outright share ownership, not stock options, should equal about two to three years' salary.

18. Thrifts were in a cyclical group and should be rotated (market timed) in response to interest rate cycles.

19. The dollar value of new institutional portfolio positions in thrift shares was about $1 to $3 million.

20. Market-makers dropped inactive stocks, those with volume of 2,000 or less shares per day.

In general, issues which surface in these studies pertain to perceptions of business strategy. For example, money managers claimed two misperceptions surrounded investment in thrift stocks. First, they contended that investors misperceived the difference in industry structure and competitive fundamentals between eastern savings banks and western savings and loan associations. Second, they believed investors misperceived the positive effect of balance sheet restructuring on thrifts' operating margins, i.e., reduced sensitivity to swings in short-term interest rates and to fluctuations in loan volume and increased stability of earnings.

Other issues which affected investors' perceptions of thrifts' future cash-generating abilities were management-related in many instances, such as perception of a lack of management depth with which to fully exploit competitive advantages or to adequately contain costs and preserve margins as capital was levered. Excess management optimism concerning operating goals was potentially problematic. And a "mutual mentality," a management attitude not geared to sharing information with outside sources, lessened the availability of information. Executives may disagree with survey research results (discussed in Chapter 5). Or they may find investors have significant misinformation, or that they significantly lack available information about the company. Recall from Chapter 1 Professor Arbel's checklist to determine the extent to which a company may be neglected:

Analysts' research coverage

Institutional ownership (number of institutions and shares owned as a percent of outstanding equity)

Trading volume

Newspaper coverage

Analyst meetings

If an entire group of peer competitors seems underresearched and under-owned, a prudent strategy may be to organize peers, a la the "London connection" mentioned in Chapter 3. The joint effort may attract sponsorship and ownership. It may infuse information and pricing efficiency.

In general, opportunities to communicate value to Wall Street are both quantitative and qualitative. The former focuses on capital strategy, value-based planning systems used in investment decision making. The latter focuses on three themes in business strategy which support a company's growth/returns profile: growth/share relationships in product/markets (the company's market opportunity), earning power and earnings quality (operating margin potential arising from competitive advantage) and management. Both capital and business strategy will be discussed more fully in chapter 5.

For thrift institutions, several opportunities to communicate value presented themselves. First, it was clear that those thrift executives with a firm grasp of their thrift's operating numbers (an understanding of analysts' information needs and a willingness to share information with them), had a communications advantage. Second, those with an ability to articulate their thrifts' competitive advantages, expected growth rates in loan volume in their lending markets, and reinvestment opportunities in which to lever owner's equity capital had a competitive advantage in the race to attract sponsorship and to reduce information deficiency. Third, introducing these executives to investing institutions put a brand identity on an equity product perceived as a commodity. And fourth, investors' ability to buy stock at the same price as executives was an opportunity to shape perception of management as buyers and owners of its equity securities.

I recommend that managements initiate a perception study at least once per year. The results highlight how investors value equities in an industry, which equities they perceive to be best positioned for future growth and profitability, and why they value individual equities differently. The findings enable executives to ask and answer questions about why their shares trade at their relative multiples and what those share prices imply about the risks investors perceive and the returns they expect. The results thus naturally highlight themes which form the core of a cash flow communications strategy (discussed in Chapter 5). The process also puts management in direct contact with lead investors and dominant sponsors around whom to form an equity valuation network.

If reasons for valuation differentials between a company and one of its peers remain unclear, then management can take a more focused approach. Returning to the Form 13F filings, executives should make contact with the largest institutional shareholders in, or in that competitor's shares and ask direct questions about how and why institutional portfolio managers and analysts perceive a valuation differential.

Answers will usually pertain to business strategy: perceptions of different rates and durations of expected sales growth, or perceived ability to expand operating margins by raising prices or lowering costs. Management experience may be an issue. These responses should eliminate all guessing about reasons for valuation disparities and make clear those themes which executives must address in communicating value to Wall Street.

DIFFERENTIATION AND POSITIONING

Executives must differentiate and position their company's equity product within its industry and, relative to the market, establish and gain market share of investors' minds and investment capital. In this chapter, I use the drug industry market/book ratios to only highlight the relative valuation of equities. I emphasize "only" because Professor Fruhan has cited evidence that the pharmaceutical industry is one in which differences between generally accepted accounting principles-calculated returns on equity and discounted cash flow calculations of economic returns on equity may be significant. Therefore drug equities are offered for illustrative purposes only.

Positioning and differentiation of equity products in equity capital markets can be done visually. They can be viewed in terms of both capital strategy, the quantitative assessment of risk and expected returns. It can also be observed in terms of business strategy, the qualitative assessment of profitability and its contribution to stock price.

Recall from Chapter 2 that portfolio risk, variations in returns on a portfolio of common stocks, can be attributed to market-related effects (31 percent), group effects (37 percent), industry effects (12 percent), and company-specific effects (20 percent). In contrast, security-specific risk, variations in returns on individual securities, can be attributed to market related effects (31 percent), group effects (14 percent), industry effects (12 percent), and company-specific effects (43 percent).

On a quantitative level, management must differentiate the company's equity product on the basis of its capital strategy. Executives must compare their company-specific risk to that in alternative investments within its industry and to the market. They must also measure their company-specific expected returns relative to those in alternative investments and to market expected returns. This requires calculation of the beta coefficient and alpha intercept of the company's stock.

For example, executives should highlight the systematic influences of those statistical attributes which may help to explain the company's returns-generating process, such as: (1) Alpha (security-specific expected returns in excess of mar-

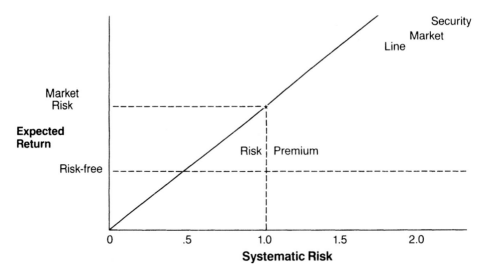

Figure 1
Risk/Expected Return (Security Market Line)

ket expected returns), (2) Beta (historical price movement relative to stock market movement), (3) Bond beta (historical price movement relative to bond market movement), (4) Yield (dividend policy), and (5) Size (market capitalization). Recall from Chapter 2 that one academic study of a returns-generating model based on these five factors found systematic influences which explained 10 percent of the variation in security returns of a New York Stock Exchange issue over a typical month and 40 percent of the variation in a typical stock over time.

Management must also assess the level of estimation risk surrounding forecasts of the company's earnings, relative to dispersion around estimates for peer competitors. Comparisons lead to conclusions about market perceptions of the company's risk relative to management perceptions. Combined with an assessment of market expectations of the company's returns potential relative to management's expectations, implied by the company's stock price (and discussed in Chapter 5), executives should be able to paint a risk/expected returns picture for the company relative to peer competitors and to the market.

Executives should graph their company's risk/expected returns profile (called a position map) and visualize it as an expression of their company's capital strategy. The relationship is called the security market line (SML) and is considered a benchmark for assessing the relative value (attractiveness) of stocks[1] (See Figure 1).

Stocks in the same risk class (beta), proportional to market risk, should earn returns similarly proportional to overall market returns, and should thus plot on the security market line (alpha appears where the regression calculation of beta intercepts the Y axis). In theory, no company's stock should be able to sell for long periods at prices which yield returns in excess of those available in other securities in its risk class. Executives should determine whether the expected returns investors can earn in their companies' shares are proportional to their risk class.

The X-axis on the risk/expected returns graph is systematic risk (beta) and the Y-axis is expected returns. Systematic risk on the overall market is 1.0 on the X-axis. Both the risk-free rate of return on Treasury bills and the expected returns on the overall market (market risk premium) can be located on the Y-axis.

The slope of the SML reflects the relationship between risk and expected returns, such that the steeper the slope, the higher the expected returns. A company's position on the SML reflects the attractiveness of its risk/expected returns relationship relative to the market and to peer competitors. Issues for aggressive investors are located further out on the security market line. Those for defensive investors are located closer in on the SML.

The graph helps to explain investors' perceptions of risk and their willingness to bear it. If investors perceive higher systematic risk relative to alternative investments of equal expected returns, then a company will move into a new risk class with higher proportional expected returns and its share price will fall relative to securities in lower risk classes. If investors require higher returns relative to alternative investments of equal risk, then the slope of the SML will become steeper and share prices of all securities in the same risk class will fall relative to alternatives. For example, at bull market peaks, the level of the security market line will be relatively flat and its slope will be gradual, suggesting that a willingness to bear more risk does not generate much higher return. At bear market bottoms, the level of both the security market line and its slope will be steep, suggesting that bearing higher risk can generate significantly higher returns.

A bull market peak, a bear market trough, and an intermediate market cycle occurred between 1972 and 1976. Measured on the security market line by extending a vertical line from beta of 1, expected return on the market was 9 percent on June 30, 1972 (peak), 15.7 percent on September 30, 1974 (trough), and 13.1 percent on December 30, 1976 (intermediate).[2] (For examples of the slope of the security market line in other market periods, see Fama/MacBeth in the bibliography.) Market risk premiums over risk-free rates of return in Treasury bills tend to be lower than average in bull markets and higher than average in bear markets. For example, the market risk premium was 5 percent in 1972, 7.7 percent in 1974, and 8.5 percent in 1976, versus a premium of approximately 7 percent from 1926 to 1972.

Companies with positions on the security market line (or close to it) offer expected returns in line with market expected returns for their risk class and (their capital strategies) are, therefore, of average attractiveness. Within the same risk class (extending from the X-axis), those above the SML by more than a minor deviation offer higher expected returns, in excess of market expected returns, than alternative securities of equal risk (positive alphas). Their capital strategies appear undervalued and attractive. Buyers will tend to drive the prices of these securities up and their expected returns down to the security market line. Those below the SML by more than a minor deviation offer lower expected returns, less than market expected returns, than alternative securities of equal risk (negative alpha). Their capital strategies appear overvalued and unattractive. Sellers will tend to drive the prices of these securities down and their expected returns up to the SML.

A company's position off the security market line by a minor deviation may result because transactions costs or taxes are disincentives to investors to buy undervalued securities or sell overvalued securities. A position off the SML by more than a minor deviation suggests information deficiency, market misperception and market mispricing.

Management should try to locate its company and its peer competitors on the security market line, even if they are in different risk classes. Executives can derive their own alpha and beta estimates. Or they can use those of securities analysts at their companies' underwriting firm, at firms which provide research coverage on the industry, or in Merrill Lynch's Beta Book.

As suggested at the start of this chapter, if a company is in a higher risk class than its peer industry competitors, executives should find out why investors perceive more risk and require higher returns to own their company's equity securities. Talking to the stock will reveal how the market perceives the company (and its capital strategy).

On a qualitative level, management should also differentiate the company's equity product on the basis of its business strategy and the contribution of profitability to stock price. For example, executives should highlight those financial attributes which may explain their company's sources of returns, such as growth in shareholders' equity, cash flow yield and change in valuation. Recall from Chapter 2 that one study of a returns-generating model based on these three factors found a better-than 90-percent correlation between estimated and actual returns by summing the values of these three components.

Management can also graph these returns-generating factors (See Figure 2). The price/performance specifications of a company's equity product can be demonstrated in an equity valuation model which plots share price as a percentage of book value (price/book) on the Y-axis against profitability (return on equity) on the X-axis. The graph (position map) shows clearly that profitability is the key to market value (growth in book equity).

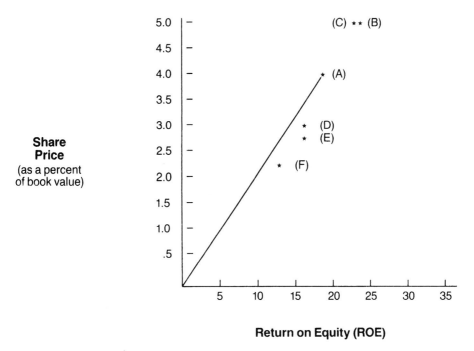

Figure 2
(Price/Book) -to- (Return on Equity)

The slope of a company's position on the graph is determined by dividing the company's share price as a percentage of book value (P/B) by its percentage return on equity (ROE) such that the higher the number (the steeper the slope), the more its profitability contributes to growth in its book equity, and the more attractive the company's equity as an investment. Positions for negative returns on equity companies are not represented on the above graph.

Profitability is the best positioning variable for any company's equity product. And the best company position on the relative valuation graph is that in which incremental profitability contributes to increases in share price (as a percent of book value) disproportionate to the industry and to peer competitors. High growth/high returns on equity companies have the steepest slopes on the graph and the most desirable perceived product/market opportunities. It is to executives' advantage to shape investors' perception of the performance slope of their business strategies so that investors can fairly value their companies' equity.

Price/book-to-return on equity seems to be a more accurate valuation tool than price/earnings models with which to begin to explain current share prices based on historical data. Assuming relatively stable and predictable operating performances, it is also a more useful method by which to compare valuation differences between companies within an industry and management estimates of expected returns with consensus expectations of returns on equity. Estimates which exceed consensus are most attractive.

One study[3] found that for the majority of companies followed by the *Value Line Investment Survey*, a valuation model of share price to historical growth in book equity (P/B) seemed a more accurate predictor of value than a model of share price to historical growth in earnings (P/E). For example, the standard error for a constant P/B model was (0.521) but improved to (0.358) in a model of P/B as a log linear function of ROE. The standard error for a constant P/E model was (0.489), not much less accurate than that of a constant P/three year average earnings growth model (0.418) or of a single variable model of P/three-year average earnings per share as a linear function of 10-year earnings per share growth rate (0.400). In addition, the mean squared error (log of the ratio of actual price to expected price) varied far less across the sample for a P/B-ROE model (0.128) than for the P/E models (0.239, 0.175, and 0.160 respectively).

The study also concluded empirically that stable earnings growth did not always lead to higher share prices. Rather, the stability of returns on equity lengthened investors' time horizons and holding periods. It also raised share prices when ROE exceeded shareholders' expected returns but lowered share prices when ROE fell short of the returns investors expected.

Results also suggested that when tests controlled for ROE stability, the effect of dividend policy might be to lower the relative valuation of companies with ROEs greater than shareholders' expected returns and to raise the value of companies with ROEs less than investors expect. Finally, leverage only sometimes seemed to hurt share prices and no positive correlation existed between shareholders' expected returns in 35 industries and average industry betas.

A Strategic Planning Institute study of 600 industrial companies between 1968 and 1981[4] found that stock price (P/B) multiples fell dramatically from 2.3 in 1968 to 0.9 in 1974 and recovered to 1.25 by 1976. Within this context, high returns on equity companies or accelerating returns on equity companies (current ROE relative to a weighted average of five-year or ten-year ROE to eliminate any distortions to ROE from leverage or inflation) within an industry commanded the highest prices per share as a percent of book values per share. For example, the Institute found that average P/B ratios for companies with returns on equity between 20 percent and 25 percent were 1.79.

In contrast, low returns on equity companies or decelerating returns on equity companies commanded the lowest prices per share as a percent of book values per share. The Institute found in the same study that for companies with returns on equity between 5 and 10 percent, average prices per share were 67 percent of book value per share.

Comparisons of companies within the drug industry (as of March 31, 1986) highlight the price/performance characteristics of a range of drug equity products. On a composite basis the drug industry's return on equity was 18.7 percent (versus a weighted four-year average return on equity of 20.1 percent), and the price of a composite share traded at about 393 percent of composite book value per share (A on the graph above). These figures suggest that a 1 percentage point increase in industry return on equity added about 21 percentage points in industry price per share (as a percent of book value). The industry's price/ earnings ratio was 21.

Mylan Laboratories, Inc. is an example of a high growth/high returns on equity, high (P/B) drug company (all of the following historical company data is from Standard & Poor's *Stock Reports*). According to *Business Week*, in 1985 Mylan's sales grew 57 percent, earnings grew 97 percent, return on equity was 46.1 percent (versus a five-year weighted average of 43.1 percent), and price per share was 1,237 percent of book value per share (it does not appear on the graph above). A 1 percentage point increase in return on equity contributed more than 26.5 percentage points to Mylan's price per share (as a percent of book value per share). The company's P/E ratio was 25.

Zenith Laboratories, Inc. is another example of a high growth/high returns on equity, high (P/B) drug company. In 1985, Zenith's sales increased 115 percent, earnings rose 440 percent, return on equity was 50 percent (versus a five-year weighted average of 37.3 percent) and price per share was 1,132 percent of book value per share (it also does not appear on the graph above). A 1 percentage point increase in Zenith's return on equity added more than 22.5 percentage points to its price per share (as a percent of book value). Its P/E ratio was 25.5.

In contrast, Abbott Laboratories is an example of low growth/relatively high returns, high (P/B) drug company. In 1985, Abbott's sales rose 8 percent, earnings grew 16 percent, return on equity was 24.9 percent (versus a five-year weighted average of 25.1 percent), and price per share was 503 percent of book value per share (B on the graph above). A 1 percentage point increase in the company's return on equity added more than 20 percentage points in its price per share (as a percent of book value). Its P/E ratio was 20.

Syntex Corporation is another example of a low growth/relatively high returns on equity, high (P/B) drug company. In 1985, Syntex's sales grew nine percent, earnings grew 36 percent, return on equity was 24.5 percent (versus a five-year weighted average of 23.4 percent), and price per share was 505 percent of book value per share (C on the graph above). A 1 percentage point move in return on equity added more than 20.5 percentage points to Syntex's share price (as a percent of book value). Its P/E ratio was 25.

C.R. Bard, Inc. is an example of a medium growth/relatively low returns on equity, relatively low (P/B) drug company. In 1985, Bard's sales rose 12 percent, earnings grew 19 percent, returns on equity were 16.3 percent (versus a five-year weighted average of 17.4 percent), and price per share was 290 percent of book value per share (D on the graph above). A 1 percentage point increase in return on equity added about 18 percentage points to Bard's price per share (as a percent of book value per share).

In contrast to these low growth/high returns and relatively high growth/low returns companies, Sterling Drug, Inc. is an example of low growth/relatively low returns on equity, low (P/B) drug company. In 1985, Sterling's sales grew 2 percent, earnings rose 8 percent, return on equity was 16 percent (versus a five-year weighted average of 15.9 percent), and price per share was 270 percent of book value per share (E on the graph above). A 1 percentage point improvement in the company's return on equity added about 16.75 percentage points to its price per share (as a percent of book value per share). Its P/E ratio was 17.

Finally, Schering-Plough Corporation is an example of another relatively low growth/low returns on equity, low (P/B) drug company. In 1985, the company's sales rose 3 percent, earnings increased 9 percent, return on equity was 13.4 percent (versus a five-year weighted average of 13.9 percent) and, price per share was 232 percent of book value per share (F on the graph above). A 1 percentage point increase in return on equity contributed slightly more than 17 percentage points to its price per share (as a percent of book value per share).

The significance of the second (valuation) graph and the performance slope calculation is that it enables executives to examine the returns-generating process as it pertains to their company's market opportunity, business strategy and competitive advantage. It helps them to pinpoint whether the economic value they are creating (operating margins in excess of the cost of capital) relative to the economic value that other companies with similar fundamentals are creating is translating to growth in book equity and market value (changes in P/B ratio).

A gradual slope on an ROE level which exceeds and is expected to continue to exceed competitors' ROE suggests that economic value is not being translated to market value. It may suggest detachment from economic reality or investors' perceptions of worsening fundamentals. Management should correct the market mispricing, thus creating value for shareholders. A steep slope on an ROE level which falls short and is expected to continue to fall short of competitors' ROE suggests that economic value is being translated into more market value than it is worth. It may also suggest valuation detached from economic reality. It may also indicate that investors perceive improving fundamentals in the future. In this case, management should capitalize on the market mispricing, thus transferring value to shareholders.

The Strategic Planning Institute suggests computation of a benchmark "par P/B" ratio for companies with similar fundamentals against which to judge a company's relative price/performance position (the success of business strategy).[5] The benchmark is the P/B value, which on average is associated with companies achieving specific ROE levels. The Institute concludes that average P/B multiples tend to approximate their benchmark P/B multiples such that those with high benchmarks tend to have high prices per share as a percent of book value per share, and those with low benchmarks tend to have low prices per share as a percent of book value per share.

Benchmark P/B multiples change over time, as mentioned above, in line with changing stock market conditions. For example, prices per share as a percent of book value relative to specific levels of returns on equity were higher in the period 1968-1973 than during the period 1974-1981.

The Institute observed that a company's actual P/B ratio relative to its ROE level may differ significantly, on the upside or the downside, from its benchmark P/B multiple for the same ROE level. A disparity may reflect differences in historical versus speculative information, in investors' perceptions of a company's returns-generating factors relative to alternative investments, in perceptions of a company's break-up value, or in shortcomings of the valuation model.

If a company's actual P/B multiple is higher than its benchmark P/B multiple, it may reflect investors' positive perceptions of a company's future competitive advantage, their perception of a company's positive changing fundamentals or their misperception and unrealistic expectations caused by some information signal. A move in a company's benchmark P/B multiple toward its actual P/B multiple at a given ROE level (multiple expansion) suggests either the first or the second explanation. A move in actual toward benchmark suggests the third, i.e., market mispricing and a value transferring opportunity.

If a company's actual P/B multiple is lower than its benchmark P/B multiple, it may reflect investors' perceptions of a company's future competitive disadvantage, their perception of its weakening fundamentals, or misperception triggered by some information signal. A move in a company's actual P/B multiple towards its benchmark P/B multiple at a given ROE level suggests either the first or the second explanation. A move in benchmark towards actual suggests the third, i.e., market misperception and market mispricing and a value creating opportunity.

The best way to differentiate any company in terms of business strategy is on the basis of profitability and competitive advantage. That is the importance of shaping investors' perception of the future. But executives must also differentiate the company on the basis of its earnings sensitivity, the sensitivity of the company's returns generating process to external factors. They must position the company in a group of stable, cyclical or growth equities. The classification will be based on the variability in its security returns relative to unexpected changes in macroeconomic factors such as industrial production, inflation, interest rates, or spreads between high and low grade bonds (mentioned in Chapter 2).

Next, management must position the company in its industry. Executives must identify the company with a recognizable industry or industry sector. In general, a company's position will be aligned with that industry or sector in which a majority of its revenues, operating income, net income or assets is concentrated.

For purposes of comparison, Fidelity Investments (Fidelity Funds) defines industry sectors for the benefit of buyers of shares in its Select Portfolio sector mutual funds. In accordance with its charter, each fund invests only in companies in particular industries. The fund manager concludes that a company is principally engaged in a specific industry if 50 percent or more of its assets, gross income or net profits are committed to, or originate with a particular business activity. Management should use a higher percentage.

Both the U.S. government and Wall Street classify companies by industry. The first uses the standard industrial classification code (S.I.C.). The second divides the Standard & Poor's 500-stock index into 10 broad industry sectors and 102 industry subsectors. In order of weighting, the industry sectors as of March 1986 were:

Consumer (26.16 percent)

Capital goods (20.5 percent)

Utilities (13.18 percent)

Energy/natural resources (13.16 percent)

Basic industrials (7.20 percent)

Finance (7.05 percent)

Health care (6.89 percent)

Transportation (2.94 percent)

Housing (.99 percent)

Miscellaneous (1.92 percent)

The technology industry alone comprises 17 subsectors:

Manufacturers of analytical instruments

Manufacturers of computer peripherals and subsystems

Computer services and software companies

Connector companies

Disk and media makers

Distributors and leasing companies

Electronic test and instrumentation companies

Electronic warfare systems makers

Makers of interactive graphics and voice communications

Mainframe computer firms

Manufacturers of micro-computers and small computer systems

Makers of microwave components

Manufacturers of mini-computers and systems computers

Office automation companies

Semiconductor and materials manufacturers

Semiconductor companies

Telecommunications companies

The retailing industry group comprises seven major sub-sectors: apparel-related retailers, diversified retailers, drug-related, food-related, general merchandisers, interest rate sensitive retailers, and specialty retailers.

An industry positioning problem for emerging companies may develop because a company may not fit into any recognized industry sector. Entre Computer Centers, Inc. (Vienna, VA) faced this challenge. The company's revenues, net income, and assets were concentrated in the computer retailing industry. Management tried to position the company in the stable group of retailing but analysts positioned the company in the cyclical growth computer industry. Management ultimately won the positioning battle through persistence and perseverance.

Since steep slope (P/B to ROE) businesses carry high valuations and high P/E ratios, it is desirable to position a company in high growth/high returns, steep slope product/markets. Managements may try to position their company by association. They try to align their company with others they consider comparable on the basis of operating characteristics, reinvestment opportunities and profitability, especially if those companies have steep price/performance slopes on the relative valuation graph. The caveat is that a company's assets must actually be concentrated in that same industry.

The management of Vie de France (Vienna, VA) tried this approach. The company manufactures both fresh and frozen baked goods, namely croissants, and also operates specialty restaurants. It is slightly more than 50 percent owned by the principals of Grands Moulins de Paris, a French milling company. A majority of the company's revenues, net income and assets were concentrated in the stable milling and baking industry which was viewed as a flat slope, low growth/low return, low (P/B) industry. Management tried to position the company in the steep slope, high growth/high return, high (P/B) specialty restaurant concept growth industry. Management lost the positioning battle.

Management may choose to posture the company as the industry's leading authority and most credible source concerning trends and developments which affect valuation for a broad sweep of companies.

Lowe's Companies, Inc. (N. Wilkesboro, NC) took this approach. The company is a specialty builder of building materials in a cyclical group which is sensitive to macroeconomic cycles. The company took advantage of the opportunity to monitor the industry's cyclical swings and its effects on industry valuations. Its data became a source of reliable analytical information with which analysts could formulate assumptions and estimate industry and company earnings.

MARKETING GOALS AND OBJECTIVES

Translating economic value into market value is the goal of any program to communicate value to Wall Street. Management may state it alternately in terms of: raising a company's valuation or lifting its price/earnings ratio or its price/book ratio to premium levels above comparable companies and above market multiples.

Information efficiency and pricing efficiency are the twin objectives of any program to communicate value to Wall Street. Management may state them alternately in terms of: broader market sponsorship from an increase in the number of securities analysts providing research coverage, greater liquidity from an increase in the number of market-makers, and greater market share of institutional investment funds from an increase in institutional share ownership.

THE MARKET OF INVESTMENT CAPITAL

Now management must prepare its marketing plan. Charles Ellis, president of Greenwich Associates (Greenwich, CT), a survey research and consulting firm, separates the marketing of corporate equities into two strategies: industrial and consumer. The former applies to retail investors and is more popular. The latter applies to institutional investors and is more efficient.

Here is his opinion, based on years of surveying the investment community:

If individual investors were defined as the target constituency, then the right marketing strategy would be a consumer strategy. Broad "reach" would be wanted to get to the largest number of actual and potential investors, and media advertising would be brought into play. The "selling proposition" would be kept simple and easy to recognize and accept. Retail brokers would be courted as "centers of influence." Marketing objectives would be set in terms of recognition and acceptance among the some 40 million individual investors.

But the stock market is dominated today by institutional investors. Large in assets, but relatively few in numbers, these easily identified professional investors are full-time, active and well-informed. The effective strategy for reaching them focuses on direct contact and is conceptually based on industrial marketing.[6]

Industrial marketing strategy is applicable to companies of all market capitalizations. It must be adjusted and tuned for smaller companies. The "industrial" market of information intermediaries and investing professionals for the shares of emerging companies is targetable, penetrable and more efficient than the "consumer" market. It can be broken down by the number of institutions, the types of institutions, the size of equity assets under management, their location and the functional specialty of institutional personnel. I supply this information for perspective only, rather than to suggest that emerging companies should undertake sweeping efforts to penetrate the industrial market.

INVESTING INSTITUTIONS

According to Technimetrics, Inc., (New York, NY), a database management and research firm, the industrial market fits into 13 categories of investing institutions. It represents a total of 1,246 institutions (as of March 26, 1986):

Bank/trust institutions (309)

Insurance groups (120)

Mutual fund management firms (51)

Investment counselors (371)

Retirement funds (88)

Savings banks (10)

Endowments/foundations (16)

Asset management subsidiaries of brokerage firms (75)

Asset management subsidiaries of banks (59)

Asset management subsidiaries of insurance companies (36)

Risk arbitrage (hedge fund) firms (111)

In general, before consideration of investment strategy and style, managements of emerging companies should concern themselves most with the following (both of which are discussed at length in Chapter 7):

1. Small and medium-sized institutions with tens of millions to several hundreds of millions of dollars in equity assets.
2. Large institutions that dedicate a portion of total managed assets to investment in small capitalization companies, those which maintain average portfolio positions which are a small percentage of total managed assets or those which buy relatively high percentages of the outstanding equity of emerging companies as passive investments.

These investing institutions can best capitalize on the excess returns potential of neglected, small capitalization companies and can also best afford the liquidity costs often associated with those issues.

There are a total of 296 institutions in the $200 million asset size category within Technimetrics' database. A breakdown indicates: 26 bank/trust institutions, 5 insurance groups, 7 mutual fund management firms, 117 investment counselors, 6 retirement funds, 2 savings banks, 4 endowment/foundations, 22 asset management subsidiaries of brokerage firms, 4 asset management subsidiaries of banks, no asset management subsidiaries of insurance companies, and 102 risk arbitrage (hedge fund) firms.

Identification of those professionals who manage less than several hundreds of millions of dollars in equity assets is difficult but several other sources may also be helpful. Of 1,195 funds monitored, Lipper Analytical Services (New York, NY) lists 136 capital appreciation funds and 33 small company growth funds that manage a range of equity assets from a low of $6.8 million by GIT Special Growth to a high of more than $1.5 billion by T. Rowe Price (Baltimore, MD) New Horizons Fund. Examples of mutual fund complexes with specialized mutual funds are Fidelity Investments (Boston, MA), the Vanguard Group (Valley Forge, PA), and Dimensional Fund Advisers (Santa Monica, CA).

In its September 30, 1985 issue (page 52) *Pensions & Investment Age* magazine listed 77 equity managers of 552 surveyed (two-thirds of whom manage less than $1 billion in equity assets) who include emerging companies as part of their investment approach. CDA Investment Technologies also follows the performance of 79 aggressive growth funds. The directories of investment advisors (counselors) mentioned earlier are also useful.

And in the category of investment counselor, the Securities and Exchange Commission and Money Market Directories, Inc. (Charlottesville, VA) publish annual directories of investment advisers registered with the SEC, under the Securities Exchange Act of 1940. Only those advisers with more than 15 clients are required to register. The Commission estimated that, in 1985, 11,146 investment advisers were registered, up from 5,485 in 1982, more than one-third of whom were also money managers.

CDA Investment Technologies, Inc. (Silver Spring, MD) tracks, by computer, the quarterly performance of more than 300 investment counselors, managing more than $331 billion in equity assets at the end of the first quarter of 1986, and 295 bank-managed common stock funds.

SIZE OF EQUITY ASSETS

Salomon Brothers, Inc., a national institutional brokerage firm, divides the industrial market by equity assets under management. The firm believes that total institutional equity funds amounted to $928.243 billion in 1985. Of that amount, the firm's research indicates that banks controlled $339.667 billion (36.5 percent); investment advisers managed $334.359 billion (36 percent); insurance companies handled $82.062 billion (8.8 percent); mutual funds ran $63.026 billion (6.7 percent); and other managers of equity assets controlled $109.129 billion (11.7 percent). Of the total, index funds made up about $150 billion in 1986, an increase from about $60 billion in 1984.

Technimetrics also breaks down its industrial market database by assets under management: greater than $10 billion (58 institutions); between $5 billion and

$10 billion (72); between $2.5 and $5 billion (144); between $1 billion and $2.5 billion (223); between $500 million and $1 billion (190); between $200 million and $500 million (258); between $50 million and $200 million (198); between $25 million and $50 million (39); and less than $25 million (59).

Pensions & Investment Age magazine tallied 72 mutual fund families with $1 billion or more in assets. Merrill Lynch is the largest with $51.8 billion under management as of March 31, 1986. The magazine also determined that 1,505 mutual funds accounted for $495.5 billion in assets at the end of 1985, up 33.7 percent from $370.1 billion managed by 1,246 funds in 1984. In addition, pension assets overseen by corporate (48.5 percent allocated to equities in 1985), public (35.1 percent allocated to equities in 1985) and union (36.9 percent allocated to equities in 1985) pension funds amounted to about $1.5 trillion as of December 31, 1985.

LOCATION (GEOGRAPHY)

The industrial market can be segmented geographically by zip code. According to Technimetrics' database of the largest investing institutions with $500 million or more in equity assets, the top 50 cities in the country, in terms of assets under management, accounted for 86 percent of those assets. More than half of the nation's equity assets was managed in the top five money centers of New York City ($250.9 billion), Boston ($106.8 billion), Philadelphia/Washington ($44.9 billion), Chicago ($44.5 billion) and San Francisco ($38.4 billion). The 50th largest center of managed equity assets was Toledo with $1.5 billion.

Investing institutions in the top five cities represented more than 44 percent of all institutions which manage more than $500 million. New York City led the country in assets managed. A total of 123 institutions, each managing more than $500 million, accounted for more than $250 billion in equity assets.

The market can also be divided by regional concentration of equity assets. Database statistics indicate that a total of 82 firms managed $142.5 billion in equity assets in New England. Another 192 managed $341.6 billion in the mid-Atlantic region; 50 managed $51.4 billion in the south Atlantic area; 137 managed $154.3 billion in the north central part of the country; 42 managed $45.9 billion in the south central region; 9 managed $7.5 billion in the mountain states; and 65 managed $92.3 billion in the pacific region.

From the perspective of retail securities sales distribution, New York, Los Angeles and Chicago rank first through third, respectively, in terms of the regional concentration of brokerage firm branch offices and of stockbrokers. Boston ranks number 10, Phoenix is 20, Buffalo is 30, New Orleans is 40 and Jacksonville ranks 50th. Standard & Poor's also helps in the identification of branch offices and broker numbers. A reference book titled *Security Dealers of North America*, details the information, state by state and city by city.

FUNCTIONAL SPECIALTY

The market can also be separated by functional specialty of institutional personnel. As of the end of March 1986, Technimetrics recorded categories for brokerage firm directors of research (1,329), brokerage firm securities analysts (2050), brokerage firm institutional securities salespersons (2,223), institutional securities analysts (5,990), institutional portfolio managers (5,011) and retail stockbrokers (66,015).

INVESTMENT STRATEGY AND STYLE

A company's equity product can best be defined by its customers in the industrial market. More appropriate, its investment characteristics are defined by the strategies and investment styles of its lead investors. Strategy affects money managers' allocation of portfolio assets and style reflects investors' perception of returns-generating attributes.

Two general strategies predominate in investment management. The two are opposite approaches to asset allocation but are often combined. One is called "top-down." It is a market timing approach to portfolio structuring and asset allocation and is geared to timing general shifts in the valuation of equities. It anticipates macroeconomic forces of change, such as those described by the Arbitrage Pricing Theory, before it considers selection of groups of stocks or individual securities. Market-related factors determine investment themes, such as inflation, disinflation, tax revision, or deregulation. They also determine the allocation of assets to those equities whose valuations may be affected by those themes.

The second strategy, called "bottom-up," is a stock-picking approach to portfolio structure and asset allocation. It is geared to fundamental securities analysis before consideration of macroeconomic forces. It seeks fundamental cash-generating ability, usually reflected either in growth in shareholders' equity or dividend yield, before consideration of macroeconomic factors. Both approaches usually minimize portfolio risk through portfolio diversification.

Patterns of portfolio returns different from those on a passive indexed portfolio distinguish investment styles. For example, in general, very aggressive portfolios tend to hold positions in low yield, high P/E small capitalization companies. Aggressive portfolios own positions in low yield, high P/E large capitalization companies. Cautious money mangers buy stock in high yield, low P/E small capitalization companies. Defensive portfolios tend to own shares in high yield, low P/E large capitalization companies.

Investment styles tend to reflect objectives for risk tolerance and total return from growth and/or income. Many incorporate considerations of both share price and dividends and, in that sense, often mix performance and price. Aggressive buyers seek to enhance total return and tend to focus on changes in share price and capital gains. Conservative buyers strive to preserve capital and tend to focus on income and dividend yield. The first differs from the second in that it seeks higher pretax total returns in excess of inflation and greater price volatility.

Mutual funds provide insight into various investment styles. Equity mutual funds offer: capital appreciation (aggressive growth, high volatility, share price increase only), high growth (high risk, emerging companies, more than 10 percent pretax total return over inflation), growth (moderate risk, mature companies), cyclical growth (risk varies with group rotation), high quality growth (low risk, blue chip stocks), growth and income (less than 5 percent pretax total return over inflation), and income (no volatility, yield only).

In the category of general equity mutual funds, as of March 31, 1986, there were 116 capital appreciation (hedge) funds, 206 growth funds, 33 small company high growth funds, 123 growth and income funds and 36 equity income funds. Of the total, big funds with net assets in excess of $250 million beat the performance of small funds with net assets less than $25 million in every category but small company growth from May 1985 through May 1986.

In terms of portfolio performance, from June 30, 1982, to April 30, 1986, small company growth funds registered a total return of 131.22 percent. In contrast, specialty sector funds, covering more than 40 industry sectors, recorded the best performance, 229.65 percent. In further contrast, growth and income funds reported 135.61 percent total return, equity income reported 134.20 percent, growth funds reported 127.59 percent, capital appreciation reported 124.12 percent, the Dow Jones Industrial Average reported 164.50 percent and the S & P 500 reported a 155.46 percent total return. Over the past 15 years the dollar value of the average equity fund increased by more than 400 percent.

Within the context of these general investment management styles, investors trade on value or expectations. Value investors buy either performance or price. Performance investors buy earnings momentum. They search for companies with real competitive advantages in growing product/markets. They want companies with rising operating profits as a result of real growth in sales due to real physical expansion in unit volume, not just because of price increases or cost reductions.

Value-oriented performance investors select companies with relatively higher risk/higher reward profiles and accelerating price/performance specifications. In up markets, they buy high relative ratios such as high P/B ratios, high P/E ratios, above market beta coefficients and low yields. They buy companies with accelerating earnings relative to trend, earnings visibility from sustainable competitive positions and price momentum relative to past moving averages of prices (rising relative price strength).

They highlight those companies which grow substantially in excess of the rate of inflation, those with inflation-adjusted returns on equity in excess of consensus expectations and those they perceive to have sustainable earning power.

Performance buyers are fundamental and aggressive in nature and buy both large and small capitalization companies.

Value-oriented price investors buy market mispricings. They search for spreads between market values and intrinsic or asset values. They search for companies in which stock price fails to reflect estimated growth in present values or enhanced competitiveness leading to positive changes in future earning power.

Buyers on price emphasize relatively low relative ratios, especially in down markets, such as low P/B ratios, low P/E ratios, high yields, and below market beta coefficients. They are contrarian, opportunistic and conservative in nature. They often trade in and out of positions as soon as market prices adjust and spreads narrow.

In bullish stock markets, investors buy performance. They buy emerging companies as primary holdings in venturesome or aggressive actively managed performance-oriented funds or passively managed value-oriented portfolios.

In bear markets, investors buy price and management. They buy emerging companies as secondary holdings in defensive portfolios of high yield, low P/E, large capitalization companies. And they apparently concentrate their holdings in relatively few industries. For example, Shearson Lehman Brothers found that during 10 bear markets since 1953, only 10 out of about 85 industry groups outperformed the S & P 500-stock index at least 70 percent of the time: beverages-soft drinks, broadcast media, entertainment, foods, oil-international, retail food chains, shoes, soaps, electric utilities, and natural gas. Of these, shoes had the best performance in bear markets. The industry's performance topped the S & P 500 index 90 percent of the time.

Information investors trade on changing expectations. Essentially, they buy or sell on discovery of positive or negative performance-oriented information. They anticipate information which will lead to investors' assessment of accelerating or slowing earnings momentum and to subsequent shifts in share price. In bull markets, they buy expectations that investors will appreciate rapid earnings growth (as in the 1986 price action in Reebok). In bear markets, they may buy expectations that investors will appreciate protected earnings in high yield, large capitalization companies in defensive industries. Or they sell or sell short on expectations that investors will depreciate equities perceived to have above average earnings vulnerability to unexpected shifts in macroeconomic variables.

Portfolios reflect any of several different asset management philosophies. Those of short-term shareholders may be actively managed and diversified with high turnover from active rotation of groups of stocks, entire industries or individual companies. Recall that information traders care about time, not price. They rotate positions in advance of changing expectations concerning macroeconomic conditions or company fundamentals.

Portfolios of long-term shareholders may be passively managed and diversified. They may exhibit relatively low turnover and may use various portfolio insurance strategies such as indexing, dedicating, or immunizing. Recall that value traders care more about price, not time. Management may also integrate fundamental analysis, quantitative screening, and technical analysis.

Equity funds which invest in emerging growth companies are usually called aggressive growth, emerging growth, growth or small company funds. The first is most actively managed. It trades on expectations and incorporates rapid rotation of positions to capitalize on rapid price changes. The second and third tend to base investment decisions on value judgments and performance prospects. The fourth may incorporate both performance and price in an actively managed, value-oriented portfolio or just price in a passively managed portfolio.

In terms of portfolio diversification, equity funds may concentrate in as few as 10 issues, diversify among hundreds of issues, specialize by company size, industry focus or geographic location, or hedge through use of options, futures or arbitrage. The Investment Company Management Institute or Wiesenberger Investment Company Service (located in business libraries) lists funds' styles and their past total return performance.

Emerging companies are usually core holdings (especially in up markets) only in diversified, aggressive portfolios with "bottom-up" investment strategies. The portfolios may be actively or passively managed and trade on value or expectations. They may buy low yield, high P/E small capitalization companies on the basis of either performance or price. This sort of portfolio may also be constructed as a part of much larger portfolio with completely different characteristics.

Institutions in the industrial market exhibit different investment strategies and styles. In general, investment advisers (counselors) and private corporate pension funds are most often equity specialists whose objective is enhanced returns. They tend to be active money managers with varying levels of aggressiveness in low yield, high P/E companies. The most aggressive want capital appreciation in all markets. It requires high turnover. They often trade on expectations but also combine market-timing with value-judgments about price in small, medium or large capitalization companies. They may also hedge their investments with stock index futures or options.

Banks and insurance companies tend to be equity and/or balanced managers and mix both equity and fixed-income vehicles in their total portfolio. These two tend to be less active than investment advisers in their asset allocation. They may adopt a top-down or bottom-up strategy or combine them. And they may take a performance/price approach to medium or large capitalization companies. They usually seek both share price gains and dividends, especially because insurance companies benefit from 85 percent dividend exclusions on taxable income.

Public pension funds (state and municipal), endowment funds, foundations, and charitable trusts have historically been oriented to income-producing securities for preservation of capital. They may use a bottom-up strategy and their style is usually growth, growth and income, income, or balanced in high yield, low P/E companies. They focus on growth in earnings and especially dividends from investment in relatively large capitalization companies. They also tend to be relatively passive value money managers who produce low turnover.

A typical owner of an emerging company's equity product tends to be more of a stock-picker than a market-timer. He or she also tends to be venturesome or aggressive, seeking share price gains, not dividend income. Either usually falls into the category of investment counselor, small-cap money manager, growth stock money manager, or investor with specialized interest in or knowledge about a market or a technology. Short-term owners sell when expectations move share prices up or down. Long-term owners usually manage diversified portfolios. They tend to actively buy performance in up markets or passively buy on price in down markets. His or her portfolio time horizons and holding periods vary with total return objectives and target selling prices.

SHAREHOLDER IDENTIFICATION

Management must analyze its shareholder base, the customer base for its equity product, and institute a shareholder records system. Identifying owners of the company's shares has obvious benefits: (1) facilitates proxy voting in support of management proposals and resolutions at annual meetings; (2) heightens defense in takeover situations and proxy battles; and (3) increases the opportunity to sell more shares to existing owners via dividend reinvestment plans or employee/customer ownership plans.

A Center for Entrepreneurial Management (New York, NY) quiz asks: what does an entrepreneur need most: an idea, capital, customers, or a plan? The answer is customers. The greatest idea, the most capital, and the best plan amount to little without customers and market demand for its products/services. A company can only sell what customers will buy. And customers will only buy goods and services which satisfy their wants and needs. As a result, a company's products or services are defined by its customers, not vice versa.

In keeping with this belief, managements of emerging companies should try to sculpt a profile of their shareholder base in the wake of their initial public offering. Executives use many resources to identify shareholders. They examine the company's transfer sheets, listings from depository trust companies which hold the company's stock in the names of nominees, and ownership data contained in Form 13F filings. They should also use the company's underwriter who should provide ownership data at no cost, or proxy solicitation firms which offer "stock watch" programs to monitor stock accumulation. And they rely on response cards attached to shareholder reports and management contacts with market-makers and analysts in Wall Street's distribution channel (discussed in Chapter 7).

Immediately in the wake of an initial public offering, management should examine its transfer sheets provided by its transfer agent. First, executives should identify which institutions bought the most stock on the company's offering. Second, they should make direct personal contact with those institutions' portfolio managers. And third, they should find out which firm sold the stock to them. It is the basis for potential sponsorship.

Results of these contacts also enable management to sculpt a profile of the company's lead investors. Management should learn the characteristics of their portfolios as a means of defining the company's equity product. For example, executives should ask portfolio managers at investing institutions:

1. What are their portfolio objectives, investment strategies and investment styles? Are they value traders or information traders?
2. Are their portfolios passively managed and indexed to the market? Or are they actively managed, diversified and rotated? What is their total return track record?
3. What is the beta coefficient on their portfolios? Their portfolio's alpha?
4. How are stock groups weighted in their portfolios?
5. Is investment concentrated in high slope industries (visible on the valuation graph)?
6. How patient are they? What are their investment time horizons? What is their annual portfolio turnover? Are they short-term traders or long-term holders?
7. What is the average yield of their portfolio? Average P/E?
8. Is their portfolio weighted by size (market value) of portfolio company?

Management should examine its transfer sheets regularly, especially after unusual block trades in its stock. And they should review ownership data contained in 13(f) filings at the end of every quarter. In addition, executives should monitor requests for the company's materials and requests to be added to the company's mailing list. New institutional names may give rise to new lead investors and to new dominant sponsors.

Beyond Form 13F filings for institutional investors, however, shareholder identification may be an immediate problem. A company's transfer sheets usually reveal the names of large individual shareholders of record and of beneficial owners of the company's shares. Beneficial owners are those who hold shares in "nominee name" or "street name." They are stockbrokers, banks or depositories. This has complicated shareholder identification for many years. Historically, managements of many companies have not been able to identify direct owners. Sometimes, 60 to 70 percent of a company's shares may be held in nominee names. Executives identified beneficial owners through use of the nominee list directory from the American Association of Corporate Secretaries (New York, NY). This procedure is changing.

SEC Rule 14b-1(c) now requires that brokerage firms provide to public companies the names of all of their accounts (usually individuals) who are non-objecting beneficial owners (NOBO) of the company's shares. In addition, the Shareholder Communications Act, to be enacted in early 1987, requires that banks provide the names of beneficial owners (usually institutions) who have active accounts as of January 1, 1987, if they approve. All accounts opened subsequently will be treated in the same manner as brokerage firms. The effort is expected to yield a paucity of names of investing institutions. The Independent Election Corporation of America (Lake Success, NY) serves as the back-office intermediary between brokerage firms and companies. IECA is expected to act in the same capacity with banks.

Many beneficial owners may object (OBO) to release of their names to a company. In this case, trading in the company's shares can still be monitored. A nominee list identifies nominee names on transfer sheets. The National Association of Securities Dealers (Washington, D.C.) sells trading activity reports to companies that trade over-the-counter. Regional repositories, such as the Depository Trust Company (New York, NY), sell security position reports. They detail only the shifts of shares among beneficial owners of the company's stock. Proxy solicitation firms sell "stock watch" programs to get behind the beneficial names. And, as already mentioned, Form 13F filings reveal institutions' portfolio activity after the fact. Ultimately, the best monitors of share shifts and ownership trends are strong relationships in the distribution channel.

A profile of the company's individual shareholder base incorporates individuals' location, average age, average share holding, average holding period, average portfolio value, average income, method of research, and attitude toward the company. The company's transfer agent can analyze shareholders of record by geographic, social and share range statistics. A survey of nominee owners via IECA contract mailings or shareholder reports helps to further define the company's equity product.

Lowe's Companies, Inc. (N. Wilkesboro, NC) has conducted annual shareholder surveys for more than 15 years. In 1982, a survey and response card were wrapped around the outside of the company's annual report. First Pennsylvania Corporation (Philadelphia, PA) also conducted a Stockholder Survey as part of its third fiscal quarter 1984 report to shareholders. The poll, managed by an outside attitude-survey firm, asked 19 questions and did not require that respondees sign their name.

Some of the company's existing audiences form a natural individual investor constituency: suppliers of materials to a company, dealers in the company's products, consultants to the company, consumers of the company's goods or services, current and past employees of the company, retirees from the company, competitors of the company, current shareholders of the company, past shareholders who sold the company's stock at a profit and even residents in communities in which the company has operations. They are natural targets of additional share ownership. Relationships with these natural investors should be nurtured and maintained. Their loyal ownership may prove helpful in times of proxy support for management resolutions and takeover defense.

Ben & Jerry's Homemade, Inc. (Waterbury, VT), maker of ice cream, went further. The company went public after a celebrated anti-monopoly war of words with Pillsbury, Inc., owner of Haagen-Dazs ice cream. Ben and Jerry believed that customers who buy its ice cream should buy its stock and that customers who buy its stock should buy its ice cream. During the offering, a motto was printed on the company's pints of ice cream "Scoop up our stock" and an 800 telephone number was installed at the company's headquarters. In contrast, Lockheed Corporation (Los Angeles, CA) discovered that college endowment funds were natural investors. The company found that these institutions not only educated future engineers and scientists but also invested in companies which employed them.

Managements consider a variety of incentives to keep natural shareholders and to attract new individual investors. Some focus on all expenses paid dividend reinvestment plans and odd lot buyback programs. Others maintain financial policies which pay out higher dividends and grant more voting power to long-term shareholders and the establishment of IRA accounts. And some, such as utilities, think in terms of customer stock ownership plans.

Dividend reinvestment plans allow shareholders to purchase additional shares without additional commission expense or at a discount from market price. At the same time, they infuse the company with additional low cost capital. Plans may not be sensible, however, if their administrative costs exceed capital contributions. About 1,300 companies offer participation in dividend reinvestment programs.

For employees, managements often initiate employee stock purchase plans. They may take the form of employee stock ownership plans (ESOP, PAYSOP or TRASOP), stock incentive compensation plans (for job performance), stock option plans or 401 (K) retirement plans.

According to the National Center for Employee Ownership (Oakland, CA), an estimated 8.6 million workers will participate in ESOPs in 1987. The management of Hospital Corporation of America proposed a $1.8 billion plan involving 20,000 employees, the largest plan to date.

Employee stock ownership plans, IRS 423 plans called ESOPs, are intended to motivate employees to work for the success of the company, and by extension, themselves. But the market does not react positively, and may react negatively, to IRS 423 plans in contrast to stock purchase plans or other managerial incentive plans (mentioned in Chapter 1).

For example, one study[7] found that stock purchase plans motivate key executives more than subordinate employees. It reviewed 69 IRS 423 plans between

1970 and 1982. The average return on the proxy mailing date was 0.13 percent versus 1.81 percent for 19 stock purchase plans over the same period. The average two-day average return was −0.01 percent versus 3.43 percent for stock purchase plans. The average two-day return from board meeting date on IRS 423 plans and the next trading day was 0.00 percent. In addition, mean announcement period returns for 19 plans which included key executives only were 4.86 percent versus 4.35 percent for plan directed at all management. Returns were 1.42 percent when those plans allowed broader employee participation and 0.79 percent when plans excluded key executives or only included non-management employees.

STRATEGY: LEAD INVESTORS, DOMINANT SPONSORS AND POPULARITY FLOW

In 1936, John Maynard Keynes likened the stock market to a beauty contest in which the objective for each judge was not to choose the contestant he found prettiest but to choose the contestant whom he thought others would find most pretty[8]. His comments pertained more to short-term information traders than long-term value investors. In other words, the winning strategy was to anticipate changes in consensus opinion.

The significance of this metaphor in terms of stock selection is that stock prices reflect expectations and consensus expectations determine stock prices. One academic study examined 919 one-year forecasts and 710 two-year forecasts of companies with December 31 fiscal years followed by three or more securities analysts.[9] It found that forecasting future consensus earnings forecasts earned higher risk-adjusted excess returns than forecasting actual future earnings and that levels of excess returns varied with the size of consensus forecast error. For example, the study determined that if an analyst were able to select stocks from among 30 percent of the companies in the study for which consensus forecasts underestimated true earnings and if the analyst's selections were right half of the time, then he or she would have earned cumulative excess risk-adjusted one-year returns of 4.54 percent. Returns would have been 9.08 percent if the selections were entirely accurate and 0.91 percent if they were only 10 percent accurate.

Keynes's metaphor raises another interesting issue which is particularly germane to this book. To affect its stock price and market value, management of an emerging company, or any company, must affect the consensus forecast of the company's future. For emerging companies, the inexistence of any forecast still represents a consensus. How? Executives must reverse the process of the beauty contest. They must identify not which judge they think is most influential in the valuation process but the judge whom others think is most influential. He or she will be the information catalyst concerning the company's returns potential. That judge will be the company's lead investor.

In the demand-creating cycle, lead investors usually attract dominant sponsors who then attract a popularity flow into a company's stock. They are what Fischer Black of Goldman, Sachs calls "information traders" versus "noise traders" and what Joel Stern of Stern, Stewart & Co., (New York, NY) calls "lead steers." Lead investors achieve superior risk-adjusted portfolio returns by identifying and capitalizing on consensus forecast errors of corporate cash-generating abilities. They perceive unrealized economic value. Lead investors force realignments of the consensus and revaluations of equities. They set equilibrium share prices and form the core around whom new consensus expectations are formed. The role of lead investors in the equity valuation process is discussed further in Chapter 7.

Who are these lead investors and what attracts them (chapter 7)? They are value-oriented investors who command a following because of their perfor-mance, their superior total return track records. From management's perspective, active growth or active value investors move more quickly than passive value investors to spread perception. Correcting market mispricings benefits their port-folio performance. Perception of enhanced competitiveness and excess returns potential, relative to alternative investments of equal risk, attracts them and their commitment of capital (usually for investment purposes only). Perception often originates with information spread by word of mouth. Chapter 9 offers examples of the behavior of lead investors in the stocks of Leisure Concepts, Envirodyne Industries, The Clothestime, and National Medical Care.

Management will know them by their commitment of capital, measured by the size of their position in a company's shares. That position will likely be large(est) in an absolute sense in terms of number of shares and percent of the company's outstanding equity. It may also be largest in a relative sense, relative to the positions of other holders of the company's shares or to the size (shares and dollar value) of the investor's average portfolio position.

Management will also know lead investors by those who try to do commission business with them. Institutional salespersons and securities analysts at major national institutional brokerage firms usually court lead investors who manage large pools of equity assets. They compete to give these investors the "first call" (service) with news which may affect their portfolio positions and returns. Re-tail/institutional salespersons at major bracket firms and broker/analysts at major and small regional firms usually court small lead investors with smaller pools of equity assets.

The identity of a lead investor varies with the market capitalization of a company. For example, among large capitalization companies, wisdom suggests that management spend its time and money in establishing one-to-one relation-ships with money managers only in three cities: New York, Boston and Chicago. These are money centers, centers of concentration of both the largest pools of equity assets and the most dominant sponsors. Wisdom also suggests that man-agement cultivate only those industry securities analysts at the most prestigious national institutional firms because they cut the greatest swath of influence with dominant sponsors.

For small capitalization companies, however, a lead investor may double as a dominant sponsor, may be located elsewhere than big money centers, and have a lower profile than money managers at large investing institutions. He or she may likely be an investment adviser, a big producing stockbroker (often the equivalent of a money manager), even a board member with a successful investment track record and an array of Wall Street contacts. They may also be influential information processors such as newsletter publishers with wide circulations (as seen in Chapter 9) or multi-industry generalists at lower bracket firms with respected reputations as stock pickers.

Peter Lynch, portfolio manager of Fidelity's Magellan Fund, is an obvious example of a lead investor with an ability to perceive changes in future earning power. Between March 31, 1977 and March 31, 1987, Lipper Analytical Services reported that the Magellan fund achieved a total return of 1,962.22 percent versus a 380.35 percent move in the S & P 500 index.

Examples of Peter Lynch's influence as a lead investor were his (Fidelity Magellan Fund) purchase of Chrysler shares at about $3 per share in 1981 or his purchase of IBM shares at about $116 in 1986. Consensus expectations for each company were cautious or low. Analysts subsequently revised their performance expectations for each. Chrysler traded to a 1986 high of $47.125 per share, declared a 3-for-2 stock split and traded to a 1987 high of $55.50 as of this writing. IBM traded to a 1987 high of $167.625. In the case of converted thrift institutions, Lynch bought thrift shares across the board because he perceived earnings momentum, earnings stability regardless of the direction of interest rates, and the opportunity to own stock at the same price as management.

It is Joel Stern's opinion that about 2,200 active money managers at U.S. investing institutions are responsible for more than 90 percent of the volume of all equities traded in the country. And he believes that only 150 or fewer of them are the most visible lead investors who are capable of affecting market-wide expectations. They are individuals such as Peter Lynch of Fidelity's Magellan Fund, John Templeton of the Templeton Funds, Warren Buffett of Berkshire Hathaway Corporation, Binkley Shorts of the Over The Counter Securities Fund, or John Neff of the Windsor Fund.

In the equity valuation process, dominant sponsors usually attract a popularity flow to a stock. Who are these dominant sponsors and what attracts them (chapter 8)? They tend to be securities analysts in a variety of forms. They command a following because of their track records of successful stock picking and research recommendations. Reported profitability and commission-generating potential inherent in companies with earnings momentum or changing fundamentals attracts them and their commitment of time. Perception also often originates with information spread by lead investors. Chapter 9 shows the behavior of dominant sponsors of the shares of the four companies mentioned above.

Management will know dominant sponsors by their commitment of time and their merchandising skill. The latter, observable on a company's transfer sheets, can be measured by analysts' ability to generate share volume in a company's shares and by annual gross commissions generated. Management will also know them by those with whom they do business, the number and tier of institutional accounts with which they do active commission business.

The identity of a dominant sponsor varies with a company's market capitalization (Chapter 9 discusses this more fully). For small capitalization companies, lead investors often also act as dominant sponsors. For medium to large capitalization companies, dominant sponsors will be securities analysts.

One should not confuse dominant sponsors of small capitalization, emerging companies with stock pushers. Dominant sponsors are professional securities analysts or broker/analysts at reputable securities firms whose credibility in spotting real growth or value attracts professional investors. Stock pushers, such as entrepreneurs or lesser quality underwriters, have vested interests in the companies they tout. They push story stocks, often called puff stocks, which carry high market capitalization-to-sales ratios, minimal sales and usually no profitability. They attract traders.

It was mentioned earlier that the breakdown of the industrial market presented here is for purposes of perspective only. There is no reason why managements of emerging companies should undertake widespread, national marketing campaigns to create investor demand. To the contrary, the share prices of emerging companies, and of any company for that matter, will be most affected at the margin by the ability of a few individuals to affect expectations market-wide.

In that sense, lead investors will probably find small capitalization companies, especially if they are neglected, before management finds them. In that case, recognizing a lead investor when one sees one is the challenge. Then, identifying dominant sponsors and shaping their perceptions requires a rifle approach using one-to-one relationships, not a shotgun approach using mass mailings.

Forming an equity valuation network around lead investors and dominant sponsors is the best equity valuation strategy. It is the shortest route to pricing efficiency and fair valuation and is in everyone's best interests (as mentioned in Chapter 1). It requires that executives be effective salespersons of their company's equity product. Good salespeople always ask for the order. Good managements always ask for the referral.

Management must do two things to lay the foundation for an equity valuation network. Executives must identify: who owns stocks in the company's industry and the location of those professional investors who buy stocks with the company's characteristics. It is at this point that managements often retain outside financial communications consultants. These consultants try to pinpoint lead investors in the industry's equities and dominant sponsors of those equities.

Management should examine ownership data for peer competitors contained in Form 13F filings. They should identify which investing institutions own the largest portfolio positions in peers' shares. They should make contact and schedule personal visits with each, only after each has received and studied the company's materials. Otherwise, they may waste portfolio managers' and their own time. And they should ask for referrals to others whom these lead investors believe should follow or own the company's shares.

Building a network also requires that management identify those information processors who attract popularity flows. They may be analysts at national institutional, national wirehouse and retail/institutional brokerage firms. But they may also be broker/analysts at major or small regional firms who have in the past attracted a flow to peer stocks in the company's industry or to stocks in the company's geographic region.

Ordinarily, management of an emerging public company should expect its underwriters' industry securities analysts to be the company's dominant sponsors. But that role may not be automatic unless management demands full sponsorship as part of its underwriting agreement as specified in Chapter 3. When executives realize research coverage is not automatic, they are bound to be disappointed, at least, and probably livid.

Brokerage economics (Chapter 8) dictates whether an underwriter assumes the role of dominant sponsor. As mentioned in Chapter 3, if a deal is hot or if the company's market capitalization is large enough to offer adequate commission potential, then sponsorship will likely be provided. But if a deal is less than hot or if market capitalization is small, an underwriter may pass on its opportunity, what management would call obligation, to act as a company's dominant sponsor. Brokerage economics aside, growth, profitability and an expanding equity capital base are the keys to expanding market sponsorship. Returns stability is the key to retaining market sponsorship.

In the event that executives find their company orphaned in the aftermarket, they should look to their board and to their shareholder list for sources of sponsorship from lead investors. In fact, I recommend that management consider electing a lead investor to its board, a professional money manager, not a so-called "trustee", in addition to or instead of its investment banker. The former will be much more attuned to how and why the company's equity is valued, to sponsorship issues and to the means by which management can affect the pricing of its shares. A banker plays a financial advisory role and tends to be passive in matters of valuation. But a money manager plays an investment advisory role and should be more knowledgeable, active and involved with management in the equity valuation process.

If orphaned, management's analysis of its shareholder list should focus on the institutional holders of the largest amount of the company's outstanding equity. Management should make contact with the portfolio manager(s) at these institutions to solicit their support in exerting pressure for aftermarket support on the company's underwriter (discussed in Chapter 9). And executives should ask these lead investors for help in organizing small gatherings with other investors whom they perceive to be valuable.

Even if a company's underwriter does assume the role of dominant sponsor, management should still strengthen and expand the company's valuation network. Executives should organize small meetings over breakfast or lunch with dominant sponsors and lead investors. Establishing one-to-one relationships and making face-to-face presentations is management's most effective means by which to shape and to spread perception of the company's future.

It is important that management organize its own meetings. Although some organizations are in the business of arranging luncheons for companies at cost, the measure of their success is the number of warm bodies they cram into a room, regardless of the importance of those bodies to the valuation of a company's securities.

An outside financial communications consultant can actually identify appropriate invitees (owners of industry stocks) and arrange the details of small gatherings. But management, not the outsider, should extend the invitations directly to those invited. I recommend this procedure because too many free lunches at shareholders' expense are served on Wall Street. By handling the invitations directly, on company letterhead, executives can qualify each participant on the basis of: existing share ownership in the industry, profiles of those who invest in companies with similar investment characteristics and coverage of companies in the industry for dominant sponsors. Consequently, they can classify their audience in terms of perceived influence in the equity valuation process. Finally, they should always ask a lead investor to bring a dominant sponsor and vice versa.

In the aftermath of these meetings, management should personally follow-up with each luncheon guest. Executives should answer any further questions, solicit constructive comments about presentation and content, ascertain his or her perception or the company, determine his or her inclination to buy the company's shares, and ask for referrals to others with perceived buying power who may not have been able to attend the meeting. These gatherings can produce meaningful results (as NEECO, Inc. found in Chapter 3).

How often should management pay attention to the structure of the company's valuation network? Thinking as owners, executives should certainly apprise existing dominant sponsors and lead investors of the company's operating results at the end of every fiscal quarter and year. Recall that predictable earnings and stable returns lengthen investors' time horizons and holding periods.

At the same time, management should also initiate contact with new sponsors and investors in their shares as well as those in the shares of peer competitors. And, at any time that management judges the company's shares to be mispriced, assessment of the structure of a valuation network is important. It is usually the time for management's initiation of a perception study.

Executives should always ask those who make new inquiries of the company, be they potential lead investors or dominant sponsors, how they learned of the company. This is discussed more in Chapters 7 and 8. Their answers help management to understand the basis on which perception of the company is spreading, who is spreading it and where the company stands in the demand-creating cycle. And, short of retaining a proxy solicitation firm, matching the names of new inquirors with nominee names on the company's transfer sheets may aid in identifying beneficial owners.

Networking with peer industry executives to identify dominant sponsors and lead investors in thrift equities worked well for the managements of New England's converted thrift institutions. In October 1986, executives at One Bancorp (Portland, ME) hosted a one-day, closed door session for peer executives at New England thrifts on communicating value to Wall Street. Officers from about 45 institutions participated.

The meeting presented the foundation and core of a thrift equity valuation network. Two buy-side institutional securities analysts from Evergreen Fund and Fidelity Select Portfolio S & L Fund sat on a panel. Each institution held thrift shares in their portfolios. Two sell-side brokerage firm securities analysts from Keefe Bruyette & Woods and Merrill Lynch, and two big producing stockbrokers from Moseley Capital Markets and E.F. Hutton also sat on the panels.

The author did not attend the meeting but expanded the valuation network by asking for referrals from some of the meeting's participants to others perceived to be influential in the thrift equity valuation process. Referrals led the author to institutional analysts at lead investing institutions in various tiers such as Wellington Management, Massachusetts Financial Services, Gray Siefert Co., Manhattan Fund, and Essex Management. They also led to securities analysts at dominant sponsoring brokerage firms in various brackets such as Moseley Securities, Coburn & Meredith (Hartford, CT) and Shearson Lehman Brothers. An examination of ownership data in SEC 13(f) filings revealed a larger built-in network of past and present institutional owners of thrift equities.

Finally, further research made clear that thrifts were divided into three market value categories. Dominant sponsors essentially neglected thrifts with market values less than $40 million. For example, of 78 thrifts covered, Shearson Lehman followed only five with market capitalizations less than $50 million. Dominant sponsors followed thrifts valued between $40 and $100 million and provided research coverage of those over $100 million.

Management is the real catalyst in the equity valuation process. Executives must manage Wall Street's channels to communicate value. They must use its networks to translate economic value into market value. Networks only come to life if management activates them. They only stay alive if management periodically talks to the company's stock. Management must make certain that lead investors and dominant sponsors play their roles in the demand-creating process.

Management can also alter, broaden or deepen its shareholder base by actively using its valuation network. For executives of large capitalization companies operating in a reasonably efficient market, this may mean that the effort may affect share volume but not share price. The end result may be the same equity pie divided into different pieces. The market value of the pie itself may be no larger or smaller.

For example, Lockheed Corporation (Burbank, CA) solved a shareholder concentration problem through use of its dominant sponsors. The company had about 65 million shares outstanding and a market capitalization of about $3.5 to $4 billion. Management discovered that 92 percent of its stock was held by 55 institutions. A shareholder shift from 10 percent to more than 90 percent institutional ownership had occurred in a period of about one and one-half years. Executives were concerned about the perceived volatility in the company's shares. They carried a beta coefficient of about 1.85.

Management developed a sponsorship strategy to broaden the company's share ownership to small institutions and individuals and to quiet its stock. For small institutions, executives held regional meetings which were sponsored by brokerage firms whose analysts were recommending purchase of the company's shares. Management also put its stock into European portfolios. For individuals, executives used a mailing list targeted only to brokers at national wirehouse firms which followed the company on a research basis.

The shareholder shift results were dramatic. In two years, institutional ownership among more than 300 banks, insurance companies and endowment funds fell to 72 percent from 92 percent. European ownership rose to 10 percent and share ownership among individual investors comprised the balance. A broader base of ownership apparently quieted the stock as its beta coefficient fell to 1.19.

ADVERTISING AND PUBLIC RELATIONS

Also on the strategy spectrum, advertising and public relations are not adequate substitutes for strong relationships with dominant sponsors and lead investors. The reason is that marketing equities differs greatly from marketing products/services. And investor demand for a company's shares differs greatly from consumer demand for a company's products or services.

Creating investor demand focuses primarily on increasing the price of an equity product independent of sales volume. In contrast, creating consumer demand focuses on increasing sales volume for a product through differentiation or price. Chapter 6 makes clear that shifts in share volume may or may not lead to share price changes with investors. Volume is not a proxy of investors' consensus about a company because risk preferences vary among investors. But managements usually expect shifts in product prices to lead to product volume changes with consumers.

Other differences are in the "tools" used to create demand. Products are bought, not sold, and marketing is based on current information. But equities are sold, not bought, and marketing is based on predictive information. Advertising and public relations support a product's current identity. They foster brand awareness and customer preference. They heighten product visibility and induce product purchases. But one-to-one relationships and valuation networks clarify perception of a company's future growth and profitability. They facilitate investment decisions.

Advertising and public relations highlight "present" features or past results. Print media campaigns such as those of Figgie International, Westinghouse and PPG Industries may creatively present past performance. But investors who set share prices look to future economic benefits. Shaping their perception must focus on the future, not the present or the past.

Executives constantly hope that positive reinforcement and added awareness of a company's products will translate into higher stock price because they translate into higher sales. They hope that exposure in print or broadcast media will be swiftly reflected in the company's market value.

Independent of a company's competitive position and operating spread, that result is wishful thinking. Companies can show reams of press clippings and video tapes marking successful use of advertising and public relations. But the campaigns may create volume demand and sales gains for a company's products while, at the same time, share price falls.

Such was the case with Kurzweil Music Systems, Inc. (Waltham, MA), maker of computer-based music synthesizers. The company's products received national media exposure as music stars such as Stevie Wonder used its products on nationally televised entertainment specials. And the company's prolific founder was the subject of innumerable print articles in major national periodicals about his unquestionably brilliant abilities in the areas of voice recogniton and artificial intelligence.

However, publicity was utterly immaterial to the company's stock price. The company offered 1.3 million shares on December 17, 1985 at $7.25 per share. Its one-day initial capital loss was 6.9 percent (closing bid price of $6.75 per share) and its one-month initial capital loss was 24.1 percent at a closing bid price of $5.50 per share at the end of December 1985. Its shares were the worst performing of all New England stocks in 1986. They closed for the year at $1.94 per share, a one-year initial capital loss of 64.73 percent.

The activity of Coleco Industries (Hartford, CT) is another dramatic example. Advertising and public relations had an impressive impact on sales of its high-margin "Cabbage Patch Kids" dolls. But the impact of those sales on the company's value-creating ability varied directly with the company's operating spread. There is no question that sales of the dolls reversed what would have been a financial disaster for the company in the wake of its failed attempt to enter the personal computer market with its "Adam" computer. But the reversal was only temporary because the company's competitive advantage with the dolls was quite short.

The example of Coleco shows clearly that sales growth creates economic value only when operating margins exceed the cost of capital. And sales growth clearly destroys value when operating margins fall short of the cost of capital. To demonstrate this, I have tried to estimate Coleco's cost of capital and operating spread for a five-year period starting in 1982, coincident with the company's introduction of its Cabbage Patch Kids dolls.

To derive these estimates, I relied on the April 24, 1987 edition of the *Value Line Investment Survey* for information concerning the company's operating margins, incremental fixed plus working capital expenditures, sales growth rate and income tax rate. For purposes of simplicity, I assumed all rates remained constant over the forecast period. By definition, these calculations are only estimates. Their accuracy is less important than their relevance to the issue of value creation.

First, Value Line estimated a beta coefficient of 1.15 on Coleco's stock as of January 29, 1982. Next, I used David Mullins's 1982 estimate of 20.35 percent for the cost of equity capital for a company with a beta coefficient of 1.15 (see footnote 10 in Chapter 2). This figure still seems low relative to the characteristics of other stocks with the same beta. For example, Mullins estimated a beta of 1.15 on companies in the drug industry and 1.50 on nondurables and entertainment companies. By 1987, Standard & Poor's accorded Coleco a beta of 1.67 and Value Line estimated beta at 1.30.

Next, Coleco's long-term debt as a percent of total capital averaged 40.45 percent between 1976 and 1981, according to S & P *Stock Reports*. The company's weighted cost of equity is determined by multiplying the equity proportion of its capital structure times expected returns of 20.35. In other words weighted cost equals 0.5955 times 0.2035, or 0.122.

In October 1982, Moody's Investor Services gave a B2 rating to Coleco's 14.375 percent subordinated debentures due 2002. Priced to yield 15.56 percent, I use this rate to calculate Coleco's after-tax cost of debt. The company's tax rate averaged 45.28 percent between 1979 and 82. Its after-tax cost of debt would have been 0.1556 times 0.5472, or 0.08514 percent. To arrive at a weighted cost of debt, the proportion of debt in the company's capital structure, that figure times 0.4045 equaled 0.03444. When added to 0.122 above, Coleco's 1982 weighted average cost of capital would have equalled 0.15644, or 15.6 percent.

Value Line's figures showed that the company's five-year annual sales growth rate, beginning in 1982, was 34 percent. Its five-year average annual rate of incremental fixed (capital spending per share) and working capital investment was calculated as the ratio of incremental fixed and working capital per dollar of sales. Between 1982 and 1986, it was 23.01 percent.

Using Professor Rappaport's formula (Footnote 3 in Chapter 2), Coleco's incremental threshold (break-even) margin on incremental sales in 1982 would have been: (0.23) times (0.156) divided by (1 plus 0.156) times (1 minus 0.4528). This translates to 0.0359 divided by 0.6326, or 0.0567. In other words, the incremental threshold margin on Coleco's incremental sales would have been 5.67 percent. Threshold (break-even) margin on total sales would have been: (1981 operating profit of $20.83 million) plus (5.67 percent) times (1982 incremental sales of $332.4 million) divided by (1981 sales of $178 million) plus (1982 incremental sales of $332.4 million). This translates to ($20.83 plus $18.85) divided by ($510.4), or 39.68 divided by 510.4, or 0.0777. The company's threshold margin on total sales was 7.77 percent. Threshold margins rise (fall) as cost of capital and/or investment to sales ratios rise (fall).

In 1982, Coleco's sales grew 186.7 percent. Incremental fixed and working capital per dollar of 1982 sales rose to 28.7 percent (82.3 percent per dollar of 1981 sales) versus 5.83 percent in 1981. Capital spending was $1.10 per share versus $.41 per share in 1981 and working capital increased to $129.6 million from $41.1 million in 1981. The company's operating margin was 19.8 percent versus an estimated threshold margin on total sales of 7.77 percent. The resulting contribution of Coleco's positive 12.03 percent threshold spread to shareholder value and shareholders' realized returns was dramatic. The company's stock price traded from a 1982 low of $3.50 per share to a 1983 high of $65 per share and management declared a 100 percent stock dividend.

It was at this point, however, that a combination of rising start-up expenses, sagging consumer demand, and production problems hit Coleco's line of "Adam" home computers. For example, the company produced only about one-fifth of its originally projected unit volume. The company's good fortunes began to reverse. Incremental fixed and working capital investment as a percent of 1983 sales was 23.8 percent (79.7 percent per dollar of 1981 sales) versus 28.7 percent in 1982. Capital spending per share rose to $2.13 in 1983 from $1.10 in 1982, and working capital increased another $107.8 million above $129.6 million in 1982.

As a result, the company's 1983 cash flow was effectively eliminated and operating margins were squeezed to 0.004 percent on a sales increase of 16.9 percent. Sales rose to $596.5 million from $510.4 million, $60 million of which was estimated to be sales of Cabbage Patch Kids dolls. With a negative threshold spread of -0.737 percent management destroyed significant shareholder value. The company's stock traded to a 1983 split-adjusted low of $16 per share and investors sold short 38 percent of the company's non-insider stock.

In January 1984, Value Line had estimated that doll sales could contribute more than $100 million to sales in 1984 and between $.50 to $.75 per share to earnings. Working backwards using 16.15 million shares outstanding in 1984 and a tax rate of 43 percent, that estimate suggested an expected operating margin between 18.8 percent and 28.2 percent on incremental doll sales versus an estimated threshold margin on incremental sales of 5.92 percent. Sales of Cabbage Patch Kids dolls soared in 1984 to about $540 million, about 69.7 percent of the company's total sales of $774.9. Incremental fixed and working capital expenses per dollar of 1984 sales was 12.3 percent and all of the company's operating profit came from doll sales. Operating margins were 10.5 percent, a positive 2.73 percent threshold spread.

Despite the Cabbage Patch Kids dolls contribution to Coleco's operations, 1984 results were dismal. Management shut "Adam" down in the last quarter of 1984 and took a $118.6 million pretax writeoff for the year. The company's net worth dropped to $10.5 million from close to $90 million, book value per share fell to $.65 per share from $5.58 per share, and debt rose to 93 percent of total capital. Coleco reported a loss of $4.95 per share in 1984, $2.40 per share from continuing operations. The company's stock fell steadily from a 1984 high of $22.375 to a low of $9.75 per share and closed at $12.125 per share.

In 1985, sales of the dolls rose to about $600 million. Incremental fixed and working capital expenses per dollar of 1985 sales was 26 percent, operating margins rose to 16.8 percent, a positive 9.03 percent threshold spread, and the company reported all time-high earnings of $3.87 per share. Coleco's stock traded in a range from $10.125 per share to $21.50 per share in 1985. It closed at $16 per share, up $3.875 per share over 1984, a 32 percent increase.

Ultimately, the company's only competitive advantage with the Cabbage Patch Kids dolls was lead time. Unfortunately for Coleco, the duration of that advantage was quite short-lived. Imitation dolls flooded the market such that 1986 sales of the dolls decreased 62 percent. Estimates were that doll sales would stabilize in the range of $200 million range. Management cut doll prices and gave rebates and increased both advertising expense and spending on new product development.

As a result, 1986 operating margins were wiped out. The company's negative threshold spread was -0.777 percent. Coleco reported a negative cash flow of $1.75 per share and a loss of $6.52 per share. The stock traded from a 1986 high of $20.50 per share to a low of $8.375 per share. It closed for the year at its low, for a 47.7 percent loss in market value from the close of 1985.

It is intuitively appealing to think that clear corporate identity and increasing product awareness in the market will have a positive effect on investor demand and share price just because they have a positive impact on consumer demand and sales. But the Coleco example shows clearly that they do not necessarily have similar effects. Identity and awareness address only sales growth rates and market share. They have no bearing on the size and duration of operating margins or operating spreads.

In and of themselves, advertising and public relations only have a direct effect on share price when they unknowingly disclose material information previously lacked by investors which alter their returns expectations. More likely, they contribute to share price indirectly only when operating margins on incremental or total sales exceed the cost of capital.

Professor Arbel draws an equation between investor goods and consumer goods. He likens companies which are underresearched and underowned (neglected) to generic products. He equates those which are broadly followed and widely held (i.e., 60 to 70 percent of a company's equity) to brand products. IBM, GE, AT&T, GM and Exxon are examples. He contends that just as in consumer markets, brand names sell at a premium to generic products. They offer greater certainty of product quality and standards and higher expectations of customer satisfaction. With brand name equities this means that some investors are willing to pay more for less earnings estimation risk and are consequently willing to accept lower expected returns. Generic products, on the other hand, sell at discounts because of greater customer uncertainty about product uniformity, performance and consistency. With generic equities, this means that some investors are willing to pay less for more earnings estimation risk and expect to register higher expected returns as a consequence.

As Chapter 6 makes clear, the greatest impact of financial advertising and financial public relations campaigns for neglected companies of all market capitalizations occurs at calendar year-ends. Information efficiency is highest and estimation risk is lowest. At that time, most corporate financial communications campaigns center around annual report advertising. It tends to focus on growth in one or more areas: revenues, earnings, dividends or total return. Strangely though, many of these advertisements ignore the one matter of most importance to shareholders either because they know no better or because they fail to compare well with peers or the market. For example, in the February 1986 annual report section of *Barron's*, only seven of about 100 advertisers boasted their total return to shareholders. Yet this is the most important corporate result to be communicated.

TACTICS

Managements of companies use a variety of tactics to execute their marketing strategy. They rely on mailing lists, management presentations at luncheons or at forums, analyst visits to company headquarters, analyst field trips, teleconferencing of analysts meetings and use of telex machines to speed data to analysts. Other companies pay for booths at investor fairs, produce corporate fact sheets and fact books, offer coupons or videotape their annual meetings and annual reports (Georgia Pacific Corporation). Some use gimmicks to attract attention.

American Family Corporation (Columbus, GA) ran a Japan Branch Tour contest for stockbrokers. Each entrant had to guess the company's earnings and revenues for the fourth quarter of 1984 and the first quarter of 1985. The winner received an all-expenses-paid round trip for two to Japan and Hong Kong in conjunction with the company's biannual financial analysts briefing tour. Management openly stated its hope that those who made estimates would conclude that the company represented a growth situation and that they would continue to follow the company after the contest was over. Another contest was available for stockholders who were not stockbrokers.

For any company, profitability is the key to sponsorship because it is the key to value. For emerging, small capitalization companies, the best tactics are solid one-to-one relationships with dominant sponsors and lead investors. They counter neglect and information deficiency. As supplements, management might also produce the equivalent of a quarterly in-house research report. It might focus on business strategy or competitive advantage in the company's product/markets and on management. A different executive per quarter might discuss competitive advantages and changing fundamentals in his or her operating division. The effect is to paint a picture of management know-how and management depth. It puts a brand identity on the company and does the work of securities analysts.

Managements of companies in small capitalization industries might also band together, a la the London Connection in Chapter 3, to attract sponsorship. Or those in poorly followed industry categories might join with peer competitors to better define their industry and their earnings prospects.

MEASUREMENTS

Execution of cash flow communications strategy yields both qualitative and quantitative performance measurements. The former is measured in terms of activities which reflect the extent of market sponsorship. The latter is measured in terms of share price.

In general, success of efforts to build market sponsorship is measured primarily by increases in information efficiency and increases in liquidity. The first takes the form of lower estimation risk due to greater consensus about future performance. Statistical success is research coverage-oriented: more securities analysts following the company, more written research reports, more research recommendations, greater page volume of research reports, more analyst requests for corporate material, larger numbers of management presentations, more inquiries about the company and greater institutional ownership in terms of number of shares held and percent ownership of equity.

The latter takes the form of lower trading costs, narrower bid-ask spreads as a percent of share price, and larger share volume per unit of price. Statistical success is market-making oriented: more market-makers making markets in a company's shares, larger share volume per percent stock price move, larger dollar value per percent move and greater average daily trading volume. Investors' success in this category is measured by buyers' and sellers' ability to execute investment decisions without paying more or receiving less than the fair economic value of a company's securities. It is also determined by their ability to transact without being concerned about the effect of the spread in a quote on the profit potential of their investment, and without stirring rumors about the reason for the purchase or sale.

Another measure of success is the extent of investor interest in the company in the form of percentage of shareholder votes represented at annual meetings, and investor support for management in the form of proxy votes in favor of management proposals.

Finally gains in pricing efficiency are quantitatively-oriented. They are completely geared to stock price. They are measured by the extent to which actual returns approximate expected returns and stock price fairly reflects investors' returns expectations. Some argue that share price is an unfair performance measurement of any program to communicate value to Wall Street because price may be affected by too many factors beyond management's control. In an absolute sense, it is true that share price is an unfair yardstick. But share price is never considered in the absolute. Therefore, in a relative sense, share price is really the only valid measure of pricing efficiency and fair valuation of a company's equity securities.

A measure of quantitative success is the spread between market value and estimated worth of equity. It is the extent to which a company's market value and multiple fairly reflect its intrinsic or asset value, its fundamentals, the risk/expected returns profile of its capital strategy relative to alternative investments of comparable reinvestment opportunities, and the price/performance specifications of its business strategy relative to alternative investments of comparable operating fundamentals.

Managements' ability to identify market misperceptions or consensus forecast errors which contribute to market mispricings is a first step to realizing economic value. Their ability to correct or to capitalize on those mispricings is the second step. Ultimately, their translation of economic value into market value, real wealth for shareholders, is management's best success.

5

Wanted: Cash Flow Communicator

"Do you feel that the current price of your company's stock is an accurate indicator of the real value of your company? If not, does the stock price undervalue the company or overvalue it?"[1] That question was asked of senior financial managers of more than 600 companies in a *Business Week*/Louis Harris & Associates Poll in February 1984. The poll was conducted five months before the market reached a two-year intermediate bottom in an otherwise protracted bull market which had begun in August 1982.

The response was uniformly dramatic. About 60 percent of the executives believed the market undervalued their company's securities. More than one third of the 60 percent thought "serious" undervaluation was more the case. Only 32 percent of the managers were satisfied that the market valued their company's securities fairly. Six percent were not sure, and about 2 percent thought their company's stock price was higher than it should be.

Clearly, the majority of executives believed that investors failed to accurately perceive their company's true future earning power and therefore incorrectly harbored lower returns expectations than management. It clearly frustrated many corporate executives.

But why should such differences in returns expectations exist or persist? Why should there appear to management to be such a gap in perception of their company's returns potential? It is usually the result of disagreement between management and information intermediaries about future corporate growth, profitability and risk. It arises for any of several reasons:

1. Differences in estimating beta to set discount rates for present value calculations.

2. Differences of opinion about optimal capital structure with which to achieve lowest average costs of capital within acceptable limits of financial risk. Investors may prefer

more leverage because they can diversify away that risk. Executives may prefer less leverage because their wealth is concentrated.

3. Differences in perspective on the strength and duration of competitive advantages over competition and product substitutes or the wisdom of business strategy to exploit those advantages.

4. Differences in perception of sales growth rate potential of seemingly disparate business units.

5. Differences in assessment of incremental fixed and working capital investment requirements of business strategies.

6. Differences in the amount and quality of information concerning cash-generating ability: prices, costs, market growth and market share.

These differences lead to disagreements about capital spreads, operating margins and operating spreads. They may subsequently lead to gaps in perception of value creating potential and future earning power. Those may translate to increases in estimation risk and wide variations from consensus estimates of corporate earnings. This reduces share prices and raises investors' expected returns.

This dispersion is a proxy of analysts' confidence (risk) in predicting a company's earning ability and returns stability. Recall from Chapter 2 that the greater the perception of potential variance in operating cash flows and net income, the greater analysts' perception of security-specific risk relative to alternatives of equal expected returns, and the greater the impact of that risk on share price. The potential for dispersion is understandable, though the valuation consequences for management may be hard to accept.

Analysts usually consider the assumptions that underlie their earnings estimates to be reasonable until the unexpected content of reported earnings leads them to conclude otherwise. Changes in operating margins usually lead to variations in reported earnings. This leads to revisions in analysts' earnings forecasts. It is this change in consensus expectations, not the change in earnings, that moves share prices. Chapter 8 discusses more fully the frequency and the impact of forecast revisions on security-specific returns.

Many financial managers are skeptical of analysts' ability to properly value their company's securities. They believe, regardless of analysts' opinions, that no one knows better about a company's future cash-generating ability and returns potential than a company's senior management. Differences of opinion on these matters between managers and analysts which reduce the valuation of a company's equity aggravate them.

Given executives' often questioning attitude about the market's valuation process, management should attempt to mollify its skepticism. But the burden of proof that their company's equity securities are mispriced is on them. They should assume the market's pricing of the company's shares is fair unless they can identify precise reasons for misperception and mispricing. Adequate explanations may be the possession of material non-public information, analysts' faulty assumptions about the future, or some break-down in the analytical function. And they should learn why the stock trades at its price and what that price implies about investors' returns expectations, rather than trying to determine why its stock does not trade at a price management may think is more appropriate.

Managements are not the only interested parties which may be skeptical of the equity valuation process. Shareholders may also question investors' perceptions and the market's valuation of their shares. In the case of Alamito Company (Tucson, AZ), an electricity wholesaler, shareholders filed suit against management for interfering with and breaking down the market's valuation process.

The company was a spin-off from Tucson Electric Power Company. It began trading in January 1985 on the American Stock Exchange at $65.50 per share. Senior executives initiated a leveraged buyout in November 1985 at $110 per share as the company's shares were trading publicly in the low $90 per share range. The company's investment banker advised management that the buyout bid was too low. Considering the perceived future earnings potential of energy wholesalers in general, the bid was deemed unfair to shareholders. Management raised its bid to $123 per share. It was accepted on November 15, 1985.

At that point, however, shareholders interceded. They believed, even at $123 per share, that investors still undervalued the future economic value of their Alamito holdings. They contended that investors misperceived the company's potential future growth and profitability and, as a result, mispriced the company's securities. A group of stockholders filed suit against the company's senior executives.

The suit alleged management's tampering with investor perception and with the equity valuation process. It charged that management had artificially depressed the company's share price by refusing to talk with Wall Street securities analysts and by intentionally releasing negative news at important times. In other words, the suit charged that management purposefully and knowingly contributed to market inefficiency in the pricing of the company's shares. The shareholder suit was settled on February 28, 1986. A total of 13 offers for the company were subsequently made. A bid of $165 per share was accepted on April 4, 1986.

A paradox often arises in the valuation process. Management questions the validity of the process but does nothing to affect it. It is paradoxical because executives devote expensive executive talent, significant intellectual effort and elaborate corporate resources to the resolution of two overriding issues: how to invest and how to compete to create maximum economic value. The process is intense, authority is delegated carefully, progress is reviewed frequently and corporate life hinges on the results. With a lot at stake, success determines the level of executive compensation and the extent of career advancement.

But managements often stop before they translate the economic value they create into market value investors realize. They impose total influence upon the internal corporate planning and capital budgeting process but ignore their ability and responsibility to influence the external equity valuation process. In effect, they neutralize the benefits of their own value creating strategy.

Financial managers offer numerous reasons for watching, but not affecting, the valuation process. Some associate communicating value to "hype," "tout" and "promotion." They think their credibility will suffer when, in fact, the reverse is true. Some consider it a matter of ethics. They associate attempts to influence the market's pricing mechanism with "market manipulation" instead of market efficiency when, in fact, the reverse is true. Other managers relate their reluctance to influence the market to their "priorities." They believe actively shaping perception is less important than actively managing assets.

Other executives fear the leak to competitors of sensitive information concerning cost structures, pricing strategies, profit margins and capital spending. Others fear personal embarrassment. They are afraid that their perception of the company's future may be imprecise or premature such that operating shortfalls may make them look foolish.

In reality, future-oriented strategy is based on assumptions, not conclusions, about the future. It requires calculated efforts to anticipate investment opportunities and risks. By definition, it is inexact. But enabling investors to understand and to appreciate the magnitude and the risk of a company's growth opportunities makes executives look smart.

A 1981 survey of corporate executives and securities analysts conducted for The Conference Board revealed several additional reasons why managements were shy about affecting the valuation process with public earnings forecasts. Some lacked confidence in their personal predictive powers. They feared legal complications associated with forecast inaccuracy. They also believed that forecast errors would contribute to the volatility of their stock and lower their company's price/earnings ratio. Some managements thought that cooperation with analysts might lead to higher visibility of the company on Wall Street and others were concerned that their refusal to cooperate with analysts might lead to negative opinions about the company.

Uncertainty and lack of control over the equity valuation process frustrates many executives. They do not trust analysts and investors to correctly value their company. They think the process is too irrational and too emotional. They consider the market too skittish, too jumpy and too much influenced by what they perceive as ancillary factors rather than by strict operating fundamentals. The irony is that without management's direct input, efficient pricing and fair valuation of a company's equity undoubtedly does rely on ancillary factors.

Some financial managers believe securities analysts waste management's time. Executives know they have to educate analysts about firm-unique fundamentals. But, even then, they think analysts may still not focus on those variables which management thinks are essential to proper understanding and valuation of the company.

Some executives adopt an attitude of "let analysts hang" by their estimates of future earnings. They adhere to this regardless of whether those estimates are wide of the consensus and add to investors' perception of the company's earnings variance. Fred Hartley, chairman of Unocal (San Francisco, CA) goes so far as to claim that securities analysts are just MBAs who know nothing about the oil business in which his company competes.

Financial managers often believe catering to Wall Street takes too much time away from managing their business. They wonder how much they have to do to satisfy Wall Street's seemingly insatiable appetite for company-specific data. Executives speak at analyst meetings and make luncheon presentations to stockbrokers. They meet with visiting portfolio managers. If this is the valuation process, they think it is very repetitive and quite cosmetic. Consequently, they rely on their corporate communications, public relations or public affairs department to protect them from Wall Street. They use others to intercede, to run interference for the chief executive officer and screen those who want the chief financial officer's time.

Ultimately, many executives conclude that, short of making forecasts and assuming that all analysts receive the same information, the only company-specific data which makes any real difference at the margin, are operating results. Management believes that is how the market valuation process should work—manage for results and watch the effect on stock price and market value.

This relatively passive management attitude suggests that executives believe that the market is reasonably efficient. It infers that they believe they do not have to exert much, if any, effort to make certain that investors agree upon the importance of available information on estimates of risk and expected returns. Yet about 60 percent of executives surveyed by *Business Week* believed that the market's pricing of their company's shares was inefficient and unfair. Communicating value demands more than communicating operating results.

Cash flow communications offers managements of both small and large capitalization companies an opportunity to affect the market's pricing mechanism, to build market sponsorship, pricing efficiency and market value. Those executives who seize the opportunity usually work extensively with securities analysts and money managers. They send signals to both about future operating cash flows. And they use analysts as indirect channels through which affect investors' returns expectations.

Even the management of General Motors believed a valuation differential separated active efforts to communicate value from passive distribution of operating data. In 1985, management of the company enhanced its cash flow communications efforts. "General Motors may start sharing more financial data with

Wall Street analysts, a move that may give a boost to GM's stock," reported the *Wall Street Journal* on December 27, 1985. "One GM financial executive acknowledges privately that he thinks the auto maker hasn't adequately fulfilled Wall Street's need for information."[2]

GM traditionally has offered to analysts little data and little accessibility to its senior executives. This contrasts sharply with other auto companies' communications policies. "In contrast to GM," wrote the *Journal*, "Ford Motor and Chrysler, as well as most other blue-chip industrials, provide elaborate explanations for most questions, analysts say, as well as personal interviews with executives and guided tours of plants."[3] Competitors clearly believed that shaping investors' perceptions positively affected their companies' relative valuation.

Analysts believed GM heightened its company-related risk and lowered its stock price by letting investors shape their own perception. "Analysts say the difference [in communications efforts] shows up in GM's stock price," and that "lacking such clues [to GM's accounting practices or investment objectives] forces them [analysts] to be more cautious about recommending GM common shares."[4] Consequently, the *Journal* reported in December 1985, that GM's stock was trading at a 15 percent discount to its 52-week high while Ford and Chrysler were trading at only 6 percent discounts.

Some analysts argued that GM's paucity of available data meant the company was more intent on managing for long-term results rather than for short-term gains. A minority thought there was plenty of public information available, although not from the company. But analysts' consensus was that the lack of available information made their efforts to fairly value the company more difficult.

"If lines (of communication) aren't installed, we may not take a chance and its value won't be fully reflected,"[5] complained one analyst. *The New York Times* seemed to support this contention. Its December 31, 1985, "Market Place" column was titled, "G.M. May Lag Behind Its Rivals." In March 1987, GM's management sent a signal to Wall Street. It initiated a $5 billion corporate share repurchase plan, the largest in corporate history, as an attempt to express confidence in the company's future cash-generating ability. It was also an effort to show concern for its shareholders.

Gulf and Western Incorporated (New York, NY) is another example of a company which restructured. At the same time, management actively reshaped investors' perceptions of its impact on the company's future cash-generating ability. Charles G. Bluhdorn founded the company in 1958. At the time of his death in February 1983, the company's stock traded at $18 per share and carried a price/earnings multiple of 3.

Martin Davis replaced Bluhdorn. Since that time, the company's shares have traded above $58 per share. As of this writing, they sell at a multiple of 16. Davis consolidated the company, improved its competitive position and enhanced its future earning power. And he increased efforts to communicate value. He actively established relationships with those investors whom he believed could affect the company's share price. Bluhdorn had been unwilling to do that.

Both General Motors and Gulf & Western would certainly be considered to exist in semi-strong form efficient information environments. Each is a multi-billion dollar corporation both in sales and market value and each benefits from broad research coverage from securities analysts. But it is interesting to note that the management of each company believed that the pricing of its company's securities was inefficient. Each took action to shape investors' perceptions of their company's future. Managements of emerging companies, which compete in relatively weak form efficient information environments, must do the same.

CHALLENGING THE VALUATION PROCESS

There are "three requirements for successful second-guessing of the market. First, management [or shareholders] must avoid the trap of equating a low P-E multiple (on a historical basis) with evidence of undervaluation. [Moderating returns on equity and elevating payout ratios may point to worsening fundamentals]. Second, the company must monitor the leading analysts' perceptions for significant variations from its own forecasts [accounting book returns on equity adjusted to economic returns on equity]. Third, the company must be able to translate these forecasts into estimates of real economic value."[6]

Ideally, executives should want their companies' shares to trade in a narrow range around intrinsic or asset value over time. Management should examine each business unit as if it were a separate stand-alone publicly-held company. Executives should relate each unit to other companies "as comparable as possible in fundamental valuation terms—profitability, reinvestment opportunities (growth), nondiversifiable operating characteristics and financial risk."[7] Recall that Chapter 4 put capital and business strategy into the visual context of a security market line and a (price/book)-to-(return on equity) valuation model.

Comparisons reveal the relationship between the economic value creating potential of a company's business units relative to one another, to outside peer competitors and to the parent. They shed light on how the market values equities with similar investment and operating fundamentals in a unit's industry. And they offer a clue to a unit's potential market value on a stand-alone basis.

Management should examine business units in terms of both capital strategy and business strategy. In the first case, executives should estimate each unit's cost of equity capital. They should examine the beta coefficients of publicly-traded issues with percentage concentrations in lines of business as similar as possible to the company to determine investors' minimum required returns per business unit (see Fuller/Kerr, Van Horne and Harrington in the bibliography). They should also calculate each unit's weighted average cost of equity and after-tax debt capital.

After estimating unit returns on equity, the expected duration of those returns (i.e., capital spread and expected duration of that spread) and unit reinvestment rates, management can plug its figures into Professor Fruhan's economic value/book value formula presented in Footnote 2 in Chapter 2. This will enable them to determine theoretically appropriate price/book ratios for each unit.

Professor Rappaport has also developed an "Index of Value Creation"[8] for use in comparing business units. A rough approximation of the average units of value a business unit creates over a forecast period can be charted on a graph. It is bounded by [(long-term average sales growth rate) times (long-term average operating spread)] on the Y-axis and (duration of the positive spread) on the X-axis.

In trying to satisfy this goal of establishing business unit capital spreads and performance standards, one study[9] calculated unit return on invested capital as a unit's net after-tax operating profit divided by its assets. In contrast, Rappaport calls "value ROI" the [(economic value created by a strategy) divided by (the present value of investment in the strategy)]. The study then attempted to estimate business units' return on equity and their dollar contribution to parent company composite value and price per share by using units' ROI and debt ratio projections. The study indicated that pro forma income statements for each unit could be devised. It also suggested that each unit's return on invested capital could be converted into estimates of its return on equity. It expressed return on equity in terms of return on invested capital plus the contribution of financial (debt) leverage to return on equity.

In this calculation, unit return on equity equalled (unit return on invested capital) plus [(unit return on invested capital minus unit after-tax cost of debt) times (the unit's proportion of debt to total capital structure)]. At this point, the study estimated unit economic value/book value ratios. It calculated unit economic income as (unit free cash flow discounted to present value by unit cost of equity) and divided it by (initial book value of unit equity). Unit value created (i.e., economic income) divided by a parent company's outstanding shares yielded an estimate of unit contribution to parent company economic value on a per share basis.

This sort of internal valuation exercise enables both senior corporate executives and divisional operating managers to develop acute awareness of the relationship between unit capital strategy and and unit value creation, between unit business strategy and unit operating profitability, between unit operating spreads and company stock price and between unit value creation and manager compensation. It leads directly to questions about whether to invest further to build market share, to harvest cash, to limit asset growth or to divest. It also leads directly to decisions about cash flow allocation to unit capital strategies and business strategies relative to their value creating potential and competitive advantage.

At this time, management should also initiate an external perception study of the company. It should clarify investors' perceptions of the returns potential of both the parent and its operating units. It should also highlight the extent to which investors perceive each unit's risk and competitive advantage and the contribution of each unit to parent share price. Results should pinpoint any sources of misperception which may contribute to mispricing of the parent's securities.

The management of General Mills, Inc. (Minneapolis, MN) began to examine corporate performance on a unit by unit basis in the early 1980s. It learned that the cyclicality of its toy and apparel units depressed the valuation of its stable growth food business. As a result, executives started to restructure the company in 1985. They sold 26 businesses with sales of about $1.2 billion and initiated a spin-off of its Kenner Parker Toys and Crystal Brands fashion units. Kenner Parker was subsequently the object of a hostile 1987 takeover attempt by New World Entertainment Ltd., but was bought by Tonka Corp. in a white knight move. The resulting effect on stock price was impressive. Between 1985 and 1986, shareholders' total return on investment in General Mills doubled.

Management can second-guess the market another way. Executives can closely monitor market expectations and learn what stock prices and price/earnings ratios imply about levels of future returns investors expect. They can judge whether those returns expectations are reasonable relative to management expectations. As a result, they can identify whether or not a company's stock is efficiently priced and can take any necessary actions to assure efficiency.

Understanding the theoretical price of a company's shares relative to its current share price or what current share price implies about future expected returns requires use of theoretical present value (multi-phase dividend discount) models. It also necessitates calculations similar to those for internal rates of return on capital projects with uneven cash flows.

Recall from Chapter 2 that conventional two-phase dividend discount models enable calculation of (1) the present value of a projected dividend stream over an initial forecast period of above-average growth plus (2) the dividend in the last year of above-average growth times the dividend growth rate discounted to the present. In contrast, recall that Professor Rappaport's affordable dividend model suggests calculation of (1) essentially the same first term plus (2) the affordable dividend in the first year after transition to normal growth (cash payout rate adjusted for any changes in sales growth) discounted to the present.[10]

Theoretical models also allow for calculation of expected returns. But Rappaport offers an alternative method which links market expectations to corporate growth opportunities, a la Miller-Modigliani in Chapter 2.

Recall that the Miller-Modigliani formulation of theoretically appropriate P/E ratios considered growth in cash flows from investment in both existing assets and new investment in positive net present value earnings opportunities. Recall also that one academic study (mentioned in Chapter 2) found that this formulation seemed to explain more of the variation in P/E ratios across firms and more of the persistence of those differences over time than the Gordon-Shapiro constant dividend growth formulation.

Rappaport recommends calculation of a "value growth option" and a "market expectations premium" on a company's shares at their current market price.[11] The first is equivalent to the capitalized value of future cash flows from new investment in future earning assets expressed as a percentage of current share price. It is the second term in the Miller-Modigliani formulation. The second is the difference between a company's required returns and investors' minimum required returns at a current price per share.

As a starting point, Rappaport suggests calculation of "prestrategy value" per share before new investment. It is the capitalized value of cash flows from investment in existing assets. It is the first term in Miller-Modigliani's formulation. The calculation of residual value is (after-tax operating profit), before commitment of new capital to fixed or working capital investment, divided by (the cost of capital). When this figure is divided by sustainable (constant) after-tax operating profit, it is the same as (1 divided by the cost of capital). It equals a company's theoretical P/E ratio on cash flow from existing assets, part one of the Miller-Modigliani formulation.

Next, the difference between current share price and prestrategy value is a term Rappaport calls a "value growth option". It is equivalent to the second term in the Miller-Modigliani P/E formulation. The relative size of this option is the above difference divided by a company's current share price. This option is important because it shows what percentage of a company's current share price is assigned to a future forecast period, to cash flows from investment in future earning assets. Rappaport offers this as proof that the stock market is more long-term oriented than the short-term behavior of investing institutions might suggest.

The Miller-Modigliani formulation is immediately helpful because it allows a quick glance at the extent of a company's future growth opportunity, its value growth option. A company's theoretical P/E ratio equals its P/E on cash flows from investment in existing assets (1 divided by the cost of capital) plus a P/E ratio on cash flows from investment in future earning assets. If management is investing only at the cost of capital, the formulation will not capitalize future cash flows because management is creating no value. In other words, current share price equals prestrategy value per share if management invests only at the cost of capital. Current share price exceeds prestrategy value, if management invests above the cost of capital.

Current price per share equals (the present value of future cash flows over a forecast period discounted by the company's cost of capital) plus (the present value of residual cash flows at the end of a forecast period discounted at the same rate). Management must calculate the discount rate which equates those same future cash flows to prestrategy value per share. Rappaport calls this spread in required returns a "market expectations premium".

After solving for market expectations premium, if executives believe that investors' expectations are too high, that corporate required returns exceed internal rates of return, they should capitalize on market mispricing. For example, executives might sell stock, exchange stock or sell out. They might accelerate plans for a public offering of stock, sell insider stock, exchange stock in an acquisition or agree to be acquired. The last may transfer value to shareholders.

If they think that investors' expectations are too low, that internal rates of return exceed corporate required returns, they should take action to correct market mispricing and to translate potential economic value into actual market value. For example, executives might buy stock, shift assets or buyout. They might plan a corporate repurchase of the company's shares, exercise insider stock options or initiate a leveraged buyout.

In an efficient market a company's current market price per share should equal its prestrategy value per share plus the dollar value per share of its value growth option. If the two are equal, it suggests that competition for a company's excess expected returns over market expected returns has eliminated those excesses. Investors only earn market expected rates of return. A company's equity is considered fairly valued.

If shares are inefficiently priced on the low side, current share price will be less than the the combination above. It suggests that investors are undervaluing the company's value growth option and underexploiting its excess returns potential. In this case, excess returns persist due to information deficiency, i.e., investors perceive that a company's investments yield more than the cost of capital but less than the internal rate of return. Management must take action to correct market mispricing and to translate potential economic value into actual market value.

If shares are inefficiently priced on the high side, current share price will be higher than the combination above. It suggests that investors are overvaluing a company's value growth option and overexploiting its expected returns. In this case, excess returns are more than eliminated. Expected return on an investor's purchase of a company's shares falls short of market expected returns. Investors perceive yield on the company's equity investment greater than both the cost of capital and the internal rate of return. Management has an opportunity to capitalize on market optimism by transferring value to shareholders.

Calculation of the theoretical price/earnings ratio on the company's value growth option using the Miller-Modigliani formulation also enables executives to judge the clarity of investors' perceptions of the company's future growth opportunities. And it allows for corrective action. For example, if executives believe that investors are overcapitalizing potential future cash flows from their company's earnings opportunities, they should capitalize on the positive market mispricing and transfer value to shareholders. If they believe that investors are undercapitalizing their company's future cash-generating abilities arising from its competitive advantages, they should strive to correct market misperception and pricing inefficiency.

Rappaport encourages the use of a few tests to determine the interrelated sensitivity of rates of return, stock prices, sales growth rates, and profit margins:

1. How sensitive are both the corporate internal rate of return and investors' minimum required return to changes in expectations for sales growth rates and profit margins? Returns rise (fall) as sales and/or margins rise (fall).

2. How sensitive are they to changes in stock price (investors' minimum required returns unchanged)? Investors' minimum required returns rise (fall) as share price falls (rises). Assuming investors' required returns remain constant, corporate required returns rise (fall) as share price rises (falls).

3. How sensitive are sales growth rates to changes in share price (assuming investors' minimum required returns remain constant)? Sales growth rates rise (fall) as stock price rises (falls).

Executives' ability to quantify differences between theoretical values and actual market values and between security-specific expected returns and market expected returns, and to identify reasons for the differences contributes to corporate decision-making and management efficiency and longevity. It invites management action to create value for shareholders in times of relative undervaluation and to transfer value to shareholders during times of relative overvaluation.

COMMUNICATING VALUE: IMPACT OF DECISIONS ON FUTURE CASH FLOWS

Cash flow communications efforts are geared to affect Wall Street's pricing mechanism. Efficient market theory claims that data become information only if, after having been processed by Wall Street's pricing mechanism, they affect a share's price. Otherwise, data remain only data. Clearly, data are not necessarily information. But information is data. Similarly, information is not necessarily communication, but communication is information.

Data about a company's cash-generating ability and earning power are only raw materials to the market until processed by Wall Street's information processors. Their interpretation of the data triggers the market's pricing mechanism. Data become information only when they affect share price. Information has an impact on share price when it affects market-wide returns expectations. It is incumbent upon management to oversee this share price assembly line. They should serve as the equivalent of data traffic managers and steer the flow of company data to those lead investors and dominant sponsors whose perceived influence affects the perception and decisions of others.

Communicating value to Wall Street combines capital strategy (finance and investments) and business strategy (marketing and communications). A formal program focuses on the future and educates investors. It clarifies the impact on a company's future cash flows of management's investment, operating and financing decisions. It is intended to lower costs of equity capital, to heighten access to capital markets and to lower fixed operating costs in the form of cash dividends. A 1976 American Stock Exchange study showed that half of the managements of companies with active value communications programs were confident of their equity financing ability whereas only about a quarter of those with passive efforts were confident.

Ultimately, the effort is established to help management to achieve a sustainably high stock price in line with management's ability to sustain a competitive advantage in positive net present value capital strategies. By definition, it strives to shape perception of risk, growth and growth duration. It is geared to increase information efficiency, pricing efficiency and market value. And it is intended to heighten liquidity and reduce trading costs and trading volatility.

A cash flow communications program also strives to differentiate and to position a company. They are real necessities for emerging companies, especially in industries in which many competitors go public in a short period. For example, results of the thrift perception study mentioned in Chapter 4 showed that respondents perceived the thrift industry as a "commodity" lending business without distinguishing or differentiating competitive features. Yet no thrift executive would agree with that perception. Nor would Theodore Levitt, Professor of Marketing at the Harvard Business School.

Levitt believes there is no such thing as a commodity product or business.[12] In other words, he is certain that all products or businesses can be defined, differentiated and positioned in terms of their customers' wants and needs. He offers perspective on product differentiation as a reflection of customer purchasing decisions.

He cites the existence of:

1. Generic products which satisfy customers' basic performance expectations.
2. Expected products with brand names which satisfy customers' minimum acceptable performance expectations.
3. Augmented products with enhanced features which broaden customers' performance expectations.
4. Potential products which stimulate new customer performance expectations.

In this framework, emerging companies fall into categories three and four.

In this chapter, positioning and differentiating a company on the basis of capital strategy (value creation potential) and business strategy (competitive advantage) is more qualitative than quantitative. It is more verbal than visual and involves discussions of strategy more than models of valuation.

For example, beginning with capital strategy, executives should differentiate the company on the basis of its value-based planning system. They should highlight the cash flow/risk and the investment/returns nature of its product/market opportunities. It is this system by which management makes investment decisions aimed at growing, harvesting or selling businesses. A company's cash flow communicator must know the risk, expected returns and capital spread for the company as a whole and for each of its business units:

1. How does management set hurdle rates for capital projects?
2. How does management calculate the cost of equity capital?
3. What is the weighted average cost of capital for each unit?
4. How great are capital spreads expected to be?
5. How long are positive spreads expected to last? before they decay to market rates of return?
6. How much capital is to be allocated to value creating strategies over those periods (reinvestment rates)?
7. How does management structure compensation packages for managers of business units with differing risks, business cycles and levels of earnings sensitivity?

Financing decisions support investment decisions. Management must prepare to discuss them because they affect a company's capital structure and financial risk. Finance literature offers no unanimity about which capital structures are optimal for corporations, except those which provide the least (minimum) weighted average cost of capital relative to its competitors's capital costs. The literature offers only shareholder-oriented theories, called shareholder wealth maximization models, in which managements act in the best interests of shareholders. It also offers management-oriented theories, called agency cost and information asymmetry/signaling models, in which managements act in their own interest though monitored by shareholders. Both try to explain firm financing behavior.

The first models above (see Miller-Modigliani 1958 in the bibliography) consider financial risk from the perspective of those, as shareholders, who hold diversified equity interests in a diversified portfolio. They are concerned with systematic risk and support the use of leverage. The second (see Jensen, Meckling in the bibliography) consider financial risk from the perspective of those, as corporate executives, who hold long-term, non-diversified equity interests, wealth concentrated in their company's stock. They are concerned with total risk and support use of conservative equity financing. Touche Ross & Co. advises that these managers consider selling shares when 20 percent of their personal portfolios are concentrated in their company's stock.

Agency theory considers the diversification/concentration differences between managers and shareholders in constructing so-called growth optimal capital structure models. In these models, acceptable upper limits of leverage[13] satisfy the profitability, risk avoidance and wealth maximization interests of both. The theory also delves into the use and structure of executive compensation plans (discussed in Chapter 1) as means by which to more closely align the interests of both managers and shareholders.

Stewart Myers of Massachusetts Institute of Technology boils the optimal capital structure issue down to taxes, risk, and asset type. He also supports Miller and Modigliani's proposition that leverage has no earnings or stock market magic.[14] The belief is that management must balance borrowing capacity with bankruptcy risk. Management's use of debt financing should be kept at manageable levels to maintain financing flexibility and to withstand adversity such as economic swings, industry downturns or competitive difficulties. In that sense, a company with relatively risky investment opportunities and potential earnings variance (such as Coleco Industries in Chapter 4) should avoid debt financing especially if it can find alternative ways to shield its income from taxes. In contrast, a company with predictable cash flows and tangible assets should benefit from a high ratio of debt to total capital.

Managements tend to prefer to raise equity capital internally through earnings retention and debt capital externally. It is a form of agency cost avoidance, called managerial capitalism. In his article "The Capital Structure Puzzle" (*Journal of Finance*, July 1984), Myers cited the heavy corporate reliance on internal finance and external debt during the decade of 1973-1982. For example, internally generated cash covered, on average, 62 percent of corporate capital expenditures, including investment in inventory and other current assets. Borrowing constituted the majority of required external financing. Equity financing in the form of net new stock issues were never more than 6 percent of external financing.

Ultimately, management should identify a target capital structure which supports the company's fundamentals and results in the lowest weighted average cost of capital. One study[15] surveyed corporate financing-decision processes in Fortune 1000 companies. It found that, measured in terms of long term debt-to-total capitalization, debt comprised 26 to 40 percent of target capital structures. A communicator must be prepared to discuss changes in that target and their impact on the company's systematic risk: business risk (operating cash flow variance) and financial risk (interest coverage).

Financial policy (dividends) has also been a source of great debate and little unanimity since 1961. At that time, the opinions of Miller and Modigliani clashed with those of Graham and Dodd. The latter believed that investors would pay more for high dividend paying companies. The latter argued that given fixed investment and borrowing guidelines and ignoring taxes and transactions costs, dividend policy was irrelevant to the determination of share prices[16] because the present value of overall cash flows were the same regardless of payout policy.

They claimed that cash distribution policy depended on cash-generating ability, not the reverse. They also contended returns of capital to shareholders depended on returns on shareholders' capital.

Another study of annual earnings and dividend information for 1,050 New York Stock Exchange companies divided into 25 portfolios running from 1951 to 1970[17] found that dividend yields had no clear effect on stock returns and stock prices. Controversy, however, continues to brew about whether higher yielding stocks offer higher returns.[18] Ultimately, the implications are that managements should be more concerned with what changes in dividends, not levels of payout, suggest about management expectations for future operating cash flows.

One study examined the dividend decisions of 1,000 companies in 64 industries between 1974 and 1980.[19] It found a predictable dividend policy behavior among companies with similar fundamentals. It theorized that dividend payout ratios were influenced by three parameters: transactions costs of external financing, agency costs of outside shareownership, and financing constraints imposed by operating and financing leverage. The study showed that lower dividend payout ratios were strongly associated with higher past and forecast growth rates (transactions costs to support growth), higher betas (financing constraints), and higher proportional inside ownership. Larger numbers of shareholders were associated with higher payout ratios (agency costs). Industry membership did not explain payout ratio.

Specifically the study's regression analysis revealed that a company forecasting a 7 percent annual growth rate could be expected to have a payout ratio about 11 percentage points higher than a company with 20 percent forecast growth. It also showed that a company with a beta of 0.75 could be expected to have a payout ratio about 13 percentage points higher than one with a beta of 1.25, that a shareholder increase from 500 to 5,000 could be expected to raise payout ratio by 6 percentage points (another 6 points from 5,000 to 50,000) and that a loosely held company could be expected to have a payout ratio about 5 percentage points higher than a company which is 50 percent closely held.

Share volume reactions to changes in dividend policy raise questions about the relevance of dividend policy and the existence of clientele effects, evidenced in shifts in shareholder base with adjustments in yield. One study reviewed 192 companies announcing their first cash dividend.[20] It found very significant volume increases on average in the week of initial dividend declarations and slight increases in volume on average in the period between announcement week and ex-dividend week (attributable to information content). It also found a positive correlation between abnormal volume and dividend size and a negative correlation between volume and prior share price appreciation. The evidence suggested that share volume increases were the result of reaction to positive management signals about future operating cash flows but lent only weak credence to clientele effects.

Other studies have argued that taxes aside, investors should be indifferent about whether their wealth builds as a result of share price increases or cash distributions. And, even in a taxable world, investors should still be indifferent because of their ability to collateralize their stock or to borrow against their insurance so as to avoid ordinary income tax liability.

However, in a taxable environment, it seems that dividend policy is relevant to investors or at least they think it is relevant. Historically, dividends have been taxed at higher ordinary income tax rates than long-term capital gains when gains have been realized. Obviously, if securities are not sold, gains are not realized and are not taxed. Therefore, investors in high marginal income tax brackets have tended to prefer investment in low cash dividend-paying companies. In contrast, investors in relatively lower marginal income tax brackets have tended to prefer high cash dividend-paying companies.

Many contend that passage of the Tax Reform Act of 1986 enhances the appeal of dividends and makes dividend policy a very relevant issue for corporate executives. The Act sets tax rates for dividends and capital gains eventually at the same ordinary income tax rate, a maximum of 28 percent versus a previous maximum of 20 percent on capital gains and 50 percent on ordinary income.

Once again, however, tax rates on dividends and capital gains are comparable only if capital gains are realized. And capital gains may be indirectly realized without being taxed by borrowing against the equity value of a portfolio, thus still lessening the appeal of dividends.

Critics of the bill claim it is pro-cash and anti-investment. They contend that it favors investment in companies with greater potential for near-term payoff with high streams of dividends over investment in companies which require patient commitment of long-term capital. They argue that the bill favors established cash-generating, high dividend-paying companies and penalizes emerging, high reinvestment, growth companies. The tax system may no longer compensate patient, long-term risk-oriented investors by taxing them less. And corporate reinvestment of capital instead of return of capital may become hard to justify. Many fear the bill may malaffect capital formation, especially venture capital investment, and the development of emerging technologies in the U.S.

Many believe that the Tax Reform Act of 1986 favors economics over tax benefits and predictable streams of future income to unpredictable gains (or losses) from risk investments. Investors may value securities more on companies' abilities to distribute cash than on their abilities to compound cash by reinvesting in opportunities with high growth/high returns potential. Equity capital may expand more through stock offerings than earnings retention.

To offer statistical perspective on dividends, the number of companies which raised their dividends in December 1986 and January 1987 rose to 305 from 284 in the prior year period. But only 626 of 9,812 corporate dividends declared in the first four months of 1987 were increases. The number of dividend increases in one year peaked in 1978 at 3,211. Only 1,515 companies raised their dividends in 1986, the lowest number since 1971. The annual dividend growth rate peaked in 1982 at 11.5 percent, was about 4 percent in the third quarter of 1986 and averaged only about 3 percent in the first quarter of 1987. Dividend payout ratios in 1986 were about 54 percent of corporate earnings, versus 56.3 percent in 1985 and 51.9 percent in 1984. They were projected to fall to 47 percent of estimated 1987 corporate earnings.

Should an emerging company, or any company for that matter, pay a dividend? It depends on a company's reinvestment opportunities. Assuming that a company's investment and borrowing policies are fixed, the rational response is that if the capital spread on incremental investment of net after-tax operating income (sustainable cash flow) is positive, then returning capital to investors is neither necessary nor desirable, especially as threshold spreads expand. A dividend should not be initiated as a means of affecting stock price. This is especially true if subsequent equity financing is required to provide adequate cash with which to execute financing decisions. Dividends are a high fixed cost.

The above response implies that, in the event that management faces only zero or negative net present value investment opportunities (at or below the cost of capital), then returning cash to owners is necessary and desirable, regardless of threshold spreads. In this case, owners must be allowed to make their own investment decisions. Otherwise, managements' hording of owners' cash can become problematic.

Clearly, management must not invest to destroy economic value. And executives must not act passively with cash. Rather, they should return it to shareholders in the form of capital gains through corporate repurchases rather than dividend income, to avoid the fixed costs of dividends. Some invest in other public companies with perceived superior earnings opportunities. But recall that shareholders do not pay managements to do (diversify) what they can do themselves. Otherwise, management risks incurring the wrath of shareholders or attracting the attention of corporate raiders. Passive cash depresses returns on equity. And, as Warren Buffett, a renowned value investor, contends, increases in owners' net worth which result from basic compound interest on passive cash is a capital sin.

Realistically, dividends may potentially broaden share ownership. Many defensive and cautious investing institutions require dividends as a criterion for stock selection. Consequently, some executives may believe that cash dividends are a necessity because institutional investors expect them.

Yet, aggressive investors do not expect cash dividends. They are satisfied with the economic value-creating ability of companies with sustainable competitive advantages and positive net present value investment in perceived high growth/high returns product/markets. Digital Equipment Corporation (Maynard, MA) is an example. Management and the board of directors have never authorized cash dividends to shareholders since the company went public in August 1966. Over that 20-year period, shareholders' realized returns on share price appreciation alone have compounded at a 25.29 percent annual rate.

Many newly converted thrift institutions declared initial cash dividends in 1986. They were more flush with new equity capital than they were with positive net present value earnings opportunities in which to put that capital to work. Declarations of initial dividends were intended as signals of management confidence in thrifts' future earning power. Thrift managements used cash signals to shape investing institutions' perceptions of their earnings stability and predictability independent of interest rate fluctuations.

Moving to business strategy, executives should differentiate the company's growth/returns potential on the basis of its strategic planning and strategy analysis. This involves examination of growth/share relationships and cash flow/strategy allocation in product/markets.

So-called product/market portfolio models are used in corporate portfolio planning by strategy consulting firms. Boston Consulting Group uses Growth/Share Matrix models. GE/McKinsey employs market attractiveness/competitive position grid models. Arthur D. Little relies on industry maturity/competitive position matrices. Shell uses Directional Policy Matrices. And Michael Porter's (Harvard Business School) industry/competitive analysis models (*Competitive Strategy*, New York: Free Press, 1980 and *Competitive Advantage*, New York: Free Press, 1985) have become helpful in the effort to associate companies with sustainable advantages (operating margins and spreads) in competitive product/markets.

A formal cash flow communications program should focus on the five themes which support a company's cash-generating ability and growth/returns fundmentals: the company's market, its product position, its competition, its pricing strategy and cost structure. The first three are a proxy for market growth/market share relationships. The last two represent earning power and earnings quality. A sixth factor is management. Executives should reexamine the company's business plan, operating plan and strategic plan. And they should review the company's business description, mission (purpose), goals and environment.

Changing trends in consumption usually give rise to market opportunities. On a macro level, many factors shape these trends. Leading economic indicators reveal changing economic conditions. Demographics change. Populations shift, technological developments occur and new products are introduced. Finally, social and cultural attitudes shift or legislation affecting taxes, trade policies, regulation or antitrust efforts offers competitive opportunities.

Porter cites the five factors above as those which dictate the returns portion of corporate growth/returns fundamentals. He claims that market entry, product substitutes, competitor intensity and the bargaining power of both buyers and suppliers can affect costs, prices, unit volume, investment and risk. They are the fundamentals which affect any company's sales and earnings growth. Within a macroeconomy, industry or segment growth/returns attractiveness must be examined in terms of issues over which management has no control:[21]

1. Economic characteristics (market size, growth rate, maturity, seasonality, cyclicality, cost structure, economies of scale, price elasticity, production lead time and capacity lead time).
2. Structure (concentration, specialization, vertical integration, horizontal integration, barriers to entry, barriers to exit, stability and competitor similarity). This limits pricing flexibility.
3. Competition (upstream/downstream participants, direct/potential participants and suppliers of substitutes). This affects variability in demand for a company's goods and services.
4. Competitive positions of participants (share, independence, predictability, aggressiveness and innovativeness). This affects prices and costs.
5. Bargaining power balances (raw material suppliers, component vendors, workers, insurers/creditors, sub-contractors, shippers, producers, distributors, dealers, endusers, after-users, repairers/scrappers and bystanders). This affects cost structures, pricing flexibility and operating leverage.
6. Product characteristics (differentiability, perishability, complementary products, buyer priorities, social constraints, regulatory constraints, obsolescence rate, standardization). This affects pricing strategy.

Company-specific market share and sales growth usually builds as a consequence of:[22]

1. Better resources (people, facilities, financial).
2. Greater product differentiation (brand awareness, preference and loyalty supported by product features, price advantages, promotion efforts, distribution steps and communication strategy).
3. Broader product lines.
4. Wider distribution.
5. Deeper market penetration.
6. Faster new product introductions.

Within the context of growth/share relationships, management must describe the growth/returns potential of its business for the benefit of money managers, securities analysts and shareholders. A business description uses active, present tense verbs to depict the company's activities. For example, a company "provides," "assembles," "manufactures," "specializes in," "manages," "develops," "designs," "constructs," "supports," "produces" or "markets." A mission statement discusses markets and market share. The company seeks "to build," "to obtain," "to establish," "to penetrate," "to enter," "to develop."

Management must also highlight the company's earnings power and earnings quality. Executives must talk about the company's and units' competitive advantage(s). They must discuss the keys to its (their) cash-generating ability: the size of its positive operating margin and spread, the expected duration of that advantage and the size of its sales growth potential at that spread. Recall from footnote 26 in Chapter 2 that a growth/share model explained only about 10 percent of cash flow dispersion across business units and a cash sources/uses model explained about 67 percent of that variation.

Managements must also discuss their companies' earnings quality (see Bernstein/Siegel and Siegel in the bibliography). The extent to which reported earnings accurately reflect earning power is a proxy for earnings variance and estimation risk in consensus earnings estimates. They must make clear the comparative reliability of reported income relative to their accounting and business decisions: liberal or conservative accounting policies relative to industry policy, discretionary costs, earnings variability and asset values.

For example, what are those competitive advantages in its markets which give rise to its cost advantages, in terms of cost of goods sold or cost of sales:[23]

1. Proprietary inputs.
2. Lead-time.
3. Process patents.
4. Know-how.
5. Scale economies.

Management must also highlight those competitive advantages in its markets which give rise to product differentiation and to long-term or short-term pricing advantages:[24]

1. Product patents.
2. Consumer franchise.
3. Know-how.
4. Lead time.
5. Exclusionary tactics.
6. Switching costs.
7. Proprietary outlets.
8. Long-term contracts.
9. Short-term pricing advantages may accrue as a result of:
   a. work disruptions (shortages, stoppages, reorganizations, natural disasters, severance, start-ups, shut-downs).
   b. changes in accounting policies.
   c. cost-cutting efforts.
   d. inventory turnover.
   e. decreasing operating rates.

    f. fluctuating currency rates.

    g. timing differences (cost or price changes).

To summarize, management must prepare to discuss business strategy in terms of:

1. What drives the growth/returns attractiveness of the company's industry?
2. What drives the company's operating decisions (growth/share and cash flow/strategy allocation): resource analysis, opportunity analysis, competitive analysis, risk orientation, time horizon or financial objectives?
3. What drives the company's cash-generating ability: cost or price advantages, growth/ share relationships, sources/uses factors? Is the company an efficient low-cost producer? Is the company a price/performance leader able to protect its market position?
4. What drives the company's returns potential: operating margins, sales growth rates, tax rates and investment intensity. Is the company able to reduce its investment/sales and/or its revenue/assets ratios?

Shaping perception of market growth and earning power are especially important in positive market conditions. For example, in bull markets professional investors buy momentum when they buy shares in the best performing companies in the best performing industries. In up markets, they hunt aggressively and swiftly for both sales momentum (real expansion in unit volume) and earnings momentum (real gains in operating profit from continuing operations).

Besides the company's market opportunity and its earning power and earnings quality, executives should use themselves to qualitatively differentiate their company. It is especially true for small capitalization companies with large shares in rapid growth markets or with small but growing shares in slow, no or negative growth markets. Management is the key to performance, credibility, visibility and to consensus-building among investors of the company's earnings predictability and returns stability.

Shaping perception of management capability and stability and of the company's asset value is especially important during bear markets. It is also significant in two-tier markets, as in 1986 and 1987. In this case, big capitalization issues benefit from popularity flow due and institutions' liquidity preferences. Small capitalization issues suffer from popularity outflow.

For example, value investors "buy management" and undervalued assets when they buy shares in the best performing companies (operating profit margin) in the worst performing (depressed) industries (relative to the market). As of this writing, Texas banks and savings and loans are examples. In other words, in down or two-tier markets, management, operating success and financial condition are the company's best points of differentiation and positioning. When markets turn or popularity flow changes course, investors will look to those companies postured for growth, profitability and stable returns.

Executives should highlight their:[25]

1. Policies
   a. Financing (discussed below) and financial policy (use of debt, payment of cash dividends, asset management/profit goals, accounting policies).
   b. Organizational structure and administrative procedures.
   c. Marketing and distribution.
   d. Research and development (engineering).
   e. Purchasing and production (integration ratios, labor relations, processes and methods, capacity levels, plants and warehouses, scheduling controls and sourcing).
2. Planning and coordination.
3. Information and controls.
4. Flexibility and responsiveness.
5. Discipline and motivation.

The issue of credibility also focuses directly upon the quality of both management and the company's board of directors:

1. Is management committed, flexible, accessible, mature, motivated, responsive, creative and analytical?
2. How are executives motivated (incentive compensation) and rewarded?
3. Who sits on the company's board? Are they reputable, good sources of counsel and wisdom, guidance, ideas and contacts?

At this point, managements of some companies select a positioning "tag line" to reflect management's philosophy about creating economic value. The management of Gillette Company (Boston, MA), for example, aims for sustainable profitable growth (versus sustainable competitive advantage). Others use advertising to reinforce their philosophy. Fuqua Industries (Atlanta, GA) boasts its past 10-year record of compound annual total returns to shareholders which compares favorably to those companies which comprise the Dow Jones Industrial Average. In an advertisement, the company claims to be a value builder instead of an empire builder. McKesson Corporation (San Francisco, CA) highlights its industry and its group (stable) in a "Wish List" of investors' investment criteria. Advertisements hail the company as a value-added distributor.

IN-HOUSE CASH FLOW COMMUNICATIONS

The result of the February 1984 *Business Week*/Louis Harris & Associates poll raises concerns about the effectiveness with which corporate managements communicate value to Wall Street. Some executives see it as a continuous need while others consider it a continuous annoyance. Some corporate executives devote much time while others spend no time.

The form of the exercise varies widely. Some companies formalize the cash flow communications process. They establish independent departments, structure a full-time position to manage the task and actively shape perception of their company's future cash-generating momentum. Others remain passively informal. They view it as a part-time responsibility of the corporate secretary, treasurer or vice president of finance and administration. They passively distribute historic operating data.

For an emerging company, a public offering usually strengthens its balance sheet, reduces its debt, decreases its leverage, increases its cash and expands its borrowing capacity. It prepares a company to more fully exploit its existing product/market opportunities. But it also imposes an additional responsibility. It forces management to link total strategy to stock price in making investment, financing and operating decisions which create economic value for shareholders. And it requires that they translate that economic value into real market value for the benefit of shareholders.

After an initial public offering is completed, management faces one of three choices about how to communicate value and support the company in the aftermarket. First, executives can manage the function in-house. In this case, either the chief financial officer, a current employee or a new recruit can assume communications responsibilities. Reporting to the company's president or chief executive officer heightens the importance of the function both to management and to shareholders. Second, management can retain an outside financial communications consultant. Third, management can do nothing. The first is most logical and the last is least sensible.

There are usually two reasons why corporate managers initiate formal in-house cash flow communications programs: performance (growth) or price (undervalued). Managements of companies in high growth/high returns emerging companies with large shares in rapidly expanding markets often initiate active cash flow communications programs to support market share strategies. They want to maintain a high stock price in order to be able to grow or diversify through mergers or acquisitions which may require the exchange of shares. On the other hand, managements of companies which believe their company's share price does not fairly reflect the earning power of its underlying assets also formalize a communications plan. They want to correct an undervalued situation.

Considering the time and the cost associated with the going public process, an organized in-house communications program is a management time-saver. Planning and making an initial public offering significantly dilute management's time and take senior executives away from operating decisions. Managements attest that the effort can be so time intensive that a company had better be prepared to manage itself for up to six months.

Establishing cash flow communications responsibility is an operating decision in itself. A formal program frees executives to devote full attention to capital budgeting and strategy analysis. In that sense, it is economic because it recaptures the opportunity cost of managements' previously lost time. And it is efficient in that it is intended to ably substitute for both chief executive or chief financial officers in direct dealings with securities analysts and money managers.

But confusion seems to surround the definition of a company's cash flow communications function. Here are some pertinent questions:

Is it a communications job or a strategy job?

Is it a public relations function or a planning function?

Is it marketing effort or a communications effort?

Is it a job for a planner, a writer or an analyst?

Is the job skill-oriented or activites-oriented?

Should the position protect or project management?

Should the position report to senior or middle management?

What should be the job's objectives?

Is the function expandable or expendable?

The effort to communicate value to Wall Street, in house or outside, has many names. They tend to fall under a public relations umbrella. The most common titles are investor relations, shareholder relations, stockholder relations, financial relations, financial communications and capital formation communications.

Individuals of varied professional backgrounds are assigned to the in-house corporate, versus cash flow, communications function. Some are ex-securities analysts. Others are ex-stockbrokers. Others are ex-journalists. The positon may begin at the level of coordinator. It may then progress to manager and on to director. Depending on the company, the position's status may rise to vice president and, in a few cases, to the level of senior vice president. In some cases, individuals get drafted by their strategic planning department.

Corporate titles for the position sound similar to customer service positions in product companies. But, unlike customer service, the effort is intended to be assertive, not responsive. Titles are as varied as individuals' backgrounds. Some are called Manager, Investor Relations and Shareholder Services; Manager, Investor Relations; Manager, Financial Relations; and Manager, Investor and Press Relations.

Others are termed Director, Investor Relations; Director of Corporate Relations; Director, Corporate Communications; Director, Financial Relations; Director of Investor Relations and Assistant Treasurer; and Director of Financial Analysis and Investor Relations. Still others receive these titles: Vice President, Investor Relations; Vice President, Corporate Relations; Vice President and Director of Investor Communications; Vice President, Public Relations; Administrative Vice President; Vice President, Investor and Public Affairs; and Vice President, Investor Relations and Assistant Treasurer.

Corporate descriptions for the in-house position usually stress coordinator instead of planner. They use verbs to describe the position's responsibilities such as respond, assist, schedule, participate, arrange, monitor, prepare, and maintain. The position often falls into the public affairs department. Position guides claim that the job is responsible for achieving favorable understanding of the company and its management among a variety of constituencies, including analysts and investors. The position is often regarded as a focal point for coordination of a broad range of communications efforts, including employee and community communications.

Professional communicators interpret literally their financial communications duties. They believe their job is to heighten the company's identity and management's credibility. They prepare to answer investors' questions, to respond to issues and to distribute the company's materials to investors. They expect to organize and conduct meetings between management and analysts or investors. They are geared to prepare press announcements and shareholder reports concerning quarterly and annual operating results. They intend to establish shareholder records systems and to identify institutional owners of the company's shares.

Finally, as a means of being able to justify their position, they hope to be able to claim direct responsibility for building the market value and market multiple of their company's equity. Sometimes, despite the company's fundamentals or its intrinsic value, they want to be able to point to their company's price/earnings ratio at premium levels to peer competitors, the industry and the market, as their measure of success.

A formal cash flow communications program should be perceived in the context of corporate development. It is a natural extension of a company's total planning effort. It is closely allied to the capital budgeting process and to the strategic planning process and links them both directly to the company's stock price. It lets executives talk to their stock. It helps management to understand investors' perceptions of their company's competitive position, cash-generating ability and returns potential. And it highlights which steps may be necessary to affect those perceptions. It is a relatively inexpensive means by which to influence the equity valuation process.

Plans for and prospects of a company's future growth and profitability are communicated most effectively to Wall Street in a strategic planning context. Responsibility for communicating value belongs more in a corporate development department, less in the company's finance department and not in a company's public relations arena. It is advantageous to management to fold cash flow communications responsibility into a strategist's or an economist's position. It is less logical to fold strategy into a communicator's position. Ultimately the combined effort of planning (in both a capital and business strategy context) and value communications warrant a corporate title which binds them. The position's title might be that of "Cash Flow Communicator" or "Equity Valuation Strategist."

A job description for an in-house value communicator should incorporate an understanding of the company's capital strategy. This means comprehension of its investment decision-making process and returns guidelines. It also necessitates familiarity with its business strategy and competitive position, on both a corporate and business unit level. Finally, it requires awareness of the rationale for its financing decisions and financial policy. It should also involve access to the company's strategic planning, finance and administration and marketing executives and departments.

On the level of capital strategy, a valuation strategist must learn how corporate and operating managers set hurdle rates. They must know managers' cash flow growth rate and duration assumptions for their forecasts. And they should be familiar with the targets to which executive compensation plans are tied.

On a business strategy level, the perception shaper must have a working knowledge of the company's market environment. The person should know its market or segment characteristics, product characteristics and protection, market competition, pricing strategy and cost structure. He or she should also understand growth/share relationships on a corporate and business unit basis. And the communicator should be able to interpret the effects on future cash flows of changes in sales growth, operating margins, tax rates, or capital intensity.

He or she should be conversant about the company's products and/or services, its distribution channels for them and its customers, suppliers of, and dealers in them. The value communicator should understand how the company sells its goods and why customers buy them. The person should be familiar with secular trends in the company's industry, why they dominate and how they may change.

The value communicator is management's window on the market. He or she anticipates the market's pricing mechanism. The person predicts market reaction and interprets market response (as seen in Chapter 6) to management's investment, financing (capital structure, financial policy, accounting) or operating decisions (earnings). The communicator also deciphers what stock price implies about investors' returns expectations.

He or she should be able to articulate management's philosophy to lead investors and to dominant sponsors concerning what to invest in and how to compete. And the person must be able to speak clearly to management about investors' philosophy concerning performance or price as a basis for investment in the company's shares. And, just as management defines the company's products in terms of its customers, the communicator defines the company's stock (equity product) in terms of its investors.

The value communicator is also the market's window on management. He or she is an educator who uses words to shape investors' perceptions of management's decisions. And to spread that perception to dominant sponsors and lead investors, the person relies on conventional marketing communications tools: reports, meetings, records, presentations, direct mail, executive compensation packages and dividend reinvestment plans and employee/customer stock owner-ship plans.

The importance of the position must be emphasized to management. Meetings of the company's (operating) policy committee, management committee and the board of directors should include the cash flow communicator in a titled or untitled capacity. Also it is highly desirable to have the person manage the company's in-house pension fund or oversee the performance of those outside money management firms that manage the pension fund. This added responsibil-ity requires close relationships with an active network of institutional portfolio managers and securities analysts. It directly complements the company's cash flow communications effort and facilitates monitoring of Wall Street's percep-tion of the company.

The person who fills the position must have the ability to analyze financial statements, to conduct market research, to develop a marketing plan and to present ideas in oral and written form. He or she should report to the chairman, president, chief executive officer or chief financial officer. Finally, the person should establish an internal policy for communicating value to investors. It should emphasize truth, credibility and consistency among all of those who may speak for the company.

Where can management recruit a capable and qualified person to be the com-pany's cash flow communicator? One method is to retain the services of an executive recruiting firm (headhunter). The firm will usually ask for referrals to prospective qualified candidates from individuals in investor relations positions in other companies.

A better method is for management to ask directly for referrals to qualified candidates from sell-side securities analysts who are industry specialists. They can recommend individuals whom, they perceive, are adept at shaping investors' perceptions of returns potential of capital and business strategies relative to alternatives of equal risk. For the analyst, helping management to hire a com-municator is in his or her best interest. He or she may perceive a potential competitive information advantage by virtue of having faster access and quicker contact with company officers through that recruit.

Realistically, emerging companies may not enjoy the luxury of access to a strong cash flow communicator. Management may have no ideal candidate al-ready in-house and may prefer not to pay a big sum to hire one. In this case, executives' usual method is to appoint someone from the company's marketing, public relations or secretarial staff area. They allocate "half of one person" to the job in an effort to relieve day-to-day time pressures from more senior executives.

In this instance, executives must ask how can they train an individual to communicate value. Training should focus on two issues: the concepts and the language of equity valuation. It should spotlight the key terms in which the valuation process is expressed. And it should highlight the premier investment, operating and financing themes on which assessment of risk and expected returns is based. The objective is to enable an appointee to comprehend how the market values equities in general so that he or she can positively affect the market's valuation of the company's equity in particular.

Training in cash flow communications at this stage does not require return to school, although further academic training at some point may be highly desirable. Rather, it necessitates reading and talking about the practice and the theory of equity valuation. Management should encourage a new appointee to gather and to read an enormous number of investment research reports produced by sell-side securities analysts at a variety of brokerage firms. Copious notes on the reports' central themes, main analytical points and language facilitate an understanding of how Wall Street values industries and companies. The enduring valuation themes of present value analysis, relative ratio analysis and asset value analysis will consistently recur.

Ideally, the reports should cover the company and its industry. But such specificity is not entirely necessary. Valuation's general themes and language ring true throughout investment literature.

Research products are easy to accumulate. Brokerage firm industry securities analysts should be pleased to forward many copies of past research reports on the industry and companies in the industry. Indirect peer competitors, especially if they are located in non-competitive markets (by geography or product), should respond positively to requests for copies of older, non-current reports. Or on-line access to databases mentioned in Chapter 4, such as *Investext* (Business Research Corp., Boston, MA) or *Exchange* (Mead Data Central, Dayton, OH) can speed recent industry and company reports via personal computer and modem. Management should also urge appointees to this position to actively make contact and to arrange visits with cash flow communicators at other companies.

Training should be rewarding. Intense reading and talking quickly broadens one's perspective and deepens one's knowledge of the valuation process. Awareness of the cash flow communications opportunity heightens dramatically and ability to speak the language of Wall Street develops quickly. Training builds the skills with which to use Wall Street and to affect market expectations and share price. The benefits accrue immediately to the company and to the individual.

According to a 1985 membership survey conducted by the National Investor Relations Institute (NIRI, Washington, DC), this is how in-house financial communicators spend their time: 36.08 percent for analyst meetings and contacts, 12.49 percent for annual reports, 9.8 percent for preparation of other shareholder materials, 6.4 percent for media relations, 3.86 percent for annual meetings, 3.78 percent for shareholder identification and 3.75 percent for strategic planning. About 2 percent or less time was devoted to such activities as internal publications, acquisition/divestiture planning, employee relations, corporate advertising, proxy solicitation and working with underwriters and government relations.

The 1985 membership survey also revealed the cost of in-house cash flow communications capability. A company's annual budget depends on the level of corporate activities. Salary, travel and entertainment and shareholder report preparation are the core expenses. The survey found that the average annual budget for a company listed on the New York Stock Exchange was $746,000. It was $557,000 for a company listed on the American Stock Exchange. The average annual budget was $348,000 for companies traded on NASDAQ. The 1986 NIRI survey found that the average budget including salaries was $507,700 and was $322,270 excluding salaries ($183,870 or $2.94 per copy for annual reports). The amount is only an average figure. The function can certainly be performed on a more frugal basis. But the figure compares well to the recaptured value of executives' previously lost time during the going public process.

The 1985 survey found that the average annual salary for the head of a corporate investor relations department was $73,700. It ranged from $90,000 in the New York area to $59,000 per year in the southeastern part of the country. A 1986 salary and budget survey was based on responses from 247 corporate investor relations officers. It found that the average annual salary for a chief investors relations person was $70, 559 ($50,407 for a subordinate). The figure adjusted to a company's sales or market capitalization. Larger companies paid more for the function.

RETAINING OUTSIDE OF THE COMPANY

Venture capitalists and underwriters believe disseminating information and shaping perception is very important for their portfolio companies and their corporate finance clients. They usually advise managements of emerging public companies to retain the services of an outside communications outfit, sometimes several months or a year in advance of an initial public offering.

An outside organization may bill itself as a public relations firm with an investor relations department, a financial communications organization or an independent investor relations firm. Firm size may range from one person to hundreds of employees. Retainer fees may vary dramatically. Large firms may quote an annual fee between $60,000 to $100,000, a rate of about $5,000 to $8,000 per month, regardless of the base of annual sales or net income of the corporate client.

There are advantages and disadvantages to retaining outside the company. The decision rests on such factors as: money, time convenience, level of desired sophistication, and organizational structure.

First, outside communications firms can pave the way for market sponsorship in the aftermarket. They can acquaint money managers and securities analysts with a company's technology, its applications and the size of its product/markets. Management should focus on growth/share relationships and competitive advantages. They can develop a trade press strategy which includes "backgrounders" on the company, its products and the industry. The intent is to strengthen underlying investor demand for a new issue and to stimulate share volume during the 90-day quiet period immediately following an initial offering.

Public relations introductions are worthwhile. They are a necessity for emerging companies in high-technology industries because investors need to understand what a company does, how it does it and why it is important to which markets. Outside organizations tend to focus on the top line of an income statement: how the company makes what it makes, what it makes and why buyers buy it. In contrast, managements focus on the bottom line: how the company makes money and why it makes money.

Second, management can take a reasonable period to adjust to the new administrative responsibilities associated with being a public company. They are time-intensive. Third, depending upon the size of the retained firm, management may expect to avail itself of a broad array of additional services and resources. Executives may be able to call on specialized communications tactics in the areas of crisis management, proxy solicitation, stock surveillance and takeover defense.

There are a few disadvantages. First, the company's cash flow communications efforts will be off the premises. Senior executives will not be able to walk into a nearby office to discuss topics of strategy, valuation, market reaction, or perception. Second, information processors prefer to talk directly to the company's senior management or value communicator, not to a third-party, once removed from the company.

For example, Wellington Management Company/Thorndike, Doran, Paine & Lewis (Boston, MA), manages more than $16 billion in institutional assets. The firm generally discourages visits from public relations firms, on retainer, in lieu of management visits. The firm's introductory meetings with corporate managements are usually through company-arranged and sponsored luncheons or independently arranged visits.

Money managers of smaller pools of equity assets also welcome invitations to management presentations and inclusion on company mailing lists. And many initiate contact with independent investor relations firms to learn of any fast-growing small capitalization companies which may have been added as new clients. It is a means of networking.

Third, outside firms' capabilities may vary dramatically. Some may be skillful in public relations and product publicity. Others may specialize in particular industries or events. From management's perspective their understanding of capital markets and the equity valuation process is of paramount importance. There is no substitute.

Fourth, firms may be oriented more toward group activities than to one-to-one relationships. It may be that they lack strong Wall Street contacts, especially with securities analysts and money managers. Or it may be that they fear that stressing that aspect of market sponsorship which management can do for itself may deal them right out of a retainer fee.

These firms may work hard to "reach" target audiences through relatively expensive mass mailings to analysts and portfolio managers and through group meetings with stockbrokers. But if they stress that approach, management should question it. That method fails to grasp the economic notion that share prices are set at the margin not by the masses, but by a few key individuals whom others perceive to be influential in the equity valuation process. Executives must also judge the effectiveness of recommended programs relative to management time and shareholder expense.

Ultimately, a communications consulting firm's proximity to Wall Street is far less important then its ability to recognize lead investors and to identify dominant sponsors, wherever they may be located. The distinction should be an important consideration in the decision concerning which outside firm to retain.

And, fifth, the impact of an outside communications firm's efforts to affect market value may be difficult to observe. For example, one academic study[26] conducted tests of market efficiency both for unlisted companies which retained outside investor relations firms and for those companies which hired one of just a few large firms. Results in both cases in this study alone demonstrated no statistically significant difference in share price in the year before, the year of, and the year after retention of an outside firm. It appears that these firms may have affected individuals' returns expectations (share volume) but they seemed to have no measurable impact on market-wide consensus returns expectations (share price).

There are two methods by which management can find a capable and qualified financial communications/investor relations firm to retain. Executives can ask for a referral from an indirect competitor in the same market but different geographic or product segment. There should be no conflicts of interest. But a better idea is to ask for referrals from money managers who own the company's shares. They will recommend a firm (or ask securities analysts with whom they do commission business to do so) which they perceive can be influential in introducing management to lead investors and dominant sponsors. Helping a portfolio company to find a reputable financial communications firm is in the best economic self-interest of a money manager. Ideally, it leads to market sponsorship, popularity flow and market value.

The investor relations and financial communications services industry is perceived as a commodity business. But management must still distinguish among firms. What can the firm do for the company that management cannot do for the company? Executives should ask several questions of any outside agency: (1) does the firm understand, in general, the equity valuation process? Does it understand the company's competitve position, and (2) does the firm know, in particular, how the market values companies in the industry? How investors perceive the company's competitive advantage in particular?

Any communications plan not based specifically and explicitly on this knowledge is useless. Management should reject it outright. And no program intended to shape, reshape or reinforce investors' perceptions of a company can do so without first determining what those perceptions are.

In equity valuation strategy, media relations means little compared to security analyst and money manager relations. For small capitalization companies, the ability to establish realtionships with venturesome and aggressive lead investors is most important to the ultimate development of market sponsorship.

Management should seek answers to more questions:

1. Can the firm recognize potential lead investors in the company? Who are they? Why are they perceived as lead?

2. Does the firm know which investing institutions own, have owned, recently bought or recently sold the shares of peer competitors?

3. With which types of money managers does the firm think management should make contact? Why? Where are they?

4. Can the firm identify potential dominant sponsors of the company? How? Why are they perceived as dominant? Do they take and return the firm's phone calls? Examples.

5. Does the firm know which analysts currently publish research of peer competitors? What is their current opinion of the industry? Of competitors? Has that opinion changed over time? How? Why?

A few more questions are appropriate:

1. What is the firm's reputation? How is the firm perceived? Ask for an unscreened list of accounts or peruse *O'Dwyer's Directory of Public Relations Firms* for a list of the firm's clients. Plan to speak to some present and past accounts of the firm, especially indirect competitors in the same industry.

2. What are the size of its annual billings? Is the figure an increase or a decrease from prior years?

3. How many clients does the firm serve? Is the number up or down from prior years?

4. Can the firm offer examples of past successes? How were they accomplished? How was success measured? Past failures? Why did they fail? How was failure measured?

5. How much does the firm charge for its services? How often?

6. What does the company get for the fee? Measured how? Management should compare a firm's fees with other firms of comparable size and with other companies of comparable revenues. But executives should not prepare to fight the fee.

7. How extensive are the firm's capabilities? Do they include takeover defense, proxy solicitation or stock watch programs?

8. How many activities with the investment community should the company expect to undertake? How many are too many? Who decides? On what basis?
9. How much of senior management's time will the firm expect to use?

The communications firm must understand the company's competitive environment, its corporate objectives and corporate culture. It must learn the company's approach to investment, operating and financing decisions in order to be able to accurately advise management about market reaction and response to them. Finally, the firm must agree with management on cash flow communications objectives. The firm must stipulate the measurements, both in terms of stock price and activities, by which management will be able to judge its efforts.

In the event of a strategy presentation, for which the company may be charged, management should make five demands upon the presenting firm:

1. Any presentation should detail precisely those variables perceived most critical to the valuation of companies in the company's industry.
2. A presentation should explain how those variables were identified, verified and prioritized.
3. A presentation should explain the objective of any proposed strategy in the context of these variables.
4. If a proposed strategy is based on variables other than these valuation criteria, how were the other variables determined and how are they relevant?
5. What will be the expected result of proposed strategy, specifically in terms of stock price?

Management should be prepared to demand service from its outside financial communications firm. Executives should demand a monthly and quarterly summary of activities, complete with explanations of each activity's significance. They should make certain they understand the communications firm's perception of the value of such activities.

The management of an emerging company may balk at an underwriter's suggestion to retain outside services. The cost may seem prohibitive. The ability to measure results may seem unclear. Executives may choose, at best, to delegate part-time authority for cash flow communications to a senior corporate officer. At worst, they may elect to do nothing. It is a mistake.

Management may believe operating results speak for themselves. Executives may think that investors already have an adequate understanding of the company. They may believe it is a waste to use excessive amounts of executives' time to determine and to clarify investors' perceptions.

This appears to have been the case with many of the top 100 performing over-the-counter companies cited in the May 1986 issue of *OTC Review* magazine. A majority of them had no organized cash flow communications program. One nationally syndicated financial columnist mused that managements of these companies made discovery of their companies' returns potential very difficult for investors. In other words, executives in these companies heightened their own information deficiency and pricing inefficiency. They penalized their personal net worth and shareholders' wealth.

There is no question that operating results speak. But they only tell about the past and lend no perspective to the future. Perception of the future is what matters most to investors. Management's interest in focusing more on the past than on the future in discussions about the company heightens investors' perceptions of estimation risk and uncertainty. Investors require higher returns to bear higher perceived risk. And if they perceive lower risk in alternative investments of equal expected returns, they will sell a company's stock. Selling pressure only contributes to potential neglect and information deficiency.

In general, executives may be skeptical of the equity valuation process. They may believe that only they know the true value of their company's equity and that Wall Street opinions to the contrary be damned. That perspective is short-sighted. Executives can isolate reasons for valuation differentials by systematically talking to their stock. They can identify breakdowns in the valuation process and implement cash flow communications programs to shape clear perception of their companies' cash-generating abilities and returns potential. Executives who understand the equity valuation process can affect the market's pricing mechanism by affecting market-wide returns expectations. They have the ability to translate economic value into market value.

6

Sending Signals to Wall Street

This chapter concerns the information content of management decisions and actions. Executives shape investors' perceptions of a company's business strategy, competitive advantage and future cash-generating ability in two ways: words and actions. Both send information signals to Wall Street which may alter market-wide returns expectations. Each may affect a company's market value.

Empirical evidence of abnormal returns (relative to expected returns) suggests that active investors anticipate information generating events. Stock prices reflect their impact both before and swiftly after they occur. Within a brief period surrounding corporate announcements of earnings, dividends, etc., share prices adjust to reflect the impact that new information has on the returns generating process. This adjustment eliminates excess returns.

Talk is a relatively inexpensive option with which to try to affect the market's pricing mechanism. In direct contact with investors, managements use words to shape perception of future earning power. Executives discuss economic assumptions which underlie estimates of their company's sales and earnings growth rates, returns guidelines which dictate their investment decisions, capital structure targets which streamline their financing decisions, and productivity and efficiency goals which motivate their operating decisions.

Management's speaking opportunity begins in pre-offering road shows. Visits to investing institutions offer a chance to shape perception of returns potential. And they offer a forum in which to highlight the maturity of management. The occasion for ongoing dialogue continues in presentations by management in one-to-one meetings, investment seminars and conferences, annual meetings and shareholder reports. For managements of high growth/high returns emerging companies, there is much to talk about. The challenge is to find those who can not only understand and appreciate the company's story but who can also afford to own its securities and lead others to do the same.

Management should approach these speaking opportunities very seriously. Stream-of-consciousness, technical jargon or technical detail presentations are a mistake. They divert attention from those matters of most importance to lead investors: market opportunities and competitive advantages. Poor presentations pose a real threat to management credibility and to market value. They waste investors' time and make executives look foolish and uninformed about growth and profitability issues. They generate no enthusiasm for or belief in the company. And potential lead investors think, if management cannot crisply articulate the company's future earnings opportunities and returns potential, why should they bother to consider it.

The intent of management's spoken word is to clarify market-wide returns expectations. The goal is to maintain a stock price that fairly reflects expected returns relative to alternative investments of equal risk. In that sense, an audience that attends a management presentation can serve as the equivalent of a valuation focus group.

Executives should always compile a list of attendees. The list helps management to define the company's equity product in terms of its potential customers. It also offers a built-in perception measurement tool. Follow-up telephone conversations will reveal investors' perceptions, reactions, concerns, opinions, conclusions and attitudes about the company's story or its management. Responses better equip executives to focus on those variables others perceive most critical to valuation of the company.

Executives can expect that four types of management actions have information content. Earnings announcements (the results of operating decisions), financing and financial policy decisions, investment decisons and decisions which alter corporate control through changes in organizational structure, or ownership structure send signals to Wall Street.

Finance theorists often conduct (time series) "event" studies to measure market efficiency and the "information content" of management signals. I refer to several of these studies in this chapter. I offer them as guidelines for executives in their efforts to anticipate share price reaction to their decisions.

Information content has been defined in terms of price as "a change in expectations about the outcome of an event." Defined in terms of volume, "the change must be sufficiently large to induce a change in the decision-maker's behavior."[1] In other words, changes in a stock's price suggest changes in market-wide returns expectations. But changes in share volume suggest changes in a narrower band of individuals' expectations.

The relationship between price and volume is such that if all investors had the same risk preferences, volume would imply a lack of consensus among investors about price. But investors' risk preferences vary. And volume does not necessarily imply a lack of consensus on price.

Event studies usually use sample periods spanning many years and sample sizes covering many companies. They analyze the magnitude of stock price changes (investor response) and the speed with which those changes occur in the months, weeks or days surrounding corporate announcements relative to other weeks of the fiscal year. A management action which contains information should have a greater magnitude of impact on a share's price and volume in the week of the action than during other weeks of the year.

Abnormal positive or negative returns (i.e., stock price changes) surrounding an announcement, relative to levels of normal expected returns, equals the actual change in share price minus the expected change. Expected change can be measured in two ways. First, from Chapter 5, [(alpha) plus (beta times the market's change)] equals the expected change (during times of normal trading). A stock's actual change over a forecast period minus this calculation of expected change equals abnormal returns. Second, using the capital asset pricing model, expected return equals [(the risk-free rate of return for the announcement month)] plus [(beta) times (the market rate of return for the month) minus (the risk-free rate of return)]. The first term is the annual risk-free rate of return divided by 12. The market rate of return for one month is the percent market index change over a month plus the market's monthly dividend yield.

OPERATING DECISIONS: EARNINGS ANNOUNCEMENTS (ANNUAL AND INTERIM)

This section is particularly important to managements because it concerns earnings announcements. Positive information contained in reported earnings attracts dominant sponsors and popularity flows. Managements may anticipate their reactions. To reflect this significance, I will begin with conclusions relevant to creating investor demand:

1. The unexpected content of management announcements moves share prices up and down.
2. Investors react to both the sign (positive/negative) and the size (small/large) of the unexpected information.
3. Market response to quarterly and annual earnings reports of small capitalization companies is greater and lasts longer than that of large capitalization companies because of information deficiency and less information availability.
4. The information environment for all companies is most efficient at year-ends. It is a prime financial advertising opportunity.
5. Investors react to the earliest information about earnings (preliminary earnings releases).

Chapter 8 examines analyst behavior relative to earnings forecasts: the information content of forecasts, the accuracy of analysts' forecasts of annual earnings relative to the fiscal quarter in which they are made, the timing of changes in analysts' forecasts, and the relative accuracy of management and analyst forecasts.

In terms of annual earnings announcements, empirical studies have found and executives can expect that annual earnings announcements have information content. Significant changes in consensus expectations about companies' prospects, and hence significant changes in their share price and share volume, occur in annual earnings announcement weeks. One study examined accounting income numbers for December 31 reporting companies between 1957 and 1965.[2] It found a positive correlation between the sign of the error in income forecasts and the sign of abnormal returns (abnormal performance index) associated with the error.

For example, positive abnormal returns over a 12-month period prior to and including the month of annual earnings release for companies with positive income forecast errors (earnings underestimated) were 7.1 percent. Negative abnormal returns over the same period for companies with negative forecast errors (earnings overestimated) were -9.3 percent. Knowing only the sign of earnings changes 12 months before their announcements, an investor could have earned a positive abnormal annual return of 8.3 percent by going long stocks with positive income forecast error signs and short those with negative signs.

The study also found that investors had largely anticipated these companies' earnings. Due to the availability of interim information (for the large capitalization New York Stock Exchange companies in the sample), all but about 10–15 percent of the information in announcements of unexpected earnings had been anticipated by the month of the announcement.

The same study mentioned in footnote 1 also reviewed the magnitude of price changes for 143 non-December 31, non-dividend announcing New York Stock Exchange companies. It found that in the week of annual earnings announcements the magnitude was 67 percent higher than the average during nonreport periods. It also found that mean volume was 33 percent larger than mean volume during nonreport periods. When adjusted for market influences, volume was still 30 percent higher than during nonreport periods and about 40 percent higher than mean volume in weeks prior to the announcement week.

Another study examined 1,200 annual earnings announcements from 397 companies (mostly New York Stock Exchange) randomly selected from Value Line between 1977 and 1979.[3] It found that the magnitude of unexpected earnings and company size were associated with the information content of annual earnings announcements. It showed that the greater the absolute value of earnings surprises, the greater the volume of trading around announcement dates. It revealed that trading reaction was greater for smaller companies than larger companies. It also demonstrated that earnings announcements for small non-December 31 reporting companies generated a greater increase in trading volume (i.e., investors' expectations may be less accurate or their certainty lower) than for large NYSE, December 31 reporting companies. Other studies have found that price and volume reactions seem greatest the day before and the day of annual earnings announcements (see Morse in the bibliography).

For example, the study revealed that unexpected trading volume increased around announcements of annual earnings. Median trading volume percentage was 0.0933 over a three-day period surrounding announcement dates versus a 0.0725 nonannouncement median level). Three-day volume reaction was greater for non-NYSE than NYSE companies, regardless of whether they were December 31 or non-December 31 reporting companies (0.0216 versus 0.0128 and 0.0241 versus 0.0222 respectively). Finally, unexpected trading volume was greater (negatively related) for non-December 31 reporting companies, which tended to be smaller than December 31 companies, regardless of whether they were NYSE or non-NYSE companies (-0.2268 versus -0.2034 for NYSE and -0.2189 versus 0.0618 respectively for non-NYSE).

Markets react to the size of forecast errors for annual earnings. A study examined 276 New York Stock Exchange companies with complete histories of security returns from April 1960 to March 1975.[4] It found a positive correlation between the size of the error in annual income forecasts (mean forecast error) and the size of unsystematic annual abnormal returns associated with the error (rank correlation of .98 and .94).

For example, the mean unsystematic portfolio return (similar to the abnormal performance index mentioned above) on 25 portfolios in one model with 2,652 observations rose smoothly from 0.1751 percent (mean forecast error of -1.5478, mean portfolio beta of 1.4766) to 0.2916 percent (mean forecast error of 1.8508, mean beta of 1.3747). In another model with 2,667 observations, it rose from -0.1355 (mean forecast error of -1.6506, mean portfolio beta of 1.5277) to 0.1886 (mean forecast error of 1.4821, mean beta of 1.3675). Trading reactions (volume) around annual earnings announcement dates also varied directly with the magnitude of unexpected earnings (forecast error) and with company size.

Turning to quarterly earnings, studies of the usefulness of interim earnings concern their role in stock selection and forecasting (discussed in Chapter 8). For example, unexpected interim earnings changes are associated with excess returns around announcement dates. And successive quarterly reports enhance the predictive accuracy of estimates of annual earnings.

Empirical studies have found that quarterly earnings reports have information content and that a positive correlation exists between the sign of interim earnings changes and the sign of abnormal returns associated with them. One study[5] reviewed the announcements of 69 New York Stock Exchange companies between 1946 and 1974. With no assumptions about the sign of earnings, it found a positive cumulative average residual of 0.0162 for all four quarters. In 21 trading days up to and including quarterly earnings announcements, average residuals were 0.0184 for the first quarter, 0.0166 for the second, 0.0197 for the third and 0.0104 for the fourth quarter. Half of the market response occurred the day before and the day of the announcement.

Assuming a direction for earnings, the study found positive (negative) abnormal returns over 60 trading days prior to and including the announcement of quarterly earnings in the *Wall Street Journal* for companies with positive (negative) forecast errors. Positive abnormal returns (earnings underestimated) were 2.13 percent for all four quarters combined. They were 2.67 percent in the first quarter, 1.56 percent in the second quarter, 3.12 percent in the third quarter and 1.11 percent in the fourth quarter. Negative abnormal returns (earnings overestimated) were −3.26 percent for all four quarters combined. They were −3.59 percent for the first quarter, −3.59 percent for the second, −3.45 percent for the third and −2.43 percent for the fourth quarter.

The study also found that the sign of interim earnings changes in successive quarters helped to explain the size and sign of annual abnormal security returns. For example, a 12.9 percent cumulative annual positive abnormal return was associated with four quarters of positive earnings changes. A 3.9 percent positive return was linked to three positive and one negative quarter. A −1.11 percent return was related to two positive and two negative interim earnings changes, a −7.4 percent return for one positive and three negative quarters and a −16.2 percent return was associated with four quarters of negative earnings changes.

Other studies have also found the content of quarterly earnings announcements to be informative and that the size of abnormal returns is positively correlated with the size of unexpected interim earnings changes. One reviewed the sign, magnitude of earnings forecast errors and market size of companies that reported results within one month of the close of their fiscal quarters over a 36 quarter period between third calendar quarter of 1971 (a low of 618 companies) and the second quarter of 1980 (a high of 1,496 companies in the first quarter of 1980).[6] It found that a significant portion of total abnormal returns, about 35 percent, occurred the day prior to and the day of quarterly earnings announcements. In addition, only about 50 percent of the information in these announcements was anticipated before the announcements were made.

The study also revealed that cumulative excess returns persisted for several months after quarterly announcement dates. Ninety-day post-announcement returns of 4.3 percent were reported for companies with the largest positive unexpected earnings. Returns of −4 percent were reported for those with the largest negative unexpected earnings. Another study found an average abnormal return of 4-5 percent could be earned over a quarter if end-of-quarter earnings were known at the beginning of the quarter.[7]

The size of abnormal trading volume is also associated with the size of unexpected quarterly earnings. One study examined 900 first, second and third-quarter earnings announcements from 195 companies (mostly New York Stock Exchange) between January 1977 and March 1980.[8] It found a positive correlation between the absolute value of unexpected quarterly earnings (the difference between actual reported earnings per share and Value Line earnings per share forecasts divided by the Value Line forecast) and the magnitude and duration of trading volume around announcements of those unexpected earnings.

For example, the median daily increase in announcement period trading (three-day period centered around announcement dates) was 0.0227 percent in first quarters, 0.0274 percent in second quarters and 0.0227 percent in third quarters. When fourth quarter and annual earnings were announced together, another study (see Hagerman/Zmijewski/Shah in the bibliography) concluded that the information content of fourth quarter earnings announcements was greater. It also helped to explain market reaction to annual earnings announcements.

The study mentioned in footnote 8 also found that the percent of shares traded over a three-day period centered on the quarterly earnings announcement date for 230 companies reporting positive unexpected earnings less than 6.7 percent was 0.0088 percent. It was 0.0176 percent for 224 companies reporting positive unexpected earnings between 6.7 percent and 16.7 percent, 0.272 percent for 226 companies reporting unexpected earnings between 16.7 percent and 42.9 percent, and 0.0496 percent for 228 reporting positive unexpected earnings greater than 42.9 percent.

The same study found a positive correlation between company size (market capitalization) and magnitude and duration of trading volume surrounding announcements of quarterly earnings. Small capitalization companies on average generated larger percentage increases in trading volume around their quarterly earnings announcements, which lasted longer, than large capitalization companies.

For example, the median daily increase in percent of shares traded over a three-day period centered around the quarterly earnings announcement date for 225 companies in the largest market capitalization quartile (the difference between a company's market value and the median market value of all firms in the sample) was 0.0111 percent. It was 0.0193 percent for 233 in the medium-large quartile, 0.0302 percent for 226 in the medium-small quartile and 0.0629 percent for 224 companies in the smallest market capitalization quartile. In addition, the duration of the trading reaction (volume) was longer for small companies (about four days) than for large companies (about two days).

Many studies have been conducted on the announcement timing of management actions. The "timing effect" of corporate announcements (early/late announcements about good/bad news relative to the timing of prior years' earnings) breeds market reaction. The popular belief is that announcement dates vary with company profitability. Good earnings reports (positive deviations from consensus) may be accelerated from expected announcement dates and bad reports (negative deviations from consensus) may be delayed beyond expected dates. Conclusions about the size of this effect differ.

One study reviewed the announcement timing of 297 New York and American Stock Exchange companies with December 31 fiscal year-ends (3,564 observations).[9] It found that five-day average return residuals for good news firms were 0.83 percent versus −0.97 percent for bad earnings news companies. Price reactions to reports published earlier than expected (three to four days ahead of the prior year's schedule for quarterly reports and one week for annual reports) were larger than those for reports published on time or later than expected. Five-day average return residuals were 0.43 percent, 0.27 percent, and 0.16 percent respectively.

These results persisted regardless of whether the earnings announcement was unexpectedly good or bad or moderately good or bad, was annual or quarterly or came from a large or small capitalization company. Other studies have found an inverse correlation between reporting lag times and size of company capitalization. They found greater reactions to earnings announcements from small capitalization companies than those for large capitalization companies.

Other findings were that five-day cumulative average return residuals for bad news/early reporting companies were 0.79 percent. They were −1.13 percent for bad news/on time companies (more bad news is announced on Mondays or Fridays than other days) and −1.02 percent for bad news/late reporting companies. Residuals for good news/early reporting companies were 1.39 percent (reflected in the distribution of positive mean market returns in the first two weeks of calendar quarters two, three and four on average over 55 years—see Penman 1987). They were 0.45 percent for good news/on time companies and 0.54 percent for good news/late companies.

Another study perused interim announcements (1,743 observations) and annual announcements (584 observations) for 100 randomly selected New York Stock Exchange companies between 1970 and 1976.[10] It confirmed that the magnitude of average abnormal returns (before transactions costs) over a 20-day holding period was 1 percent for short sales of stocks which reported later than their expected quarterly reporting date and for long positions in those which reported earlier than their expected reporting date. Returns were greater for small capitalizaton companies and were positively related to the length of reporting delay. Results suggested that investors did not fully anticipate pending bad news when companies reported earnings later than expected.

One study examined 68 instances of earnings estimates by officials of December 31 companies between 1968 and 1970.[11] It found that investors react to the earliest earnings-related announcements. Trading reactions from individual investors in the week of announcements of pre-audited preliminary earnings estimates resulted in a 47 percent increase in the weekly average of daily percentage of shares traded relative to the average of 16 weeks prior to the announcement. In contrast, when management estimated earnings, reaction in the week in which the estimate was made showed a 51 percent increase in the weekly average. Only a 1 percent reaction occurred in the week in which preliminary earnings were released after management's estimates versus 6.5 percent if management's earnings estimate announcement weeks were deleted.

On an aggregate market level, trading strategies surrounding announcements of earnings estimates generated abnormal positive returns. Knowledge of earnings estimates five days before their public release resulted in 1.61 percent abnormal positive return for annual estimates versus 0.31 percent after estimates were announced. Abnormal positive returns were 1.48 percent for quarterly estimates versus 0.31 percent after estimates were announced.

Earnings per share numbers hold no magic, in and of themselves, as a means of influencing shareholder response. Studies have shown that investors are not fooled by accounting changes which alter the appearance of financial statements and state reported income differently (manipulate earnings) but which have no effect on a company's future cash-generating ability. These changes take many forms from shifts in accounting policies to capital structure changes. Policy shifts seem to be initiated by companies with poor operating records and thus, on balance, send negative signals.

Research has shown that, on average, the market may react positively in the very short-term around the date when a company announces earnings inflated by a change in accounting treatment. But it reacts negatively in the long-term. One study reviewed 332 New York and American Stock Exchange companies[12] reporting increases in earnings from such moves as adopting the flow-through method of accounting for investment tax credit or switching to straight-line depreciation. It found that any positive market reaction to these reported earnings seemed to be neutralized by the end of the immediate subsequent fiscal quarter. By that time, it became apparent that the companies could not sustain their cash-generating abilities.

Investors react negatively, however, to accounting related disclosures which reflect poor quality of earnings. For example, announcements of financial statement revisions result in negative abnormal returns. Those which reduce realizable asset values are associated with larger two-day abnormal negative returns and larger prediscovery stock price declines than releases concerning the impact of fraud, mistakes, or failure to disclose transactions in financial statements (see Kellogg in the bibliography).

Abnormal negative returns surround qualified opinions from auditors. They occurred three to six months before announcement date in the annual report or Form 10-K. The information content at announcement date was small (see Dodd/Dopuch/Holthausen/Leftwich). However, media disclosures of qualified opinions in the *Wall Street Journal* or on the *Broad Tape* resulted in three-day negative abnormal returns of -4.7 percent (see Dopuch/Holthausen/Leftwich). Finally, auditor changes which included disagreements with auditors produced a negative market reaction (-7.55 mean residual) in the week of Form 8-K filing with the SEC (see Smith/Nichols).

Earnings numbers may not be magical but forecasts of earnings breed investors' response. I review empirical studies of the information content and accuracy of analysts' and management's forecasts in Chapter 8.

Finally, of most importance to the managements of emerging companies, stock price change and volume reaction seem inversely tied to the frequency of information availability. The information content of annual earnings announcements (measured by volume and price changes) seems inversely related to both the amount of interim information available between those announcements and the size of announcing company (market capitalization). One study examined annual earnings announcement dates between 1960 and 1964.[13] It found that the mean and median information-content measures for over-the-counter companies in the week of annual earnings announcements were 2.596 and 1.066 respectively versus 1.282 and 0.454 respectively for New York Stock Exchange issues.

New York Stock Exchange companies tend to have many outlets for dissemination of interim information (between announcements of annual earnings). They relay information through shareholder reports, analyst reports, industry journals, offering prospectuses, etc. As gauged by the number of their interim news announcements appearing in the *Wall Street Journal* (a proxy for the amount of information available from all sources), over-the-counter companies have fewer information pipelines. As a result, the information content of annual earnings announcements of OTC companies in the week of and on or about the actual date of annual earnings announcements is greater than that of NYSE companies.

Studies in the early 1970s confirmed that market efficiency in the shares of over-the-counter companies was weak, that today's share prices essentially bore no relation to tomorrow's prices. However, later studies concluded that market efficiency for OTC companies was semi-strong relative to the information content of their annual earnings announcements. This is significant to communications strategy (discussed later) for emerging companies.

Abnormal price changes and trading volume seem to surround management communications with shareholders. One study reviewed these communications for 120 randomly chosen British companies with share price data available between 1974 and 1979.[14] It found that abnormal return residuals averaged across all companies in the sample tended to be greatest in the week of preliminary earnings estimate announcements, 0.0683, 0.0642, and 0.0641 percent in three successive years. They were next largest in the week of release of interim results, 0.0510, 0.0482, and 0.0562 percent and third largest in the week of annual reports (0.0476, 0.0486, and 0.0501 percent). Residuals were smallest in the week of annual meetings (0.0356, 0.0372, and 0.0378 percent). Annual meetings seemed to possess less information content, probably because they followed on the heels of annual reports.

Another study examining market reaction to shareholder reports 34 American Stock Exchange companies between 1961 and 1968.[15] It found that these reports, both annual and quarterly, carried information importance in the week of their publication greater than that of an average week. And it revealed that the marginal information content (variance in returns) of annual reports on annual report announcement dates was greater for those companies who did not publish quarterly reports than for those who did publish them.

The issue of information content becomes especially interesting relative to a stock market anomaly called the "January effect." In 21 of the last 23 years, stock market performance in January has been consistently associated with high abnormal positive returns to investors. And in seven of 14 years in which the OTC composite index has increased in January, the monthly gain has foretold gains in the index for the entire year. In those years, January moves have comprised between 21 to 56 percent of full-year gains.

Explanations for this persistent year-end seasonality in stock prices vary. They include selling pressure on share prices to personal tax considerations (many institutional investors are tax-exempt). And they range from year-end cash needs associated with holiday gift giving or travel, to portfolio window dressing on the part of money mangers.

Professor Arbel of Cornell believes the inverse relationship between information quantity, quality, and acceptability and estimation risk explains the January effect.[16] He theorizes that the interim information deficiency surrounding emerging companies imposes investment costs on investors. But at the turn of each year, the information environment surrounding small capitalization companies strengthens. This is due both to managements' annual earnings announcements and media coverage of stock market winners/losers. Lower estimation risk leads to less dispersion in analysts' earnings forecasts. This leads to higher share prices in January.

For example, Arbel analyzed monthly changes in analysts' consensus estimates between 1976 and 1981 (about 60,000 observations). He found that the seasonal variance in earnings forecasts for popular stocks (followed by more than 15 analysts) was low in January (about 0.70) versus May (greater than 1.75) and December (about 0.75). But the decline in information deficiency was greater for neglected stocks (followed by only three to five securities analysts). January variance was about 0.97 versus a high in April of about 2.16 and a December variance of about 1.25.

The average January gain for highly researched S & P 500 companies was 2.48 percent. This contrasts with 4.95 percent for moderately researched S & P

500 companies and 7.62 percent for neglected S & P 500 companies. However, January returns for neglected non-S & P 500 companies were 11.32 percent, five times greater than the first category above.

The average January gain minus the average monthly return for the rest of the year was 1.63 percent, 4.19 percent, 6.87 percent and 10.72 percent respectively. The average January gain after adjusting for systematic risk was −1.44 percent, 1.69 percent, 5.03 percent and 7.71 percent respectively. In other words, the January effect was largest for companies with the most information deficiency (see also Lakonishok/Smidt in the bibliography).

The empirical results of these event studies suggest cash flow communications strategy for the managements of emerging companies plagued by too little market sponsorship and too much pricing inefficiency. The strategy is geared to attract sponsorship and to translate economic value into market value.

First, executives should manage the merchandising process. They should use their underwriters' securities analyst to the fullest extent possible. Merchandising reduces information deficiency surrounding announcements of the company's quarterly and annual earnings. Recall from Chapter 3 that the underwriter should be under contract to provide research coverage.

Executives should make certain that the analyst's written reports on each of the company's quarterly earnings announcements, especially in the third and fourth quarters, are widely distributed to the firm's brokers and clients. They should be sure that the analyst makes his or her full complement of calls to owners or prospective buyers of the company's shares and that the analyst refers management to those money managers perceived to be potential lead investors. Executives should make direct contact with current institutional owners of their shares.

Second, management should follow up on operating, financing and investment signals (discussed in succeeding sections) which contain unexpected information. These announcements carry unexpected implications, especially about expectations of the company's future net operating cash flows. Lead investors and dominant sponsors search for and are attuned to these signals concerning competitive advantage and returns potential, and the signals which offer management built-in opportunities to stimulate the equity valuation network.

Third, management should capitalize on environments of relatively greater information efficiency and lower estimation risk. These surround corporate equities at the end of calendar years (regardless of the company's fiscal year-end).

For example, Professor Arbel claims that 60 percent of all popular business magazines publish a list of stock market winners/losers only at year-end. And he contends that about 57 percent of all shareholders identified by the New York Stock Exchange are exposed to at least one year-end list. Exposure is believed greater for investors in higher income brackets.[17]

Managements of emerging companies should make certain that their companies are included in relevant year-end stock market lists pertinent to the company's industry, region, and size (sales, assets or employees). Executives should go so far as to check the editorial schedules of industry trade journals, business magazines oriented to emerging companies, and local metropolitan newspapers. They should also make certain that research directors and broker/analysts at small/major regional brokerage firms in the company's region are aware of the the company's stock market performance in the year just concluded.

Fourth, managements should try to capitalize on the relatively greater information content associated with quarterly and annual (especially non-December 31) earnings announcements for small capitalization companies. They should consider advertising annual earnings in one or two major investment publications and in industry trade journals, especially at the end of fiscal years. For companies with low coverage and institutional ownership, managements should consider a trade press strategy for quarterly earnings announcements. It is a means by which to create coverage of operating progress. It it is a source to which lead investors who do their own primary research turn for information about competitive positioning in growth markets. And it heightens the signal which dominant sponsors look for in their search for future earning power.

Management might also strategize and capitalize on the timing of its annual and quarterly earnings announcements. They might plan to make positive earnings announcements as early as possible, preferably before peer industry competitors make their announcements. The effect of their company's information may transfer to the share prices of other companies within the industry.

For example, management of Nynex Corporation (New York, NY) competes to report its numbers earlier than its competitors so that they will be read first by analysts at the more than 30 firms which follow the company. Executives allocate 10 working days after the end of a fiscal quarter to work up the company's operating numbers and 15 days to report them. Earnings releases jibe with the schedule of the chief executive officer, i.e., no conflicts. Upon release, executives distribute press releases and make personal contact with the 25 largest sell-side brokerage firm securities analysts to review highlights only. They prepare the chief executive officer for discussions with Wall Street within one week of the release of the numbers.

There is another reason to speed the release of earnings. One study of 75 companies in 10 standard industrial classification four-digit categories[18] found that earnings information has an intra-industry transfer effect. Earnings announcements have an impact on both the announcing company and non-announcing companies in the same industry, but have the greatest impact on companies with large percentages of their revenues in the same lines of business as the announcing company. The effect of information transfer from earnings release companies in the study produced two-day abnormal returns for non-announcing companies of 1.5 percent.

Early earnings announcements may not only affect the share prices of companies in homogeneous lines of business but may also draw the attention of industry information processors. This may occur, especially if the size and sign of earnings results vary significantly from expectations either for the industry or for peers. Therefore, executives should make certain that the information in those positive announcements is hand-delivered to Wall Street. Dominant industry information processors such as analysts, trade journals, and associations and money managers who own stock in the industry, according to Form 13F filings, should receive it.

The information transfer effect and the January effect were evident in price changes in the stocks of Massachusetts' thrift institutions in January 1987. As a group, thrifts' stock prices rose an average of 60 percent in 1986, versus an S & P 500 increase of 14.62 percent. At year-end thrifts' prices per share traded at about 86 percent of book values per share. Then two events sent strong signals to investors: annual earnings announcements and successful takeovers. The second signal was stronger.

Managements of companies that share fiscal year-end dates with their peer industry competitors may find that the information content of their annual earnings announcements is weaker than expected. A clustering effect around many announcements at the same time weakens information content. This is the case in the banking and thrift industries in which all competitors usually close their books on December 31. Therefore, the information content of positive annual earnings announcements for Massachusetts' thrifts was relatively indistinct. But the content of industry "take-outs" at impressive multiples to book values and earnings was very distinct.

A signal with the noise of a sonic boom was sent on January 12, 1987. Home Owners Federal Savings Bank (Boston, MA), in a white knight move, paid a price per share of 170 percent of book value per share and 28 times earnings for the stock of Union Warren Savings Bank (Boston, MA). Two weeks later Cooperative Bancorp of Concord (Concord, MA) paid a price per share of 160 percent of book value per share and 18 times earnings for the stock of Quincy Cooperative Bank (Quincy, MA).

The combination of takeouts and earnings revised consensus returns expectations and revalued thrift equities significantly. During January 1987, the average return (share price appreciation) in the common stocks of Massachusetts' 45 converted thrift stocks was 38 percent. By the end of January 1987, thrifts' prices per share traded at about 106 percent of their book values per share.

Fifth, regardless of when during the calendar year a company goes public, management is almost immediately offered an opportunity to send a returns signal to Wall Street. Quarterly earnings must be released within 45 days after the close of every fiscal quarter as a public company. Management should use this occasion to establish lines of communication with lead investors and dominant sponsors.

Some managements think they can regulate market efficiency in their company's shares surrounding their company's quarterly earnings announcements. For example, in times of strong quarterly earnings comparisons, some executives release earnings on the earliest possible announcement date or in line with prior years' announcement timing but stagger publication of the good news in quarterly reports to shareholders. In an environment in which relatively little interim information on emerging companies may seem available, they believe the equivalent of a second announcement of a company's good news may strengthen the information content of its quarterly earnings announcement.

In times of weak quarterly earnings comparisons, some executives make earnings announcements in line with prior years' announcement dates but coincide publication of their quarterly reports to shareholders with their original earnings announcement date. They believe the equivalent of one announcement weakens any residue of negative information content associated with their bad news as much as possible.

The company's first annual earnings announcement and annual report to shareholders are major information opportunities for emerging companies. To maximize the information content of the announcement of their annual earnings, managements should again put their investment banker to work. They should expect a written research report on the company's results and prospects very soon after release of preliminary results and a follow-up report very soon after adjournment of the company's annual meeting.

In both instances, executives should expect maximum distribution of the report to the firm's brokers and to the analyst's commission-paying clients and prospects (potential lead investors). Executives should check to be certain that the analyst has made all of his or her calls to those investing institutions. And they should ask the analyst for referrals to those institutional money managers whom the analyst perceives to be potential buyers of the company's shares. It is to the advantage of both analysts and managements that executives conduct this merchandising check. Management can swap market intelligence with analysts. And follow-up can lead to new commission business for the analyst (and for his or her firm) and greater institutional share ownership for the company.

In addition, management should make personal contact with lead money managers who already own stock in the company. They should keep them completely current on the company's performance and returns potential. And they should ask them for referrals to analysts whom they perceive to be potential dominant sponsors for the company. Executives should make personal contact with current institutional owners and money managers who own large positions in the shares of industry competitors.

The annual report can become management's prime business strategy piece, a showcase of the company's earnings opportunities. But it is also an investors' scorecard. Lead investors compare management promises made in past annuals with actual results. A persistence of discrepancies reduces management credibility. Some companies, such as Lowe's Companies, Inc. (N. Wilkesboro, NC), use them to make securities analysis a redundant exercise. They indulge in heavy statistical work, both on an industry and corporate level. They facilitate intra-industry comparisons and estimates of changes in present values among competitors.

An annual report's focus should always be on the future. It should concentrate on the nature of the company's competitive advantage, management's plans to use that advantage to the benefit of shareholders, and the expected end-result of the plan to capitalize on the advantage (shareholder value). Some companies, such as Quaker Oats (1985 annual report) and Libbey-Owens-Ford, now Trinova (1983 annual report), devote extensive time to their philosophy and approach to creating shareholder value. Before preparing an annual report, management should review prevailing industry trends and central issues of immediate concern to investors with their underwriter's industry securities analyst. The annual report should address these issues.

The corporate information committee of the Financial Analysts Federation (New York, NY) offers help in annual report preparation. It evaluates and publishes a review of annual reports of companies in about 20 industries. The publication, at cost, offers an annual report checklist.

Post-annual report critique sessions are also helpful exercises. Arranged over lunch with a dominant sponsor (industry securities analyst) or lead investor (shareholding institutional investor), they are the equivalent of a valuation focus group. They offer an opportunity for management to receive direct and immediate feedback about the content, direction and usefulness of the company's annual report. And they offer management a chance to strengthen its one-to-one relationships with key members in the company's valuation network.

Immediately after an initial public offering, managements of emerging public companies usually get barraged by vendors of all sorts of information dissemination related services, such as mailing lists and financial advertising outlets. The obvious question is, which are worth their price. The answer is, not many. Only those on which lead investors rely for information about competitiveness and dominant sponsors rely for information about reported earnings should be considered. Management should ask money managers and securities analysts which sources they use for information signals about future growth and profitability. No vendor's services substitute for one-to-one relationships. They are most important in the equity valuation process.

FINANCING AND FINANCIAL POLICY DECISIONS

Empirical studies show and management can expect that investors will respond negatively to announcements of sales of corporate securities. One study[19] summarized the results of many other academic studies on the topic. It reported that average abnormal negative two-day announcement period returns surrounding the voluntary sale of corporate securities were: (-3.14) percent for the sale of common stock by 155 issuers, (-2.07) percent for the sale of convertible bonds by 73 issuers, (-1.44) percent for the sale of convertible preferred stock and about (-0.19) percent for the sale of either straight preferred stock by 53 issuers or straight debt (-0.26) percent by 248 issuers. Recall from Chapter 5 that over one decade managements preferred external financing of debt and internal financing of equity. The sale of minority equity interest (equity carve-out) in a wholly-owned corporate subsidiary by 76 issuers was the only instance of positive abnormal returns. Five-day announcement period returns surrounding a public offering of these securities were 1.8 percent.

Several general hypotheses have been offered to try to explain the pattern of investors' responses to corporate financing decisions. First, the optimal capital structure hypothesis suggests that investors react negatively to changes in the liability structure of a company's balance sheet which alters a company's optimal financial structure and firm value. Second, the implied cash flow theory suggests that financing decisions contain information about management expectations for future levels of net operating cash flows.

Third, the unanticipated announcements hypothesis implies that stock prices adjust in proportion to the unpredictability of the content of financing announcements. Fourth, the information asymmetry theory contends that corporate managers have more information about the intrinsic value of corporate equity. They are likely to sell overvalued securities and buy undervalued stock or sell debt intead of equity (see Myers/Majluf in the bibliography). And fifth, the ownership changes hypothesis suggests that decisions which alter corporate control affect share prices.

In the case of public stock offerings, both the optimal capital structure relevance (and irrelevance) hypotheses cannot adequately explain negative average abnormal returns. In contrast, the implied cash flow theory suggests that investors may associate the need for cash inflow from the sale of securities with smaller than expected future net operating cash flows. And, the unanticipated announcement hypothesis contends that the unpredictability of new equity issues (versus debt issues) is directly related to the unpredictability of corporate earnings (versus the predictability of debt service).

In addition, the information asymmetry theory implies that the extent to which management's information about intrinsic value is perceived to be better than investors' information, the greater investors' sensitivity to perceived changes in company value suggested by public offerings. This inference holds even though the proceeds may be directed towards high growth/high returns investment opportunities. And, finally, the corporate control theory suggests that transactions which dilute ownership concentration lower share prices.

These hypotheses take on meaning in the real world of Wall Street. For example, the choice of department of an investment banking firm which hosts a management presentation sends signals to investors about a company's future. Investors cue on research or corporate finance. If the research department of a company's underwriter is the sponsor, then customers expect a briefing on the cash-generating ability of its business strategies. But if the corporate finance department hosts management, investors expect a public offering in the near future (even though none may be planned). They pick up an implied cash flow or information asymmetry signal and often sell off the stock.

In the case of equity carve-outs, positive market reaction may also be tied to expectations of positive future operating cash flows and information asymmetry. For example, one study examined 76 equity carve-outs.[20] It found that in 94 percent of the cases, incentive compensation plans attached to the subsidiary's stock market performance were adopted. Recall from Chapter 1 that academic studies found positive market reaction surrounding announcements of both short-term and long-range executive compensation plan adoption. Several hypotheses suggest that plan adoption offers incentives to increase earnings more than expected. They also infer that managers are signaling their anticipation of unexpected positive earnings and want to pass incentive plans before earnings are announced. Finally, they imply that plans which increase management ownership contain information about future cash flows.

The relevance of these theories is that they emphasize management's need to talk clearly about business strategy and the reasons for executive decisions which directly shape investors' perceptions. For example, they must discuss financing decisions and the intended uses of the proceeds raised in financings. As this chapter shows, investors' reactions vary with management's decisions about capital allocation, capital structure, organizational structure, and ownership structure.

Sales of corporate securities which represent a change in financing policy are a cash signal. They suggest expectations of lower future net operating cash flows. The same study above found that two-day weighted average returns surrounding announcement of these changes were: −2.1 percent for 80 sales of convertible debt, −1.6 percent for 262 sales of common stock, −1.4 percent for 30 sales of convertible preferred stock, −0.2 percent for 221 sales of straight debt, and 0.1 percent for 102 sales of preferred stock.

Dividends and repurchases of corporate securities (discussed later) are also cash signals. In the case of changes in financial policy, price and volume effects surround dividend announcements. Dividends also send cash signals about implied changes in expected levels of future net operating cash flows. They thus affect investors' expectations and share price. As with earnings announcements, investors react to both the size and the sign (positive/negative) of the unanticipated content of dividend change announcements, not to the announcements themselves.

A previously mentioned study[21] summarized research into the information content of dividends. It found that two-day weighted average abnormal returns surrounding announcements of dividend increases were positive, implying increases in expected operating cash flows. They were: 3.7 percent for 160 initial dividend declarations, 2.1 percent for 164 announcements of specially-designated or labeled dividends (special, year-end or extra), and 0.9 percent for 280 unexpected increases in regularly paid dividends (more for unexpected resumptions of previously paid dividends).

Investors' reactions to unexpected decreases in regularly paid dividends were negative, implying expectations of lower future operating cash flows. Two-day negative abnormal returns were −3.6 percent for 48 decreases. And another study reviewed 129 companies in the midst of major shifts in dividend policy between 1971 and 1978.[22] It found that investors react more negatively to unexpected dividend decreases than positively to unexpected dividend increases. Two-day abnormal returns were: −9.6 percent for 32 large dividend reductions (mean decrease of 44 percent), −7.7 percent for 28 dividend omissions, 1.4 percent for 34 large dividend increases (mean increase of 52 percent) and 4.3 percent for 45 dividend declarations (22 initial and 23 resumed after one year of omission).

Another study perused 1,039 dividend changes for 668 New York Stock Exchange companies between May 1977 and February 1979.[23] It concluded that companies which increased their dividends generally experienced positive abnormal returns. But it found that those which increased their dividends but decreased their dividend payout ratio at the same time (reduced financial risk) achieved higher abnormal returns than those which increased both their dividends and their payout ratio (increased financial risk).

A Strategic Planning Institute study[24] found that dividend payout boosted the stock prices of high returns companies much more than those of low returns companies. Those with returns on equity of about 20 percent and payouts less than 25 percent commanded prices per share which were 149 percent of book values per share. When payout ratios rose above 40 percent, prices per share for high returns companies rose to 192 percent of book values per share.

In contrast, companies with returns on equity below 10 percent and payouts of 25 percent commanded prices per share which were only 60 percent of book values per share. When payout ratios rose above 40 percent, prices per share for low returns companies rose to only 66 percent of book values per share. As a corollary to this issue of financial risk, high interest coverage raises prices per share as a percent of book values per share. Low interest coverage lowers stock prices.

Bristol-Myers Company (New York, NY) has used financial policy changes (dividends and payout ratios) to send cash flow signals to investors for years. The company has paid a cash dividend every year since 1900. Since 1972, management has raised the company's dividend every year (coincident with 13 years of improved operating margins). Dividend growth has compounded at a 19 percent annual rate since about 1980 and a 17 percent rate since about 1975.

The company has achieved more than two decades of increased sales and earnings and profit margins have improved for 13 consecutive years (to 1985). Results for 1985 showed revenues up 6 percent to $4.44 billion and net income up about 12.5 percent, to $531.4 million, or $3.86 per share, from $472.4 million, or $3.45 per share.

In early 1985, management raised the company's dividend by 17.5 percent, to $.47 per share. The stock was then selling at its all-time high of $56.625 per share. In early 1986, management raised it again, by about 17 percent, to $.55 per share. The payout ratio rose slightly from about 13.9 percent to 14.5 percent.

Institutional investors and managers of index-programs picked up the signal loudly and clearly. Bristol-Myers's shares traded to an all-time high of $72 per share. Average daily volume increased more than 50 percent from 200,000 to 400,000 shares per day to 400,000 to 600,000 shares.

Finally, a 1981 study examined 76 dividend announcements made at least five days after the predicted date.[25] It found that dividend announcements made later than predicted confirmed investors' expectations of bad news. Results showed that the proportion of dividend decreases associated with late announcements was significantly greater than the proportion of dividend decreases associated with on-time announcements. It also revealed that the mean excess return on the expected dividend announcement date (though the announcement was made at least five days later) was about zero and that gradual declines in stock prices preceded late announcements.

Although the operating cash flow implications of the unexpected content of dividend increase announcements seem positive, many claim that cash dividends send negative signals. The contention is that cash diverted to dividend distributions reduces the amount available for cash reinvestment. By extension, cash distributions implicitly suggest that management cannot identify positive net present value reinvestment opportunities either inside or outside of the company with returns potential superior to alternatives of equal risk.

Cash dividends are a fixed operating cost. They are a far more expensive method of signalling than effective cash flow communications. But there are a few reasons why the signalling effect of dividends appeals to managers. First, dividends are a simple and regular cash event. Dividend payments assume a regular, four times per year, announcement schedule. They offer management a ready-made forum in which to shape investors' perception of business strategy and future cash-generating abilities. Investors come to expect quarterly cash signals from management. Second, they require that corporate executives put their cash on the barrel and their money where their mouths are to back up their expressions of confidence in their company's future.

In other dividend related decisions, announcements about stock dividends, stock splits, and reverse splits also have information content for investors. Studies associate positive returns signals with the first two and negative signals with the third. All are accounting maneuvers which, in and of themselves, have no effect on companies' cash-generating abilities.

The classic empirical study on the information content of stock splits was conducted in 1969. It examined up to 940 split announcements of New York Stock Exchnage companies over 60 months.[26] The conclusions were that splits tend to occur most often during periods of both rising stock markets in general and positive firm performance in particular. And investors react more to the anticipated dividend increases associated with stock splits than to splits themselves.

For example, in the 29 months prior to splits, average residuals were uniformly positive for all splits regardless of whether they were accompanied by dividend increases. Cumulative average residuals rose from 0.0062 to 0.3713. For decreases, cumulative average residuals rose from 0.0033 to 0.2730 in the month prior to the split and dropped to 0.2640 in the split month. The largest positive average residuals appeared over a three to four month period immediately before a split.

In the 30 months after splits, average residuals were randomly distributed. Cumulative average residuals rose steeply up to the split month but changed less than one-tenth of 1 percentage point in the first year after the split and less than 1 percentage point in the 29 months following a split. Cumulative average residuals for splits/dividend increases peaked at 0.3999 in post-split month 14 and drifted down to 0.3870 by month 30. Residuals for splits/dividend decreases dropped to a low of 0.1899 in post-split month 22 and drifted to 0.1946 by month 30. In other words, investors seemed to expect that dividend increases (confidence in future cash flows) would accompany stock splits. They were disappointed otherwise.

Another study reviewed 1,762 announcement events and 1,740 ex-date events.[27] Empirical evidence suggested that significant positive abnormal returns occurred on and around both the announcement dates and ex-dates of both stock dividends and splits. It implied that announcement and ex-date returns were larger for stock dividends than for stock splits. Mean three-day and five-day abnormal positive returns around stock dividends were 0.0186 percent and 0.0193 percent respectively for New York Stock Exchange companies versus

0.0255 percent and 0.0237 percent for American Stock Exchange companies. Mean three-day and five-day abnormal positive returns around stock splits were 0.0077 percent and 0.0144 percent for NYSE companies versus 0.0222 percent and 0.0268 percent for AMEX companies. Ex-date returns for both were, on average, larger than those for companies with cash dividends. Mean three-day and five-day abnormal positive returns were 0.0134 percent and 0.0178 percent respectively. But they were smaller for those companies which resumed dividend payments after three-year disruptions. Mean returns were 0.0218 and 0.0267 percent respectively.

In terms of risk, another study examined moving betas on 219 securities between 1945 and 1965.[28] It observed that average moving betas (systematic risk) for splitting securities were less than 1, regardless of whether dividends were increasing or decreasing. They tended to increase about 10 percent (.88 to about 0.97) in the year prior to split announcement months. In post-split months, average moving betas on split/dividend increasing companies tended to return to pre-split levels, about 0.85. It reflected confidence in the size of future operating cash flows. Betas on split/dividend decreasing companies tended to remain high (about 0.93), above normal levels over post-split months.

Managements traditionally believe that stock dividends and stock splits appeal to investors because they positively affect their shares' trading liquidity (up) and trading costs (down). Both actions increase the number of shares outstanding and the size of a company's float, shares available for public trading, by the proportion of the dividend or split. Executives believe that an increased supply of shares increases the volume of shares traded, thus improving liquidity. And they think that increased share volume narrows spreads in price quotes, between bid and ask prices, and thus lowers trading costs (spread as a proportion of stock price).

Results of academic studies, however, seem to contradict managements' traditionally stated goals in initiating either action. For example, one study of 25 splits between 1963 and 1973[29] found that they resulted in relatively lower liquidity. Post-split total dollar trading volume declined by about 20 percent, brokerage commissions rose an estimated 7 percent and the bid-ask spread as a percent of the dollar value of stock traded rose from a pre-split level (40 days before) of 4.95 percent to a post-split level (40 days after) of 6.79 percent.

Another study reviewed post-split liquidity of 181 companies between February 1972 and February 1977.[30] It found that liquidity (proportional post-split trading volume) for stock splitting companies declined significantly in the short-term, the month of distribution of split shares. It also revealed that liquidity was essentially unaffected by splits in the long-term. In contrast, liquidity for stock dividend-paying companies also declined in the short-term, though not as greatly, but also declined in the long-term. Neither action narrowed or widened spreads in share price quotes in the short or long-term.

Managements' primary rationale for reverse splitting a company's stock is to gain greater institutional investor acceptance. The belief is that a company with fewer shares outstanding and a higher proportional price will appeal to a broader audience of fiduciaries who may otherwise be precluded from buying and holding low-priced shares.

However, reverse splits induce significant negative investor response. One study examined all New York Stock Exchange and American Stock Exchange reverse splits between 1962 and 1981.[31] It found that they reduced a company's market value and its trading liquidity, and did not seem to draw institutional interest. Negative signals seemed to occur on proposal dates, approval dates and effective dates. Three-day abnormal negative returns centered around announcement dates were − 7.29 percent for proposals, − 9.89 percent for approvals, and − 2.09 percent on effective dates. Share prices seemed to fall more in the split month than in prior months and continued to fall after the effective date.

INVESTMENT DECISIONS

Unexpected changes in investment policy also send information signals to investors about management's confidence in a company's future earning power. Capital budget announcements have a "corporate finance" effect on market valuation. Market reaction to them varies directly with the size and sign (increase/decrease) of the announcement, especially in conjunction with the fundamentals of the industry in which a company competes.

One study reviewed 547 corporate financing announcements by 285 New York and American Stock Exchange-listed companies between 1975 and 1981.[32] It found that investors positively revalued equities in line with unexpected increases in capital spending. Two-day weighted average abnormal positive returns were 1 percent for 510 companies. Investors apparently capitalized the perceived net present values associated with the incremental cash investments. They negatively revalued companies in line with unexpected decreases in capital spending. Two-day weighted average abnormal negative returns were − 1.1 percent for 111 companies. Investors apparently perceived fewer positive net present value earnings opportunities. Studies also concluded that this investor response was in line with wealth maximization, versus size maximization, objectives.

The Strategic Planning Institute found that increases in capital budgets translated to higher market values for high returns companies than for low returns companies.[33] Those with returns on equity of about 20 percent and less than 8 percent annual growth in investment in capacity commanded prices per share which were 114 percent of book values per share. When annual growth in investment rose above 12 percent, prices per share of high returns companies rose to 183 percent of book values per share.

In contrast, companies with returns on equity of less than 10 percent and less than 8 percent growth in capital investment commanded prices per share which were only 57 percent of book values per share. When annual growth rates in capital investment rose above 12 percent, prices per share of low returns on equity companies rose to only 81 percent of book values per share.

Recall from Chapter 1 (footnote 2) that Professor Fruhan found similar valuation results. In a study of almost 1,500 companies, he found that those with returns on equity between 18 and 25 percent and rates of earnings reinvestment of 19 percent or less commanded median prices per share which were 140 percent of book values per share. When rates of reinvestment rose to 120 to 160 percent of earnings, median prices per share rose to 300 percent of book values per share.

In contrast, companies with returns on equity between 8 and 12 percent and earnings reinvestment rates of 19 percent or less commanded median prices per share which were only 40 percent of book values per share. When earnings reinvestment rates rose to 120 to 160 percent of earnings, median prices per share of low returns on equity companies rose to only 80 percent of book values per share.

The Strategic Planning Institute also observed that increases in research and development intensity (as a percent of sales) translated to higher market values for high returns companies than for low returns companies.[34] In its study, companies with returns on equity of about 20 percent and R & D as a percent of sales of 0.5 percent or less commanded prices per share which were 135 percent of book values per share. When (R & D/sales) ratios rose above 2.0 percent, prices per share of high returns companies rose to 202 percent of book values per share.

In contrast, companies with returns on equity of 10 percent or less and (R & D/sales) ratios of 0.5 percent commanded prices per share which were only 59 percent of book values per share. When (R & D/sales) ratios rose above 2.0 percent, prices per share of low returns companies rose to only 73 percent of book values per share.

Common stock repurchases are another cash signal concerning expectations about higher future net operating cash flows. Viewed once as a financing decision, corporate repurchase plans are now considered viable investment decisions. And market reaction to them is usually stronger than that to cash signals through dividends (see Offer/Thakor in the bibliography). Repurchased shares are usually designated for use in executive stock options, employee stock ownership plans, and potential acquisitions. Companies repurchased a total of about $45 billion in common stock in 1986 and about $8 billion within the first two months of 1987.

Corporate repurchase is perceived as a reasonable cash investment decision if managements' returns expectations exceed investors' expectations implied by the company's stock price. It is also reasonable if estimated costs of equity exceed expected returns on equity. Executives must weigh the cost of cash investment against the cost of releasing information which might correct market misperceptions and mispricings. If a share repurchase is authorized, net after-tax profit spread over fewer shares outstanding results in higher earnings per share and higher returns on equity.

One study examined various forms of corporate repurchases. For example, 148 intrafirm tender offers were initiated for an average of about 15 percent of the repurchasing firm's outstanding shares at an average premium above pre-offering prices of about 23 percent. They generated weighted average abnormal positive returns of 16.2 percent during a two-day period surrounding tender offer announcement dates.[35]

In contrast, share repurchases in 182 open market transactions were associated with two-day abnormal positive returns of 3.6 percent. General Motors' shares rose 4.7 percent in price within two days after a March 1987 announcement of its plan to repurchase about $5 billion of its shares in the open market. And 15 targeted repurchases of small holdings registered two-day abnormal positive returns of 1.6 percent.

The information asymmetry hypothesis is offered to explain stock market reaction to transactions which purely affect corporate capital (financial) structure. Empirical studies have found that abnormal returns surrounding transaction announcements explicitly associated with sources and uses of funds which alter a company's financial structure were the same as the sign of the leverage change associated with the alteration. The absolute value of abnormal returns increased as leverage changes increased. Changes implied management's positive or negative expectations for future profitability and financial risk.

In descending order of magnitude of positive reaction to leverage increases, 45 repurchases of common stock with the proceeds of the sale of debt securities generated abnormal positive returns over two-day announcement periods of 21.9 percent. Abnormal positive returns for 52 debt/common stock exchange offers were 14 percent. Those for 9 preferred/common stock exchange offers were 8.3 percent. Abnormal returns for 24 debt/preferred stock exchange offers and income bond/preferred stock exchange offers were 2.2 percent. Debt/debt exchange offers (36 transactions) or debt repurchases with proceeds from debt securities sales (83 transactions) had no leverage effect. Abnormal returns were 0.6 and 0.2 percent respectively.

In contrast, in ascending order of magnitude of negative reaction to leverage decreases, 57 calls of convertible preferred stock (resulting in the issuance of common stock) registered insignificant abnormal two-day returns of −0.4 percent. For 113 calls of convertible bonds (also resulting in the issuance of common stock) abnormal negative returns were −2.1 percent. Repurchase of debt with proceeds from the sale of convertible bonds generated negative returns of −2.4 percent in 15 transactions. Returns for 30 common stock/preferred stock exchange offers were −2.6 percent. Those for 12 repurchases of debt with proceeds from the sale of common stock were −4.2 percent. Negative returns for

9 preferred stock/debt exchange offers were -7.7 percent. And 20 common stock/debt exchange offers generated negative abnormal returns of -9.9 percent.

One study of 50 companies traded on the New York Stock Exchange and over-the-counter[36] offered a summary perspective on the impact of corporate events on stockholder returns. Two-day abnormal returns surrounding corporate announcements in the *Wall Street Journal* were: 0.436 percent for 70 dividend increase announcements; 0.231 percent for 71 product sales; 0.626 percent for 52 forecasts of positive earnings; -1.719 for 12 forecasts of negative earnings; 0.305 percent for 24 construction or building project announcements; 1.132 percent for announcements of stock splits; and -0.173 percent for announcements of labor strikes.

CORPORATE CONTROL (STRUCTURE AND OWNERSHIP)

One academic study defined the market for corporate control (the takeover market) as "the arena in which managers compete for resources to manage."[37] Empirical studies have found that corporate restructuring generally benefits shareholders (positive abnormal returns). They have also found that increases in ownership concentration generally raise stock prices while reductions in ownership concentration generally lower stock prices. Ultimately changes in corporate control tend to increase the combined market value of assets of target and bidding firms.

Mergers and divestitures are two prominent forms of organizational restructuring. Mergers are perceived as positive net present value investment opportunities. The present value of the resulting company's future cash flows is expected to exceed the combined market value of the bidding and target company. Gains from takeovers seem to stem from enhanced operating efficiencies in the form of lower production or distribution costs than from increases in market power in product markets or from eliminations of inefficient target managements. Those gains are only realized if target company assets are transferred to the bidding company.

One study[38] summarized the results of research on the effects of merger announcements on stock prices. It found that weighted average abnormal returns for target and bidding companies involved in attempted mergers over a two-day announcement period, a one-month announcement period and through merger outcome were: 7.72 percent for 339 target companies, 15.90 percent for 457 targets, and 20.15 percent for 282 target companies in successful mergers. They were 9.76 percent/200 targets, 17.24 percent/219 targets, and -2.88 percent for 188 target companies in unsuccessful merger attempts. Abnormal returns for bidding companies in successful mergers were -0.05 percent/358, 1.37 percent/784, and -1.77 percent/256. They were 0.15 percent/212, 2.45 percent/251, and −4.82 percent for 171 bidding companies in unsuccessful merger attempts.

These results suggest that about half of total abnormal positive returns surrounding merger announcements occurred before the attempts were announced. Target companies in successful mergers registered significant abnormal positive returns from merger announcement through merger completion. Target companies in unsuccessful merger attempts seemed to surrender all previously generated abnormal positive returns and to generate abnormal negative returns at the time a failed merger was announced. Bidding companies in successful merger attempts earned virtually no abnormal returns while bidding companies in failed mergers earned abnormal negative returns.

Management opposition to mergers harms shareholders. One study reviewed 151 merger proposals over a seven-year period ended December 31, 1977 (71 completed/80 cancelled).[39] It examined unsuccessful merger attempts, when management of 26 target companies opposed and terminated a pending merger proposal. It revealed that although cumulative abnormal positive returns were 11 percent over a 20-day announcement period, two-day abnormal negative returns for the target company surrounding the termination announcement were −5.57 percent. It also examined unsuccessful attempts in which managements of bidding companies terminated a pending merger. It showed that although cumulative returns were 0.2 percent over a 20-day period, two-day abnormal negative returns to target companies were −9.75 percent. These results suggest that managements of target companies which terminate pending mergers do not act in their shareholders' best interests and that target company share prices return to pre-offer levels when managements of bidding companies terminate mergers.

Divestitures are another form of organizational restructuring. They take the form of either spin-off, carve-out, or sell-off. The first establishes a new company from a parent company's existing assets in a tax-free exchange with shareholders. The second involves the sale of assets and is a complete taxable exchange of cash flows for cash. A sell-off may generate positive net present values to both buyer and seller. Both actions tend to receive positive investor response but abnormal positive returns around spin-off announcement dates tend to exceed those for sell-offs.

One study found that managements initiate spin-offs for one or combination of at least three reasons: greater focus of operations/product lines, greater ease of merger terms, and reduced regulatory interference (anti-trust).[40] They tended to initiate them after periods of positive investor perception, reflected in positive abnormal returns. In contrast, equity carve-outs create a new shareholder constituency. It often differs from that of the parent in investment objective, attitude and time horizon their growth/returns profiles differ.

Regardless of the reason for a spin-off, investor reaction to spin-off announcements seems positive. Cumulative positive abnormal returns were 3.4 percent for 76 transactions in one study.[41] And in carve-outs several valuation benefits may accrue to the parent company. The independent market value of a carve-out may enhance the market value of the parent. For example, Allied Signal's carve-out of the Henley Group was believed to have added about $5 per share to the shares of the parent, and as a defensive move, it may make the parent more expensive to buy.

Finally, the market may value the initial public offering of a business unit at a greater multiple to cash flow than an offering from the parent. Proceeds from the carve-out may represent a fresh source of new capital for the parent at less cost than directly available to the parent. This may spark a reassessment of capital strategies previously considered uneconomic. However, both the market value of the carve-out and its value as a percent of the parent corporation's market capitalization must be large enough to affect the parent.

Studies indicate that investor response to voluntary sell-off announcements is also positive. Sell-offs seem to follow periods of negative investor perception, reflected in abnormal negative returns. Both sellers and buyers perceive sell-offs as positive net present value transactions. Both earn similar cumulative abnormal positive returns around transaction announcements:[42] 0.7 percent for 279 sellers and for 118 buyers respectively.

Other types of corporate restructuring also benefit shareholders. Cumulative abnormal positive returns surround announcements of joint ventures (0.7 percent for 136 agreements), leveraged buyouts (30 percent for 81 transactions), voluntary liquidations (33.4 percent for 75 completions), and proxy fights (1.1 percent for 56 fights).[43] The study mentioned in footnote 41 found 1.2 percent two-day announcement returns and 8.2 percent cumulative returns to target company shareholders from two months before proxy announcement through election outcome regardless of result. Two-day outcome returns are higher if dissidents obtain seats.

The previously mentioned study above also found that changes in ownership (ownership restructuring) benefit shareholders in target companies of tender offers and seem not to penalize shareholders in bidding companies. It summarized the results of thirteen studies of the effects of tender offer announcements on stock prices. It found that weighted average abnormal positive returns to target companies in successful tender offers were 29.1 percent for 653 tenders versus 3.81 percent for 478 bidding companies. For companies involved in unsuccessful tender offers, the study found that weighted average abnormal returns to 283 target companies were 35.17 percent versus −1.11 percent for 236 bidding companies. Two-day returns to bidding companies in unsuccessful takeover attempts were positive regardless of whether termination was initiated by the target or the bidder. These results are consistent with the notion that takeovers are zero net present value transactions for bidders.

Positive abnormal returns to target companies in unsuccessful tender offers seem to reflect anticipation of follow-up offers. Once a company goes into play, the likelihood of a subsequent takeout is high. The same study above found that average abnormal returns (including announcement effects) over a two-year period beginning with the announcement month of the initial unsuccessful tender offer were 57.19 percent for 86 target companies which were subsequently tendered for. Abnormal returns were -3.53 percent for 26 which received no further tender offers.

The study also found that management opposition to takeovers benefits target company shareholders in successful takeovers but harms target company shareholders in unsuccessful takeovers. The average abnormal announcement month return to target company shareholders in 44 successful manager-unopposed takeovers was 16.45 percent versus 19.8 percent in 21 successful manager-opposed takeovers. These abnormal positive returns turned to abnormal negative returns if manager-opposed takeovers ultimately failed to result in takeover.

Management actions to terminate takeover bids which do not require shareholder approval generate abnormal negative returns to non-participating shareholders.[44] In one study, 61 targeted repurchases of blocks of previously acquired stock, averaging 11 percent of the repurchasing firm's outstanding shares, were made at an average of 9.8 percent premium to the market. They registered two-day abnormal negative returns around purchase announcements of -2.85 percent for single blocks (-3.8 percent one-month return). Three-day announcement returns for 21 repurchases associated with merger bid cancellations were -5.5 percent (-12.5 percent one-month return). They were -1.39 percent for 40 repurchases unassociated with merger cancellations (0.6 percent one-month return).

In addition, 41 targeted repurchases of single blocks of stock, averaging about 11 percent of total outstanding equity, were made at average premiums of 16.4 percent above pre-offer prices. These resulted in two-day abnormal negative returns on the purchasing firm's stock of -1.76 percent (-6.3 percent one-month return). Two-day announcement returns for 17 non-premium repurchases were -0.34 percent. Two-day negative abnormal returns on the repurchasing firm's stock of 34 companies which obtained standstill agreements were -4.52 percent. They were -4.04 percent for 19 companies entering standstill agreements unaccompanied by share repurchases. The above figures should be compared to the abnormal positive returns associated with intrafirm share repurchases mentioned earlier in this chapter.

Managements often take action to reduce the probability of takeovers with antitakeover amendments. On average, these actions seem not to decrease shareholder wealth. There is only weak evidence that they increase shareholder wealth.[45]

In general, changes in a company's state of incorporation seemed to be made after periods of superior performance. Abnormal positive shareholders' returns over a 24-month period prior to and including announcement month for 140 companies were about 30 percent. And managements' adoption of antitakeover amendments at 100 companies seemed to have no negative effect on shareholder wealth. For example, super-majority provisions, staggered boards, fair price amendments and lock-up provisions generated statistically insignificant abnormal negative returns of −0.16 percent over two days and −0.90 percent over 20 days surrounding proxy mailing dates. However, removal of previously adopted antitakeover amendments by 49 companies resulted in abnormal negative returns of −3.63 percent between board approval and proxy mailing date.

Securities and Exchange Commission studies tend to disagree about the effect of takeover provisions on shareholder wealth. One study examined market reactions to more than 600 companies adopting takeover amendments and 37 companies adopting poison pills between 1979 and 1985.[46] It found that average cumulative net-of-market stock returns surrounding proxy statement-signing dates (20 days before to 10 days after) were: −0.65 percent for fair price amendments proposed by companies with 29.7 percent institutional ownership, and 12.8 percent insider ownership and −2.95 percent for companies 25.7 percent institutionally held and 14.1 percent held by insiders.

In addition, market reaction was −1.31 percent for pure super-majority provisions for companies with 22.6 percent institutional and 16.6 percent insider ownership. It was −4.92 percent for super-majority board provisions in those with 16.5 percent institutional and 19.5 percent insider ownership. It was −3.67 percent for authorized preferred amendments (32.5 percent institutions, 8.7 percent insiders) and −1.29 percent for classified board provisions (40 percent institutions, 6.6 percent insiders). Composite results indicated abnormal negative returns of −1.25 percent for companies with an ownership breakdown of 28.6 percent institutions and 13.1 insiders. Two-day abnormal negative returns of 1.42 percent were found for those companies announcing poison pill provisions.

Interfirm equity ownership in the form of acquisitions of large blocks of stock (5 percent or more of another company's equity securities) tend to increase both acquiring company and target company returns.[47] Two-day abnormal returns (by type of outcome) to acquiring companies surrounding announcement of 13D filings (when no takeover attempt was announced) were: 2.04 percent for 43 completed takeovers (1.07 percent average total return); 1.50 percent for 39 targeted repurchases of shares (5.69 percent average total return); 1.48 percent for 47 instances in which shares were sold (5.10 percent average total return); and 0.87 percent for 45 third party takeovers (2.25 percent average total return).

Two-day abnormal returns to target firms were: 6.34 percent for 25 targets (21.10 percent average total return); 4.64 percent for 30 targeted repurchases

(1.69 percent average total return); 3.65 percent for 38 instances in which shares were sold (6.32 percent average total); and 2.46 percent for 30 third party takeovers (15.98 percent average total return).

Two-day abnormal returns (by type of outcome) to acquiring companies surrounding announcement of 13D filings (takeover attempt was announced) were: −0.59 percent for 136 firms (−0.30 percent average total return); −0.62 percent for 114 completed takeover attempts, close to zero net present value investments for acquiring firms, (−0.72 percent average total return); and −0.45 percent for 22 failed takeover attempts (1.83 percent average total return). Two-day abnormal returns to target firms were: 14.90 percent for 69 firms (16.35 percent average total return); 15.55 percent for 60 completed takeovers (17.69 percent average total return); and 10.56 percent for 9 failed takeover attempts (9.16 percent average total return).

In general, antitrust merger actions (complaints, convictions and merger cancellations) impose significant costs on shareholders in both target and merged firms. In addition, security regulations governing takeovers, such as the 1968 Williams Act and state antitakeover tender offer laws currently enacted in 22 states, increase average abnormal returns to target companies and reduce average abnormal returns to bidders. They reduce both the profitability of takeovers and the equity values of bidding firms. As of this writing, the Senate Banking Committee has approved "The Tender Offer Disclosure and Fairness Act of 1987." Its aim is to prevent "creeping tenders" and "street sweeps." It limits open market stock purchases to 25 percent before formal tender, extends tender offers to 35 days (now 20) and closes the 10-day window between 5 percent purchase and SEC notification.

One study reviewed returns to 47 target firms prior to passage of the Williams Act, 90 targets subject to the regulation, and 20 targets subject to both federal and state tender offer laws.[48] It showed that abnormal positive returns from 40 days before through five days after takeover announcement to the former were 22 percent, 40 percent and 35 percent respectively. It also studied returns to bidders in 28 unregulated offers, 51 federally regulated offers, and 9 offers regulated by both federal and state laws. Abnormal positive returns from 40 days before through 20 after takeover announcement were 9 percent, 6 percent, and 4 percent respectively.

Managements and registered exchanges often debate the issue of dual classes of common stock with unequal voting rights. Closely-held family-founded businesses use this method to raise capital in public markets without having to give any voice in the company's affairs to the buyers of those shares. According to the Securities and Exchange Commission and Deloitte Haskins & Sells, 14 companies created dual classes of stock between 1976 and 1982, another 14 did so in 1983, eleven in 1984, seventeen in 1985 and 9 in 1986.

Some state takeover laws create the equivalent of dual classes of voting shares to protect managements and employees of public companies within their borders at the expense of shareholders in those companies. For example, executives at Arvin Industries (Columbus, IN), who were threatened by takeover by the Belzberg Brothers of Canada, lobbied for passage of takeover laws in Indiana. And executives at the Gillette Company (Boston, MA), who were threatened with takeover by Ronald Perelman of Revlon, lobbied for enactment of Indiana's law. Antitakeover laws establish "many share, no vote" precedents. They destroy the "one share, one vote" system, the cornerstone of the nation's capitalistic ideals and corporate democracy.

The Securities and Exchange Commission (office of the chief economist) conducted a 1987 study of the market reaction to this phenomenon. It found that shareholders in companies considering the adoption of dual classes of stock did not want to reduce the possibility of takeovers at higher prices. The study also found two-day announcement abnormal negative returns of -0.93 percent for 92 companies which announced dual class recapitalizations since 1976 (34 of which announced recapitalizations after March 1986). It appeared that dual classes of stock with unequal voting rights reduced shareholder wealth.

As of this writing, it is unclear whether state antitakeover laws will truly discourage takeover attempts, though Congress seems willing to let state laws preempt the Williams Act. It worked in one case. Ohio legislation was hastily enacted to protect Ohio companies from unwanted takeovers. The legislation was viewed negatively by free market supporters and was "dubbed the management entrenchment act."

It was introduced during the takeover attempt of Goodyear Tire and Rubber Co. at $49 per share by Sir James Goldsmith. Goodyear ultimately bought back his 11.5 percent position in the company's stock in a targeted premium repurchase at $49.50 per share ($618.8 million) and initiated a self-tender at $50 per share for another 36.5 percent of its outstanding equity. The company's stock unenthusiastically traded up $1.25 per share to $43.

It may not work in the Gillette case. As of this writing, Revlon has made three runs at the company. The first was a $4.12 billion takeover attempt at $65 per share initiated on November 14, 1986. It resulted in a November 24 targeted repurchase, at a $2.875 per share premium over market price, of Perelman's 13.9 percent position in Gillette's stock at $59.50, with a standstill agreement. At the announcement, the company's stock fell $10.75, from $56.625 to $45.875 per share. The last two approaches were rejected by Gillette's board. But Revlon seemed undeterred.

Distributions of stock also constitute ownership restructuring. Investors' react negatively to secondary stock distributions. The response is related to implied expectations of lower future operating cash flows and information asymmetry rather than to any price pressure effect. These distributions are associated with permanent reductions in stockholder wealth. Two-day abnormal negative returns associated with 146 registered secondary offerings were found to be -2.9 percent (-1.53 percent cumulative 11-day return). They were -0.8 percent for 321 non-registered secondaries (-3.96 percent cumulative 11-day return).[49]

One study examined daily data on 345 secondary distributions between July 1961 and December 1965.[50] It found that distributions usually occurred after periods of positive abnormal returns. It also revealed that investors' response was most negative to sales of stock by company officers. Negative abnormal returns were -2.9 percent for 23 observations over a 20-day period surrounding distribution and seemed to continue to build up to 18 months after distribution. Negative returns for mutual funds and investment companies were -2.5 percent for 192 observations over a 20-day period. Reaction was mildly negative for short periods to sales by individuals (-1.1 percent for 36 observations over a 20-day period). It was also mildly negative to sales by trusts or estates (-0.7 percent for 50 observations over a 20-day period) and banks and insurance companies (-0.3 percent for 31 observations over a 20-day period).

Market statistics indicate that repurchases, mergers, acquisitions and divestitures set a record pace of activity with record value in 1985. A total of 3,001 transactions were valued at an all-time high of $179.6 billion. In 1984, a total of 2,543 deals carried a market value of $122.2 billion. A record of 128 deals in 1985 was valued at more than $100 million, up from 87 in 1984. And 36 transactions in 1985 were valued at $1 billion or more.

The cumulative effect of corporate restructuring in recent years on the nation's supply of capital stock has been startling. The Federal Reserve System annually measures the amount of capital raised in new stock sales and the amount retired in various corporate transactions. In 1983, the value of new stock sales exceeded the value of retired stock by approximately $31 billion. In 1984 and 1985, the Federal Reserve estimated that the value of retired stock exceeded the value of new stock by about $72 billion and $77 billion, respectively.

Salomon Brothers, Inc. calculated that the value of equity capital stock removed from the market between 1984 and 1986 was a huge net $216.6 billion and was about $160 billion in 1986 alone. The positive effect of a shrinking capitalization on industry composites and stock market indices is the same as it is on a single company. Growth in book values accelerates and returns on equity increase. In times of more money chasing less stock, a liquidity-driven market, price appreciation of market indices apppears impressive. But bull market advances must be closely scrutinized. They may not be solely attributable to improved prospects for inflation, interest rates or future corporate earning power.

Management's words and actions send signals about executives' expectations for a company's future cash flows or their perception of intrinsic value. Words are cheaper than actions and therefore more desirable in any plan to communicate value to Wall Street. But actions speak louder than words and investor response to management signals is reasonably predictable. Executives' understanding of how their words and actions affect investors' perceptions and ultimately their company's share price better enables them to anticipate market response to their investment, financing and operating decisions. Open cash flow communications with dominant sponsors and lead investors about the reasons for those decisions facilitates translation of economic value into market value.

7

Lead Investors—Prioritizing Buying Power

Cash/assets ratios usually define institutional buying power. But portfolio economics governs money managers' purchases of corporate equities. Most investing institutions ($100 million or more in equity assets) devote the greatest amount of their research effort and time to the efficient sector of big capitalization companies. That sector offers both information (lower estimation risk) and liquidity. For example, *Business Week* data showed that as of March 31, 1986, an average of 166 institutions owned an average of 43 percent of the outstanding shares of each of the 1,000 companies with the largest market capitalizations (over $322 million).

The National Association of Securities Dealers offers ownership data on companies in several market capitalization categories traded over-the-counter on the National Market System (NMS). The data show that in 1986, institutional investors owned an average of:

Market Capitalization	Companies	Institutional Ownership
Less than $10 million	237	9 percent
$10 to $25 million	496	12.9 percent
$25 to $50 million	486	17 percent
$50 to $100 million	456	21.6 percent
$100 to $250 million	397	28.1 percent
$250 to $500 million	177	33.3 percent
Over $1 billion	35	45.7 percent

The data also revealed that 2,367 NMS over-the-counter companies (of a total of 2,695 NMS issues and 5,189 total NASDAQ issues) had at least one institutional holder of their shares. Collectively, institutions held a total of 55,595 positions in NMS companies at the end of 1986.

Research coverage and ownership of stocks in the nonefficient (weak form efficient) sector costs too much for managers of large pools of equity assets. The time intensity of analysis and investment decision-making must be measured against the potential of that analysis to yield portfolio returns at least in excess of the costs of research.

For example, Stephen Timbers, past director of research for Mutual Life Insurance Co. of New York, past vice president of MONY Advisors, Inc., and current chief investment officer of the Portfolio Group Inc., estimated (in 1977) an institution's cost of research coverage:

An organization managing $1 billion of common stocks might typically employ 12 analysts and have a research budget of $800,000. This group would follow the approximately 100 companies owned in the portfolios and 200 more that would be possible candidates, meaning about 25 companies per analyst [versus 11 per analyst in the top 25 brokerage firms in 1985]. Currently almost all of these 300 companies would enjoy relatively efficient characteristics as stocks.[1]

He supposed further:

A serious program of investing in non-efficient sector stocks [small capitalization companies] probably would entail a switch of 20 percent of the portfolio into these kinds of stocks. Because of the smaller market capitalization and the dearth of available information about these stocks, prudence would dictate holding a greater number of stocks in the new 20 percent of the portfolio than the old. I contend that this ratio would be at least three to one. The result would be a new portfolio of 140 stocks or 40 percent more and probably a comparable increase in the stocks followed but not held.[2]

Timbers put numbers on his hypotheses:

The complications are obvious. An analyst would now have to follow 35 instead of 25 stocks or the institution would have to hire another five analysts to maintain the same intensity of coverage as before. Since these newer companies would be more difficult to follow [because of less available information] than the efficient sector stocks, more travel, industry conferences, subscriptions, field work and perhaps specialized analytical techniques would be required. To be specific I estimate the cost of five analysts and necessary support today [1977] might run conservatively $250,000.[3]

Offsetting the incremental cost of adding analysts to an institution's research department is no easy task. Even in 1977 dollars, when Timbers's observations were made, an institution charging an annual half of 1 percent management fee to manage $1 billion in assets needed to earn an additional 5 percent return per year, or $50 million, just to cover the $250,000 cost. Yet common stock returns have only compounded at an anuual 9.1 percent rate since 1926. Consistently superior annual gains in portfolio performance would be required to fund and support an expansion in an institution's research coverage. An institution's performance burden would be unrealistic.

Research also suggests that the economics of trading in the shares of small capitalization companies for institutional investors is overwhelmingly negative. One study examined 180 issues from the Wilshire 5000 spread across several market capitalization groups.[4] It showed that market-makers' spreads increased sharply as a company's market capitalization decreased. It also revealed that the cost of trading in the shares of small capitalization companies increased significantly as the dollar value of trades increased.

The study established a matrix of market capitalization, block size (dollar value of trade), and trading costs (spread/price). In the matrix, companies with market capitalizations between $0 and $10 million had an average price of $4.58 per share. The spread/price cost in this category of trading stock valued at $5,000 was 17.3 percent. The cost of the same size trade in the shares of a company with a market value of $1.5 billion was 1.1 percent, or 15.7 times less. The costs of trading stock valued at $25,000, and $250,000 in this market value range were 27.3 percent and 43.8 percent respectively. The cost of the same size trade in a company with a $1.5 billion market capitalization was 1.3 percent, or a 22.7 times less.

Between $10 million to $25 million, the average price was $10.30 per share. The spread/price costs in this category of trading blocks of stock valued at $5,000, $25,000, $250,000 and $500,000 were 8.9 percent, 12.0 percent, 23.8 percent and 33.4 percent respectively.

Between $25 and $50 million, the average price was $15.16 per share. The costs of trading blocks of stock valued at $5,000, $25,000, $250,000, $500,000 and $1,000,000 were 5.0 percent, 7.6 percent, 18.8 percent, 25.9 percent and 30.0 percent. Between $50 and $75 million, the average share price was $18.27 per share. The costs of trading blocks of stock valued at $5,000, $25,000, $250,000, $500,000, $1,000,000 and $2,500,000 were 4.3 percent, 5.8 percent, 9.6 percent, 16.9 percent, 25.4 percent and 31.5 percent.

Between $75 and $100 million, the average price was $21.85 per share. The costs of trading blocks of stock valued at $5,000, $25,000, $250,000, $500,000, $1,000,000, $2,500,000 and $5,000,000 were 2.8 percent, 3.9 percent, 5.9 percent, 8.1 percent, 11.5 percent, 15.7 percent and 25.7 percent. Finally between $100 and $500 million, the average share price was $28.31. The costs of trading blocks of stock valued at $5,000, $25,000, $250,000, $500,000, $1,000,000, $2,500,000, $5,000,000 and $10,000,000 were 1.8 percent, 2.1 percent, 3.2 percent, 4.4 percent, 5.6 percent, 7.9 percent, 11.0 percent and 16.2 percent. The study's remaining categories did not apply to emerging companies.

Another study reviewed New York Stock Exchange companies with requisite bid-ask spread data between 1961 and 1980[5]. It found that liquidity (spread) had a highly significant impact on stock returns and thus, investment decisions. It showed that over the 20-year period monthly excess return on a stock with a 1.5 percent spread was 0.45 percent greater than the return on a stock with a 0.5 percent spread. However, it revealed that monthly excess return on a stock with a 5 percent spread was only 0.09 percent greater than the return on a stock with a 4 percent spread. In other words, returns on low-spread stocks were lower but more sensitive to changes in spreads than returns on high-spread stocks.

Several other portfolio constraints restrict some money managers from buying the shares of emerging companies. Investment policy and fiduciary responsibility may limit portolio exposure to companies on the basis of size of float and market capitalization. Other restrictions may be earnings record, whether the company pays a dividend or where a company's shares trade.

Avoidance of small capitalization companies by some investing institutions, however, is an important portfolio opportunity for lead investors. Research suggests that analyst concentration in the efficient sector of stocks offers opportunities for abnormal excess returns in the inefficient sector. Recall that results of the Goldman, Sachs study of the results of stock selection strategies mentioned in Chapter 2. Lead investors capitalize on neglected, small capitalization companies, those with little research coverage and low institutional ownership.

One study examined 510 New York and American Stock Exchange companies grouped by institutional holding between 1971 and 1980.[6] Professor Arbel et al. found a significant "neglected firm effect." It is a market anomaly in which, over time, investment in the shares of neglected companies generates risk-adjusted returns greater than investment in the shares of popular, widely-owned companies. For example, in the the decade 1971–1980, the study found the average annual return for institutionally neglected stocks was 20.8 percent versus 10.4 percent for those most widely held by institutions. Results for neglected and popular S & P 500 companies were 16.4 percent versus 9.4 percent respectively.

Arbel et al. determined that total risk (standard deviations of returns) increased with neglect, 0.337 for widely held stocks to 0.536 for neglected stocks. But systematic risk (beta) declined from 0.99 to 0.90. On average, portfolios of neglected stocks earned twice to four times the return per unit of risk than portfolios of popular stocks. And on a risk-adjusted basis, the average annual excess return on a portfolio of popular stocks was -0.0580 percent versus 0.0564 percent on a portfolio of neglected securities.

Arbel et al. also studied the relationship between neglect and company size. They found that a neglected firm effect persisted across all size groups of companies. But a systematic "small firm effect" was not evident. This is a market anomaly in which, over time, investment in the shares of small capitalization companies generates risk-adjusted returns in excess of investment in the shares of large capitalization companies.

In other words, all measurements of risk (systematic, unsystematic and total) declined as company size rose. Mean beta factor was 1.24 on small company portfolios versus 0.70 on large company portfolios. But risk was largely unaffected by changes in institutional holdings. On the other hand, returns rose as institututional holdings decreased. They increased from 0.147 percent to 0.201 percent on portfolios of small companies. They rose from 0.086 percent to 0.173 percent to 0.260 percent on portfolios of medium-sized companies. And they lifted from 0.109 percent to 0.232 percent on portfolios of large companies. Arbel et al. concluded that small firm effects may be a reflection of neglected firm effects rather than vice versa.

Small firm effects seemed to disappear when excess returns were measured relative to an equally weighted market index. They fell from 0.0314 percent to 0.0098 percent to -0.0532 percent as company size decreased. But neglected firm effects seemed to persist as risk-adjusted excess returns rose as neglect increased (institutional holdings fell) and popularity decreased. They increased from -0.0612 percent to 0.0029 percent on portfolios of small companies, from -0.0793 percent to -0.0073 percent to 0.116 percent on portfolios of medium-sized companies, and from -0.0404 percent to 0.1020 percent on portfolios of large companies.

Liquidity and trading costs aside and abnormal returns potential considered, the importance of small capitalization companies to institutional portfolios seems to be rising. A Wharton School of Finance study examined market values of companies as a percentage of the market value of total portfolios. It found that between 1979 and 1985 the percentage of over-the-counter companies held in institutional portfolios rose from about 5 percent to about 8.5 percent.

The importance of institutions is also clear in NASDAQ trading volume. In 1986, volume was 28.7 billion shares (19.7 billion shares of NMS issues). About 41.8 percent of that volume occurred in block transactions the average size of which was 20,469 shares. The average share price of an NASDAQ issue was about $13.25 versus an average price about $38.50 per share on the New York Stock Exchange through mid 1986.

Institutional ownership of emerging companies has grown primarily for diversification and liquidity reasons. Institutions have allocated portions of portfolio assets to investment in small capitalization companies for diversification purposes. Pension funds have directed portions of their equity assets to "small cap" money managers also for diversification. Growth in equity mutual funds (especially sector funds) has increased available cash for investment. And liquidity (trading costs) in actively traded over-the-counter markets has been comparable to listed exchanges. Management should measure the extent of institutional interest or neglect in its company's shares by those yardsticks used by Professor

Arbel mentioned in Chapter 1. It is a basis for concern about trading costs, information costs, and pricing inefficiency.

Chapter 2 discussed the impact of diversification on portfolio risk. Recall that finance theory claims that portfolio managers only get compensated for bearing nondiversifiable, systematic, market-related risk. The systematic risk of their portfolios varies in proportion to market risk (beta) and with portfolio exposure to unexpected changes in macroeconomic variables such as industrial production, inflation, interest rates and competing yields. Money managers do not get compensated for bearing company-specific risk because portfolio diversification can virtually eliminate it.

For purposes of perspective on adequate portfolio diversification in this book, I assume that money managers set an average maximum ownership limit of 2 to 3 percent of a company's outstanding equity securities. Purchase of 5 percent or more requires Securities and Exchange Commission apprisal in a Schedule 13D or 13G. In the document, the manager must specify the intent of the investment, for investment purposes only, for additional future purchases of the issuer's stock or for takeover. I assume most money managers prefer to avoid this filing. By extension, I assume that 5 percent ownership is a threshold of potential portfolio concentration (lack of diversification) which they also prefer to avoid.

Ownership limits can, of course, vary. Equity mutual funds, for example, may limit portfolio positions to 10 percent maximum ownership of any class of securities of any single company. However, a position of such size in a small capitalization company, by virtue of risk and illiquidity, is viewed as a passive long-term investment. But limits should enable money managers to achieve the highest risk-adjusted returns while maintaining portfolio liquidity and flexibility.

Money managers usually set ownership limits in terms of actual shares as a percent of a company's outstanding stock or of average trading volume over a specified period as a percent of shares outstanding. Guaranty Trust Company of Canada (Toronto, ON), for example, which managed total assets of $889 million in 1985, limits exposure to 2 percent maximum ownership. And Fred Alger Management, Inc. (New York, NY), which manages about $3 billion in pension assets, owns no positions in the shares of one company larger than eight days' trading volume.

Managers of large actively or passively managed, diversified portfolios of equity assets (billions of dollars in market value) often diversify to such an extent that the dollar value of the average positon is usually a very low percentage of total portfolio assets. An average figure per position between 0.002 and 0.005 percent of total managed assets is realistic. The dollar value of the average position in actively or passively managed, concentrated portfolios varies with the degree of concentration. It is usually a much higher percentage of total portfolio assets.

I use the nation's top 50 money managers in 1983 to illustrate portfolio diversification. They managed total equity assets of $315.4 billion. In contrast, in 1985, the nation's top 10 money managers alone managed equity assets totaling $189.6 billion. In 1986, the top five managed $124.6 billion. The dollar value of the average portfolio among 1983's top 50 money managers was $6.413 billion. The average number of stocks held in each portfolio was 610. The average market value of the average portfolio position was $10.51 million and the dollar value of each average portfolio position represented 0.00164 (0.002) percent of the dollar value of the total portfolio.

If the 3 percent average maximum ownership limit is applied to the portfolios of 1983's top money managers, a $10.51 million average portfolio position equalled a 3 percent position in the shares of a company with a market value of $350.33 million ($10.51 million divided by 0.03). Therefore, on average, assuming a 3 percent top ownership limit, only companies with market values greater than $350 million would have been acceptable additions to an average 1983 portfolio.

Of the top 10 money managers among the top 50 in 1983, each managed equity assets of $10.46 billion on average. The average number of stocks in each portfolio was 885 and the market value of the average portfolio position was $11.82 million. The weight of the average position in any portfolio was 0.00113 percent. In this case, the 3 percent rule limited investment choice, on average, to those companies with market values greater than $394 million ($11.82 divided by 0.03).

Of the bottom 10 money managers among the top 50 in 1983, each managed equity assets of $4,090.25 billion on average. The average number of stocks held in each portfolio was 352 and the market value of the average portfolio position was $11.62 million. The weight of the average position in any portfolio was 0.00284 percent. Threshold market capitalization for acceptable companies began on average at $387.33 million.

Liquidity minimizes trading costs and contributes to portfolio flexibility. These are two bonafide concerns of money managers. Professionals want to be able to "get in" or "get out" of a company's securities on a "real time" basis. They do not want to receive or pay relatively exorbitant discounts or premiums (eighths and quarters of points) from last sale bid or ask prices per share to trade stock.

Measured as a percent of share price, these discounts/premiums from last sale prices are a trading cost. Illiquidity manifests itself especially when selling stock. Traders at brokerage firms will buy a piece of a seller's block of stock to wrap up and to "work" a portfolio manager's sell order. But even this can produce a down stock in an up market. It can destroy an orderly market in the trading of a company's shares, shrink potential portfolio returns, or induce money managers to avoid these relatively more costly shares completely. Illiquidity is an origin of neglect and inefficient pricing.

Liquidity requirements and systematic risk objectives often conspire against small capitalization companies. Money managers of actively managed portfolios with growing assets face a portfolio diversification problem. Fewer companies are available in which investment can remain at or under maximum ownership limits. As a result, managers must raise the market capitalization threshold below which they can realistically commit capital.

Assuming the number of portfolio positions and maximum ownership limits remain constant, portfolio size alone can "crowd out" emerging growth companies from actively managed portfolios. An inverse relationship exists between assets under management and opportunities for investment. Managers of the smallest equity asset bases can make investment choices from the largest number of available companies. They can invest in large or small corporations. As assets increase, however, investment opportunities decrease. Managers of the largest equity asset bases make investment choices from the least number of available companies. They can invest only in large capitalization companies which offer liquidity and meaningful position sizes.

There are three parameters to consider: size of assets under management, weightings of average portfolio positions and maximum ownership limits. These highlight portfolio diversification or concentration. Portfolios with increasing (decreasing) assets under management, increasing (decreasing) weighting per average portfolio positions, or average weighting which represents decreasing (increasing) maximum ownership limits must concentrate (diversify) assets in relatively fewer (more) securities.

It was mentioned earlier that the dollar value weighting of the average position in the portfolios of 1983's top 50 money managers was 0.00164 percent of the dollar value of the total portfolio. If both ownership limits and portfolio weightings are held constant across changes in portfolio sizes, the number of companies available for investment increases as portfolio size decreases. The following example is illustrative only. It is unrealistic in that portfolio position weightings may vary significantly over time and across portfolios.

For example, assume that both the top limit of 3 percent ownership of a company's common stock and the 0.00164 percent average portfolio position weighting are held constant in a portfolio. With $25 billion in equity assets under management, the size of an average portfolio position will be $41 million ($25 billion multiplied by 0.00164). Threshold capitalization of companies for portfolio investment will begin at $1.367 billion ($41 divided by 0.03).

Portfolio assets of $20 billion will maintain average positions of $32.8 million. Money managers can invest in companies with market values no less than $1.093 billion. A portfolio of $15 billion will average positions of $24.60 million and invest in companies capitalized by the market at $820 million or more. Assets of $10 billion will establish average portfolio positions of $16.4 million and seek companies greater than $547 million in market value. A portfolio of $5 billion will keep average positions of $8.20 million and buy shares in companies with market values no less than $273 million.

An asset base of $1 billion will oversee average positions of $1.64 million and invest in companies with market values of $54.7 million or more. Portfolios of $800 million will keep positions which average $1.31 million and buy companies with minimum market values of $43.7 million. Money managers with $500 million under management will average portfolio positions of $820,000 and look for companies with market values which start at $27.3 million. Finally, port-folios with $100 million of equity assets will average positions of $164,000 and invest in companies with minimum market capitalizations of $5.47 million.

If the number of portfolio positions is held constant across changes in portfolio size, the result is the same inverse relationship. Stephen Nesbitt, senior associate of Wilshire Associates, Inc. (Santa Monica, CA), made the point clearly. He claims:

The "typical" institutional equity firm [in 1983] manages approximately $800 million and holds roughly 50 stocks. As a result $16 million ($800 million divided by 50) must be invested in every common stock the manager purchases. For liquidity purposes, managers would avoid holding more than 2 percent to 3 percent of a company's outstanding shares. Using the 3 percent maximum holding as a rule of thumb, the smallest company this equity manager can invest in has a market value of $533 million ($16 million divided by .03). Using this capitalization requirement would restrict the "typical" manager to the largest 640 stocks.[7]

Although the actual universe of publicly traded issues exceeds 26,000, Nesbitt segmented 5,000 actively traded companies into six groups by size of market capitalization. At the time of his study, the top group of 500 companies ranged in market value from $61.3 billion to $676 million. The second group of 500 companies covered market values from $676 million to $250 million. The third group of 500 spanned values from $250 million to $125 million. The fourth group of 500 included companies with market values of $124 million to $69 million. The fifth group of 500 companies ranged from $69 million to $42 million. And at the time, the bottom group of 2,500 companies incorporated those with market values of $41 million to zero.

The number of companies available for investment shrank dramatically under the stated portfolio conditions: 50 stock holdings per portfolio and 3 percent maximum ownership of a company's outstanding shares in any single position. For example, a successful money manager with $100 million in equity assets under management had the most choice. He or she could have invested in companies with minimum capitalizations of $67 million ($100 million divided by 50, divided by 0.03). There were approximately 2,000 companies from which to choose according to Nesbitt's study.

A firm managing three times the assets would have almost halved its invest-ment choices. With $300 million equity assets, a money manager must have invested $6 million on average ($300 million divided by 50) in every common stock position. When the smallest investable company had a market value of $200 million ($6 million divided by 0.03), the number of available companies slipped to 1,200 from 2,000.

A manager overseeing $500 million in equity assets would have cut his invest-ment alternatives further. On average, $10 million must have been invested. But market values for the smallest companies which could have been considered rose to $333 million. There were only 860 companies available. An asset manager with $800 million under management would have had $16 million on average to invest. And the smallest investable company would have had a minimum market value of $533 million. The choices were among 640 companies in Nesbitt's universe.

The trend worsened. A portfolio manager with discretion over $2 billion would have had, on average, $40 million to invest in every common stock purchased. Threshold market value would have started at $1,333 billion. No more than 275 companies would have fit the bill. Finally, portfolios with $5 billion or more in equity assets under management would have had the least choice. Up to $100 million, on average, must have been invested in every new portfolio position. Market value of the smallest companies began at $3,333 billion. There were only 95 companies, in Nesbitt's study, from which to choose.

In real life money management, size of assets, average portfolio position weightings and ownership limits usually do not remain constant over time or across broad bases of equity assets. They vary significantly. Variance depends upon whether a portfolio is diversified or concentrated, actively or passively managed, performance (growth) or price (value) oriented, aggressive or defen-sive.

The implications of the inverse relationship between asset size and investment opportunities for pricing inefficiency are great. Potential information deficiency about and pricing inefficiency in a company's shares increases as a company's market capitalization decreases. This occurs for two reasons. First, fewer institu-tional portfolios can own enough shares of a small capitalization company (with-out approaching or exceeding 5 percent ownership) at a satisfactory trading cost to meaningfully contribute to a portfolio's overall total return performance. And, second, fewer information processors compete for information about excess returns in small capitalization companies because fewer investing institutions demand it, i.e., no popularity flow.

The irony of this inverseness is that high excess risk-adjusted returns are usually available in the shares of those public companies which suffer from information deficiency and pricing inefficiency. For, example, one market anomaly, called the "small firm effect," was mentioned earlier in this chapter. Simply stated, over time, small capitalization companies offer opportunities for risk-adjusted returns in excess of those available in large capitalization companies. Between 1926 and 1981 common stock returns ran at an annual compound rate of 9.1 percent. But return on the common shares of small capitalization companies, in the bottom quintile of the New York Stock Exchange, ran at an annual compound rate of 12.1 percent.

Small capitalization companies tend to outperform the overall market in good market conditions but tend to underperform the market in bad conditions. Research indicates that there have been 34 up-market years and 16 down-market years since 1933. In up markets, annual returns on the Standard & Poor's 500 stock index averaged 22.4 percent, compared with a 35.3 percent return for small capitalization companies. In down markets, the S & P 500 fell an average of 11.1 percent a year, compared with a 13.1 percent drop for small companies. When grouped into 10 five-year periods, average annual compound returns for small capitalization companies beat the S & P 500 seven times.

This relationship does not always hold true. Big capitalization stocks outperformed small capitalization stocks in 1984 and in 1986. In 1984, for example, risk-free Treasury bills returned 9.9 percent to investors, the S & P 500 achieved a total return of 6.1 percent, the largest 500 companies achieved a total return of 5.5 percent and the smallest returned −9.4 percent. In 1986, the NASDAQ composite gained 7.36 percent versus a gain of 14.62 percent for the S & P 500, and a gain of 22.58 percent for the Dow Jones Industrial Average.

On both occasions, however, small capitalization issues staged comebacks in the new year (as predicted by the January effect). The relative ratio of the price/earnings ratio of the T. Rowe Price New Horizon Fund to the P/E ratio of the S & P 500 is considered a signal of market turns in small capitalization companies. The ratio fell from 2.16 in June 1983 to about 1.35 in November 1984. At that time, emerging growth stocks turned up. And they roared back in January 1985. The NASDAQ industrials gained 12.7 percent versus 7.4 percent for the S & P 500. In January 1987, the NASDAQ composite was up more than 12 percent in the first 10 trading days. And as of March 1987, the NASDAQ composite had risen by about 25 percent.

Capitalizing on pricing inefficiencies in the non-efficient sector of stocks can heat up a money manager's portfolio. Money gets "hot" when quarterly portfolio performance is consistently superior to that of pre-selected or broad market indices, such as the Standard & Poor's 500-stock index. Hot money is most impressive in bull markets. Managers are usually venturesome or aggressive. They buy performance in the securities of low yield, high P/E, above-average beta, small capitalization companies. Superior performance attracts millions of dollars in new equity assets such that managers of small pools of equity assets can quickly find themselves managing big funds. The experience of the fund managers at Fidelity Investments (Boston, MA) is a good example.

But the inverse relationship between portfolio size and investable companies becomes a problem for hot money managers. Money flows into hot funds faster than it can reasonably be invested in the shares of high growth/high returns emerging companies. Cash builds faster than it can reasonably be put to work. Portfolio diversification becomes more difficult. Potential portfolio concentration in fewer securities poses a very real portfolio performance problem because those fewer positions are usually in larger capitalization companies with relatively more modest returns potential. As a result, a hot portfolio's total return tends to moderate and hot money cools.

Fidelity Investments's Over-the-Counter (OTC) Fund was hot in 1985 and in the first quarter of 1986. It is a small company performance fund which used a stock-picking approach to maximize total return on share price appreciation. Its portfolio was diversified and actively managed. In 1985, the mutual fund's total return rose 69 percent. That ranked it very highly among the 768 mutual funds monitored by Lipper Analytical Services. It was up another 14.1 percent between January 1 and March 16, 1986. These results compare to a 1985 increase in total return of the S & P 500-stock index of 31.57 percent, and a first quarter of 1986 gain of another 13.72 percent.

Superior performance, coupled with Fidelity Investments' marketing muscle, catapulted fund sales. Amounts in excess of one million and up to several million dollars per week flowed to the fund. The fund began with $2 million in assets in January 1985, grew to about $81 million in equity assets by October 1985, and to $162 million by January 1, 1986. Its asset base jumped to $300 million by February and to $460 million by the week of March 10, 1986. Assets under management had increased almost 185 percent in less than three months. By June 1986, the fund's assets had increased to $946.5 million, a more than 10-fold increase in eight months. By November 1986, net redemptions had lowered the fund's assets to $659 million.

As Fidelity's OTC Fund grew, it faced the irony of its investment success. "When you have 50 or 75 stocks in the fund it's one thing," said Paul Stuka, portfolio manager of the OTC Fund, "but when you have to have 300 or 350 it gets a lot harder."[8] As equity assets rise, continuous portfolio diversification becomes more difficult. A portfolio manager may literally be unable to either invest new cash fast enough or to find enough high growth/high returns performance companies in which to even invest to positively affect portfolio performance. Ironically, at this point of rapid portfolio asset growth, the whole premise on which a portfolio's superior performance was based begins to undermine its success. Closing a fund to new sales is the only way to retain the opportunity to earn superior risk-adjusted returns in small capitalization emerging companies.

I use the specifications offered above by Stuka to measure the impact of portfolio concentration on market capitalization thresholds. Assuming portfolio diversification among 300 positions at the start of 1986, the value of the OTC Fund's average position would have been $540,000. The weight of the average portfolio position would have been 0.0033 of total portfolio assets. By June 1986, the $946.5 million OTC fund was diversified among about 550 positions. The dollar value of the average position size was $1.72 million and the weight of the average portfolio position was 0.0018 percent of total managed assets.

Assuming 300 portfolio positions and an average limit of 3 percent ownership of the outstanding shares of any portfolio company, the market value threshold in January 1986, below which, on average, the OTC Fund could make no investment, was $18 million ($540,000 divided by 0.03).

By February 1986, the numbers had changed against the portfolio's fast fund sales-generating manager. He was no longer able to invest in a broad array of emerging companies. With $300 million under management, assuming 300 portfolio positions, the dollar value of the average position was $1 million. But the average market capitalization threshold had increased to $33.33 million. When the fund's assets rose to $462 million, opportunities for investment contracted further. The size of the average position increased to $1.54 million and the portfolio's average market value threshold rose to $51.33 million. By June, the minimum market value threshold, with about 550 positions, was $57.33 million.

In contrast, if the OTC Fund's $162 million in assets (as of January 1, 1986) had been concentrated in only 50 positions, each position would have averaged $3.24 million. Constant portfolio weighting per average position would have been 0.02 of total portfolio assets. The market value threshold below which, on average, the OTC Fund could make no new additions to the portfolio, would have been $108 million. At the $300 million level in equity assets, the dollar value of the average position would have been $6 million and the average market capitalization of portfolio additions would have begun at $200 million. When assets reached $460 million, portfolio positions would have averaged $9.2 million per holding and market value barriers would have risen to $306.67 million. And at $946.5 million and 50 portfolio positions, average portfolio size would have been $18.93 million while market capitalization thresholds would have risen to $591.33 million.

In recent years, portfolio managers have tried to contend with this portfolio concentration challenge. They have allocated a portion of their total managed assets, sometimes as much as 20 percent, solely to investment in the shares of high growth/high returns small capitalization companies. In essence, they have created mini-"small cap" equity funds within larger diversified portfolios. This strategy has enabled them to capitalize on the positive abnormal returns potential available in the shares of small capitalization companies (the small firm effect) within a portfolio broadly concentrated in medium to large capitalization issues.

For example, Value Line, Inc. manages money in addition to publishing investment advisory publications. It controls nine mutual funds with assets estimated, in mid-1985, at $1.4 billion. It also oversees another $1.2 billion for pension and profit-sharing accounts. That brings total assets under management to approximately $2.6 billion.

Value Line allocates slightly more than 10 percent of that total asset base to investment in small capitalization companies. As of January 1986, it invested $330 million of clients' funds in its "Small Capitalization Program." It was a diversified and actively managed portfolio which used a market-timing approach to maximize total return on share price appreciation. Market values of portfolio companies ranged from $10 million to $250 million. As of April 1986, more than 5,139 actively traded public companies fit into this market capitalization category. Value Line restricted its universe of small capitalization companies to about 2,000. The portfolio never had less than 100 positions.

According to these statistics, the maximum weight per average portfolio position in Value Line's "Small Capitalization Program" was 0.01, or 1 percent, of the total portfolio. The maximum average market value of the maximum average position was $3.3 million ($330 million divided by 100 minimum positions). Assuming 3 percent maximum ownership of any one company, the portfolio's average minimum market value threshold began at $110 million ($3.3 million divided by 0.03). Portfolio strategy clearly would have called for heavy investment in companies with market values between $110 million and $250 million (approximately 866 companies fell into this narrow market value range). It obviously would have allowed for light investment in companies with market values between $10 million and $110 million (1,134 companies were in this smaller category).

Tukman Capital Management (San Francisco, CA) stands in stark contrast to Value Line and to most money management firms in terms of portfolio concentration. The firm used a market-timing approach and stressed price (asset value) in stock selection in a very highly concentrated and actively managed portfolio. In 1986, the firm managed equity assets of $200 million but held only nine stocks. The weight of the average portfolio position was 11.11 percent of the portfolio's total dollar value. The average market value of the average portfolio position was $22.22 million. On average, assuming maximum 3 percent ownership, the firm's investment was limited to companies with market values greater than $741 million. According to *Business Week*'s 1986 tally of companies with the largest market capitalizations, only 585 public companies were available.

Fidelity Investments' Mercury Fund is another example of variation in portfolio characteristics. It used a market timing approach and stressed performance in a diversified and actively managed portfolio. As of November 30, 1985, the market value of the fund's investments was $133.2 million. It maintained portfolio positions in 232 companies. The average number of shares per position was approximately 34,000. The average price per share was $16.89 and the weight of the average portfolio position was 0.00431 of the portfolio's total market value. The average market value of the average position was $574,000. Assuming 3 percent maximum ownership, on average, the fund's purchases were limited to companies with market values greater than $19.132 million. This eliminated more than 2,200 companies from the total universe of 6,453 actively-traded issues as of April 1986.

Capitalization and liquidity parameters vary with money manager, investment objective, investment policy, investment strategy, investment style, and portfolio characteristics. But the inverse principle still dominates. If weight per average portfolio position and maximum ownership limits are reasonably held constant, the number of companies in which a money manager can invest decreases as equity assets under management increase. Managers of small portfolios enjoy the greatest investment choice. Those who have discretion over big portfolios have the least choice.

It clearly behooves corporate managers of neglected small capitalization, emerging companies to establish relationships with and seek word-of-mouth support from two sorts of venturesome or aggressive lead investors: 1) those who manage relatively small to medium-sized pools of actively managed equity assets (from tens of millions to several hundreds of millions of dollars); and 2) those who actively manage large pools but who allocate a portion of total assets to small capitalization companies. These money managers can establish portfolio positions in the company's shares. And they are eager to spread perception of the returns potential of those holdings to dominant sponsors in the equity valuation network. As a company's value spread narrows, management should focus more on managers of passively managed, diversified portfolios.

One of the problems in achieving the above objective, however, is that senior executives of emerging companies often do not know how to recognize lead investors and to identify dominant sponsors. And they lack perspective on the interrelationships of Wall Street's players. They are unclear on the investment community's spheres of influence and networks of prestige. They tend not to be aware of which lead investors influence which dominant sponsors and which dominant sponsors attract popularity flows. As a result, executives risk spending significant amounts of time with those who might be of least importance in their efforts to create investor demand.

Sponsorship strategy prioritizes both selling power and buying power in Wall Street's distribution network. Buying power is management's best prioritization screen for lead investors. It is usually defined literally in terms of institutional dollars available for investment (cash/assets). But I refer to the absolute and relative percentage equity ownership which may result from that investment. It may seem semantic. It is the best way for management to determine which money managers can most serve its needs.

Management should screen the purchasing power of money managers on an absolute basis and on a relative basis. Executives should determine the weight of an institution's average portfolio position and its average maximum limit on ownership of one company's equity securities. They should measure the size of an institution's potential equity position in their company as a percent of both the company's outstanding equity and of the dollar value of the institution's total portfolio. And they should compare the size of this potential position to the position sizes of other institutional holders of the company's outstanding equity and to the dollar value of the money manager's average portfolio position. These calculations will highlight buying power and capital commitment. Recall from Chapter 4 that this is how management can recognize lead investors.

Market value divided by share price determines the number of shares which a money manager may purchase. For example, the average position in Fidelity's Mercury Fund was valued at $574,000. The average market value threshold was approximately $19 million. Given the Mercury Fund's portfolio characteristics, the fund's manager must buy more than 19,000 shares of a $30 stock (0.03 percent of a company's 633,000 outstanding shares) to equal the size of an average position. At $20 per share a manager must purchase 28,700 of a company's 950,000 shares outstanding. At $10 per share a portfolio manager must acquire 57,400 shares of a company's 1.9 million outstanding shares.

Management and money managers may differ markedly in their opinions about the relative importance of a portfolio position in the company's shares relative to the company's shares outstanding. For example, the dollar value of an average portfolio position for the Mercury Fund carries a 0.00431 percent relative level of importance (average weighting) to the dollar value of the total portfolio. But the same position carries a 3 percent relative level of importance to a company's executives (3 percent of the company's outstanding stock). And, considering that a mutual fund's charter may allow ownership of 10 percent of a company's outstanding securities, the difference in this relative importance between management and money managers is not small.

The extent to which management should be nervous about an institution's purchase of shares depends on the intent of the purchase. Corporate managers of emerging companies must interpret an investing institution's purchase in light of its strategy and style. Money managers of passive, diversified portfolios who buy either performance or price are usually not a source of concern. Their time horizon may be long-term and their annual portfolio turnover may be relatively low. In contrast, those who manage active, diversified portfolios and who aggressively buy performance or price or trade on expectations may be a source of concern.

For example, Wellington Management's Over-the-Counter Securities Fund manages a passively managed, diversified portfolio. It is a value-oriented (price), stock-picking fund. It invests in companies with relatively small capitalizations and maintains a very low annual turnover of about 20 percent. Assuming market value approximates intrinsic or asset value, this sort of investor is desirable.

Ultimately, stability of returns on equity is the best way to attract long-term holders instead of short-term traders. It is the best means by which to lengthen portfolio managers' investment time horizons for their portfolio positions in a company's shares. A company's record of profitability must be considered in light of operating margins, relative to the use of leverage and the impact of inflation. But a record of stable returns on equity is the best way to calm nervous hands and to build a loyal shareholder base.

It is also imperative that management understand the size of the potential buying power which may lurk behind one money manager's portfolio. In Fidelity's case, the fact that the Mercury Fund was a $133 million part of a $16.5 billion mutual fund complex must also be considered. For example, portfolio managers of separate funds within the same complex occasionally compete against one another unknowingly to own a company's shares (mentioned also in Chapter 9). This can result in nervous owners who feel overexposed to a company. It also creates artificial demand which can result in stock price volatility.

Close scrutiny of buying power and capital commitment help executives to prioritize institutions' importance in the demand-creating process. It reveals which can be most useful to management in building an equity valuation network. And close relationships with both lead investors and dominant sponsors keep management plugged into that network. It keeps executives aware of investors' perceptions of the company's growth, profitability and relative value.

INVESTING INSTITUTIONS

Recognizing and using lead investors is important to corporate managements of companies of any size. They may be managers of actively or passively managed, diversified portfolios at investing institutions. But in the competition to exploit security returns potential, active managers set share prices.

Investing institutions form a four-tier structure based on size of equity assets managed. The significance of this structure, in general, is that specific brackets of brokerage firms do commission business with specific tiers of institutions. For example, top tier institutions manage the largest pools of equity assets (billions of dollars). They are: very large banks (such as Wells Fargo Investment or Bankers Trust Co. with $35 billion and $29.7 billion respectively under management in 1986), very large mutual fund managers (such as Fidelity Investments), very large investment counselors (such as Batterymarch Financial), very large insurers (such as Aetna), very large private pension funds (such as IBM), very large public pension funds (such as the California Public Retirement System), very large endowments (such as Harvard University), and very large broker affiliates (such as Lehman Asset Management with $12.3 billion under management in 1985).

Second tier institutions manage large pools of equity assets (middle to high hundreds of millions of dollars). They are: large banks, large mutual funds, large investment counselors, large insurers, large pensions, large endowments, and large broker affiliates. Third tier institutions manage medium-sized pools of equity assets (low to middle hundreds of millions of dollars). Fourth tier institutions manage relatively small pools of equity assets (tens of millions of dollars).

There is a winner and a loser on every stock trade. Ironically, professional money management, as practiced by large investing institutions, is acknowledged to be a loser's game. For example, in 1985, many money managers' total return performances beat the market (S & P 500 returns) for only the first time in three years. All of their gains occurred in the fourth quarter. Indata (Southport, CT) surveys the performance of about 1,000 equity money managers. It measures portfolio total returns in two ways: on equities only and on equities plus cash reserves. Through December 13, 1985, its survey indicated that about 56 percent of money managers had beaten the S & P 500's 26.33 percent gain on the equity portion of portfolios. Including cash reserves, however, only about 36 percent reported superior results. Through November 30, 1986, the firm found that median returns on professionally managed portfolios (20.6 percent) lagged the S & P 500 (21.6 percent).

Part of the reason for such disappointing performance is that professional money managers essentially are the market. By competing against the market, they compete against themselves. In so doing, active managers turn over their portfolios more than may be necessary and incur heavy transactions costs in the process. This negates portfolio gains. Acknowledging this performance dilemma, institutional equity assets indexed to the market (passive management) increased to about $150 billion in 1986 from about $60 billion in 1984.

The National Center for Policy Analysis studied the performance of pension funds between 1961 and 1981. It found they averaged a 7.8 percent rate of return versus 8.3 percent for the overall stock market. The study attributed inferior performance to active management and frequent shifts in investment strategy by sponsoring companies. It claimed that the average annual turnover rate in pension fund assets climbed from 25.8 percent in 1974 to 70.7 percent in 1983. It essentially concluded that passive portfolio management is a more prudent investment style. In apparent agreement, stock indexing by the nation's 200 largest pension funds rose 44 percent in 1986 from $75.62 to $108.9 billion, or 30.08 percent of about $362 billion allocated to stocks.

The buy-side distribution channel comprises institutional securities analysts and portfolio managers. Unlike his sell-side brokerage firm counterpart, the buy-side analyst is invariably a multi-industry generalist. He or she performs similar information processing functions but his or her time is much more diffused. The person darts among many stocks and across many industries and also serves as a data filter for the institution's portfolio managers.

When a buy-side institution's securities analyst makes contact, management should ask several questions:

1. Size of institution
   a. What size of equity assets does the institution manage? In which tier of institutions does it fit? Have assets increased or decreased in recent years?
   b. What has been the institution's total return performance, versus the S & P 500, over the past year? Past two years? Past three years? Past five years?
   c. How many analysts are in the institution's research department? Has the number increased or decreased in recent years? How many portfolio managers? More or less than prior years?
   d. How many portfolio positions, on average, does the institution maintain? What is the dollar value of the average portfolio position? Share size of the average portfolio position? Weight of the average portfolio position as a percent of the total dollar value of the managed portfolio? Does the institution maintain an average maximum ownership limit?
   e. What is the institution's investment time horizon? What is its annual portfolio turnover?

2. Methodology of Analyst
   a. How did the analyst find the company? Word of mouth (from whom)? Which computer screen? Which brokerage firm analyst? Institutional securities salesperson? At portfolio level?
   b. Does the analyst's institution already own the company's shares? How many? Is it a new position? Have additions been made to existing positions? Does it own other equities in the industry? Which? For how long? Why? Have there been any intra-industry switches? Why?
   c. Which valuation models does the institutional analyst use to value corporate equities? Why? What biases do they incorporate? Has the institution changed use of valuation models? Why?
   d. How are investment decisions made in the institution?
   e. How many total companies does the analyst follow? How many companies in the industry? How many industries? How often is the analyst in telephone contact with these companies? In personal contact?
   f. On what basis does the analyst recommend purchase of a company's shares? Sale?

   g. How many sell-side analysts or institutional salespersons call on the institution? With how many brokerage firm analysts does the buy-side analyst do commission business? What characterizes the best brokerage firm analysts with which the analyst does commission business?

   h. Can the institutional analyst refer management to brokerage firm analysts (dominant sponsors)? Other institutional analysts (lead investors)?

Sell-side brokerage analysts have characterized the personalities of buy-side institutional analysts.[9] The former break the latter down into several categories. For the best use of management's time, it is valuable to know which is which.

The "scared" buy-side analyst seems confident but lacks specific knowledge about companies or industries. "Egotistical Ed" is superconfident about his past performance even though he manages little money. "Minutiae Mike" dwells heavily on a company's small points in the belief they are significant to a company's big picture. "Details Dan" wants all of the assumptions which underlie management actions.

"Louise Libber" focuses on corporate politics instead of securities analysis because she thinks she is not taken seriously in her own organization. "Bitter Bill" holds grudges. He always bad-mouths the investment decisions of his portfolio managers. He is an angry, unpleasant sort. "Evasive Ellen" does not return phone calls. "Bottom-Line Bob" wants the "net net" of the situation: should he buy or sell? Finally, "Relentless Rick" is logical, aggressive and informed. But he is in the minority. Sooner or later executives of emerging companies may cross paths with one of the above.

Lead investors function differently than brokerage firm or institutional securities analysts. The former want the "right stock." The latter want the "right company." The difference may seem subtle but it is enormous in investment practice. In contrast to both perspectives, stockbrokers want the "right story." Lead investors address total return issues of "when" to buy/sell equities, "what" (groups) to buy/sell, and "how long" to hold equities, in addition to fundamentals issues such as "why" to buy.

Maryann Keller, an ex-first team *Institutional Investor* All-America Research Team securities analyst for the auto industry with PaineWebber, made the point about these differences very clear. She quit the ranks of analysts to join the ranks of money managers as a portfolio manager at Vilas-Fischer, a New York-based money management firm. She observed that an analyst can be well versed in industry minutiae but poorly versed in his or her relevance to portfolio performance (the big picture). In her opinion, analysts can be right on companies (operations) but dead wrong on stocks (investments).

In support of this opinion, one study examined 5,441 buy and sell recommendations made by one brokerage firm to its investing customers between January 1964 and December 1970.[10] It confirmed the apparent inability of analysts to anticipate market direction and market moves. For example, three major market upturns and two downturns in New York Stock Exchange and American Stock Exchange indices occurred between January 1964 and December 1970. Yet the ratio of buy recommendations to sell recommendations hardly varied over the 7-year period, regardless of reversals in market direction. There was no indication of market timing insight by analysts and sell advice was slightly more frequent in rising markets.

In pursuing the "right stocks," the mission of lead investors is to achieve a record of total returns consistently superior to that of the performance of a market index or preselected indices. Success requires that they presciently market-time the allocation of their equity assets, wisely pick stocks, or both. For portfolio decisions, lead investors look to analysts as sources of information on new investment ideas and to confirm that right stocks are also right companies. They rely on analysts for numbers, to make certain that a company's fundamentals are intact and support a buy decision. And they use them for clues about consensus expectations and estimation risk.

But their mission is also to attract dominant sponsors to support (appreciate) their portfolio positions. They need them to attract a popularity flow to their portfolio companies. As seen in Chapter 8, market sponsorship in the form of broad research coverage results in greater information efficiency and broader institutional ownership. The combination raises share prices and lowers expected returns. It eliminates security-specific expected returns in excess of market expected returns. When pricing becomes efficient, lead investors search for other investments with excess returns potential.

Many financial communications consultants advise corporate executives to think as securities analysts (sellers of equities) in assessing their companies and in preparing to communicate value to Wall Street. I do not agree. Creating investor demand requires that management develop the perspective of a buyer of equities. Executives should think, as professional investors, in terms of expected returns.

Buyers of equities think in portfolio terms of total return, not just reported earnings. Similar thinking enables executives to self-assess their company in buyers' terms, to understand who can buy their shares and why (economic incentives) they should buy them. It helps them to enhance the features of their companies' equity product and to be aware of how perception of the returns benefits of ownership can be spread to others in the equity valuation network.

The basis for my contention is the role of lead investors in the investor demand-creating process. Most investors can spot growth situations, especially after they unfold. But lead investors are the first to spot spreads between market values and intrinsic or asset values. They are first to perceive changing fundamentals (positive and negative), causes of value-enhancing competitiveness in existing markets, or value-creating competitive advantages in new growth opportunities.

Perception of competitiveness and excess returns potential attract lead investors. And their successful exploitation of perceived errors in consensus expectations attracts dominant sponsors usually through direct word of mouth. Lead investors capitalize on security-specific excess returns potential. They stimulate competition for those returns in the equity valuation process.

Dominant securities analysts then attract a popularity flow of other investing institutions through direct merchandising efforts. The effect of the flow is measured both in terms of numbers of institutions and percent ownership of a company's outstanding equity. This flow forces an upward revaluation of equities and establishes new levels of consensus expectations. Optimism and popularity flow can raise consensus expectations to lofty levels. They can detach a company's market value from economic reality on the upside. On perception of these unsustainable negative value spreads, lead investors sell or sell short.

As popularity flows, institutional holdings of a company's securities correlate positively with the intensity of research coverage from securities analysts. It remains positive until a future time when fundmentals no longer support returns in excess of industry or market returns. Recall from Chapter 2 the economic principle of reversion to the mean. At that time, pessimism and popularity outflow lower consensus expectations to great depths. They detach market valuations from economic reality on the downside. On perception of these unsustainable positive value spreads, lead investors buy.

Low consensus expectations or neglect result in higher expected returns relative to alternative investments of equal risk. Those returns may more than compensate for information and trading costs. If they do, lead investors will again identify value spreads and exploit security-specific excess returns potential. This will again attract dominant sponsors who will again attract a popularity flow. The flow will again eliminate those excesses and result in pricing efficiency. The investor demand-creating process follows a predictable cycle. Executives can observe it by watching changes in relationships among companies in their industry on the graphs mentioned in Chapter 4.

How do lead investors learn of companies with unappreciated fundamentals and excess returns potential? Management either finds them or they find the company. Management finds them through the sorts of efforts undertaken by Neeco, Inc. in Chapter 3, or mentioned in Chapter 4. Executives arrange personal visits or gatherings with those who own positions in the industry's equities or who specialize in equities with the company's investment characteristics. The first set of investors will understand industry fundamentals by virtue of being invested in, recently having established a position in, recently added to a position in, or once having owned (or followed) and preferably sold at a profit the shares of peer competitors. The second set can appreciate the returns-generating factors of companies that fit their investment strategy and style.

Lead investors find companies in numerous ways. They are usually voracious readers who tend to do their own primary research on industries and companies. They search for clues and signals about industry attractiveness and company competitiveness. They carefully observe trends, decide which industries may benefit and focus on neglected companies or those whose share prices fail to reflect their future earning power. They hunt for changing growth/share relationships and improving cost/price advantages in these markets. They scan for announcements of new products, technologies, processes, ventures, managements, reductions in discretionary expenses and organizational or ownership restructurings. They also rely on computer screens and word of mouth from other lead investors. And they solicit referrals from executives in companies in which they are already invested and from those which are suppliers or customers of companies.

In terms of computer screens, money managers usually customize them to their investment style. They use screens to fish through entire universes of actively traded issues contained in databases such as Standard & Poor's Compustat Services Inc. They look for companies which match their specific performance or price criteria.

Value investors screen balance sheets and income statements for returns-generating factors such as: profitability ratios, relative ratios, debt and liquidity ratios, net asset values, yields, payouts, dividend growth rates, and multiples. Performance buyers screen for betas, alphas, earnings/returns momentum and relative price strength.

At this point, money managers may gather information and opinions from information processors to confirm they are buying the right stock. And they may establish a position in a company's shares without making contact with management. This is why it is so important for management to learn which screens or which contacts money managers are using when they appear in person or on transfer sheets. It helps management to define the company's equity product in terms of its customers. It helps them to clarify investors' perceptions of the company. And it uncovers those information sources whom others perceive to be influential.

Recognizing lead investors is a competitive advantage in battle for share of investment capital. Executives should ask several questions of money managers who establish positions or express interest in their company. Recall that management will know them by their commitment of capital on an absolute and relative basis:

1. Portfolio Size:
    a. What total size of equity assets are managed by the whole money management firm?

In the money manager's fund? Has asset size increased or decreased over the last year? Three years? Five years? By how much (percent and dollar value)?

b. How many portfolio positions in how many different issues, on average, does the money manager maintain? What is the size of the typical position: number of shares? Dollar value? Has that increased or decreased over time?

2. Portfolio Importance: Capital Commitment

a. What is the firm's typical cash/assets ratio? Current ratio?

b. What is the weight of the average portfolio position? Has that changed over time?

c. What is the firm's typical maximum ownership limit? Has that changed over time?

d. How many brokerage firms compete for the money manager's commission business? Is that up or down in recent years? In which brackets are those firms?

e. How many analysts or broker/analysts, not institutional salespersons, does the money manager speak to directly on a regular basis? Is that up or down in recent years?

f. How much annual commission business does the money manager generate on average (see Chapter 8)? Is that up or down in recent years?

3. Portfolio Objectives

a. What are the fund's objectives: enhanced returns (share price changes) or preservation of capital (income-oriented)?

b. What was the money manager's total return performance record last year? Last three years? Last five years? How does that performance compare to the S & P 500? What is the fund's alpha?

4. Portfolio Strategy:

a. Does the money manager trade on value or expectations?

b. Is the money manager a market-timer? How does he or she currently perceive the company relative to macroeconomic forces of change? Or is the manager a stock-picker? Has portfolio strategy changed from the past? Why?

c. Does the money manager buy performance (growth), price (value) or combine them? Has management style changed from the past? Why? What portion of total portfolio assets is oriented to small capitalization companies. Is this an increase or a decrease from past years? Why?

d. What attracted the money manager to the company? Who or what influenced the money manager?

e. Does the money manager specialize in any industry? Has the orientation changed over time? Specialize in types of companies?

f. Does the money manager currently own or has he ever owned the company's stock? For how long? Ever sold it at a profit? Other equities in the company's industry? Has he or she owned or sold portfolio positions in the equities of peer competitors? Why? After holding them how long?

g. On what basis are purchases made? Why are positions sold?

5. Portfolio Style:

a. Is the portfolio venturesome, aggressive, cautious or defensive (risk, yield, P/E and capitalization of company). Recall that returns different from a passively managed, indexed portfolio highlight variations in portfolio style.

b. What, on average, is the portfolio's beta? Portfolios of median common stock managers had betas of 1.09 in 1985, down from a 1984 peak of 1.20 (1.07 at the start of 1981). Has the portfolio's beta changed over time? Why?

    c. What is the portfolio's average yield? Its average P/E ratio? Its group weighting?

    d. What is the sensitivity of the portfolio's returns to unexpected changes in macroeconomic variables mentioned in Chapter 2?

6. Portfolio Activity:

    a. Which characterizes the money manager's fund: actively managed, diversified portfolio, actively managed, concentrated portfolio, passively managed, diversified portfolio, passsively managed, concentrated portfolio?

    b. What is the portfolio's annual turnover rate? Has it increased or decreased over time? For how long a period, on average, are portfolio positions held? Is this longer or shorter than in the past?

How can managements induce lead investors to make their calls to attract dominant sponsors? Executives cannot force them to do so. But if the stock is right, lead investors will naturally spread perception because it is in their best economic self-interests. Several criteria must be met. Lead investors must:

1. Believe they are right on the stock.

2. Believe a company's fundamentals are intact.

3. Believe a company's story and confirm it with outside checks.

4. Trust management and its ability to meet operating goals.

5. Have access to adequate information from the company.

7. Have filled their portfolio position in a company's shares.

8. Believe they can sell the idea.

A money manager may or may not own the company's stock at the time of a visit to a company. If lead investors have not established a portfolio position before visiting or speaking with management, and if they like the company's story, management should expect that they will fill that position first before spreading perception of the company's returns potential to dominant sponsors.

In this case, management should watch the company's transfer sheets for the name of the lead investor. It might appear in nominee name. Regardless of whether they own stock at the time of contact, executives should follow-up within a reasonably short period for reactions (perceptions) and comments. They should answer any further questions, learn whether the investor bought the company's shares and request referrals to analysts at brokerage firms with which the money manager does commission business. This expands the equity valuation network.

Money managers can be characterized. D. F. King & Co. (New York, NY), a proxy solicitation firm, has identified five types of money managers. The "latent conservative" is first. He was the most common type of money manager in the decade of the 1970s. Securities analysis tended to be fundamental and value-oriented. The portfolio objective was preservation of capital. Time horizons were long-term and the tendency was to support management resolutions and slates.

The firm contends that the "passive opportunist" money manager prevails today. Neither an indexer nor a shareholder loyalist, the opportunist is value-oriented. The objective is capital gains (enhanced returns) through share price appreciation by almost any method including proxy fights and tender offers. He or she maintains an actively managed portfolio, buys on price and is pro-shareholder rights and anti-management entrenchment. King claims, in general, this type targets share price appreciation between 15 percent and 25 percent within 18-month periods from time of purchase.

Chapter 6 mentioned a wave of institutional investors' proxy resolutions were up for shareholders' vote in the 1987 annual meeting season. Their intent was to repeal poison pill defense (antitakeover) mechanisms. Georgeson & Co., a proxy solicitation firm, conducted a study titled, "Corporate Conflicts: Proxy Fights in the 1980s," for the Investor Responsibility Research Center (Washington, D.C.). It found that although institutions generally opposed antitakeover measures, they did not necessarily vote against management in proxy fights.

The study reported that institutions supported resolutions to change corporate control (ownership restructuring) if the effects of those resolutions were to generate abnormal positive returns to shareholders. Chapter 6 showed that merger bids and tender offers benefit shareholders. But it also showed that increases in share ownership, either by institutions or other holders with at least 5 percent positions, resulted in a greater probability that incumbent managements would win proxy fights. This seemed true, especially if their support forced management to create value for shareholders through an ownership or organizational restructuring. This might take the form of a corporate repurchase self-tender, a sell-off, or significant cost-cutting efforts.

The "social capitalist" is the third type of money manager. King claims this group is the fastest growing. His objective seems to be protection of shareholder rights and attack on perceived executive excesses. The group uses its proxy power to vote against management resolutions.

The "impersonal technician" is fourth. He is epitomized by firms such as Batterymarch Financial Management (Boston, MA). The technician manages an active, diversified portfolio. He or she screens stocks, executes portfolio strategy and makes investment decisions by computer. He or she cares neither about nor for relationships with management.

The "aggressive analyst" is fifth. He or she assumes roles similar to corporate raiders. The person buys 5 or more percent of a company's outstanding shares and, ultimately, puts a company "into play." Such activities attract passive opportunists, value buyers or other raiders.

Investing institutions dominate the American investment scene. But they are not very popular with corporate managements for three main reasons. First, their time horizons for portfolio performance tend to be short. Annual portfolio turnover rose from about 20 percent in 1976 to about 60 percent by 1985. Second, they exert pressure on executives for short-term earnings growth in the form of linked and year-to-year quarterly results. Third, their loyalty is to the investors whose money they represent, not to the managements of the companies in which they invest.

Egon Zehnder International, an international executive recruiting firm, conducted a survey of 100 chief executive officers. The results indicated that executives blamed institutional investors' short-sightedness for part of America's lost edge in world business competition. A full 92 percent of those surveyed claimed the investment community's pressure for consistent positive quarterly earnings comparisons was harmful to management's long-term ability to compete worldwide.

Obviously, executives see a conflict between portfolio strategy time horizons and capital/business strategy time horizons. The first may be months, days, hours or even minutes. But the second may be years. Executives may believe that this conflict leads investing institutions to trade stocks more than to hold them. And they may think that this portfolio activity contributes unduly to high volatility in their company's shares.

But academic research into daily and monthly data between 1972 and 1981[11] asserts that the reverse is true. Institutions' block trading (as a percentage of total trading volume or as the total number of shares traded in blocks) actually lowers stock price volatility and adds liquidity to trading markets. Institutions trade both sides of the market, not in parallel. On the other hand, total trading volume reactions to the information content of unanticipated events (management signals) do seem to add to stock price volatility.

The reason for management dissatisfaction with investing institutions is that institutionalization of capital markets has heightened competition for portfolio performance. It seems to have shifted professional investors' focus from long-term growth strategies to short-term trading profits. It seems to have shifted trading from value to expectations. Stocks seem to trade more on liquidation value and less on future earning power.

Yet this should not lead managements to believe that the stock market is no longer long-term oriented. Capital markets reflect, not affect, future asset returns potential inherent in company fundamentals. Recall Miller-Modigliani's formulation of price/earnings ratios on growth and growth opportunities versus growth in earnings and assets in Chapter 2. A breakdown of a company's P/E ratio into the P/E multiple on cash flows from investment in existing assets and the P/E multiple on cash flows from new investment in future earning assets quickly reveals that portion of a company's current stock price assignable to the future. It shows the rate at which investors are willing to capitalize a company's future cash flows. As Chapter 4 discussed, management must decide whether they perceive that growth and its duration correctly.

More appropriate, money managers are under great pressure to build clients' wealth at a greater rate than competitive benchmarks. If they fail to record superior rates of total return, they lose clients' assets. Money managers' pressure on corporate managers reflects investors' pressure on money managers. It is a bit of a vicious cycle.

For example, corporate pension funds are the toughest and most demanding of money managers' accounts. Corporate managements are under pressure to reduce pension liabilities so that they can report increased earnings. Growth in the market value of pension assets in excess of actuarial requirements accomplishes this. They are therefore aggressive and want to enhance total return under all market conditions. They want capital gains through active portfolio management. They are tough on selection and review of money managers' total return performance. They choose among money managers on the basis of portfolio performance in the last calendar quarter, not the last calendar year or last market cycle.

At the same time, the changing structure of money management fees has intensified that pressure. They are trending away from fixed rates toward performance-based fees. SEI Corp (Wayne, PA), a pension consulting firm, examined 1986 money management fees. The firm found that equity money managers on average charged 0.56 percent of assets. In 1982, that figure was 0.42 percent. The firm estimated that the value of U.S. pension assets approached $2 trillion. Based on equity and bond management fees, it also estimated revenue of about $10 billion for the money management industry.

Managers of public pension plans from such states as California and Minnesota favor a performance-based fee structure. They believe that money managers should only be rewarded for superior performance. The two most common performance-based fee structures rely on venture capital formulae or fulcrum formulae. The trend suggests that money managers may soon receive only a small fixed fee, associated with matching a preselected market index. In addition, they will receive a portion of the positive spread between the fund manager's total return and that of the preselected index. In other words, money managers may soon be rewarded only if their total return performance beats the market. They might actually have to repay client fees if performance is consistently inferior.

Portfolio performance is king in the money management business. Total return is the only quarterly and annual measure of the quality and wisdom of a money manager's strategy and style. Those who specialize in the shares of small capitalization emerging companies usually compare their portfolio's total return performance against the quarterly and annual total return performance of several "market" indices.

Comparisons with returns on the S & P 500 and S & P 400 are basic. But venturesome or aggressive growth money managers may also compare their results to the Value Line Index (1700 stocks), the American Stock Exchange HiTech Index, the Nasdaq Composite Index, the Wilshire 5000 Index (5,000 stocks), the Lipper Growth Fund Index (mutual funds), the American National Bank SmallCap Index (Chicago) and the New Horizons Fund (T. Rowe Price).

Portfolio performance is also a "Sword of Damocles." Money managers of mutual funds, pension funds and hedge funds can never rest content with yesterday's total return performance. Complacency or rigid investment strategy in changing capital markets may spell disaster. Investors want returns in excess of preselected market indices. If performance fails to meet their expectations, they respond quickly and negatively.

It happened to the 44 Wall Street Fund. It was an actively managed, concentrated portfolio. Stocks were picked for aggressive performance. Over a five-year period, entering 1980, it boasted the best performance of 421 funds monitored by Lipper Analytical Services. Over a 10-year period it was third best of 319 funds. Investor demand for the fund's performance warranted the launch of a second fund: the 44 Wall Street Equity Fund.

But the next five years were a nightmare for the Fund's managers. For the period ending September 30, 1985, the first fund was the worst performing of 464 funds. For 1984, it ranked last and the second fund ranked second to last of all funds monitored. And through December 26, 1985, the first fund ranked 761 out of 763.

Investors' reaction to such poor performance was severe. The number of the fund's active shareholder accounts declined from more than 13,000 in mid-1982 to less than 11,500 in June 1986. The fund's assets fell from a peak level of more than $300 million in 1983 to $39.9 million at the end of September 1986. And money management fees, 1 percent of assets under management before adjustments, fell to $642,000 in the fiscal year ended June 30, 1986, from $2.3 million in 1984.

INVESTORS' TIME HORIZONS

Corporate managers believe that active value-oriented or expectations-oriented money managers of portfolios demand a lot from them but give no loyalty in return. Loyalty is defined in terms of both proxy support for management proposals and long-term share holding periods. Managements know that dominant sponsors do not vote proxies. But they also learn that strong relationships with active lead investors are no guarantee of loyalty. It seems unfair to executives that these investors demand consistent access to them, ongoing openness from them, and immediate answers to tough questions about operations in both good and bad times, but that they give no loyalty in return for management's compliance.

Institutional investors are loyal to those who pay them to manage their money, not to those in whose shares they invest that money. As a result, loyalty to corporate managements is largely a function of realized returns. Capital commitment to a company's equity securities reflects the notion that a sell decision is half of any money manager's buy decision. Professional investors tend to have target sale prices in mind when they buy stock. Target sale prices correspond to target contractions in value spreads or target shifts in investors' expectations. Their loyalty to a portfolio company lasts as long as necessary to realize target portfolio returns or to perceive that those expected returns will not be realized.

Creating stable and predictable economic value over time is the best way for managements to command the loyalty of institutional investors. That loyalty translates into long-term ownership, so-called "quiet stock." Ideally, corporate executives prefer equity ownership in the strong hands of passive investors with long-term time horizons. They support management. Executives do not want their stock in the weak hands of active investors or traders with short time horizons. They support opportunism.

Definitions of investment time horizons vary. Consensus suggests that a short-term investment falls between 12 months and 18 months. It further suggests that a long-term investment extends to about 24 months. A longer-term horizon runs two to three years or more. Annual portfolio turnover and annual commission volume are two measures of portfolio time horizons.

In general, active, value-oriented performance investors tend to be more patient and have longer time horizons than active, value-oriented investors who buy on price. For example, in the category of growth funds, Fidelity Investments manages two growth and two value funds. The Mercury Fund and the Trend Fund are the two performance funds. The first invests in emerging growth companies. The second identifies and invests in emerging growth trends. The Discoverer Fund and the Contrafund are the value funds. The first buys undervalued, asset-rich companies. The second is contrarian and tries to perceive and to capitalize on errors in consensus expectations.

Annual portfolio turnover statistics reveal that Fidelity's value funds turn their portfolio holdings over at twice the annual rate of its growth funds. Stated another way, its growth funds hold their portfolio positions twice as long as the value funds.

In fiscal 1985 for example, the Mercury Fund's share holdings turned over 129 percent; the Trend Fund turned over 62 percent. The Discoverer Fund turned over 246 percent, and the Contrafund turned over 135 percent. In 1984, the respective turnover figures were 143 percent, 57 percent, 389 percent, and 234 percent. In 1983, the respective turnover rates were 136 percent (annualized), 71 percent, 353 percent, and 452 percent.

Annual commission volume is a proxy for conservative or aggressive portfolio management style. In general, retirement funds, endowment funds, foundations, charitable trusts, and profit sharing plans tend to be conservative. They invest for income and long-term security. Banks and insurance companies tend to be more aggressive. Mutual funds tend to be most aggressive. They invest for short-term price change.

Greenwich Associates monitors trends in commissions paid by investing institutions to brokerage firms. The typical institution in its study generated average commissions of $3.7 million in 1985. The figure was an increase from $3 million in 1984 and was expected to approach $3.9 million in 1986. Of the 1985 total, a typical institutional investor allocated an average of 38 percent of total commissions, about $1.3 million, to brokerage firms' research services versus about 39 percent, or $1.2 million in 1984. The figure was expected to increase in 1986.

The survey research firm separated the tiers of domestic institutions into 12 categories: very large banks, large banks, medium banks, small banks, mutual fund managers, large (investment) counselors, medium counselors, small counselors, large insurers, small insurers, pensions and endowments, and broker affiliates.

Commission trends for investing institutions have changed since 1979. Through 1982, very large banks generated the most average annual commissions. They slipped to second in 1983 and to fourth in both 1984 and in 1985. Large counselors were second most active from 1979 through 1981 and again by 1985. Mutual fund managers were third in 1979 and 1980 but first in 1984. By 1985, their average annual commission volume was almost double their nearest rival. Large insurers have steadily remained within a narrow band between third and fourth. Broker affiliates have consistently been fifth in average annual commissions since 1979.

The typical mutual fund managers paid the most commissions in 1985, by a wide margin. They paid more than $15 million versus an average of $11.7 million in 1984. Their median and mean commission costs were 9 cents and 10.7 cents per share in 1985 versus a mean average of 11.4 cents in 1984. Large counselors paid the second most in commissions, more than $8.5 million. Their median and mean commission costs were 8 cents and 7.9 cents per share versus a mean average of 8.4 cents. Large insurers were third, at about $7.7 million (8 cents and 8 cents per share versus 8.8 cents). Very large banks were fourth, at about $7.0 million (9 cents and 10.7 cents per share versus 11.4 cents). Broker affiliates were fifth, $6.8 million (8 cents and 9.1 cents per share versus 9.1 cents). The top five were expected to remain the same in 1986.

Among the balance of investing institutions, in 1985, medium (investment) counselors were sixth in average annual commissions. They paid about $3.1 million (10 cents and 10 cents per share versus 10.3 cents). Pensions and endowments were seventh, at about $3 million (8 cents and 8.4 cents per share versus 9.2 cents). Large banks were eighth, at about $2.1 million (12 cents and 12.6 cents per share versus 12.4 cents).

Medium banks and small insurers were about even in ninth and tenth spots, at about $1.6 million. The first paid median and mean commission costs of 12 cents and 14.4 cents per share versus a mean average of 13.8 cents. The second paid 10 cents and 10.6 cents per share versus 10.7 cents. Small counselors were eleventh, at about $1 million (10 cents and 12 cents per share versus 13.1 cents), and small banks were twelfth, at more than $350,000 average annual commissions (14 cents and 14.8 cents per share versus 16.8 cents). Their positions have remained relatively steady since 1979.

In percentage terms, small insurers allocated the highest portion of their 1985 average annual commissions, 62 percent, to research services. Small (investment) counselors and large banks allocated 47 percent. Pensions and endowments and small banks allocated 42 percent. Very large banks apportioned 40 percent of their average annual commissions. Mutual fund managers and large insurers allocated 39 percent. Large counselors dedicated 35 percent to research. Medium counselors targeted 34 percent. Medium banks allocated 31 percent and broker affiliates directed 22 percent of their annual commissions for research services.

In dollar terms, mutual fund managers allocated the highest portion of average annual commissions to research services in 1985, about $6 million. Large counselors spent about $3 million, large insurers about $2.9 million, very large banks about $2.8 million, broker affiliates about $1.4 million, pensions and endowments about $1.3 million, medium counselors about $1.1 million, small insurers about $1 million, large banks about $1 million, medium banks about $500,000, small counselors less than $500,000, and small banks spent about $200,000.

Commission expense varies with portfolio management style. Capital Research & Management Co. (Los Angeles, CA) was the nation's fourth largest institutional equity money manager near the end of 1985. Capital Group managed approximately $19 billion in equity assets. Those were divided between about $9 billion in equity mutual funds and $10 billion in a range of institutional stock portfolios. Wells Fargo & Co., a leader in indexed funds, was the nation's largest money manager in 1985 with $26.6 billion in equity assets under management. It was also the leader in 1986 with $35 billion under management. Capital Group was value-oriented. Fund managers tended to buy earnings performance and dividend growth, stressed fundamental securities analysis and active portfolio management. The Group maintained a research staff of 40 securities analysts worldwide and allocated $12 million to its annual budget for investment research and execution.

Steinhardt Partners (New York, NY) stands in contrast. By early 1986, the investment counseling firm managed more than $600 million in three hedge funds. The firm traded on expectations. Fund managers were aggressive buyers on information and stressed trading profits from rapid share price changes. Portfolio turnover averaged 17 times per year and the firm paid $22 million per year for research and execution services.

Corporate managers believe overseas investors have quiet hands. Foreign investing institutions are value-oriented. They tend to buy performance: earnings and dividend growth. They invest for both capital growth (capital appreciation) and income. And they tend to manage relatively passive, diversified portfolios.

By definition, foreign investors employ an initial top-down (market-timing) investment strategy to asset allocation before they apply a stock-picking approach to security selection. They must first assess market-related macroeconomic and political influences on share prices in each country in which they might invest before they pick stocks to buy in those countries. They tend to support management resolutions but may not actually vote their proxies.

For the first three calendar quarters of 1986, the Securities Industry Association (SIA) believed net foreign purchases of American equities amounted to $18.1 billion versus $4.9 billion in 1985 and $5.8 billion in the prior record year of 1981. In 1984, the SIA claimed foreign investors were net sellers of about $3 billion of American securities. These figures must be viewed relative to U.S. institutional equity assets valued at $928.243 billion at the end of 1985.

Of total net purchases of equity securities in the first nine months of 1986, the Association estimated that European investors accounted for $10.6 billion versus $2.1 billion in the same period in 1985. Britain was responsible for about half of the portfolio activity. Swiss investors were second with purchases of about $2.2 billion. West German, French and Dutch investors participated to a lesser extent.

The SIA estimated that Japanese investors were also net buyers of about $2.5 billion of U.S. equities in the first nine months of 1986. They had been net buyers of about $298 million of U.S. equities in 1985 and net sellers of about $2.4 billion in 1984. Latin American and Caribbean investors also participated. They had been net buyers of about $1.7 billion in 1985.

There are six major types of institutional investors in the United Kingdom. Investment trusts invest for capital growth, income, or a combination of the two. Their investment style focuses on performance. They tend to buy shares in large capitalization companies for domestic investment but small capitalization companies for international investment. Portfolio managers often double as securities analysts. And they tend to rely on small and major regional U.S. brokerage firms for investment ideas on, and research coverage of, emerging U.S. companies.

There are two types of mutual funds among approximately 800 in the UK. The first and best known is the Scottish Investment Trust. It is the equivalent to a closed-end mutual fund. The second type is the British Unit Trust and is also a mutual fund equivalent.

Managers of these funds' portfolios tend to focus on big capitalization domestic companies or on smaller capitalization companies which are market leaders in industries unavailable in domestic economies. Of several billion in equity assets under management, they may commit as much as half or more to investment in U.S. equities and half or more of that total to investment in emerging companies. And the dollar value of average positions may range between $5 to $10 million. Their value-oriented style combines performance and price. Portfolios are diversified and relatively passively managed, and annual portfolio turnover is as low as 20 percent per year, considerably less than most U.S. funds.

Directly managed, self-administered pension funds are third. Their objective is capital growth. They buy performance and manage diversified and passively managed, but not indexed, portfolios. Insurance companies are fourth. They tend to invest for capital growth and income in portfolios which are diversified and actively managed. Merchant banks are fifth. Corporations are sixth. They are acquisition-oriented and tend to avoid equity investments.

In their investment decision-making, British investors place great emphasis on corporate executives' relationship with their shareholders. They weigh managements' treatment of the company's owners and their perception of management's influence on earnings predictability and returns stability. Company credibility is very critical to any commitment of their capital. They seriously consider management's depth, goals, leadership capabilities, reliability and past record of delivering results to shareholders. They dwell on the company's accounting philosophy and the advisory strength of the company's board of directors. British institutions tend to shun companies which appear to be managed for short-term results.

Swiss and German money managers tend to pursue different investment objectives than their UK counterparts. They are also value-oriented and usually focus on preservation of capital, investing for performance with a primary focus on dividend growth. They tend to own shares of large capitalization, dividend-paying companies.

There are four types of institutional investors in Japan: insurance companies, banks which manage pension assets, investment trusts (similar to mutual funds) and investment counselors who also manage pension assets. Most are value-oriented and tend to invest for preservation of capital. They emphasize income and balanced portfolios. Within the context of investment style, they tend to favor a performance approach which stresses long-term investment in dividend growth and yield stocks. They focus on large capitalization companies which are market share leaders and have names with which they are familiar. Analysts and portfolio managers tend to be multi-industry generalists.

These styles may explain the performance of the U.S. equities market in 1987. Recall from Chapter 2 that a stock selection strategy focusing on overvalued, high yield, high P/E, large capitalization companies performed best between June 30, 1986 and June 30, 1987. All other stock selection strategies did worse. It was the first time in 19 years of one firm's data that that had happened. Part of the reason was that the market was liquidity-driven. One need only compare the P/E on Japan's equities market (about 50) to that of the S & P 500 (about 20). To value investors, U.S. equities looked cheap.

Some corporate executives consciously try to park their company's shares into quiet and friendly hands. They prefer that aggressive expectations-oriented money managers with short-term time horizons and high portfolio turnover not own their company's stock. They try to direct share ownership to more passive value-oriented money managers with patient attitudes, long-term time horizons and low turnover.

Hercules, Inc. (Wilmington, DE) adopted this share ownership strategy. Management intentionally placed about 20 percent of its shares into the long-term oriented portfolios of college endowment funds, state retirement (public pension) funds, and European trusts. Executives tried to steer ownership away from short-term traders such as mutual funds, banks and insurance companies, and they tried to restrict ownership by any of the three to less than 1 million shares.

For example, Kemper Financial Services, Inc. (Chicago, IL), bought about 1.6 million of Hercules' shares. It managed about $6.5 billion in tax-exempt assets in 1985 and used a stock-picking approach to buy performance. But Hercules' management talked the fund manager down from that level. Kemper lightened its position by selling one million shares.

Envirodyne Industries, Inc. (Chicago, IL), a maker of cellolosic casings for perishables in supermarkets (about 9 million shares outstanding), also tried to influence ownership of its shares. Management consciously encouraged share-ownership among conservative, value-oriented, long-term holders and discouraged it among short-term, expectations-oriented opportunists. Executives strategically avoided painting rosy pictures of their company's future. They intentionally infused uncertainty about the future into their discussions with interested investors. The result of its realism, management believed, was that only those investors with patient attitudes toward long-term growth and profitability would be willing to bear the risk of uncertainty to own the company's shares. Those with preferences for short-term price changes would look elsewhere.

Estimation risk (information deficiency) and illiquidity (high trading costs) preclude many money managers from owning the shares of small capitalization, emerging companies. These costs threaten potential portfolio gains. The challenge for executives is to reduce these costs.

They must think as buyers of their stock. Besides those institutions which already own stocks in the industry, they must understand which investing institutions can own their company's shares and why they should buy them. They must judge their company in terms of its value-enhancing or value-creating competitive advantages. They must consider their companies' returns potential relative to alternative investments of equal risk.

Furthermore, they must prioritize the buying power of institutions. Management's time must be spent most productively with those lead investors who can directly affect the demand-creating process. They must deal personally with those who have the financial resources to establish positions of absolute and relative significance in the company's shares. It is their capital commitment which makes them credible and motivates dominant sponsors to become active in the stock. Subsequent popularity flow raises institutional ownership and broadens research coverage. That reduces information cost and raises pricing efficiency. Broadened ownership and greater share volume improves liquidity and lowers trading costs.

8

Dominant Sponsors—
Prioritizing Selling Power

The process of sponsoring equities in the securities industry is similar to the process of sponsoring products in the packaged goods industry. In the latter, shelf space is at a premium and competition for it is tough. Shelf space can either make or break a product. Positioning means visibility or obscurity for a product. Shoppers tend to think in generic terms as they prepare to shop but tend to select particular brands based on what they see. Shelf space means that a product either has a chance to appeal to impulse buyers or never has a chance to tickle their fancy.

What shoppers see on shelves is not the result of random product placement. It reflects sales volume potential. Product turnover is supported by manufacturers' advertising, off-price retail coupon campaigns and purchase discounts to retailers. In modern supermarkets, cash registers measure sales volume trends by product category and by brand. Merchandisers of consumer products award prime physical shelf space to unit volume sellers.

In the investment business, people shop with their minds. Perception is in their mind's eye and they use computer screens as their shopping lists. Just as shoppers rely on grocers to display consumer items, investing institutions rely on brokerage firms to display equity products in the form of securities research. In brokerage firms, research directors measure commission volume by industry and by company. Merchandisers of research products award prime mental shelf space to share volume sellers.

There is an important three pronged process in consumer product sponsorship. The first is to reach the supermarket buying committee and get on the approved list. The second is to convince regional and local store managers to display the approved product. And, finally, probably most important, the third is to convince end-users of the product, individual shoppers, that they should select and buy the product when they actually visit the supermarket.[1] Merchandisers respond to indications of consumer interest.

There is a similar three-pronged process in equity product sponsorship. The first step is admission to a firm's universe of followed stocks. Entry for emerging companies is often bounded by certain "minimum" brokerage parameters. One SEC broker-dealer survey found some national firms used minimum coverage criteria of $32.3 million market value ($11.6 million for regionals), 1.8 million shares outstanding (1 million for regionals), $30.5 million annual sales ($15.7 million), asset size of $15.8 million ($13.8 million), reported earnings of $1.6 million ($1.2 million for regionals) and an earnings growth rate of 13 percent (11 percent for regionals). Finally, the maturity, depth and quality of management are very important. After an analyst qualifies a company for potential research coverage, a stock selection committee must usually approve the initiation of coverage.

Analysts usually initiate research coverage as a function of line of business or market value. Either they believe they perceive earnings growth and commission-generating potential from purchase or sale recommendations of a company's securities, or they think they can generate fee income by locking up a company's investment banking business.

Reported profitability in the form of earnings per share attracts analysts. They key on a variety of sources such as growth/share relationships in product markets (market leaders) and word-of-mouth from lead investors. They pay attention to cash signals which imply expectations of greater future earning power: unexpected positive earnings announcements, unexpected dividend increases or quarterly sales/earnings momentum. And they also rely on ownership signals which imply greater future market capitalization: planned equity financings and popularity flow into a security represented by the dollar value of trades on upticks (above last sale prices).

The second step is access to the firm's Recommended-for-Purchase list. It is here that a firm's research department displays its best research products. Assignment to the list confirms two opinions. First, it suggests that a brokerage firm's portfolio (market) strategist believes that market timing favors a company's "group." This makes it a right stock for purchase. And second, it infers that a firm's industry securities analyst (or multi-industry generalist) believes that fundamentals favor a company's returns potential. This makes it a right company for purchase.

Removal from the list most likely represents an analyst's perception of a company's worsening fundamentals and moderating returns. It may represent an opinion that a company is fully valued, that a narrow, neutral or negative value spread exists. This suggests perception of lower risk in alternative investments of equal expected returns, or higher returns in alternative investments of equal risk.

Removal may also stem from negative unexpected earnings announcements, erosion of market share, worsening financial condition, management instability, or popularity outflow represented by the dollar value of trades on downticks (below last sale prices). Deletion may also occur because an analyst may believe he or she lacks adequate information from a company's management. This cripples his or her ability to make earnings forecasts with any degree of confidence.

Entering the universe of stocks followed by a firm's research department is easier than getting on the firm's Recommended List, though both are difficult. For example, Kidder, Peabody & Co. followed 540 companies in its universe. But the stock selection committee put only 43 of those 540 on the firm's Recommended List as of July 15, 1986. Another 12 companies were on the firm's High Risk Recommended List.

The third step in the market sponsorship process is convincing lead investors that they should buy or buy more of a company's shares when they ask for recommendations and ideas from the research departments of brokerage firms with which they do commission business. In that sense, executives' efforts to communicate value to Wall Street are designed to gain prime "shelf space" for their company's equity product in the minds of investors. They are also intended to move that product off of brokers' shelves in volume.

Information is the main ingredient in equity products. There are three types of company-specific information. In ascending order of importance, companies release details about their past results, their present operations and their future prospects.

Past information is historical and accounting-oriented. It may inadequately explain a company's future performance potential. Present information is current event-oriented. It may already be reflected in a company's share price. Future information is predictive and assumption-oriented. It is the essence of management forecasts and analyst estimates of earnings.

Historical information appears in most companies' annual and quarterly shareholder reports. It answers the questions "What?" "Why?" and "How?" about a company's past operating history. It gives financial results of past periods. It also offers an accounting of a company's past success or failure in executing business strategy and meeting stated objectives. It is only a benchmark against which to compare future corporate performance.

One academic study tried to explain price/earnings ratios (market expectations) by comparing the accuracy of analysts' forecasts with estimates based on published accounting data or past growth rates.[2] It compared results of a regression incorporating growth rates, dividend yield and risk versus an average of analysts' forecasts from nine brokerage firms. The study found that historically-based estimates explained only about half of market expectations for the future, about 49 percent of variation in price/earnings ratios.

Present information appears in corporate disclosure announcements. It answers the questions "Who?" or "What?" about a company's current operations. Managements of public companies must, by law, comply with Securities and Exchange Commission guidelines for materiality and disclosure. Those guidelines obligate them to publicly disclose any current information which may have a materially positive or negative effect on the conduct of the company's business. These include financing and investment decisions, cash signals, and organizational or ownership restructuring.

Predictive information is the subject of management forecasts and analysts' earnings estimates. It is expectatative and shapes investors' perceptions of a company's future profit momentum. It hints at answers to the questions "How?", "When?", or "How Much?" about a company's returns potential. It fills research reports from brokerage firm analysts and investment advisory services. The same study mentioned above found that "expectational variables" contained in analysts' forecasts explained about three-quarters of market expectations, about 75 percent of the variation in price/earnings ratios.

In this chapter, I review several academic studies pertinent to the information content and to the predictive content (accuracy) of management and analysts earnings forecasts. The results help management to anticipate market behavior. The issue is of enough importance so that I will begin with significant general conclusions before examining specific findings. For example:

1. Changes in consensus estimates of future earnings, not changes in earnings themselves, affect market-wide expectations. They move share prices. Market reaction varies with the size and the sign of forecast deviations.

2. Changes in operating margins lead to changes in earnings forecasts. Forecast revisions account for significant variations in returns among specific securities.

3. The accuracy of analysts' forecasts of annual earnings made in first fiscal quarters tends to be low. But it tends to improve as fiscal years progress. Misestimates (over/under) vary with perception of rates (high/low) and predictability of earnings growth.

4. Managements' forecasts of earnings tend to be relatively more accurate than analysts' forecasts. Analyst accuracy varies with time of year of management forecast and size of analyst following.

5. Absolute accuracy of management and analyst forecasts is low.

6. Analysts are adaptive. They tend to revise their estimates up/down after earnings announcements make clear that they underestimated/overestimated earnings.

7. Analysts tend to overestimate earnings growth rates of high growth companies. They tend to underestimate earnings growth rates of low growth companies. This is often the basis for value spreads and for trading on expectations.

8. Analysts tend to change their estimates (and affect consensus expectations) after quarterly earnings are reported. More analysts tend to revise forecasts later in fiscal years than early in fiscal years.

9. Investors react to forecast revisions.

10. Voluntary earnings forecasts are intended to guide market expectations.

Academic studies show empirically that predictive information affects investors' expectations and stock prices. This information stems from "expectational" data in the form of consensus earnings estimates. Studies reveal that earnings forecasts from both managements and analysts have information content. It is measured by price reactions when earnings forecasts deviate from expected earnings. Results also suggest that the information content of voluntary forecasts, and not the forecast disclosures themselves, move share prices.

Management can expect changes in analysts' earnings estimates to have a pronounced effect on investors' expectations. Executives can also anticipate a positive correlation between the sign and the size of analysts' forecast revisions and market response to them.

One study[3] found that actual and unexpected revisions in analysts' estimates explained up to 20 percent of the variation in individual security returns. In addition, revisions of 5 percent or more up or down explained significant abnormal returns during the year in which the revision was made and that forecasts for eventual top-performing companies became more optimistic as time passed. Those for the worst-performing issues became more pessimistic.

For example, average monthly compound returns were compared to a mean monthly return value-weighted index over the same period. Returns on securities experiencing a positive revision ranged from 0.57 percent to 2.04 percent greater than the index over the rest of the year. Returns on those experiencing negative revisions ranged from −0.26 percent to −2.12 percent worse than the index over the rest of the year. In addition, returns on portfolios of positive revision companies significantly exceeded the return on portfolios of negative revision companies. The figures were 0.82 percent to 3.53 percent on portfolios with 5 percent revisions and 0.45 percent to 2.37 percent on portfolios with 2 percent revisions.

Another study examined 49 New York Stock Exchange companies with actual earnings data, earnings forecast data, and monthly stock returns data between 1967 and 1974.[4] It found that significant abnormal positive returns formed up to two months prior to analysts' revisions of earnings estimates. Holding a stock over a four-month period surrounding announcement of an upward revision of 5 percent or more resulted in an average abnormal positive return of 4.7 percent, 2.7 percent of which occurred in the two months after the revision. See also Hawkins/Chamberlin/Daniel in the bibliography.

Executives must carefully manage expectations created by analysts' forecasts, especially those which vary widely from consensus on the upside. Analysts' optimism can detach expectations from economic reality. On the negative side, such detachment can lead to downward revisions and sharp share price volatility.

Share prices fall sharply when analysts revise their estimates just to be in line with consensus expectations. They also fall when earnings announcements deviate from the expected.

This was the case with Digital Equipment Corporation. In the week of July 20, management reported record 1987 earnings (June 30) of $8.53 per share versus $4.81 in 1986, but on a lower than expected tax rate. Margins were less than expected. Investors knocked the stock down about 7 points. The stock later lifted as analysts concluded that management wanted to defer recognition of revenue to the following fiscal year.

Chapter 4 discussed what management should do when investors' expectations diverge from managements' expectations. Executives should take one of two steps. They should either take corrective action through voluntary direct earnings forecast disclosures, or they should transfer wealth to shareholders by capitalizing on market mispricings.

Investors (and securities analysts) react to management forecasts of earnings made either directly to the market or indirectly through information intermediaries. One academic study reviewed 725 forecast announcements.[5] It found that investors tended to believe that earnings forecasts for coming year(s) had predictive value. They thought that they contained more information about a company's future performance than that contained in prior years' earnings reports.

The study observed that returns on those firms which made forecasts was higher in the year in which the forecast was made than returns for the overall market. Investors seemed to associate low earnings potential with those companies which made no forecasts. The implicit notion was that if relative earnings potential were high, these companies would make forecasts. Investors also seemed to associate low earnings volatility with those companies which repeated forecasts.

The same study showed that abnormal returns correlated positively with the sign of forecast deviations. For example, "good news" firms (589 forecasts) tended to be upwardly revalued during the weeks before a forecast and then revalued sharply upward on or about the actual date of the forecast. Two-day abnormal positive returns for companies with positive forecast errors from three days to one day prior to the forecast date were 0.4069.

In contrast, "bad news" companies (136 forecasts) on average lost value during the weeks before an earnings forecast announcement and tended to be revalued sharply downward on or about the actual forecast date. Two-day abnormal negative returns including the announcement date for companies with negative forecast errors were −0.3528 percent. Managements appeared willing to disclose information which revalued their company downwards.

Another study examined 479 point projections of annual earnings per share published in the *Wall Street Journal* from July 1969 through December 1973.[6] It showed a positive correlation between abnormal returns and both the sign and the size of forecast deviations. "Good news" portfolios had a sign of forecast deviation greater than zero. They showed abnormal positive returns of 0.01421 percent from the day before through the day after forecast disclosure date. No systematic price revisions occurred from 100 days to two days prior to disclosure date. "Bad news" portfolios had a sign of forecast deviation less than zero. They showed abnormal negative returns of −0.00524 percent over the same period. Cumulative abnormal returns were −0.05929 percent from 100 days prior to two days prior to forecast disclosure date.

The same study measured positive price reaction to the size of forecast deviations. The portfolio with the largest magnitude of positive forecast deviation (0.28340 percent) showed the largest positive cumulative average return residual (0.04756 percent) from one day before through one day after the forecast disclosure date. The portfolio with the largest negative forecast deviation (−0.11540 percent) showed the largest negative cumulative average return residual (−0.01926 percent) over the same period. A positive association was found between preannouncement price revisions and forecast deviations. But little correlation was found between forecast deviations and postannouncement price revisions.

Results also indicated that negative price revisions may be undetectable when positive news disclosures accompany negative forecast deviations. A portfolio with conflicting signals had a forecast deviation less than zero with good news disclosures. It earned positive abnormal returns of 0.00923 percent from the day before through the day after the forecast disclosure date. In contrast, a portfolio with negative forecast deviations with no additional news disclosures earned negative abnormal returns of −0.01558 percent over the same period.

One study examined 336 voluntary earnings forecasts released by 258 companies between 1963 and 1967.[7] It showed that firm-specific price changes around management forecasts were greater in the third fiscal quarters (0.333), than around first quarter disclosures (0.316) or second quarter forecasts (0.067).

As part of their role in trying to accurately predict future changes in present values, securities analysts bear the burden of potential forecast errors. Empirical studies show that forecast errors are greatest at the beginning of fiscal years. Forecast accuracy improves as a fiscal year progresses due to the availability of information such as interim earnings. And knowledge of errors in consensus estimates of earnings growth, rather than knowledge of errors in actual growth, leads to abnormal positive returns.

For example, one study reviewed 919 one-year and 710 two-year forecasts for companies followed by three or more securities analysts (mentioned in Chapter 2, footnote 9).[8] It used March data because that was the earliest date on which financial data from the previous year was reported. It also used September data because it was a time when significant evidence on company performance should be available.

The study found that the average March forecast error for 30 percent of the companies for which earnings growth was most underestimated was 63.6 percent. This contrasted with a September forecast error of 26.4 percent. In addition, the average error in March for 30 percent of the companies for which earnings growth was most overestimated was 38.9 percent versus 20.3 percent in September.

Another study examined 414 calendar fiscal year companies followed by three or more securities analysts between 1976 and 1978.[9] It showed that analysts make the majority of forecasting errors in estimating industry and company growth, not economy-wide growth. The percentage of error due to industry misestimates declined steadily from 37.3 percent in January to 15.5 percent in December. But the percentage of error attributable to company misestimates rose steadily from 60.7 percent in January to 83.7 percent in December. In other words, analyst forecast accuracy improved in general as fiscal years progressed. But their industry performance forecasts tended to be more accurate than their company performance forecasts over the year.

The same study also determined that analysts had a tendency to overestimate earnings growth rates for perceived high growth companies. But they tended to to underestimate earnings growth rates for perceived low growth companies. They also tended to repeat errors for companies with unpredictable growth rates (see also Niederhoffer/Regan in the bibliography). These results are applicable to the economic concept of reversion to the mean mentioned in Chapter 2. These patterns open value spreads and expectations gaps for value and information traders.

The study also showed that dispersion of analysts' earnings estimates decreased most in the first four months of fiscal years (0.104 to 0.086). But they did not decrease appreciably after that point (0.080 to 0.067), even though the accuracy of analysts' consensus estimates was improving. Finally, it revealed that dispersion was largest around companies in growth and cyclical groups of stocks and smallest around defensive issues.

One study recorded the impact of first, second and third quarter reported earnings on analyst forecasting behavior for 78 of the largest Fortune 500 companies (in terms of sales) between 1973 and 1976.[10] These companies were followed by an average of 10.5 securities analysts. No company was followed by fewer than three analysts. It found that analysts reacted to quarterly earnings announcements. Almost one more analyst changed his or her earnings estimate in months immediately succeeding quarterly earnings announcement months than in announcement months themselves.

The study also revealed that quarterly earnings announcements affect expectations. Adjustment in the absolute value of both the dollar change and the percentage change in mean earnings estimates was greater in succeeding months than in announcement months. It also showed that analysts adjusted their earnings forecasts most after third quarter earnings announcements (2.35 mean rank difference). They made fewest adjustments after first quarter announcements (1.69 mean rank difference versus 1.96 for the second quarter).

Management forecasts are usually issued to guide market expectations toward management expectations. They are believed to have predictive ability superior to that of analysts. One study confirmed that managements seem to prefer to voluntarily "forecast" their earnings expectations indirectly through securities analysts. In contrast, direct earnings forecasts from managements of companies in semi-strong information environments are perceived as correctional. They are intended to neutralize overly positive or negative investor expectations and to bring them in line with management expectations.

In addition, management forecasts seem more accurate that those from analysts. One study reviewed 259 forecasts for 191 New York Stock Exchange calendar fiscal year companies between 1970 and 1977.[11] It found that the average absolute management forecast error was 0.115 versus 0.135 for securities analysts.

However, conclusions about the comparative accuracy of management and analyst earnings forecasts have historically been contradictory and ambiguous. With this in mind, one study examined the relative forecast accuracy of each as a function of the timing of reported analyst forecasts. It found that management forecasts released after analyst forecasts were significantly more accurate, regardless of the time in the fiscal year in which they were released. Moreover, the relative accuracy of analyst forecasts made after management forecasts depended on the time of the year in which management forecasts were released and the size of a company's analyst following.

The study covered 25 weeks surrounding the week of management earnings forecast announcements (at least one month before year-end). The majority of these were released in the third and fourth fiscal quarters. It included 124 New York Stock Exchange, calendar year companies with management forecasts and complete analyst forecast data between June 1979 and December 1982.[12] Coverage ranged from one to twelve analysts.

In general, the study found that analyst forecasts reported before the release and up to four weeks after the release of management forecasts had, on average, significantly higher forecast errors than management forecast announcements. Mean analyst forecast error ranged from 0.224 in week 12 prior to announcement to 0.171 in week four after announcement. In contrast, mean management forecast error was 0.150. The accuracy of each was approximately equal accuracy in weeks five through eight (0.166 to 0.150). And analysts' forecasts were significantly more accurate starting in week nine after management forecast announcements (0.141 to 0.124).

In particular, the study found that analyst forecasts made after first and second fiscal quarter management forecast announcements were not significantly more accurate than management forecasts. In contrast, analyst forecasts made after third and fourth fiscal quarter management forecast announcements were significantly more accurate beginning in the seventh week after announcement weeks.

The study looked further at the relative accuracy of forecasts made in the first and second fiscal quarters versus those made in the third and fourth quarters. It revealed a smaller error distribution for forecasts made late in the year. Mean management forecast error was 0.80 late in the year versus 0.241 early in the year. A mean 25- week analyst forecast error ranged from 0.189 to 0.057 in late quarters versus 0.289 to 0.209 in early quarters. This seems consistent with the findings in footnote 3 about declines in analyst forecast errors as fiscal years progress.

The relatively narrower range of mean analyst forecast errors occurring in early in the year forecasts also suggested that analysts stayed with their estimates made early in fiscal years. They seemed not to be swayed by primarily good news management forecasts in the sample. Revised forecasts in line with reported earnings later in fiscal years seemed consistent with the findings in Footnote 5 about the timing of analysts' changes of earnings estimates.

Finally, the study examined information environments surrounding companies in which managements made forecasts. It found that the difference between management and analyst forecast accuracy for companies with a high analyst following (greater than seven analysts) was insignificant in each of the four weeks after management forecast announcement weeks. And analysts' forecasts became more accurate in the eighth week. But forecast accuracy was significantly in favor of management for those companies with a low analyst following (less than seven analysts) until the tenth week. At that time, analysts' forecast accuracy became superior.

In reality, neither managements nor analysts seem able to predict the future with great or consistent accuracy. Actual earnings often differ markedly from forecast. David Dreman cited this phenomenon in his book *Contrarian Investment Strategy*.[13] He cited results of four studies which found that the mean error in management forecasts of one year or less for 266 companies was 14.5 percent. In contrast, the mean error in seven studies of analyst forecasts of one year or less for 650 companies was 16.6 percent.

Some look to insider trading as the most accurate signal of executives' confidence in the future and the tool with the most predictive ability. But one study[14] found that insider trading was less discriminating than management forecasts of company returns potential. Results indicated that the timing and the size of insider sales relative to earnings forecasts had information content. The study found a direct relationship between high forecasts and insider trading. Mean return on a portfolio of high forecast/high insider trading companies was 1.13 percent versus 1.05 percent on a portfolio of high forecast/low insider trading companies. But it reported a reverse relationship between low forecasts and insider trading. Mean return on a portfolio of low forecast/high insider trading companies was 0.004 percent versus 0.32 percent on a portfolio of low fore-cast/low insider trading companies.

Most executives do not voluntarily predict sales, earnings, dividends, capital spending, or anything associated with the company's future, especially if they can do so indirectly through securities analysts. Those who make voluntary forecasts do so for one of several reasons. They may have no indirect channels through which to make forecasts. They may wish to signal their anticipatory skill. For example, they may want to announce their ability to adjust output (production) to unexpected shifts in macroeconomic variables which may alter market demand and expected levels of future operating cash flows, or they may want to guide investors' expectations.

Should the managements of emerging companies (or any company) make voluntary performance forecasts? These would take the form of estimates of ranges and trends, not specific numbers. The answer depends on whether execu-tives can satisfy two of the requirements for second-guessing the market sug-gested by Professor Fruhan in Chapter 5. First, can management identify a breakdown in the analytical process? Does management possess information which the market lacks? And, second, does management's monitoring of the leading analysts' perceptions reveal significant variations in consensus expecta-tions from its own forecasts?

Executives may respond positively to the above questions. But any decision to voluntarily forecast should be made within the context of perceived earnings volatility. Those companies which maintain sustainable competitive advantages in their product/markets are likely to experience highest earnings predictability and lowest earnings volatility. Managements of these companies will likely be most able to estimate future levels of parent/unit operating cash flows and operating margins within acceptable limits of certainty.

If deemed necessary, they should consider making "good faith" voluntary forecasts of ranges of sales and earnings. And they should make them over relatively short forecast horizons to further lessen potential forecast error. They might issue forecasts after the end of fiscal third and/or fourth quarters before the release of preliminary earnings or shortly before the end of fiscal years.

This advice is certain to meet with opposition from corporate secretaries (in-house legal counsel). But, if managements' voluntary forecasts are made in good faith, they will be based on perceptions of reasonable predictability, beliefs of reasonable accuracy, and certainty of market mispricing. Forecast disclosure falls under the Securities and Exchange Commission's safe harbor rule which became effective on July 30, 1979. Within this context, management can effec-tively restore the valuation process and guide expectations. It is a higher vis-ibility approach to information content than simple distribution of press releases to news services. And a forecast may serve as a noticeable proxy of management's confidence in future company performance. Voluntary forecasts may also send valuable signals concerning future industry performance to industry analysts.

Companies spend money on past and present information. The cost of annual and quarterly reports to shareholders depends on volume and gloss. The cost of press releases depends on the breadth of distribution and method of delivery.

Investors spend money on predictive information (discussed by type of institution in Chapter 7). They buy estimates and forecasts. Their level of spending depends on stock market conditions. In up markets, investors live by a "make more" investment philosophy. They pay handsomely for "primary" research to divine future performance. In down markets, they adopt a "lose less" mentality. They buy "maintenance" research to preserve and protect portfolio gains.

Predictive information is processed by two types of professional information processors. The sell-side of Wall Street comprises investment information services, investment advisory services, and brokerage firm securities analysts. They process and sell predictive information for hard or soft (commission) dollars. Brokerage analysts process the greatest volume. Buyers of processed information are either professionals or amateurs, institutions or individuals. The buy-side of Wall Street comprises institutional securities analysts. They process proprietary predictive information for internal use only.

Professional investors spend a lot of money on predictive information. They obviously believe that paying Wall Street fortune tellers to predict future cash flows and future changes in present values is worth the price in potentially superior portfolio returns. Charles D. Ellis, of Greenwich Associates, put a figure on institutional investors' annual expense.

Investing institutions each year pay more than $1,500,000,000 in commissions [more than 10 percent of total commissions] to brokerage firms for their research and execution services. (This figure matches the intelligence budget of the CIA, equals the total combined budgets of the Ivy League universities and is four times the R & D expenditure of Bell Labs.)[15]

The figure is interesting, but, from corporate executives' perspective, there is a more distressing piece of data. Those commission dollars are paid to relatively few dominant sponsors who provide research coverage of relatively few public companies.

LOW SPONSORSHIP OF SMALL CAPITALIZATION COMPANIES

The U.S. equity capital market has historically been the largest in the world in terms of market value. However, Japan may have surpassed the U.S. as of April 1987. Morgan Stanley Capital International Perspective (Geneva, Switzerland) estimated the total market capitalization of the U.S. equities to be $2.171 trillion as of April 30, 1986. That figure represented a drop to 43 percent of the world's equity markets from 66 percent. The value as of April 1987 was estimated to be $2.672 trillion, about 63 percent of the nation's gross national product.

Wilshire Associates Incorporated (Santa Monica, CA) measures the market value of about 5,000 equity securities traded on the New York Stock Exchange, the American Stock Exchange and over-the-counter. The Wilshire 5000 Equity Index is the broadest measure of domestic stock market activity in use. The market value of the index at the end of the first calendar quarter of 1986 was $2.455 trillion.

Japan has been the second largest of the world's capital markets. It had an estimated market value in early 1986 of $1.332 trillion. That was 61 percent of the size of the United States equity market. In April 1987, that estimate was $2.688 trillion (versus an estimate above for the U. S. of $2.672 trillion). That value was 129 percent of Japan's gross national product. The United Kingdom is third. Its market value was estimated to be $419 billion. Investing institutions consider these markets most liquid for investment.

In April 1986, West Germany was the fourth largest of the world's equity capital markets ($230 billion). Canada was fifth ($156 billion), France was sixth ($130 billion), Italy was seventh ($116 billion), Switzerland was eighth ($104 billion), Australia was ninth ($72 billion), and the Netherlands was 10th. Its $61 billion capitalization was approximately two-thirds that of IBM.

The U.S. equities universe comprises the securities of more than 26,000 issuers. At the end of April 1986, a total of 1,499 companies were listed on the New York Stock Exchange, 819 companies were listed on the American Stock Exchange and 4,135 companies traded over-the-counter on the NASDAQ system (National Association of Securities Dealers Automated Quotation). In addition, the March 1986 issue of *OTC Review* magazine estimated the existence of more than 20,000 non-NASDAQ companies. They trade over-the-counter in local or regional securities markets. The figures aggregate to more than 26,000 issuers. Worldwide, they may exceed 30,000 issuers.

The New York Stock Exchange (NYSE) is the world's largest auction market for securities in terms of market value, dollar volume and share volume of traded securities. As of May 30, 1986, the market value of its listed securities was approximately $2.26 trillion. That was an increase from $1,950.33 trillion at the end of 1985. In 1985, the NYSE accounted for total share volume of about 27.5 billion shares, valued at about $970.5 billion. In contrast, share volume was about 21.6 billion shares, valued at about $765 billion in 1983.

The over-the-counter market is the world's third largest exchange, in terms of the dollar volume of traded issues. It stands behind the NYSE and the Tokyo Exchange in Japan. It is a negotiated market. The aggregate market value of NASDAQ common stocks was $368.959 billion as of May 30, 1986. That was an increase from $306.3 billion at the end of 1985. The National Association of Securities Dealers reported that share volume in 1985 was about 20.7 billion shares, valued at about $233.5 billion. In 1983, share volume was about 15.9 billion shares, valued at about $188 billion.

The American Stock Exchange is the nation's third largest securities market. It is the world's eighth largest in terms of dollar volume of annually traded issues. It has slipped to fifth largest in terms of number of annual traded issues. The AMEX is also an auction market. The dollar value of shares listed was $97.231 billion at the end of May, 1986. That was an increase from $83.824 billion at the end of 1985. In 1985, the exchange's share volume amounted to about 2.1 billion shares, valued at about $26.7 billion. Both the Midwest Stock Exchange and the Pacific Stock Exchange exceeded the American Stock Exchange in annual number of traded issues.

Financial managers at the vast majority of public companies face one major problem with traditional market sponsorship. Research coverage from securities analysts in all brackets of brokerage firms is very hard to secure. From a brokerage firm's perspective, perception of earnings growth potential aside, coverage is based on a company's market capitalization and commission potential relative to the costs of coverage. From an investing institution's perspective, coverage is based on liquidity and returns potential relative to the costs of coverage. Most small capitalization companies cannot satisfy either's needs simultaneously. As a result, five out of six public companies did not benefit from any sponsorship (research coverage) as recently as 1982.

Arithmetic tells the story. Traditonal market sponsorship is concentrated in the shares of relatively few public companies. Data from Lynch, Jones & Ryan's *Institutional Brokers Estimate System* (I/B/E/S) clearly show the relationship between market value and sponsorship. Of 3,175 U. S. companies in the firm's database:

Companies (#/cumulative)	Average Market Capitalization ($ million)	Average Analyst Coverage
159	9.763	1.4
158/317	19.371	1.6
159/476	28.877	1.7
159/635	37.703	2.1
159/794	48.481	2.3
158/952	61.133	2.6
159/1111	75.417	2.9
159/1270	91.322	3.8
159/1429	111.230	3.8

158/1587	139.193	4.1
159/1746	175.027	5.3
159/1905	216.270	5.7
159/2064	273.618	6.9
158/2222	350.783	7.6
159/2381	465.010	8.3
159/2540	655.935	10.8
159/2699	955.034	13.7
158/2857	1475.590	16.6
158/3016	2722.340	20.8
159/3175	20284.906	29.1

Differences in the intensity of research coverage from securities analysts significantly affect the market's pricing mechanism. They raise/lower stock prices
and lower/raise corresponding expected returns. One 10-year study (1970-1979)
examined coverage of all S & P 500 companies.[16] It found that annual returns
(including dividends) on portfolios of neglected stocks (zero or one analysts)
were greater than returns on portfolios of widely followed stocks (four or more
analysts) in every year. Lead investors capitalize on this inefficiency. They
exploit potential consensus forecast errors inherent in the information deficiency
surrounding the shares of neglected companies.

In the study, the (risk) unadjusted annual returns gap ranged from a low of 0.8
percent in 1978 to a high of 21.9 percent in 1978. Average annual returns ranged
from 16.4 percent to 9.4 percent. A previous 5-year study (1972-1976) had also
found the persistence of an annual risk-adjusted returns gap. It had ranged from a
low of 9 percent to a high of 14.4 percent. Average annual returns had run from
18 percent to 7 percent. The securities of neglected companies did not seem to
carry higher risk. The pattern of risk-adjusted and unadjusted returns was similar. And volatility increased with neglect. But it increased far less on a proportio-
nate basis than returns per unit of total risk (monthly standard deviation of
returns).

The study also found that the market anomaly called the neglected firm effect
(mentioned in Chapter 7) dominated the small firm effect. Volatility (total risk)
adjusted returns on portfolios of neglected companies exceeded those on portfolios of widely followed companies of the same size (market capitalization).
Risk-adjusted returns for small widely followed companies increased from
−0.03 percent (0.05 percent unadjusted) to 0.04 percent for small neglected
companies (0.158 percent unadjusted). Risk-adjusted returns for large widely
followed companies increased from −0.019 percent (0.084 unadjusted) to 0.088
percent for large neglected companies (0.153 percent unadjusted).

When dominant sponsors initiate research coverage and attract a popularity flow to a company, it becomes clear that analysts' consensus estimates affect stock prices. There is disagreement, however, whether securities research can produce superior risk-adjusted returns to investors. Evidence suggests that selection of stocks on the basis of consensus estimates does not lead to superior returns. But it does suggest that the ability to forecast changes in consensus estimates of earnings, rather than changes in actual earnings, generates abnormal positive returns.

Yet academic studies have found that analyst research recommendations have information content. The size of response seems to vary with the credibility and influence of the securities analyst, the strength of the recommendation, and the extent to which the recommendation gains public recognition.

One study examined 597 buy and 188 sell recommendations (almost all of which were for New York Stock Exchange companies) between 1970 and 1971.[17] It found that mention of a positive research recommendation in *The Wall Street Journal's* "Heard on the Street" column resulted in an abnormal positive return of about 0.92 percent in a company's shares on the day of mention. Appearance of a negative recommendation in the column resulted in about a −2.4 percent abnormal negative return in a company's shares on the day of mention.

Results further indicated that the information effect of analysts' recommendations may have lasted for up to 20 trading days. Evidence was also found that the effect of an analyst's primary release of information to commission-paying clients was not fully reflected in share prices before the mention of the same information in *The Wall Street Journal*. In other words, information availability continued to affect market-wide expectations, and popularity flows.

Studies find that research recommendations have an effect on share volume of those companies recommended. The effect is measured by number of transactions, the number of shares traded and the market value of traded shares. One study reviewed 6,000 research reports and trading recommendations and 175,000 transactions in 4,000 different securities in 2,500 customer accounts between January 1964 and December 1970.[18] It found a rise of 36.2 percent in trading activity in recommended stocks during a 25-day "research-response" period around a security's recommendation date.

The study also observed that the proportion of total trades by one brokerage firm's customers accounted for by trades in recommended stocks over the same time was 17.3 percent versus a regular proportion of 13.5 percent. The average dollar trading volume in recommended stocks was about $73,500 per day versus an estimated $54,000 per day. And the dollar value of total trading in all securities during the period was estimated to increase from about $400,000 per day to about $425,000 per day.

TYPES OF SPONSORSHIP AND BRACKET STRUCTURE OF SPONSORS

Market sponsorship comes in the form of information coverage from investment information services or research coverage from securities analysts. The first
charges a fee to the company. Coverage is usually short and oriented more
toward news than analysis and more toward individuals (retail) than institutions.
The second is usually oriented more toward analysis of corporate developments.
It may be geared either to institutions or individual investors and carry purchase
or sale recommendations.

Investment information services are the lowest common denominator of coverage for emerging public companies. They are distinct from investment advisory
services. For example, Standard & Poor's Corporation is an information service.
Value Line, Inc. is an investment advisory service. The former will initiate
information coverage for a fee. The latter will only initiate coverage at its own
discretion.

Information processors at information services usually issue one page, two-
sided, quarterly summaries of a company's operating results and recent corporate
developments. The mini reports provide quick historic background information
only. They make no investment recommendations. The services charge an annual fee for coverage to companies and an annual subscription fee to subscribers.

Public relations firms, on retainer, also release historical "background reports" on client companies. But these reports tend to be perceived as neither
third-party nor objective. Each must carry a disclaimer that the firm is being paid
a retainer fee by the client company.

There are currently two fee-based investment information services. Standard
& Poor's Corporation (New York, NY) is the larger of the two. It publishes *Stock
Reports* on all companies listed on the New York and American Stock Exchanges
and about 2,300 of more than 4,100 actively traded over-the-counter companies.
Stockbrokers call these reports "tear sheets" because they can easily tear the
sheets from an S & P notebook for quick use in telephone conversations with
customers. S & P's initiation of coverage of a company depends upon levels of
investor interest, measured by monthly share volume and subscriber requests. In
other words, new coverage depends upon investor demand.

The second source of information coverage is The Unlisted Market Service
Corporation (Glen Head, NY). It publishes *The Unlisted Market Guide*. It specializes in small emerging public companies which may not qualify for trading on the
National Association of Securities Dealers' (NASD) National Market System. It
also charges a fee for information coverage to companies and an annual fee to
subscribers. As of this writing, Moody's Investors Service has also started a
Moody's OTC Unlisted Manual and news service for unlisted companies.

Investment newsletters and investment advisory services' special publications also provide research coverage on companies. Approximately 900 newsletters, read by about 500,000 subscribers, cover investments of all sorts. The *Newsletter Yearbook* or *Oxbridge Directory* lists them.

Value Line, Inc. is the nation's largest investment advisory service. The *Value Line Investment Survey* is its best-known product. As of mid-1985, the *Survey* alone claimed approximately 95,000 subscribers at an annual fee of $395 per subscription. Value Line publishes five additional investment advisory publications. Total subscriptions fell to about 115,000 in mid-1985 from about 133,000 at the end of 1984. The decline was attributed to the growing stock market dominance of institutional investors over individual investors.

Several academic studies have concluded that the system by which Value Line ranks securities covered by its *Investment Survey* has information content. They have found that the effect of Value Line rank changes on share price change varies with the size and sign of the rank change.

For example, one study[19] compared performance of portfolios ranked first and fifth for timeliness. Ranking is based on estimates of growth in earnings, price momentum and the P/E ratio of a stock relative to its historical P/E and to the market. Empirical results showed that a portfolio of stocks ranked first and revised monthly over a five-year period (beginning in April 1965) consistently achieved returns in excess of market returns of about 10 percent per year. Returns on a portfolio of stocks ranked fifth were − 10 percent per year. A second study conducted rank change tests for 1,427 companies.[20] It found that small firms achieved more than 5 percent abnormal positive returns over a three-day period from rank change announcement dates.

The second study also found that changes in timeliness rank from level 2 to level 1 were perceived as very good news. Changes in rank from level 5 to level 4 were perceived as no news. And market reaction to steps up in rank was greater than that for steps down in rank. Observed investor reaction to a change from rank 2 to 1 was about three times greater than a change from 1 to 2. Finally, the speed with which share prices changed in relation to rank change announcement dates seemed slower than for other information signals. A possible explanation was that all investors were not apprised of Value Line rank changes at the same time, as they might be with *Wall Street Journal* announcements.

Whether Value Line rankings cause or predict changes in share prices is subject to debate. But it seems clear that its ranking system has the ability to affect consensus (market-wide) expectations and share prices.

Managements of emerging companies should try to attract coverage from Value Line. For example, executives of Heilig Meyers Co. (Richmond, VA) seized the opportunity when Levitz Furniture went private. Management wrote a letter to Value Line. Executives highlighted the void in coverage of the retail furniture industry as a result of the Levitz buyout and offered the company as a worthy substitute. Officials at Value Line agreed. The *Investment Survey* initiated research coverage of the company and ranked it highly for timeliness. The company's share price rose about 7 points in the aftermath of the ranking.

Investment advisory firms and trust departments of large money-center commercial banks also wholesale their research products. For example, Argus Research Corporation (New York, NY) has offered investment advice since 1934 and publishes research reports on companies and industries. Small regional brokerage firms buy the service's investment information to supplement their existing in-house research efforts.

Commercial banks, such as the Provident National Bank (Philadelphia, PA) also sell their research department's research products to other information processors. Again, the purchaser's usual intent is either to supplement an existing research effort or to fill the void of a nonexistent research product.

Brokerage firms' research departments are Wall Street's most visible sources of market sponsorship. They are the central information-processing units of the investment community. They package and sell the greatest amount of investment information and the greatest volume of research reports. And they budget the most money on information accumulation, analysis, and distribution in the hope of attracting the greatest commission-generating popularity flow.

"Brokerage analysts are the first tier in the institutional [investor] market," claims Charles Ellis. He states:

Their research output is widely disseminated. Broker analysts' written reports are distributed to thousands of institutional analysts and portfolio managers. In addition, their firms' salesmen spend most of their time calling and visiting institutional investors, stressing the key points in the analysts' written recommendations. And broker analysts themselves merchandise and communicate their own research through visits and phone calls to institutions, talks to groups of institutional investors, letters and follow-up reports, and answers to questions put to them by institutional analysts and portfolio managers. Broker analysts are recognized experts and they command a hearing.[21]

Each central processing unit employs securities analysts to process information. They fall into one of two categories. Analysts are either industry specialists or multi-industry generalists. The former focus on one industry only. They process information either as part of a larger overall securities sales effort within a large national brokerage firm or as the sole effort within a boutique firm. The latter cross industry lines to process information and may tailor their coverage either by geographical location of company or by size of company (capitalization). In contrast, as mentioned in Chapter 7, investing institutions usually maintain a staff of only multi-industry generalists.

Research departments fall under the umbrella of securities sales in brokerage firms' organizational structures. They complement the work of brokerage firms' corporate finance and syndicate departments. Securities analysts focus on corporate and industry activities in the context of a broad economic and market environment. The extent of their activities varies with the size of their brokerage firm.

In national institutional firms, industry specialists conduct company and industry-related analyses. They present their findings to their firm's securities sales staff in seminars, in printed research reports and by voice via live satellite communications networks which link all branch offices worldwide. In efforts to generate commission volume, generalist and specialist sales professionals continuously relay analysts' interpretation of expected and unexpected changes in macroeconomic and security-specific variables to institutional and individual customers throughout the world. It may affect their portfolio performance.

Research coverage from brokerage firms takes many shapes. Analysts' information is packaged in the form of: basic analysis, comments, recommendations, statistical summaries, status reports, and updates on industries and companies. Research departments also issue studies on relative market values, macroeconomics, business economics, financial economics, investment strategy, investment policy, political insight, and retail (individual investor) investment opportunities.

A firm's corporate finance department also processes information. It is called corporate finance research or corporate client research. As its name suggests, such coverage is a client service and is usually for informational purposes only. It provides historical perspective and current updates but usually carries no recommendations. It is an expected service in support of corporate finance clients. And it is also used as an initial effort to wrest investment banking clients from other underwriters.

Six brackets of brokerage firms (including the five presented in Chapter 3) provide traditional research coverage of public companies. They process and sell the most investment information and analysis to investing institutions. The list includes five brackets of commission-generating firms and one bracket of non-commission research boutiques. Each bracket varies in the size of its research staff, the extent of its investment research production, and the extent to which it specializes by geography, market capitalization or industry. Each bracket "speaks to" a tier structure of investing institutions (mentioned in Chapter 7), and each has its share of dominant sponsors. This is discussed more fully in Chapter 9.

Technimetrics, Inc. defines the parameters of brokerage firms' securities research departments. An active department, for its database purposes, must have a minimum of two full-time securities analysts. They must be analyst/analysts, not broker/analysts. Of domestic brokerage firms monitored by the database management firm, only 155 met the definition in 1985. The figure was an increase from 115 in 1984 and 105 in 1983. As of June 1986, the total number of brokerage firm (sell-side) securities analysts in those 155 firms' research departments was 2,050. It was an increase from the previous tally of 2,011 analysts in 115 firms. The total number of institutional (buy-side) analysts in mid-1986 was 5,990. It was an increase from 5,862 in 1985 and 5,614 in 1984.

In ascending order of perceived prestige and influence with investing institutions (from bottom bracket to top bracket), about 150 small regional brokerage firms are in the bottom bracket. There are one or more in every region in the country. Small local firms maintain small research staffs. Their broker/analysts are multi-industry generalists who develop their own investment ideas. Their research departments are entrepreneurial and loosely structured. Their valuation approach tends to combine relative ratio and asset value analysis. They tend to be best known for their familiarity with public companies in their region or for their specialized knowledge of industry niches.

For example, Adams, Harkness & Hill (Boston, MA) is known for its research coverage of New England based companies. Investment Company of Virginia (Norfolk, VA) is noted for its coverage of mid-Atlantic companies. Investors know Prescott, Ball & Turben, Inc. (Cleveland, OH) for its coverage of companies in the Great Lakes region, and B.C. Christopher & Co. (Kansas City, MO) follows mid-western companies. Firms in this bracket tend to influence small money managers and investment advisers as well as top tier institutions which have specific portfolio exposure to areas or niches in which these firms specialize.

Research boutiques are in the second bracket. Technimetrics defines research boutiques as having: fewer than three investment professionals who do no commission business but sell their research product for hard dollars. The firm's database cites a total of 17 research boutiques. They are usually founded by ex-industry specialist securities analysts with extensive research followings. Boutiques are not brokerage firms. They tend to be industry-specific, usually specialize in heavy capitalization industries, and serve major investing clients. La Fountain Research (Bayhead, NJ) and Daniel Morton & Co. (Stamford, CT) are examples.

Major regional brokerage firms, with a branch office network, comprise the third bracket. There are about 57 firms in this category. Technimetrics' data suggest that research departments in major regional firms number five to 50 securities analysts. They follow companies in their region and industries in which regional companies compete. Their research departments are structured. Their valuation approach tends to combine relative ratio and asset value analysis. In total, these firms employ over 13,000 stockbrokers, more than 80 percent of whom are retail-oriented. Moseley Capital Markets, Inc. (New York, NY) and Advest Incorporated (Hartford, CT) are examples.

Piper, Jaffray and Hopwood, Inc. (Minneapolis, MN) also is an example of a major regional firm. Its research department comprises 30 securities analysts and is divided into three broad functions. Some analysts provide research coverage of companies. Others follow technical trends in the market, and a branch information center answers brokers' questions concerning companies and industries.

Piper, Jaffray exemplifies the research coverage effort of a major regional firm. The *Investor Relations Update* newsletter of the National Investor Relations Institute reported that in 1984 the firm followed a universe of 2,800 public companies and provided research coverage on about 200 of them. The firm divided the stocks into 11 major macro-sectors and subdivided them into more than 320 micro-groups. Piper's technicians used computer-aided-analysis to chart the price performance of the groups and sectors. The firm sold its research product to institutional investors. Research product sales equalled half of the firm's total commissions from securities sales.

About 10 retail/institutional firms are in the fourth bracket. Although regional in origin, their reputations for research and underwriting lift them above the major regional category. They are known for the depth of their research coverage of emerging technologies such as computer hardware and software, health care, telecommunications, biotechnology and others. They focus on emerging growth companies in emerging markets. Their research departments are structured. Their valuation approach tends to combine relative ratio and asset value analysis, and their securities analysts are industry specialists who maintain an institutional presence. Examples are L. F. Rothschild & Co. (New York, NY), and Alex. Brown & Sons (Baltimore, MD).

The fifth bracket comprises about 10 national wirehouse brokerage firms. Large numbers of industry specialists staff their research departments and follow medium-sized to large capitalization companies. Their departments are highly structured. Their valuation approach combines present value, relative ratio, and asset value analysis to identify value spreads. Examples are Dean Witter (Sears Financial Network), Kidder, Peabody & Co. (General Electric Financial Services), E. F. Hutton, Prudential-Bache Securities, and PaineWebber, Inc.

E. F. Hutton is an example of the research coverage effort at the national wirehouse level. The *Investor Relations Update* newsletter reported that the firm had about 40 industry specialist securities analysts, six economists/portfolio strategists and 40 institutional salespersons. The firm conducted both primary research and maintenance research. It complemented research with trading capability (order execution) to attract greater commission business at lower trading cost.

The top (sixth) bracket comprises about 15 national institutional brokerage firms. They maintain large research departments in which the average number of analysts is about 50. Industry specialists cover mostly big capitalization companies, although some follow special situations. Their departments are also highly structured. Their valuation approach combines present value, relative ratio and asset value analysis. Some firms, such as Merrill Lynch and Morgan Stanley, maintain a group which specializes in emerging growth companies.

Six brackets of firms may sponsor and provide research coverage on public companies to various tiers of investing institutions. But arithmetic also tells a distressing story. The most visible market sponsorship of public companies is concentrated in the hands of a few dominant firms perceived to be most influential with investing institutions.

According to Technimetrics, Inc., the number of brokerage firms with active research departments has increased almost 48 percent since 1983, to 155. But the number of brokerage firm analysts has increased less than 2 percent since 1984, to 2,050. The increase in firms occurred in the small regional bracket. Their number rose from 76 in 1979 to 148 in 1985.

The *Directory of Wall Street Research* claimed that the number of equity securities analysts at the top 20 brokerage firms (969 of a total of 2,055) remained essentially unchanged in 1985 from 1984. In other words, about 13 percent of all brokerage firms with active research departments, the top 20 in terms of size of research staffs, employed about 47 percent of all analysts. The *Directory* determined levels of analyst coverage by number of research reports, not by number of earnings estimates.

In its 1982 survey, the *Directory of Wall Street Research* reported that "only" 3,157 public companies, of more than 20,000, in the United States and Canada were covered by at least one brokerage firm securities analyst. Of that total, 743, or about 24 percent, were followed by four analysts or more. Up to 1,557, or about 49 percent were covered by three or less analysts, and 857 companies, or about 27 percent, were covered by only one analyst. Collectively, analysts wrote 7,428 research reports in 1982 on 1,724, or 54.6 percent, of those 3,157 companies.

The 1983 survey reported that of more than probably 25,000 public companies worldwide, only 3,561 U.S. companies had any "following" from brokerage firm securities analysts. It was an increase of about 13 percent. And it claimed that only 462 foreign corporations had a following. Still worse, research reports were published on only 2,116 companies. Results for 1984 indicated that 3,800 domestic public companies, up 7 percent from 1983, benefitted from Wall Street research coverage. And coverage of foreign public companies rose to about 1,000 from 462 in 1983.

By 1985, about 4,200 U.S. and Canadian companies had a following. It was an increase of about 13 percent from 1984 and 33 percent from 1982. And about 1,100 foreign companies were covered. Assuming the same proportions of coverage as in 1982, then 24 percent, or 1,008, of those companies would have been covered by four or more analysts. According to the *Directory*, AT & T was covered by 53 analysts, IBM was followed by 51, Exxon by 49, and Mobil Oil by 49. About 49 percent, or 2,058 of the companies would have been covered by three or fewer analysts, and about 27 percent, or 1,134, of the companies would have been covered by only one analyst. The balance of all public companies would, presumably, have had no following.

The numbers suggest that the largest amount of sponsorship is concentrated among the smallest number of brokerage firms. The top 10 brokerage firms, by size of research department, maintained an average staff size of 58 securities analysts in 1985. Staff size was about 57 per department in 1984 and about 53 per department in 1983. Each department covered an average of about 678 companies in 1985 versus about 656 in 1984. Each analyst covered an average of about 11 companies versus about 10 per analyst in 1984.

Average research staff size of the top 20 brokerage firms dropped to about 48 analysts in 1985 from 51 in 1984. Each department covered an average of about 585 companies versus about 559 in 1984. Each analyst covered an average of 12 companies versus about 11 in 1984.

Highly structured research staffs at national institutional bracket firms looked like this in 1985:

1. Merrill Lynch: 114 analysts followed 1,149 companies. The firm was also first in size in 1984.

2. Drexel Burnham Lambert: 58 analysts followed 626 companies. The firm was also second in 1984.

3. Goldman, Sachs: 54 analysts followed 741 companies. The firm was fifth in 1984.

4. Salomon Brothers, Inc: 51 analysts followed 489 companies. The firm was also fourth in 1984.

5. First Boston: 46 analysts followed 642 companies. The firm was sixth in 1984.

6. Shearson Lehman Brothers: 44 analysts followed 531 companies. The firm was third in 1984.

7. Oppenheimer: 39 analysts followed 445 companies. The firm was also seventh in 1984.

8. Morgan Stanley: 37 analysts followed 526 companies. The firm was also eighth in 1984.

9. Donaldson Lufkin Jenrette: 32 analysts followed 487 companies. The firm was also ninth in 1984.

10. Bear Stearns: 31 analysts followed 435 companies. The firm was also 10th in 1984.

Each analyst followed about 12 companies both in 1985 and 1984.

Research staffs at national wirehouse firms showed the following breakdown in 1985:

1. E. F. Hutton: 55 analysts followed 576 companies. The firm was sixth in size in 1984.

2. Smith Barney, Harris Upham: 53 analysts followed 528 companies. The firm was third in 1984.

3. PaineWebber: 53 analysts followed 732 companies. The firm was first in 1984.

4. Dean Witter: 47 analysts followed 588 companies. The firm was also fourth in 1984.

5. Kidder, Peabody: 46 analysts followed 605 companies. The firm was second in 1984.

6. Prudential-Bache: 33 analysts followed an unspecified number of companies. The firm was fifth in 1984.

Each analyst also followed about 12 companies in 1985 and 13 in 1984.
  In the retail/institutional bracket, staff size at two firms was:

1. L. F. Rothschild: 44 analysts followed 533 companies. The firm was also first in size in 1984.

2. Alex Brown: 34 analysts followed 491 companies. The firm was also second in 1984

Each analyst followed about 13 companies.

  In 1985, the *Directory* counted approximately 14,500 brokerage firm research reports of two or more pages. The top 20 brokerage firms produced 6,415 research reports, about 321 reports per firm. In the national institutional bracket, First Boston was first with 773 reports. Goldman, Sachs was second with 428 reports. Salomon Brothers, Donaldson Lufkin & Jenrette and Bear Stearns were third, fourth, and fifth respectively.

  In the national wirehouse category, Dean Witter was first with 635 reports published. E. F. Hutton was second and Kidder, Peabody was third. In the retail/institutional bracket, L. F. Rothschild was first with 768 reports. That represented an average of 18 reports per securities analyst, down from 21 per analyst in 1984.

  Several conclusions can be drawn from this market data:

1. The top 20 firms dominate the securities industry's research sponsorship function. They maintain large analyst staffs, cover the most companies, produce the greatest volume of research reports and are perceived to have the greatest influence with investing institutions.

2. The largest and most influential firms in top brackets often follow the same companies in the same industries. A minority of companies attracts the majority of sponsorship. These companies function in semi-strong form efficient environments.

3. Attracting dominant sponsors from top bracket firms is a real battle for emerging growth companies. The numbers work against them.

4. Smaller firms have broadened the horizons of research sponsorship.

5. A majority of public companies attracts a minority of sponsorship. They function in weak form efficient environments.

DISTRIBUTION CHANNELS: PRIORITIZING DOMINANT SPONSORS

Wall Street is the packaged goods industry of investment ideas. Research departments of investment banking firms are profit centers in which securities analysts are information processors and product managers. Their presence with investing institutions sells stocks and generates commissions.

An analyst's mission is to sell equity products. To maximize sales, he or she must attract as great a commission-paying popularity flow as possible to his or her recommended products. An analyst's job is to process company information, package and merchandise it in the form of investment ideas to investing institutions and to service the portfolio wants and needs of institutional customers. Brokerage firm sell-side analysts at national institutional firms, national wirehouse firms and retail/institutional firms estimate that they spend up to 70 percent of their time merchandising their packaged ideas.

The pressure to merchandise tends to vary with the size of the brokerage firm. In the race to package and sell investment ideas, analysts at top bracket, prestigious national institutional firms are the most aggressive. They are under the most pressure to curry influence with institutional investors and to generate commissions.

For example, here is a description of an industry specialist securities analyst at Merrill Lynch:

[The Wall Street analyst] has 700 institutional clients, people who receive his research reports and seek his counsel. He averages 125 to 150 contacts a month, sometimes as many as 20 a day. He is on the road close to 10 days a month, dropping in on clients and companies, running up travel bills of nearly $20,000 a year. He churns out about 30 reports a year. More than 2,000 copies of each get mailed, gratis, to clients. [22]

In "up" or bull markets, active underwriting firms with securities research departments package and sell performance. They merchandise the stocks of companies in industries with relative price strength and positive earnings momentum. Bull markets add time to analysts' merchandising efforts but take time from their analytical efforts. Market euphoria disguises the resulting analytical void. In "down" or bear markets, active underwriting firms with research departments package and promote price and value spreads. They merchandise those companies with market values which do not adequately reflect the future earning power of their underlying assets or the replacement cost of those assets.

Both Greenwich Associates and *Institutional Investor* magazine conduct an annual poll of institutional portfolio managers to determine how they rank the quality of analysts' packaged products and merchandising efforts. Research rankings determine which analysts get paid which commission sums for which research services. The prevailing belief is the higher an analyst's ranking, the greater the amount of commission dollars allocated to his or her firm and the greater the size of the analyst's annual bonus.

Investing institutions judge brokerage firm securities analysts on a multitude of levels. Portfolio managers usually place greatest weight on the quality, accuracy and contribution of analysts' investment ideas to their portfolio's total return performance. Ideas include both buy and sell recommendations. And portfolio managers value "real time" service, fast relays of information pertinent to portfolio positions.

Institutional securities analysts scrutinize their brokerage firm counterparts differently. They judge on the accuracy of their earnings estimates, the reasonableness of the assumptions which underlie their forecasts, the detail of the analysis which supports their assumptions, the success of their recommendations, and analysts' basic accessibility.

Both commission and fee income motivate brokerage firm securities analysts to perform. Commission income is the name of the research game. It is the reward for high ranking, professional visibility and perceived influence. Brokerage firms maintain attractive incentive compensation schedules to motivate their analysts to sell first and sell often.

For example, according to the *Wall Street Letter*, Laidlaw, Adams & Peck (New York, NY), a retail/institutional brokerage firm, set a new compensation schedule in September 1985 to attract new research talent. The firm was prepared to pay analysts a base salary supplemented by monthly bonuses from institutional securities sales and quarterly bonuses from retail sales. The firm's goal was to reward analysts immediately for commission-generating research recommendations.

Executives of emerging growth companies may find it hard to get a hearing from top bracket dominant sponsors for several reasons. Big name analysts at national institutional, national wirehouse and retail/institutional brokerage firms try to build their annual payout from many sources. They compete aggressively for commission volume from institutional investors. And they work for fee income from other departments within their firm. Corporate finance will pay a portion of the underwriting fee on new banking business. Trading will pay a portion of commissions on blocks of stock. And money management will pay a portion of annual management fee for new equity assets. They may also consult for 'hard' dollars in the industry they cover. In terms of research coverage, this means that the amount of time they can afford to spend processing information on companies which only offer moderate commission potential is limited.

Traditional market sponsorship eludes many emerging companies because of brokerage economics. The first tenet which governs commission-generating ability is that stocks are sold, not bought. This means that investors tend not to initiate the purchase of equities but rather respond to the sale of stocks which satisfy their portfolio objectives. A second tenet is that stocks trade to supply. This means that trading volume and liquidity in a company's shares vary directly with the supply of shares available for trading.

This suggests that analysts must measure the time required to package, promote and sell their research products in terms of potential for commission income from those sales. Potential commission volume is a function of two variables. It varies with the size of public float (supply of shares available for trading) and the annual turnover in institutions' portfolios.

It clearly behooves a brokerage firm analyst to recommend or to follow the stocks of those companies in which all of his or her institutional clients can "take a position". Their investing, and reinvesting, will generate trading volume and commissions for an analyst and his or her firm.

The industries with the greatest potential for generating commission income are those with the biggest market capitalizations and largest floats. They benefit from the most extensive research coverage.

According to the *Directory of Wall Street Research*, electronics was the most heavily researched industry in 1985, for the fourth consecutive year. It was covered by analysts at 261 brokerage firms. Business data processing was second (237 brokerage firms). It was followed by banking (154), health care (146) and telecommunications (127). Analysts at an average of 139 brokerage firms followed the top 10 industries. In 1984, oil & gas services, hotels/motels/restaurants, oil & gas production, oil refining & marketing and the building industries were also closely followed.

According to the *Directory*, AT&T was the most heavily researched company in 1984. It was followed by analysts at 51 brokerage firms. Behind it were:

Texaco (47 brokerage firms)

Exxon (45)

Mobil (45)

Hospital Corporation of America (43)

Phillips Petroleum (43)

Schlumberger (43)

ARCO (42)

Chevron (42)

IBM (42)

Northern Telecom (42)

Unocal (42)

Bell Atlantic (41)

Digital Equipment (41)

Boeing (40)

Standard Oil-Ohio (40)

Standard Oil-Indiana (40)

Brokerage economics changed dramatically on May 1, 1975 when negotiated commission rates came to Wall Street (the Securities Act of 1975). Until that date, the New York Stock Exchange had charged non-negotiable commission rates per share for trades of any size. Rates were on a sliding scale and varied with a share's price. Brokerage firms charged the fixed rate per trade and investors paid it.

When rates became negotiable, institutional investors, who trade in the greatest volume, became hard bargainers. According to SEI Corp., institutional commission rates on trades of 1,000 to 9,999 shares plummeted from an average of $.25 per share in 1975 to an average of $.072 per share in 1986. Greenwich Associates reported that the median average commission for all institutions in 1985 was 9 cents per share versus 11.3 cents per share in 1984. The mean average was 10.6 cents per share (not available in 1984). Institutions feared that decreases in their commission (transactions) costs might increase their trading costs (bid-ask spread as a percent of share price). They feared it might force brokers to cut their execution services and their willingness to commit capital for liquidity purposes.

Brokerage firms hoped a decrease in institutions' transactions costs would increase the volume of transactions. Volume did increase, though not due solely to reduced transactions costs. Share volume on the New York Stock Exchange jumped from an average of less than 20 million shares per day in the early 1970s to an average of 140 million shares per day in 1986.

In 1985, the volume of domestic exchange-listed and NASDAQ-traded issues was 50.3 billion shares versus 6.6 billion shares in 1975. Trading in the shares of the top 30 issues on all exchanges amounted to 4.624 billion shares. That was about 9.2 percent of total share volume in 1985.

AT&T was the 1985 share volume leader on the New York Stock Exchange with 406,014,000 shares traded. The top 10 issues traded a total of 2.392 billion shares. MCI Communications Corporation was the 1985 share volume leader on NASDAQ with 368,468,000 shares traded. The top 10 issues traded a total of 1.537 billion shares. BAT Industries PLC was the 1985 share volume leader on the American Stock Exchange with 183,696,000 shares traded. The top 10 issues traded a total of 694.7 million shares.

Recent Securities Industry Association research suggests that investing institutions account for approximately 50 percent of total share volume. That meant that in 1985, they would have accounted for the trading of about 25.15 billion of a total of 50.3 billion shares. Assuming that share volume was divided evenly among the 155 brokerage firms with research departments (classified by Technimetrics), each firm would have been able to claim credit for about 162.3 million institutionally-traded shares. Average share volume per analyst would depend on size of research staff.

In 1985, the top 20 brokerage firms accounted for 49.3 percent of all analysts (according to the *Directory of Wall Street Research*). If held proportional to share volume, the top 20 firms in 1985 would have accounted for about 12.4

billion shares (49.3 percent of 25.15 billion). Each firm, on average, would have accounted for 619.9 million shares (12.4 billion divided by 20). Each firm had an average of 48 analysts. Therefore, each analyst would have accounted, on average, for about 12.9 million shares. At an average commission rate of $.072 per share, average gross commissions per analyst would have been $928,800. Average net commissions per analyst would vary with his or her firm's payout policy. Actual average gross commissions for institutional salesmen in 1986 were reported to be $1.1 million. Average net commissions per salesman were reported to be $227,412.

The actual amount of annual share volume creditable to any one analyst varies with the perceived influence of the analyst and the perceived prestige of the brokerage firm. A dominant sponsor at a top bracket national institutional firm may do business with and have commissions directed from several thousand investing institutions from each of the four tiers mentioned in Chapter 7. And large share volume, in the form of block trades, may be allocated as a combined result of research coverage and a firm's order execution capability.

These statistics pose a problem for small capitalization, emerging companies. The average share volume figure of 12.9 million shares per analyst in the top 20 brokerage firms may be a multiple of the total number of outstanding shares of most emerging companies. Average annual turnover in the shares of *Business Week's* Top 1000 companies (by market value) was 74.2 percent of 46 million average shares outstanding. Annual turnover in the shares of emerging companies would have to be alarmingly high to satisfy the liquidity needs of institutions and the commission needs of institutionally-oriented brokerage firm securities analysts.

Research directors at national firms often believe that small capitalization companies can be too expensive to follow on a research basis because of their lack of commission potential. In some cases, entire industries may have market values only a fraction of the Standard & Poor's 500 stock index. They may cost too much to cover. Recall from Chapter 4 that the market value of the 80 largest thrift institutions was only slightly higher than that of American Express Company. Commission potential from trading in the shares of these companies is too limited. Research coverage cannot adequately pay for itself.

Traditional research coverage of small capitalization companies can also be very time-consuming. Little financial or business information may be available with which to forecast earnings. And estimation risk surrounding a forecast may be too great for the reputation capital of the analyst making it. And, even after gathering data, there may be little basis for comparison of the relative valuation of an emerging company with those of more mature companies. A lack of consensus and comparability heightens investors' perceptions of earnings uncertainty. It adds to relative neglect of, and pricing inefficiency in, the shares of emerging companies.

Entrepreneurial professionals who can afford the time to discover small capitalization, emerging companies tend to be entrepreneurial. They are often found in lower bracket regional firms which maintain relatively loosely structured research departments. Their firms tend to specialize in knowing the fundamentals and managements of emerging companies in their own backyards. These firms maintain relatively low overhead. Their analysts can profit from identifying pricing inefficiencies and value spreads in these neglected companies. They can sell these stocks to venturesome or aggressive money managers in relatively lower tiers who trade on value or expectations. These investors can exploit the potential for excess returns.

Managements of small capitalization, emerging companies will usually find dominant sponsors in lower brackets and lead investors in lower tiers. In that sense, there are two reasons to establish relationships with newsletter/analysts at investment advisory firms (which may also manage money) and broker/analysts at lower bracket small regional brokerage firms. First, as discussed earlier in this chapter, research recommendations in many forms affect market-wide expectations. And they continue to affect share prices as information becomes more available. And second, these sponsors may network with lead investors from several tiers. These investors can buy the company's shares, spread perception of the company's returns potential and significantly broaden a company's valuation network to other money managers and analysts.

ANALYTICAL METHODS OF DOMINANT SPONSORS

There are two types of predictive analysis around which research products are packaged and sold: fundamental and technical. Present value, relative ratio, and asset value analysis are fundamentals-oriented. They are used to identify value spreads. Fundamental analysis is structure-oriented. It seeks structural causes for a company's cash-generating ability. It assesses value-based planning systems and competitive advantages. It evaluates financial condition, tests for quality of earnings and the impact of inflation on operations. And it ranks the results of analysis.

Recall that present value analysis relies on assumptions of growth in cash flows, duration of that growth, and discount rates to derive specific estimates of expected returns and share prices. On the other hand, relative ratio and asset value analysis relies on historical trends by which to judge current relative relationships and to derive estimates of ranges of future earning power. Those who practice either focus on price or time, independent of share volume.

Fundamental securities analysis relies on human relationships with corporate executives and logic to explain variations in cash-generating abilities among companies, and the persistence of those variations over time. It is a disciplined approach to stock picking, and it is geared to relatively long-term stock price performance. Analyst reaction to IBM quarterly earnings announcements may suggest a more short-term reaction. But that reflects the fact that analysts do business with customers who trade both on value and on expectations.

Fundamental securities analysis is both quantitative and qualitative:

The predictive process is based primarily on the quality and depth of management, market dominance, presence of a sound strategic plan and planning system, and the strategic credibility of a company. In assessing the quality and depth of management, analysts look at management's performance record, presentations, evidence of sound strategic planning, and ability to meet stated objectives by processing all such information. Along with assessments of the external economic and industry environments [group and industry effects], analysts develop a systemic appraisal of the firm. This evaluation becomes the foundation for a long-term financial performance in terms of EPS and ROE, which determine the investment value analysts place on a stock.[23]

In the context of the overall equity valuation process, good fundamental securities analysis is bottom-up and security-specific. It addresses capital and business strategy over a two- to three-year time horizon. And it focuses on the actual "how" and the "why" of a company's cash-generating ability: how a company makes money and why a company makes money.

Good analysis concentrates on fundamentals. It studies market growth and entry/barriers, product positions, competition, pricing strategies and cost structures. It is also flow of funds-oriented. It examines growth/share relationships looking for market leaders. It scrutinizes sources/uses of discretionary cash flow from rising prices or falling costs. It is a key proxy of management quality. And it judges the efficiency of capital employed.

Fundamentals-oriented analysts search for information about earnings growth. They divide their company-specific challenge into four parts: "what I know [about a company] that nobody else knows [discovery], what nobody knows [the future], what I know that everybody else knows [the past], and what I don't know that everybody else knows."[24]

In their attempts at discovery, good fundamentals-oriented analysts may identify the right "companies" but not necessarily the right "stocks." The difference lies in the fact that analyst recommendations can favor purchase of the right companies at the wrong times. They tend to focus on stock picking rather than market timing and an orientation to long-term growth versus short-term trading.

Good fundamental analysis judges the calibre and credibility of company managements and verifies its findings. It identifies the skills and motivations of corporate executives. It strives to avoid being charmed or misled or becoming a parrot for management, especially by executives of "tomorrow stocks" who talk a good story of future but never deliver. It balances management opinions, perceptions and forecasts with "checks" made outside of the company. These inputs come from objective third parties such as suppliers to the company, customers, competitors, and past employees of the company. A good analyst is like an investigative journalist. He or she verifies sources and checks facts before recommending a company.

The surprise demise of the Atari video-game division of Warner Communications is an example of analyst checks which were never made. Analysts claimed that visits to toy stores would have shown rampant discounting of and clear weakening in market demand for the company's products, regardless of management's opinion about Atari's prospects. The collapse of Warner's stock should not have been the surprise that it was.

The demise of National Healthcare, Inc. (Dothan, AL) also should not have been a surprise. A hospital management company, it grew by aggressively acquiring rural hospitals. In 1986, the company managed 33 hospitals and nine nursing homes. Its annual revenues rose from $206,000 in 1982 to $115.7 million in 1986. Offered in 1985, the company's shares traded to a 1986 high of $17, equal to a $177.9 million market capitalization.

But checks with hospital employees or former employees by any of the six brokerage firms which followed the company would have revealed that the company's success was not all that it seemed. Numbers were doctored, accounting was creative and creditors were stiffed. The company took a $9.1 million write-off in 1986. It reported a loss for the fiscal year versus a *Forbes* magazine earnings estimate of $4.3 million ($.53 per share). The company's stock dropped to $.625 per share as of September 3, 1987, equal to a market value of $6.5 million.

The interests of good analysts often conflict with the desires of executives. The former usually want to speak to senior management and operating managers. The latter prefer to restrict those visits. Some aggressive brokerage firm analysts may even go so far as to try to telephone a company's strategists or operating people in the evening at home. Management's best policy is to brief senior executives on a monthly or quarterly basis about how management should communicate value to Wall Street. This involves a discussion both of what management should give to analysts and what they should take from them.

When their travel plans take them to cities with shareholding money managers and industry following securities analysts, senior executives should schedule personal visits as a regular part of a business trip. When analysts visit company headquarters, their visits should be restricted to those senior executives who are regularly briefed. Plant tours should be conducted and technology described. But discussions should always be in terms of trends, ranges or consensus expectations versus specific numbers, projects or progress.

Analysts rate companies and industries based on their research and analysis. The ratings usually appear on a scale from 1 (highest) to 5 or 6 (lowest). They represent an analyst's estimate of the attractiveness of a company or industry relative to the overall market. A rating reflects relative confidence in potential share price appreciation out 12 months.

A 1 rating spreads perception of high expectations that a company or industry will significantly outperform the market. A 3 indicates an expectation that performance will be in line with the overall market. And a 5 (or 6) rating spreads expectations that a company or industry will substantially underperform the general market.

Money managers often think that fundamental securities analysis has other weaknesses besides a reputation for occasional poor stock selection. They think it, and those who practice it tend to be too optimistic. It favors positive outlooks for earnings and dividend growth rates. They claim that since stocks are sold, not bought, and positive earnings prospects sell stocks, the vast majority of brokerage recommendations are buying ideas.

Sell recommendations are less frequent for several reasons. Analysts do not want to turn off their information sources. They do not want to offend corporate executives on whom they rely for detailed data. It would affect the quality of their earnings estimates and harm their ability to generate trading volume and commission income. And numbers work in favor of recommending purchase instead of sale of securities. There are simply fewer sellers. Any investor can buy a stock but only those who already own a stock can sell it.

For example, a money manager can make any of four positive and two negative investment decisions about a company's stock. He or she can establish an initial position in the stock, maintain an existing position, add to an existing position, or reestablish a liquidated position. On the negative side, he or she can reduce a position or eliminate a position in the company's stock. Clearly, any institution that doesn't already own a company's stock could buy it and those that do own it could buy more. But only owners can sell long positions.

Lead investors usually prefer to do their own original primary research. Especially in bull markets, they fear faulty analysis and forecast errors because most analysts are merchandising instead of analyzing. They get nervous about potential for earnings surprises from analysts who do not make their checks thoroughly. They contend that bull market conditions only disguise problems of poor analysis and hide a lot of valuation mistakes. Money managers support the adage, "don't mistake brains for a bull market."

The other form of predictive analysis is technical analysis. It is behavior-oriented. It seeks associations between share volume and share price, especially in relation to historical volume/price relationships. It watches for changes in these relationships to predict future share prices. Those who practice it focus on share volume, independent of share price.

This method flies in the face of the "random walk theory" of stock prices. That theory states that stock market prices have no memory and that tomorrow's prices have no connection to yesterday's prices. Yet practitioners of technical analysis consider it reliable. In fact, recommendations based on technical analysis caused a record 61.87 point one-day drop in the Dow Jones Industrial Average on July 7, 1986. Technical analysis should not be confused with the effect of triple witching hours and program trading on stock market and stock price volatility.

Technical analysis is based upon the belief that share prices move in trends which are continuous until disrupted by share volume imbalances. Supply/demand analysis measures how many shares can be traded at a given price and how much price changes for a given trade. The approach is geared to market timing. By definition, it is oriented to relative changes in share price in the near term. In that sense, technicians believe that fundamentalists may win long-term wars in their search for value but can lose near-term total return battles by their vulnerability to share price swings.

Technical analysis is also a disciplined valuation approach. It is based on statistical associations between volume and price. These pertain to issues such as volatility, liquidity and marketability, momentum, relative strength, on-balance volume and buying power/selling pressure. They use these indicators to divine strengthening or weakening "value" trends in share prices. This form of analysis involves no fundamentals, no human relationships and no judgments of a qualitative nature. Technicians are called "chartists." They use charts and graphs of historic patterns of share volume/share price relationships to market time the selection of stocks.

On a market-related basis, technicians examine several sentiment indicators to measure market breadth. They watch to see if fewer issues participate in market advances (declines). They watch for gaps (positive or negative) that may open between the Dow Jones Transportation Average and the Industrial Average. As a measure of speculative sentiment, they observe share volume in over-the-counter markets which usually amounts to about 80 percent of the NYSE. Before the Dow's price drop mentioned earlier, that percentage was up to 97 percent.

The advance/decline ratio compares stocks going up to those going down. Changes in the ratio indicate investors' sentiment and behavior. The ratio usually hovers around 50/50. A stray in either direction may signal a trend reversal. Short sales, short interest, odd-lot sales and purchases, and the ratio of "put" volume to "call" volume in the options market also offer market signals to chartists.

On a company-specific basis, the discipline examines several trends by which to time purchases or sales in a company's stock. Technicians look at a stock's volatility (beta) relative to the overall market. They examine a share's liquidity and marketability. Liquidity measures the number of shares which can be bought or sold at a given price or price range. They calculate its "beta liquidity" ratio. It is a measure of the amount of stock historically required to move a stock up or down by 1 percent. And they examine its annual "volume turnover ratio." This measures annual trading volume divided by shares outstanding, adjusted for any changes in capital stock. This calculation can also highlight seasonal and monthly trading patterns.

"Momentum indicators" gauge rates and directions of change in market indices as a base from which to predict future price changes in a stock. And "relative strength" measures a stock's price performance relative to a moving average index of overall market momentum. An S & P ratio index (of monthly prices divided by a 3-month or 6-month average index) more than 1 is bullish and less than 1 is bearish.

Finally, chartists measure the average index of money flows into and out of a stock. It indicates "buying power and selling pressure." A 1-month, 3-month, 6-month, or 12-month index of moving average price divded by moving average volume is a gauge of long-term price/volume trends. It tries to quantify the amount of volume necessary to move a stock up or down by a set percentage. It also identifies trends in investors' accumulation or distribution of a company's shares. "On-balance" volume is another moving average index. It also quantifies trends in accumulation and distribution. It assumes volume trends lead price changes.

In the equity valuation process, management will usually have most direct contact with fundamentals-oriented securities analysts. But the effect, not necessarily the logic, of technicians' work on market-wide expectations and on a company's share price and share volume should not be minimized. Their work is less visible than that of fundamentalists. But many investors often consider their predictive quality equally as reliable and accurate. Chapter 9 makes these points more clear.

It was mentioned earlier in this chapter that perceived earnings growth potential attracts dominant sponsors. But commission-generating potential, the ability to sell stock to commission-paying customers, determines the amount of time an analyst spends researching, writing and merchandising. Methods by which sponsors find emerging companies with adequate commission potential were also mentioned earlier. Management may find them. But lead investors are more likely to apprise them of saleable small-cap performance or price stories.

When approached by analysts, management should ask many questions: who are these analysts, where are they from, how important are they and how much time do they warrant? Recall from Chapter 4 that management will know dominant sponsors by their commitment of time and the breadth of their merchandising. Executives should prioritize their influence:

1. Size of firm
   a. In which bracket does the analyst's firm compete? In which tiers are the institutions with which the firm does the majority of its commission business?

    b. How many total analysts are in the firm's research department?

    c. How many registered representatives work for the firm?

    d. How many branch offices does the firm maintain? Are they spread nationally or regionally?

2. Importance of Analyst: Coverage

    a. How many companies, in total, does the research department follow? Publish research reports on?

    b. Is the analyst an industry specialist or multi-industry generalist?

    c. How many companies does the analyst follow? How many industries (if applicable)? On how many companies does he/she actively publish research reports? Actively follow?

    d. How many other companies in the company's industry does the analyst follow? Actively publish reports on?

    e. Of those companies followed, how many does the analyst currently recommend for purchase? For sale?

    f. What is the range of market capitalization of companies followed?

3. Importance of the Analyst: Merchandising

    a. To how many institutions in which tiers does the analyst merchandise his or her investment ideas?

    b. The analyst is on the "research list" for commission payments at how many institutions? This is an indication of the size of an analyst's following, how large a popularity flow the analyst can attract. Have appearances on research lists increased or decreased?

    c. When merchandising a research recommendation, how many shares of a company, on average, does the analyst put away into clients' portfolios? Management should plot changes in its (P/B)-to-return on equity ratio relative to peer competitors to see if analysts' merchandising efforts affect share price or only share volume.

    d. How many companies are on the analyst's current list of recommended stocks? Why are they recommended? How long have they been recommended? Which are no longer recommended? Why?

    e. How often does the analyst pick up a new stock? What criteria must that stock meet?

4. Methodology of the Analyst

    a. How did the analyst discover the company? By computer screen (which one)? Through a network? From a money manager (word of mouth)? Another analyst? Other industry executives? Announcements? Disclosures?

    b. Which valuation models does the analyst use? Why? For how long have they been used? What biases do the models incorporate? What is his or her record of accuracy in estimating earnings?

    c. On what basis does the analyst initiate/terminate research coverage? Recommend purchase/sale?

    d. How often does the analyst visit followed companies? Visit commission-paying institutions?

    e. How often does the analyst write research reports on followed companies? What does the analyst do with those reports?

   f. To how many of the firm's commission customers are hard copies of those reports distributed? To how many brokers?

   g. When a report is published, how long does it take the analyst to make all of his or her "calls"?

   h. If an analyst picks up the company: to which other money managers and institutional analysts who buy stocks with the company's characteristics can the analyst refer management?

What can executives do to induce an analyst to make his or her calls and to speed the popularity flow into a company's shares? What can management do to get an analyst to write and to merchandise a research report(s) on the company? For small capitalization companies with limited commission potential, he or she may make calls but not write reports. Management cannot force an analyst to publish a report on the company. An analyst's decision to write will depend on several factors:

1. Belief that the company is right.
2. Belief in the company's fundamentals: perception of the strength of its competitive advantage and potential for real earnings growth.
3. Trust of management: assumptions, forecasts, quality of information.
4. Belief in management: operating skills, internal controls.
5. Existing competition to cover the company: the desire to be first and to be right on the company.
6. Belief in ability to sell the shares to investing institutions.
7. Potential to get the company's banking-related business.

Ultimately, an analyst must balance the quality of a good performance or value idea with the ability to generate commissions with it. Commission potential may be too limited due either to a small float or big competition among many analysts. In either case, an analyst probably will not publish on the company unless he or she believes he or she can "steal" the company's banking business. In that case, potential fee income for the firm and the analyst may outweigh the limited commission potential.

When an analyst publishes a research report on a company, managements of some companies do nothing with it. Others actively merchandise an analyst's opinion on their company to institutions. The latter include these reports in corporate information kits. They send them to current and prospective shareholders and large institutional holders of the shares of peer competitors. Lawyers contend that management must be prepared to send both good reports and bad reports. I recommend that managements heed that advice. But they should also prepare to personally follow-up on any mailing of such third-party opinions with perspective on the reports' highlights concerning the company.

Executives should be aware of the limited circulation of an analyst's report through a brokerage firm's distribution channel. Reports are not printed and shipped in volume to retail brokers in branch offices. Short written summaries of lengthy reports or conference call summations may be delivered. But the odds are high that most retail brokers, and their individual customers, will not see hard copies of analysts' research reports. The obvious potential problem associated with limited distribution is limited retail sales of the company's securities.

Managements of many companies counter this merchandising limitation. They often use published research reports to lubricate and broaden the retail distribution channel. They underwrite the expense of printing and direct-mailing an analyst's research report on the company to all of the retail stockbrokers throughout the analyst's firm. They make certain that a firm's stockbrokers know the research opinion of their firms' analyst on their company so that they can more easily sell it to their individual customers.

Management can perform a small test to assess the breadth of an analyst's retail merchandising effort within his or her own firm. I recommend that executives make anonymous telephone contact with any broker in several offices of a firm whose securities analyst has recently published a research report on the company. Play the role of a person who heard a stock tip (on the executive's company, of course). Ask what the broker's firm knows and thinks of the company. The broker will either respond in terms of "our research department thinks. . ." or quote from an S & P *Stock Report* on the company, if one exists. Or the broker may try a "bait and switch" tactic. He or she may not know a lot about that company but, "there is another company. . . ."

I think it is important that executives monitor analysts' merchandising ability, not just their analytical skill. Three indicators highlight their success in attracting a popularity flow:

1. Share price, independent of share volume. Shifts in P/B-to-return on equity ratios (mentioned earlier).
2. Share volume (money flow), independent of share price. Dollar value of all daily trades on upticks (inflow) versus downticks (outflow). Management should examine exchange daily trade reports.
3. Share holders. Management should examine transfer sheets from its transfer agent.

Executives should keep in contact with analysts who publish research reports on the company. They should ask which types of institutions are buying stock on the analyst's recommendation. And they should ask for referrals to them. It enables analysts to heighten commission flow at the same time as management heightens popularity flow. And it offers management an opportunity to swap market intelligence with analysts, valuable information about institutions' portfolio activity, possibly before buy or sell orders are actually submitted. That may enable analysts to steal commission business.

Management should be mindful of the fact that dominant sponsors also merchandise sell recommendations. These sponsors may tend to be broker/analysts at lower bracket firms or be newsletter publisher/analysts. Both are able to affect market-wide returns expectations and attract popularity outflow. For example, Baldwin-United (Cincinnati, OH) was brought to its knees by the dogged pursuit of a young analyst at a small, Chicago-based regional brokerage firm. And Thornton O'Glove, publisher of the *Quality of Earnings Report*, wrote about inventory buildups, sales declines, and squeezed margins in wake of retail store expansion at Crazy Eddie, Inc. It led to a precipitous stock price drop to about $4 per share from $20 per share.

SELL-SIDE DISTRIBUTION: THREE CHANNELS

There are three channels of distribution on Wall Street. Information about the returns potential of corporate equities passes from the sell-side brokerage firms to the buy-side institutions through: securities analysts, institutional salespersons, and retail stockbrokers. Of these three, analysts and big-producing retail stockbrokers are of most relative importance to managements of emerging companies. Institutional salespersons are second and average producing retail stockbrokers are least important.

Brokerage firm securities analysts are most important. The buying power and potential capital commitment of the audience to which they merchandise are greatest. To maximize their commission-generating potential, analysts aggressively compete to process information and to service the portfolio needs of lead investors in any or all tiers. For corporate executives, this means that analysts, as dominant sponsors, are the intermediaries through which to attract the largest popularity flow.

Big producing retail-oriented stockbrokers are the second most important channel. In contrast to retail/institutional salespersons at national institutional firms, they are usually found at national wirehouse or regional brokerage firms. Every brokerage firm has a few. Big producers generate millions of dollars in gross annual commissions. The largest produce tens of millions in annual commissions. They are often the equivalent of small money managers. They often have discretion over tens to hundreds of millions of dollars in hundreds of retail customers' accounts. The dollar value of their annual commissions on trading these accounts is often similar to the annual management fee for a third or fourth tier institutional money manager.

Big commission-generating retail stockbrokers may also function in the same way as broker/analysts at small regional brokerage firms. They often have a staff of assistants which conducts independent research for them. And they can often put out more stock into the portfolios of low tier institutions and of individuals than industry analysts at major regional brokerage firms. They can attract a large popularity flow to an emerging company and spread perception widely.

Andrew Lanyi is an example of a relatively big commission-generating stock-broker in the retail/institutional brokerage firm of Ladenburg, Thalmann & Co. (New York, NY). He manages about $55 million in about 570 accounts. In 1985, he generated about $2.3 million in gross commissions. That is roughly the equivalent of a money manager's fee (half of 1 percent) for managing about $450 million in equity assets. Estimates for 1986 gross commission income were around $3 million. The firm named a division for him.

Management should seek referrals from big producing stockbrokers and ask questions on these subjects:

1. Size
   a. What approximate level of annual gross commissions does the broker generate? Is that an increase or decrease from past years?
   b. Commissions on sales of equities represent what portion of the broker's total annual gross commissions?
   c. How many clients does the broker do active business with? What is the total dollar value of active customers' assets? How much of those assets does the broker have discretion over? If treated as a small fund, what record of total return performance would the broker have achieved for his or her clients?
   d. How many shares of a company, on average, does the broker put into customers' portfolios? That represents what dollar value and share size per portfolio? It represents what average weighting per customer portfolio?
2. Activities
   a. How, specifically, did the broker discover the company?
   b. What research sources does the broker use? Does his firm's analyst follow the company? Does the broker subscribe to any technical or fundamental newsletters which have mentioned the company. Ask for copies of these newsletters.
   c. With whom does the broker network? Other brokers in the firm? Money managers? The firms' analyst? Big producers at other firms?
3. Referrals
   a. Can the broker refer management to the firm's industry specialist securities analyst who covers the company's industry? Or to the firm's multi-industry generalist? Or to the firm's "emerging growth" group of analysts? Does the firm cover any other companies in the industry
   b. Can the broker refer management to any money managers, to whom they may have referred substantial individual investors? The money manager represents what size of equity assets?
   c. Does the broker subscribe to newsletters which follow emerging companies? Can the broker refer management to any newsletter/publisher/analysts?
   d. Can the broker refer management to any other big producing brokers in the firm? In other firms?

Institutional stockbrokers are third in importance to management in the sell-side distribution channel. They are usually associated with national institutional, national wirehouse, and retail/institutional firms. They are relatively few in number (about 2,200). They act as research liaisons between their firm's securities analysts and portfolio managers and analysts at institutions. Their job is to know portfolio level investment decisions before portfolio managers send buy/sell orders to the institution's trading desk for execution. In that sense, they are secondary to and take direction from securities analysts. They also serve as trading liaisons between their firm's trading desk and institutional traders. Their job is to "ask for the order" which comes from portfolio level.

Small producing retail stockbrokers are of least importance to management in the distribution channel. Their primary audience is the individual investor. Their annual gross commission levels are usually low to medium hundreds of thousands of dollars. For example, Alex. Brown & Sons has set minimum annual commission production levels for its retail brokers at $150,000 and annual production goals at $400,000 to $500,000.

In relation to the work of retail brokers, much debate concerns the importance of individuals to corporations as sources of investor demand. Many argue in favor of their loyalty to management, their long-term time horizons and their being a source of liquidity and low volatility for a company's shares. But two trends directly suggest the waning influence of individual investors in the equity valuation process. And, by association, they infer the declining importance of retail stockbrokers in the distribution of equities.

First, individuals have, for about 14 years, been direct net sellers of stocks. In general, they prefer indirect ownership (professional management) of equities, perhaps as a consequence of the institutionalization of equities markets. And, second, the financial services industry has eclipsed and engulfed the securities industry. Equity products are now only a part of a much larger financial asset package.

Federal Reserve Board data suggest that individuals have, on balance, been on the sell-side of public transactions for many years. They have sold more stock than they have bought in every year since 1972. They have been net buyers in only 17 calendar quarters since 1954 and in consecutive quarters on only four occasions since that time. No net buying trends of any duration have ever developed. Figures compiled by Salomon Brothers, Inc., a national institutional brokerage firm, confirm the trend.

Under the title of "Direct Household Acquisition of Equities," the Fed estimated that American households' net sales of equities amounted to about $121.6 billion in 1985. That was an increase from $79.3 billion in 1984. And, of the total market capitalization of U.S. equities, estimated to be about $2.727 trillion as of May 31, 1986, the Federal Reserve Board estimated that individual investors held, at the end of 1985, about 23.6 percent of the U.S. equities universe. That was a decrease from a level of about 44.9 percent in 1968 and was virtually unchanged since 1974.

The New York Stock Exchange survey found that about 47 million Americans, one in every five, owned shares either in a publicly traded company or in an equity mutual fund in 1985. That was an increase from 42.4 million in 1983. The survey also found that half of all shareowners had a brokerage account. It further revealed that the median value of individuals' portfolios was $6,200. The median value for those who maintained brokerage accounts was $9,200 and the value of their 1985 stock transactions was $7,300. The median value for those who did not maintain a brokerage account was $3,600, and the value of their 1985 stock transactions was $2,300.

The NYSE survey found that between 1983 and 1985 about 6.8 million individuals invested in equities for the first time. Although many Americans may own shares, the real question is how many individuals who own equities buy them directly or indirectly. On a direct basis, they may make their own purchase decisions. They buy their first stock through a broker/dealer, an insurance agent, in Individual Retirement Accounts (IRA), or through Keough Plans. According to the 1985 NYSE survey of shareholders, only 49.5 percent of adult shareowners who bought stock for the first time bought it directly.

On an indirect basis, individuals owned their first stock primarily through third-parties. One of four shareowners made their first stock purchase through an employee-sponsored plan. It may take the form of an employee stock ownership plan (ESOP), a 401(k) retirement plan, a profit sharing plan, stock options, or a company bonus. Or they may have received it through gifts or inheritances. In 1985, a full 50.5 percent of adult shareowners who bought stock for the first time bought it indirectly. In addition, estimates were that mutual funds represented the indirect equity ownership of about 35 million adults, up from 10 million in 1980.

The trend in individuals' market participation is clearly toward indirect ownership of corporate equities. The number of individuals who are direct owners has risen. But on balance, individuals have been direct net sellers of equities. The only conclusion is that increases in ownership of equities has occurred indirectly, through professional money managers.

A January 1987 report from IDS (Investors Diversified Services, Minneapolis, MN) confirmed the trend. Called "The Source," the newsletter reported that households sold more than $100 billion in equities in 1985, primarily because of mergers, leveraged buy-outs, and corporate share repurchase programs. At the same time, the net acquisition of mutual fund shares by individuals in 1985, excluding money market funds, amounted to slightly more than $100 billion. The Investment Company Institute estimated that more than $210 billion went into mutual funds in 1986.

Changes in the structure of brokers' compensation undertaken by Merrill Lynch lend credence to these trends of indirect ownership and institutionalization of individuals' equity assets. The firm is evolving into a money manager. In early 1986, Merrill was believed to hold about $15 billion in IRA and other retirement accounts and expectations were that that figure would triple by 1990.

Its financial services for sale now encompass pension and retirement planning, estate planning, insurance, municipal bonds, futures, business financing, tax planning, cash management, home equity credit lines, financing, funding and credit, more than 300 mutual funds and, finally, investment research (common stocks).

To reflect this evolution from brokerage firms to financial services supermarkets, stockbrokers are not stockbrokers any longer. Now they are called financial consultants or financial planners. Merrill Lynch employs about 10,600 of them and they do not just sell equities any longer. Now they sell equities and equity derivatives. Merrill Lynch's goal is to lock up individuals' total assets, not just their commission business. The firm wanted customers loyal more to the firm than to the firm's representatives.

The firm altered its commission structure to reflect that objective. Bonus incentives to brokers were intended to shift their selling focus from stocks and bonds to the accumulation of total customer assets and the extension of consumer credit. The incentive for brokers was to capture the total assets of high net worth/high profit individuals.

By implication, attempts to create demand among individual investors through small producing retail stockbrokers, in general, is ineffective. Most do not sell enough stock, generate gross annual commissions of enough consequence, or wield enough perceived influence to be of any use to corporate managements in their efforts to affect Wall Street's pricing mechanism. And shareownership by individual investors is of far less importance to managements than equity ownership by lead investors. Investing institutions tend to manage individuals' assets anyway. By capturing a share of institutional investors' equity assets, management actually gains a share of individual's assets. The reverse, however, is not true. If executives focus time and money on individuals, they waste resources on those who have minimal bearing on and involvement in the equity valuation process.

Finally, stockbrokers want the right "story," as opposed to the right company or the right stock. They classify companies in terms of whether their stories can be sold. Here are some examples:

"Concept" stocks: restaurant companies.

"Story" stocks: companies with a competitive development such as new management, new product, new technology or new process.

"Theme" stocks: companies with earnings sensitivity to economic themes such as inflation or disinflation.

"Niche" stocks: companies with growing shares in small markets.

"Deal" stocks: companies involved in public equity financing.

"Event" stocks: companies in organizational or ownership restructuring.

Companies are also "plays" on the market. They may be "pure" plays (monopolies), "asset" plays (long-term assets on corporate books at cost instead of market), "margin" plays (falling costs or rising prices), or "interest rate" plays (interest-rate sensitivity).

TRADING AND LISTING

The National Association of Securities Dealers (NASD) claims that the number of market-makers in a company's shares varies with a company's market capitalization. For example, on average, companies with:

Market Value	Market-Makers
Less than $10 million	6.4
$10 million to $20 million	7.4
$20 million to $50 million	8.1
$50 million to $100 million	9.3
$100 million to $250 million	10.2
$250 million to $500 million	13.8
More than $500 million	more than 16.2

There are six categories of firms which actively make markets in over-the-counter securities. First, small regional brokerage firms tend to trade local, small capitalization industrial and financial issues. They tend to be trading firms. They profit on trading the spread in share price quotes. Volatility and wide spreads heighten their potential trading profits. Second, major regional firms tend to concentrate on corporate finance client issues or companies in their geographic market area. They may trade between 50 to 250 separate issues. Third, retail/institutional firms may trade up to 500 separate issues.

Fourth, national wirehouse brokerage firms may make markets in between 400 to 1,500 individual issues. Fifth, national institutional firms may trade a similar number of issues. Both of the above commit capital and "position" blocks of stock to heighten institutional liquidity. And they use trading to highlight and to capitalize on their investment banking capabilities and research relationships. Sixth, wholesale market-makers strictly make markets and trade the spreads in share price quotes. They compete for agency business in high share volume, liquid stocks.

Emerging companies need support from dominant market-makers. They are perceived to be dominant providers of liquidity, price continuity, price stability and share marketability. These are proxies for low institutional trading costs. Greenwich Associates annually surveys institutional investors to determine which brokerage firms offer the best order execution services (lowest trading costs). Management must market its stock to these dominant market-makers. They are usually in the top two brackets.

The measure of trading cost and quality of market in the shares of a company is the spread in a quote between bid and ask prices. It is expressed as a percentage of share price (spread/price). It is an economic "spread," the price a dealer charges for providing liquidity and rapid order execution. It is also the price of illiquidity in companies' shares.

Mention was made in Chapter 7 that empirical studies have shown that trading in the shares of small capitalization companies costs much more than trading in the shares of large capitalization companies. Spread/price increases as the dollar value of a trade in the shares of a small capitalization company increases. This cost threatens investing institutions' portfolio returns and bars them from owning the shares of small capitalization companies. However, dominant market-makers' sponsorship of the shares of emerging companies enhances the potential for greater liquidity and lower trading cost. This helps to attract broader share ownership and greater pricing efficiency.

Managements can market their equity product to dominant market-makers. They should write letters and make follow-up telephone calls and in-person visits to the heads of over-the-counter trading departments of brokerage firms. The *Securities Industry* (Association) *Yearbook* and Standard & Poor's *Security Dealers of North America* list the names and telephone numbers of those who head equity trading and, in some cases, OTC trading departments.

Trading departments are product and profit centers of brokerage firms. Markets are made in securities on an agency basis, by matching buyers and sellers. They are also made on a principal basis, by using firm capital to provide liquidity to customers with whom the firm maintains a commission, corporate finance or new business relationship.

Trading is customer-driven. A department's decision to start making a market in the shares of a company reflects customer interest and perceived potential trading profit. It usually depends upon the size of a company's float (liquidity), its potential share volume (volatility), its past operating track record (stability), its number of shareholders, and the number of competing market-makers in the stock (liquidity). About five competing dealers is desirable. These considerations help to reduce trading risk. For example, PaineWebber avoids securities which trade below $3 per share with floats less than 500,000 shares.

A trading department will usually stop making a market in the shares of a company if there is a lack of customer demand. That reduces trading profit potential and leads to idle inventory positions. For example, trading may be inactive. No one in the firm, from research, banking or sales departments may have expressed an interest in the stock on the behalf of customers. In the case of the converted thrift industry, market-makers generally dropped stocks which traded 2,000 or fewer shares per day. A firm may recommend that management list its shares. It is an acknowledgment that the company's shares do not trade and that the firm wants to remove a slow-moving item from the firm's inventory.

Academic studies have found that market-makers tend to act rationally in setting bid prices below and ask prices above what they perceive to be investors' perceptions of an issue's fair value. One study[25] found that (dealer) spreads widened with greater share price volatility, higher share price and lower share volume. They narrowed with liquidity attributes such as high share volume, number of shareholders, number of competing market-makers and extent of price continuity. Studies have also determined that market-makers tend to be buyers on price weakness and sellers on price strength. They tend to be net buyers on days prior to price decreases and net sellers on days prior to price increases.

Managements' relationships with market-makers is important. The information content of management announcements may have an effect on the market value of dealer inventories and firmness of dealer quotes. Executives should be certain to include market-makers on company mailing lists and to alert them to the content of announcements as announcements are made.

Wall Street's perspective on the relationship between share price and share volume is conventional. The investment community believes that the two are positively correlated, that share volume leads and moves share price both up and down. Academic literature tends to agree but suggests that the relationship is more complex.

As mentioned in Chapter 6, the information content of share price differs from that of share volume. Changes in share price are considered market-related. They infer changes in market-wide expectations for a company's returns relative to alternative investments of equal risk. But changes in share volume are considered security-specific. They infer changes in the expectations of only a narrow band of investors. In other words, new information may have no effect on overall market perceptions of competing returns among alternative investments. But it may affect the perceptions of individuals. In this case only share volume would be affected.

Studies have identified a positive correlation between share volume and the arrival of new information. They have also isolated a positive correlation between share volume and the absolute value of share price changes. One study examined 131 New York Stock Exchange companies between June 15, 1981 and August 21, 1981.[26] It found that on the arrival of new information, share volume associated with price increases was greater than that associated with price decreases. But studies have also shown that neither the correlation between price and volume nor the size of market reaction suggests consensus perception of and agreement among investors about the significance of new information to security returns. Otherwise, investors would not trade.[27]

Management should become aware of the liquidity and trading pattern (price variability) in its company's shares. It is management's form of market surveillance. The most common measure of liquidity is the average liquidity ratio. That is the dollar volume of trading (trade size) divided by average absolute percentage change in price. Some think there are better measures (see Bernstein in the bibliography). One is the ratio of change in price to the absolute number of transactions in a stock (controlling for total market value and trade size). Another is the sensitivity of unsystematic risk to changes in trading volume.

To determine liquidity in a company's shares, management should find answers to questions such as:

1. How much share volume (thousands of dollars) is required to move the stock price by 1 percent?
   One study compared liquidity ratios for companies in 10 market value categories across exchanges.[28] It found that the average liquidity ratio for the smallest capitalization NYSE stocks was 7.9 versus 3.369 for the smallest AMEX stocks, and 7.42 for the smallest OTC stocks. It was 15.545, 12.636 and 30.135 respectively for companies in the next smallest market capitalization category.

2. How does the above relationship compare to that of other comparable companies traded in the same location? Is it more or less volatile?
   The ratio in number 1 above rises as trade sizes increase. As a result, comparing companies across exchanges may reflect differences in trade size, not necessarily liquidity.

3. Do the company's shares exhibit any seasonal pattern?
   Divide adjusted average monthly trading volume divided by the adjusted average number of shares outstanding.

4. What happens to volume and price around annual/interim earnings/dividend announcement dates?

5. What is the stock's relative beta in up markets? In down markets?

6. How does its beta change over time? Management may want to maintain a daily graph of the price/volume relationship in the company's stock relative to peer's stocks and to the overall market.

7. What do alterations in an observed trading pattern imply?
   For example, after the management of Norton Co. (Worcester, MA) had completed an oil industry-related acquisition, executives identified a shift in its stock's trading. It moved from a pattern in line with the machine tools industry composite to a pattern in line with the oil industry composite.

Market-makers are a focal point of market intelligence about shifts in share ownership and trends in share accumulation/distribution. Traders can identify which brokerage firms are most active in the trading of the company's shares. For example, some brokerage firms are known for their "warehousing" of shares for the benefit of corporate sharks. Traders may speak to their counterparts at active firms to learn not so much for which accounts trades are being made, but from which part of the country the orders originate.

If the trades are large enough and abnormal buying activity lasts long enough, the industry specialist or multi-industry generalist securities analyst at a firm active in the company's stock (on a trading basis) may be able to give more information about the origin of buying activity. The analyst may know which of the firm's accounts is the actual buyer or seller. That information, per se, is confidential and will probably not be made available. But the analyst may be able to suggest the type of buyer and the intent of the purchase.

By the process of elimination, management may be able to identify the actual buyer or seller of its shares. If a buyer, management should plan to establish a relationship. Executives should learn who or what influenced the purchase and how it fits his or her overall portfolio strategy.

If executives are nervous about or suspicious of the reason for the purchase of their company's shares, they may investigate the background and trading (portfolio) habits of the buyer. They might make contact either with industry peers in the same city as the buyer. Or they might inquire of executives in other companies in which the buyer has held shares. Finally, it is a service opportunity for the securities analyst at the company's underwriting firm. One of the firms' salespersons may do commission business with the buyer or know someone who does.

If a seller, management should determine how much of the seller's position remains, why the seller sold, and the seller's disposition toward the balance of the position. The remainder of the position may be significant as a percentage of the company's float and relative to position sizes of other institutional holders. If it is for sale, executives should apprise their market-makers of the potential for additional selling activity in the stock. It is the sort of market intelligence which market-makers appreciate. They can anticipate a liquidity squeeze and can protect their inventory positions.

Executives can also help their company's liquidity cause. They should keep records of all unsolicited buy and sell inquiries in their shares. At the same time, they should request that their dominant market-makers make contact when they are going to "cross" a trade in the company's shares. They should request this information, regardless of whether traders act as agent or principal. Management may be able to add liquidity by helping market-makers find "the other side" of a trade. Or through an effective share repurchase program, executives may participate on the buy-side of a block.

Trading is a prime source of rumors. Financial journalists key on unexpected jumps in share volume or unexpected changes in share price for leads to stories. For example, *The Wall Street Journal*'s "Heard on the Street" column often focuses on revised analysts' earnings estimates for story leads.

Management may not be the least bit aware of the birth of a rumor until its effects appear in both share volume and share price. But executives will want to learn of its origins as soon as possible because unsquelched rumors can do irreparable damage to or even kill a company's product and share price. From a legal perspective, the issue will be whether management started a rumor, knowingly or unknowingly, through selective disclosure of material non-public information.

There are various sorts of rumors and they begin in a variety of ways. Many rumors carry a "contamination" theme. Worms in Wendy's hamburgers or urine in Corona beer are examples. Others promote a "conspiracy" theme. Satan in the corporate logo of Procter & Gamble is an example. These themes often begin their circulation as hearsay. But, as they spread, they hurt product sales.

On more sophisticated levels, securities analysts may change estimates, publications may publish articles, "old news" may recycle in more public sources and competitors may spread stories in road shows. In addition, arbitrageurs may feed the press, a large block of a company's shares may trade at a significant discount or premium from the last sale price, or insider buying or selling of stock may trigger rumors. Money managers, analysts, brokers and the press will inquire about the reasons for abnormal share volume or price change.

Relationships are of paramount importance in the squelching of rumors. Since the distribution channel is a prime source of market intelligence, management should call on money managers, analysts and market-makers to isolate the source and content of the rumor.

Management may observe that a rumor significantly disrupts an otherwise orderly market in the trading of the company's shares. To neutralize the effect, executives might request a trading halt to issue a press release concerning the contents of the rumor. The New York Stock Exchange usually halts trading pending news announcements or an order imbalance so that investors can interpret and react to new information. Currently the New York and American Stock Exchanges can halt trading and NASDAQ can halt price quotes but not trading. Quotation halts tend to last between one and two hours.

Should management list its shares on a registered exchange? It is a frequent question. The answer varies with representatives from each trading location (New York Stock Exchange—NYSE, American Stock Exchange—AMEX, and National Association of Securities Dealers—NASD). In 1980, the American Stock Exchange and Drexel Burnham Lambert conducted a "Capital Markets Study." The results suggested that executives of both listed and unlisted companies perceived listing to be potentially helpful in increasing their company's trading liquidity (gains in share marketability), its access to capital markets, and its research coverage by securities analysts. These reasons infer executives' use of listing as a positive signal of confidence in their companies' future.

Academic studies find and management can expect that listing announcements (on the NYSE) have information content. Stock returns around listings follow two patterns. Share prices seem to rise immediately before listing and seem to fall immediately after listing. One study examined 319 companies which moved from the over-the-counter market to the New York Stock Exchange between

January 1966 and December 1977.[29] It found that pre-listing returns were positive over a 52-week period before listing announcement. They were also positive over the announcement week and between the listing announcement and the listing week. Postive market reaction may be attributable to investors' expectations of greater information availability and share marketability.

But post-listing stock returns, on average, have been negative over a four to six week period following listing since 1926.[30] One study reviewed eight-week cumulative market-adjusted returns using the same data as above. It included 446 American Stock Exchange companies which also listed on the NYSE between July 1962 and December 1982. It found that negative returns persisted regardless of whether a company generated positive pre-listing cumulative returns. Returns were -4.65 percent for OTC companies and -3.05 percent for AMEX companies. They also persisted with negative pre-listing cumulative returns which were -3.79 percent for OTC and -3.11 for AMEX companies.

Most explanations of this persistent post-listing phenomenon concern price pressure. It is supposedly the result of the "excess supply" of stock brought about by offerings of new equity issues shortly after listing, sales of shares by insiders, or sales of stock (inventory) by market-makers. None of these explanations is considered fully adequate.

One study documented that positive market response (abnormal positive returns) to New York Stock Exchange listing announcements during pre-NASDAQ days was far greater than that during post-NASDAQ days.[31] It suggested that NASDAQ may have reduced the liquidity benefits, previously perceived to be associated with listing on a major exchange, for those companies which qualify for listing. And listing seemed to have no effect on a company's systematic risk (beta) and cost of equity capital, according to a study of 38 NASDAQ companies listing on the NYSE between 1978 and 1979.[32]

Some investors advise managements of emerging companies to list on the Big Board for visibility and liquidity purposes as soon as possible. There is evidence, however, that the suitability of a trading marketplace may vary with a stock's liquidity characteristics. For example, one study examined 88 over-the-counter non-financial companies moving to the New York Stock Exchange between 1975 and 1981.[33] It found that listing may contribute to gains in share marketability for low liquidity, thinly traded (wide spread) OTC stocks. But it may not contribute anything for high liquidity, actively traded (low spread) OTC companies. Low or high liquidity was measured by the average percent median bid-ask spread. It was expressed in terms of trading cost as a percent of average bid and ask prices. In the study, the spread for the most liquid stocks was less than 1 percent. The spread for the least liquid stocks was greater than 6 percent.

The study found abnormal positive returns around the week before listing application for low liquidity OTC stocks (0.634), and negative abnormal returns for high liquidity OTC stocks (-0.258). It attributed negative returns to the costs of listing or the perceived reduction in capital commitment in the shift to a specialist system from a competing market-maker system. The results also suggested investors' perceptions of a gain in share marketability for low liquidity companies which listed on the NYSE. But they also seemed to infer expectations of no net gains in marketability for high liquidity companies which listed.

How can managements of emerging companies measure the reasonableness of the spread/price cost in their shares in order to decide whether or not to list? A study mentioned in Chapter 7 (footnote 4)[34] offered insight into the average stock price, average bid-ask spread, and average spread/price cost (round-trip trading cost for 100 shares excluding commissions) for companies in a variety of capitalization groups:

Market Value	Average Stock Price	Average Bid-Ask Spread	Average Spread/Price Cost
$0 to $10 million	$ 4.58	$0.30	6.55 percent
$10 to $25 million	$10.30	$0.42	4.07 percent
$25 to $50 million	$15.16	$0.46	3.03 percent
$50 to $75 million	$18.27	$0.34	1.86 percent
$75 to $100 million	$21.85	$0.32	1.46 percent
$100 to $500 million	$28.31	$0.32	1.13 percent

Other capitalization categories did not apply to emerging companies.

Authorities of one international exchange offered perspective of a reasonable upper limit on bid-ask spreads and spread/price costs on small capitalization issues. Officials of the Singapore Stock Exchange established new trading rules to stimulate volume in second-tier stocks and to impose accountability on market-makers who trade them. The goal was to speed the growth of Sesdaq (Stock Exchange of Singapore Dealers Automated Quotation system) as quickly as possible. Market-makers were required to maintain bid-ask spreads of 5 percent or less.

Trading in a negotiated market (NASDAQ) instead of an auction market (an exchange) may be appropriate for that genre of high liquidity, actively traded issue which qualifies for both. But several reasons pertinent to gains in share marketability support exchange listing for low liquidity, thinly traded OTC companies.

A small order flow reduces the fixed cost of a specialist's market-making activities. The absence of competing market-makers allows greater flexibility in adjusting inventory positions and in reducing trading risk. At the same time, limit orders on a specialist's book help to keep trading markets orderly. Competing public bids above specialist bids or competing public offers below specialist offers tighten quotes. They reduce the bid-ask spread in a company's shares (unlike a negotiated market).

And, finally, an exchange's mission to provide orderly trading markets (price stability/continuity) in its listings requires that a specialist commit a determined amount of capital to making a market. Making money on that capital requires that a specialist create demand by narrowing the bid-ask spread (buyers' costs) and attracting an order flow. The effect increases share marketability for low liquidity companies.

Executives' ability to prioritize Wall Street's distribution channels leads to effective use of its resources in translating economic value to market value. Dominant sponsorship of the shares of emerging companies comes in the form of research coverage and market-making. Management can reduce information costs (estimation risk) and trading costs (liquidity) relative to alternative investments of equal expected returns. This creates institutional demand for the company's equity.

9

Market Value, Sponsorship, and Ownership

At a recent investment conference, a securities analyst from a national institutional brokerage firm was asked if he applied any market capitalization minimum to companies he covered on a research basis. He said his market capitalization cutoff was $200 million. He only followed companies with market values greater than $200 million. He was asked what smaller capitalization companies should do to attract Wall Street sponsorship. His response was swift and simple, "Get bigger."

That sort of advice seems a bit flippant. Yet it is realistic. A company's market capitalization determines the breadth of its access to market sponsorship and research coverage. Market value equals stock price times shares outstanding. A company's float is distinct from total shares outstanding. It is that portion which is available for public trading. Market value draws certain kinds of analysts to a company. And analysts draw certain kinds of investors. The bracket structure of Wall Street's brokerage firms "talks to" the tier structure of Wall Street's investing institutions.

Chapter 7 mentioned that the total capitalization of the U.S. equities markets, as of April 1987, was $2.622 trillion. That market comprises a total of more than 26,000 public companies. Of that number, 6,453 comprised the universe of actively traded exchange-listed and NASDAQ-traded public issues.

That figure can be divided into four market-value classifications. Each applies to one of four quadrants on figure 3. The graph's X-axis is shares outstanding. The Y-axis is share price. Every public company falls into one of the four quadrants.

The first quadrant (A), lower-left on the graph, represents companies with market values less than approximately $50 million. It is, by far, the largest of the four quadrants, in terms of number of companies. Of 6,453 actively traded

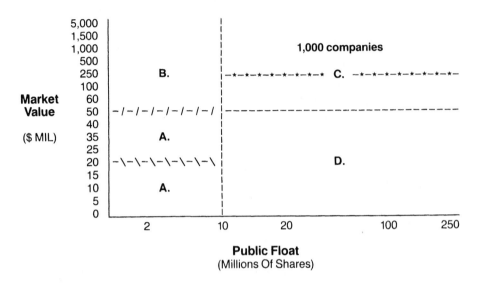

Figure 3
Market Capitalization—Market Sponsorship

issues, 3,419 are in quadrant A. I further subdivide quadrant A into companies with market values less than $10 million, between $10 million and $20 million, and between $20 million and $50 million. Start-up American companies which place a flotation in London's Unlisted Securities Market would be in this quadrant.

There were 1,496 companies which had market values less than $10 million as of May 1986. Most of them, 1,329 issues, traded on NASDAQ. The American Stock Exchange was second, with 153 companies. The New York Stock Exchange was third, with 14 companies.

Another 757 issuers had market values between $10 million and $20 million. Most of them, 606 companies, again traded on NASDAQ. The American was second, with 122 companies. And the New York was third, with 29 companies. A total of 1,166 had market values between $20 million and $50 million. NASDAQ had 853 companies. The AMEX had 238 companies and the New York had 75 companies.

Quadrant A companies usually have a relatively low stock price and a relatively small float. Both are characteristic of new issue companies. Low is defined as $10 dollars or less per share. Established companies usually go public at $10 or more per share. Low-priced stocks sell between $1 and $5 per share and are usually perceived as speculative. Penny stocks trade for $1 or less per share and are perceived as very risky. A small float is about 5 million or fewer shares available for public trading.

The second quadrant (B), upper left on the graph, comprises companies with market capitalizations more than about $50 million and less than approximately $250 million. A typical 1985 NASDAQ company fit into this quadrant. It had a 5.4 million share float, 8.1 million shares outstanding and a market value of $73.4 million. Average share price was slightly more than $13.50 per share.

Of the universe of actively-traded issues, 1,720 companies were in quadrant B. A total of 854 had market values between $50 million and $100 million. The largest number, 548 companies, traded on NASDAQ. The New York was second, with 170 companies. The American was third, with 136 companies. Another 866 companies had market values between $100 million and $250 million. Most of them (457) again traded on NASDAQ. The New York was again second, with 310 companies. And the American was third, with 99 companies.

Companies in quadrant B are usually characterized by a relatively high stock price and small float. Small is defined as less than 10 million shares, and high may be anywhere from tens to thousands of dollars per share. Berkshire Hathaway, Inc. (Omaha, NB) is a glaring example. At the end of 1985, the company had about 1.15 million shares outstanding, but its shares traded over-the-counter for about $2,930 per share. That amounted to a market value of $2.8 billion, second largest of all NASDAQ securities.

These traits also apply to closely-held companies. For example, a family concern of Arnold Bernhard, founder of Value Line, Inc. (New York, NY), owned 81 percent interest in the company. Robert Gray, founder of Gray & Company (Washington, DC), owned 67 percent of his company's 2.4 million shares outstanding before he sold the company in June 1986 to Hill & Knowlton, a division of JWT Group. New Brunswick Scientific Co. (Edison, NJ) is 27 percent controlled by officers and directors, and Wm. E. Wright Co. (West Warren, MA) is 56.6 percent owned by an outside investor, Newell Company (Freeport, IL). Finally, these traits also pertain to companies which altered their ownership structure. Approximately 35 percent of Fortune 500 companies are controlled or partly owned by founding or acquiring families.

The third (C) and fourth (D) quadrants, upper right and lower right in the graph, comprise companies with market values in excess of approximately $250 million. A total of 1,314 companies fit into both quadrants. A total of 452 had market values between $250 million and $500 million. The majority (219) traded on the New York Stock Exchange. NASDAQ was second, with 202 companies. And the American Stock Exchange was third, with 31 companies.

Finally, 862 companies had market values in excess of $500 million. Most of these traded on the New York (682). NASDAQ was second, with 140 issuers and the American was third with 40 companies. In its special April 18, 1986 issue,

Business Week covered the 1000 American companies with the largest market values. It reported that 466 public companies were valued by investors in excess of $1 billion, 769 in excess of $500 million and 1,000 (all companies on the list) in excess of $322 million.

Corporations in quadrant C usually have a high stock price and a large float. High is defined as a high-end two-digit or three-digit price per share. The highest priced of all publicly-traded common stocks, as of this writing, is Berkshire Hathaway Corp. As mentioned earlier its shares trade over-the-counter for about $2,930 per share. In contrast, the shares of Teledyne, Inc. (Los Angeles, CA) trade on the New York Stock Exchange for about $350 per share. IBM's shares trade at about $135 per share. Large is usually defined in terms of tens of millions to hundreds of millions of shares outstanding. And it is viewed in terms of hundreds of millions to billions of dollars in market value.

The range of shares outstanding of companies in quadrant C is great. IBM is on the high end. It has about 615 million shares outstanding. Teledyne is on the low end. At the end of 1971, the company had the equivalent of 88.8 million shares outstanding. But management initiated eight share repurchase plans in 13 years. By mid-1984, Teledyne had only 15 million shares outstanding.

IBM (Armonk, NY) is the king of quadrant C. It is the most heavily capitalized of all public companies. *Business Week* reported that IBM's market value represented $.04 cents of every dollar invested in common stocks. As of this writing, IBM's market value, the largest of any public company, is about $91.7 billion (on sales of about $50 billion). That is about 2.25 times the market value of Exxon, the second most highly valued company (with annual sales of about $86.7 billion). And it is about equal to the combined market values of the top five oil companies. Cross & Trecker Corp. (Bloomfield Hills, MI) was number 1,000 on the magazine's list. Its market value was about $322 million on 1985 sales of $434 million.

Companies in quadrant D have low share prices but large floats. Low may be defined on an absolute and relative basis. In absolute terms, a low price may be less than $20 per share. In relative terms, share price may be low in relation to its historic range. Large is defined in terms of high-end tens of millions or hundreds of millions of shares outstanding. These companies are usually in stages of disinvestment or turnaround. Examples of companies in this quadrant are Bank-America, Navistar, the resurrected International Harvester, and Wickes Companies.

Most of the universe of actively traded issues clearly comprises small capitalization companies. Quadrant A was the largest, in terms of numbers of companies. With 3,419, it equalled 53 percent of the entire universe. Quadrant B was second largest, with 1,720 issuers. Together, about 80 percent of all public companies fell into quadrants one and two. But they represented the minority of the market value of all actively traded equities.

Quadrants C and D comprise the smallest number of companies (1,314). But those issues carry the largest market value. About 20 percent of all public issues fell into these quadrants. But they comprised the majority valuation of U.S. equity capital markets. In other words, more than approximately 25,000 companies were valued at less than $322 million. A relatively few public companies attracted a disproportionate amount of investment, research coverage and trading volume.

A company's market capitalization category is dynamic. Share price and market value may fluctuate daily, in line with investors' changing perceptions of risk and expected returns. At the end of every trading session, every public company fits into one of the above four market value quadrants. Vertical shifts within or between quadrants occur as share prices change independent of share volume. Horizontal shifts occur as shares outstanding change, independent of share price. Diagonal shifts occur as both change proportionately. Proportional capital structure changes only result in different locations of equivalent market value on the graph.

An upward move within quadrant A or between quadrant A and quadrant B suggests investors' perceptions of improving company fundamentals. Earnings multiples expand due to perceptions of returns momentum relative to alternative investments of equal risk. Revaluation may also be triggered by announcements of positive unexpected earnings. Those which imply increases in future net operating cash flows or increases in leverage may also be a catalyst. And announcements of organizational or ownership restructuring may also affect market-wide expectations.

Some companies are born into quadrant C by virtue of large market capitalization-to-sales ratios at the time of their initial public offerings. But in terms of natural growth, a move for a small capitalization emerging company between quadrant A and quadrant C may take many years of consistent growth and stable profitability. The support of a dominant sponsor also helps.

A shift between quadrant A and quadrant D is unlikely. A company's common shares outstanding (equity expansion rate) would have to increase too dramatically. A lateral shift within quadrant A is more likely. It occurs as shares are sold in primary offerings, secondary offerings, in Rule 144 (restricted stock) sales, in exercises of executive stock options, out of dividend reinvestment plans or as executives and employees exercise stock options.

A downward move within quadrant B or between quadrant B and quadrant A suggests investors' perceptions of weakening company fundamentals. Earnings multiples contract due to perceptions of moderating returns relative to alternative investments of equal risk. Devaluation may also be triggered by announcements of negative unexpected earnings. Those which imply decreases in future net operating cash flows or decreases in leverage may be a catalyst. And announcements of management opposition to organizational or ownership restructuring or initiation of ownership restructuring in the form of secondary offerings of the company's stock may negatively affect market expectations.

This downward share price move is obviously unpopular. It causes a flight of investment capital and market sponsorship. The risk of information deficiency and pricing inefficiency increases. High-technology companies made this downward move in 1983. Silicon Valley corporations (California) such as Eagle Computer, Fortune Systems and Kaypro went from quadrant B to A. Route 128 companies in Massachusetts such as Computervision, Genrad, and Automatix, Inc. also suffered major market value reversals.

Lateral shifts between quadrant B and quadrant C occur as a company's equity capital base expands. A diagonal shift in location between quadrant B and quadrant D may occur as a result of a stock split. Stock price falls in direct proportion to the rise in the number of oustanding shares but market value remains unchanged. If the split is accompanied by an unexpected dividend increase, then share price should rise. If not, share price may fall.

Diagonal shifts between quadrant C and quadrant A are uncommon. A company's shares outstanding are unlikely to contract so precipitously. Such shifts could occur indirectly, however, through reemergences from Chapter 11 or as a result of reverse leveraged buy-outs (LBO). Lateral shifts between quadrant C and quadrant B may result from contraction in a company's capitalization. Corporate repurchases of stock in intrafirm share repurchases, open market repurchases or targeted repurchases of small share holdings shrink a company's equity.

Downward shifts between quadrant C and quadrant D occur for reasons similar to those for shifts between quadrants B and A. Investors perceive weakening fundamentals and moderating returns relative to alternative investments of equal risk. These shifts may also be triggered by the same sorts of unexpected earnings, implied cash flow, capital structure and organizational/ownership restructuring announcements mentioned earlier.

These moves bring visible problems to companies which already benefit from broad market sponsorship. A company's institutional shareholder base changes. Consensus expectations may focus on liquidation value per share as management's credibility suffers. Distress signals attract aggressive value-oriented corporate raiders. And arbitrageurs may hoard stock in anticipation of takeover attempts. In recent times, such big cap companies as USX (U. S. Steel) and BankAmerica have made this downward shift. They have also suffered the consequences of siege.

Downward shifts between C and D also result from proportional capital structure changes such as stock splits or stock dividends. For example, Walt Disney (Burbank, CA), split its stock 4-for-1 at $120 per share. The stock resumed trading at $30 per share on a float four times greater. And Subaru of America (Pennsauken, NJ) split its stock 8-for-1 after its shares had climbed from $17 per share in 1981 to close to $250 per share early in 1986. It was one of the most expensives issues traded at the time.

A lateral shift between quadrant D and quadrant A is highly unlikely. A company's capitalization would have to shrink too dramatically. It could occur indirectly as described earlier. Reverse splits are usually undertaken only by small capitalization companies with very high floats and very low share prices. They produce lateral shifts only within quadrant A. A diagonal shift between quadrant D and quadrant B is also unlikely.

An upward shift between quadrant D and quadrant C may occur for reasons similar to those for moves between quadrants A and B. Investors perceive improving company fundamentals and returns momentum potential relative to alternative investments of equal risk. They may also be triggered by the same sorts of unexpected earnings, implied cash flow, capital structure and organizational/ownership restructuring announcements mentioned earlier.

Moves between D and C have both long-term and short-term implications. In the former case, they imply investors' positive perceptions of a company's enhanced competitiveness through organizational restructuring. Lead investors exploit errors in low consensus expectations for these turnaround situations. They draw the attention of dominant sponsors who attract a popularity flow of other investing institutions. Sponsorship and ownership broaden. Management credibility resurges and stock price and market value rise. The resurrection of Chrysler is an example.

On a short-term basis, however, a move between quadrant D and C may have more to do with short-term trading opportunities resulting from ownership restructuring than long-term fundamentals. Potentially rapid share price changes associated with contests for corporate control in takeover attempts, tender offers, leveraged buyouts or leveraged cashouts attracts short-term opportunists. Gillette is an example.

Recall from Chapter 6 that Revlon attempted to take over Gillette in November 1986 at $65 per share. Management bought back Revlon's shares at $59.50. Executives also refused Revlon overtures at $40.50 per share (adjusted for a 2-for-1 split) in June 1987 and at $47 per share. Between June and September 1987, virtually all of Gillette's 114 million shares traded. And management conceded that about 80 percent of its shares were held by short-term, aggressive information traders. For example, Bear Stearns, Goldman, Sachs, Oppenheimer, Shearson Lehman, Bankers Trust, Prudential Bache, Citibank, Manufacturers Hanover Trust and Merrill Lynch held about 22.5 percent of the company's outstanding equity.

In another context of ownership restructuring, Teledyne, Inc. is a classic example of a company's upward shift from quadrant D to quadrant C. It resulted from open market corporate share repurchases. In 1971, the company earned $.61 per share and its shares traded at $8 per share. By mid-1984, management had repurchased close to 85 percent of the company's shares outstanding (about 74 million shares of a total of about 89 million shares). Earnings per share rose to about $20 and both book value and returns on equity rose. Teledyne's stock traded close to $200 per share, an appreciation of 2,300 percent from 1971.

Brokerage economics is the tie that binds market sponsorship to market capitalization. Commission-generating potential in the shares of public companies in certain quadrants attracts sponsorship from information processors at brokerage firms in certain brackets. And portfolio economics is the link between market sponsorship and share ownership. Returns potential in the shares of companies with particular investment characteristics in certain quadrants attracts ownership from lead investors in certain tiers. Analysts in certain brackets of brokerage firms speak to money managers at institutions in certain tiers.

In ascending order of their beginning market capitalization, I review the sponsorship and ownership record of four public companies. Recall from Chapter 4 that patterns of portfolio returns different from an indexed portfolio distinguishes investment styles. Recall also the description of venturesome, aggressive, cautious and defensive investors.

Lead investors in companies in the lower half of quadrant A, emerging companies of approximately $20 million or less in market value, are venturesome. They buy low yield, small capitalization companies with above market betas. These money managers are usually bottom up stock pickers who buy performance (high P/E) or price (low P/E). They may most likely be investment advisers or newsletter publisher/analysts who also manage equity capital. And they are often dominant sponsors of those same companies. Their word-of-mouth support is the key to market value and market sponsorship. At this stage, lead investors are the prime source of information processing and consensus expectations. They form the core of an equity valuation network and are management's route to dominant sponsors.

Dominant sponsors of companies with market values less than $20 million tend to be multi-industry generalists and broker/analysts at small regional firms. Their research is entrepreneurial and based on relative ratio and asset value analysis. They pride themselves on being able to find dynamic emerging companies and can generate adequate commissions from sponsoring their shares.

Dominant sponsors of companies of this size may also be independent publisher/analysts of investment newsletters. These newsletters offer advice for an annual subscription fee. They are called "say for pay" advisers. They may be oriented toward quantitative, technical or fundamental analysis. In most cases, newsletter publishers will probably never make contact with management. But the information content of their recommendations attracts a popularity flow from both retail and institutional subscribers. And if they also happen to manage small-cap equity funds, they may double as lead investors in recommended companies.

OTC Insight (El Cerrito, CA) is an example. It has about 1500 subscribers, about 300 of which are investing institutions. It specializes in emerging companies and is a stock picker. It screens for high growth/high returns companies or high alpha/low beta companies.

Management will probably never know that a newsletter publisher is a dominant sponsor of its shares and is recommending them for purchase. The impact of the information may appear clearly in share price, though not necessarily share volume. If executives learn of a newsletter recommendation of the company, they should try to obtain a copy of it. The recommendation will define its equity product in terms of customers' specifications.

Newsletter titles convey the investment philosophies of their publishers: *Emerging Growth Stocks, Growth Stock Outlook, High Tech Investor, High Technology Growth Stocks, Junior Growth Stocks, Ground Floor, The Informed Speculator, The Prudent Speculator, Low-Priced Stock Digest* and *Low-Priced Stock Survey.* Subscription to these newsletters may run high.

Leisure Concepts, Inc. (New York, NY), is an example of a company which moved vertically within quadrant A. The company is the only publicly-held licensor of commercial rights to properties and personalities. It was a neglected, low P/E, high growth/high returns, small capitalization issue. This example shows the equity valuation process in action. Profitability is the key to value. Perception of competitiveness and excess returns potential attract lead investors. They find dominant sponsors who attract a popularity flow. This demand-creating cycle raises stock price and market value. The company had a protected position in a growing market. It was a play on both performance and price.

The company's operating record showed that sales grew at about a 30 percent compound rate from 1983 through 1985. They rose from $1.03 million in 1983 to $1.38 million in 1984, $1.78 million in 1985 and $2.56 million in 1986. Earnings rose from $.12 per share (from continuing operations) in 1983 to $.23 per share in 1984, $.27 per share in 1985 and to $.16 per share in 1986 (adjusted for a 2-for-1 split). The company's net worth turned positive in 1984 and increased 350 percent in 1985. Management reported returns on equity of 164 percent in 1984 and 72 percent in 1985, on almost five times more equity outstanding.

At the same time (1984), the company's shares traded at a high of $.75 per share bid over-the-counter. With less than one million shares outstanding, it represented a market value of about $600,000 and a market capitalization-to-sales ratio of about 0.43-to-1. Although price/book-to-return on equity ratios are useful for companies with adequate historical data and predictable future performance, I use it here for comparison purposes. The company's shares traded at about 860 percent of book value per share. A 1 point increase in the company's return on equity moved its share price (as a percent of book value) by only slightly more than 5 percentage points. Its price/earnings ratio was about 3.

On this basis, the equity of Leisure Concepts was clearly undervalued, relative to the fundamentals of other publicly-traded companies with licensing departments. For example, (from *Business Week*) trailing 12-months sales of American Greetings Corp. (Cleveland, OH) grew 8 percent through the third quarter of 1985 and earnings grew 5 percent. Its return on equity was 16 percent (versus a weighted five-year average of 15.14 percent) and its price per share was 244 percent of its book value. A 1 percentage point move in its return on equity moved American Greetings' price per share (as a percentage of book value per share) by 15.25 percentage points. Its price/earnings ratio was 16.

In another example, sales (including other income) of Hasbro, Inc. (Pawtucket, RI) rose 72 percent in 1985 and earnings rose 89 percent. Its return on equity was 25 percent (versus a weighted five-year average of 23.14 percent) and its shares traded at about 286 percent of book value per share. A 1 percentage point increase in return on equity moved Hasbro's share price (as a percent of book value per share) by about 11.5 percentage points. Its price/earnings ratio was 13.

One retail stockbroker had recognized that Leisure Concepts' stock was inefficiently priced. But the broker was neither a lead investor nor a dominant sponsor. He lacked influence by which to affect the equity valuation process.

Pacific Partners (Oakland, CA) also spotted the pricing inefficiency. The principals of the firm had been referred to the company by executives at another company for which Leisure was a supplier. It was an offshoot of a money management firm with about $60 million in equity assets under management. It emerged as the lead investor in the company.

Principals of Pacific Partners visited with Leisure Concepts' management as interested buyers of the company's shares. Executives recognized the money manager as a potential lead investor, by virtue of the firm's buying power and willingness to commit capital. Management made certain that the money manager was "real." To satisfy themselves that the firm was of quality and high repute, executives checked the firm's references extensively with brokerage firms with which it did active commission business. Pacific Partners bought 5 percent of Leisure Concepts' outstanding equity (for investment purposes only).

The lead investor also became a dominant sponsor. The money management firm activated its valuation network. It arranged for management presentations with investors who actively bought stock in companys with Leisure's characteristics. The impact of word-of-mouth support on the valuation of the company's equity became apparent. Other money managers and analysts bought the company's shares for their own accounts. They then spread perception of the company's growth and returns potential to others who could appreciate its story.

Demand for the company's stock pushed its price up. It rose from a high bid of $.75 per share in the fourth quarter of 1984 (mentioned earlier) to a high bid of $7.00 per share in the fourth quarter of 1985, an increase of more than 800 percent. Its market capitalization-to-sales ratio rose to 3.32 to 1. At that level, the company's shares traded at almost 1,900 percent of book value per share. A 1 percentage point increase in the company's return on equity moved its share price (as a percent of book value per share) by more than 26 percentage points. Its price/earnings ratio was 19.

The lead investor also took a hand in the company's financing decisions. Leisure Concepts made a 550,000 share public offering in March 1986. It was priced at $9 per share and managed by William K. Woodruff & Co. (Dallas, TX), a small regional brokerage firm. The company's lead investors also found dominant sponsors for the company. Members of the underwriting syndicate with the largest share allotments initiated research coverage. These included William K. Woodruff, Furman Selz Mager Dietz and Birney, and Arnhold and S. Bleichroeder, Inc. Another firm, Oppenheimer & Co., also started to follow the company.

The resulting popularity flow into Leisure Concepts detached the company's shares from economic reality. The stock moved to a high of $35.75 bid per share over-the-counter in May 1986. Management split the stock 2-for-1 in June 1986. The company's market value had risen from under $1 million to about $56 million in about one and one-half years. At the end of 1986, the company's share price closed at $4 bid (post-split) per share over the counter.

Envirodyne Industries (Chicago, IL) is an example of a company which shifted between quadrant A and quadrant B. It is also another example of the fact that profitability is the key to value and that lead investors attract dominant sponsors. The company is the world's leading low-cost producer of cellulosic casings used in packaging processed meats. It is also a major producer of shrinkable plastic bags for food products. Envirodyne was a play on price and performance through restructuring. Its acquisitions strategy established its dominance in new markets and propelled its earnings momentum.

Primarily the result of its Steel and Mining division, the company went through a period of significant operating difficulty between 1977 and 1982. Operating margins were neglible and net worth was negative. The division was liquidated in bankruptcy in 1981. Through 1985, the company was a neglected, low P/E, small capitalization turnaround situation. Its shares traded as low as $.25 bid per share and were quoted at a $.50 point spread in 1982, for a market value of $2 million. At the time penny stock outfits and small, retail-oriented over-the-counter brokerage firms traded the company's shares at wide spreads with high volatility.

In 1983, management acquired a major producer of disposable plastic flatware and eating utensils. As a result, operating margins jumped to 11.5 percent, the highest in eight years. Net worth turned positive for the first time in five years, also the highest in eight years. Return on assets tripled to 10.3 percent, the highest in eight years, though return on equity was not meaningful. The company's shares traded from a 1982 low of $.25 per share to a 1983 high of $4.50 per share.

Operating results improved further in 1984. Operating margins rose to 14.3 percent. Long-term debt fell to 15 percent of total capital from 28.4 percent. Return on assets rose to 13 percent and return on equity to 22 percent. Management was successfully demonstrating consistent earnings growth.

The company was headed toward another year of stable operating success in 1985. Operating margins rose to 17.7 percent. Long-term debt as a percent of total capital remained stable at 15.4 percent. Return on assets increased to 14.3 percent and return on equity remained stable at 22 percent. The company's shares traded in a narrow range between $2 and $3.375 per share throughout 1984 and at the start of 1985, but traded to a 1985 high of $8.25 per share.

In the $4 to $6 per share range, penny stock brokers stopped making trading markets in the company's shares. Small regional West Coast brokerage firms started to follow the company. In the case of Bateman Eichler, Hill Richards (Los Angeles), the president of the company had been introduced to one of the firm's stockbrokers. For Wedbush, Noble, Cooke Inc. (San Francisco), a trader made a market in the company's shares. As the stock moved up in price, sponsorship moved up in brackets.

Organizational restructuring attracted two lead investors to Envirodyne in 1985 ($4.375 per share). The company's 1983 acquisition had generated steady earnings growth ($.12 per share in 1983, $.23 in 1984 and $.34 in 1985, adjusted for a 2-for-1 split). And in February 1986, management bought a leading manufacturer of cellosic packaging for $215 million from Union Carbide. As a result of the acquisition, Envirodyne's sales sextupled ($50.62 to $316.62 million) and earnings per share tripled ($.34 to $1.01). Sales were expected to top $400 million in 1987, including a $35 million acquisition of a leading producer of plastic film from RJR Nabisco Inc. in late 1986. Earnings were expected to grow at about 20 percent per year. The stock carried a P/E of 12. Its stock moved from $8 to $32 per share, to a market value of about $200 million.

A portfolio manager of Fidelity's Capital Appreciation Fund and a trust officer at a major bank perceived the company's value-enhancing competitveness and excess returns potential. The latter bought stock for his own account because the stock was too speculative for the bank's portfolio. They spread perception of that value through word-of-mouth. The stock went into several of Fidelity's funds. That ownership ultimately grew to 9.9 percent of the company's outstanding equity.

OTC Insight was both lead investor and a dominant sponsor of Envirodyne. The newsletter publisher/analyst and money management firm had discovered the company through a performance screen. It stressed bottom up strategy and stock picking with earnings growth filters, asset allocation models, quantitative risk measures (beta and alpha) and no contact with management. Envirodyne's management knew of the newsletter publisher's original request for information on the company. But executives never knew about the newsletter's active sponsorship of the company until an article about the sponsor's recommendation appeared in the *New York Post*.

Envirodyne offered 1.34 million shares at $16 per share in 1986 through Salomon, Inc. and Merrill Lynch. After the offering, both firms were dominant market-makers in the company's shares. But they were not dominant sponsors. For example, neither firm published research reports on the company, though each followed it "internally." Part of the reason was that the company's float was too small to offer adequate commission potential. Of 9 million shares outstanding, about 41 percent was closely held by the president of the company and by a voting trust. Two relatively small institutional firms provided "external" coverage.

Recall from Chapter 7 that the juxtaposition of assets under management, maximum ownership limits and average position weightings determine threshold market capitalizations for money managers' new portfolio additions. Thresholds (increase) decrease as assets under management (increase) decrease (the other two parameters held constant). They also (increase) decrease as maximum ownership limits (decrease) increase (the other two parameters held constant) and as average portfolio position sizes (increase) decrease (the other two parameters held constant).

In keeping with parameters discussed in Chapter 7, I assume an average maximum ownership limit of 3 percent. I also assume an average position weight of 1 percent or less of total managed assets. In this case, popularity flow into the shares of companies in the lower half of quadrant A will come from venturesome money managers who manage roughly $60 million or less in equity assets.

According to these specifications, these investors maintain minimum market capitalization thresholds of $20 million or less ($20 million divided by 1 percent divided by 3 percent). Those who manage $120 million in equity assets, whose average portfolio position is half of 1 percent (0.005) or less, and whose average maximum ownership limit is 3 percent also maintain minimum market capitalization thresholds of $20 million or less per position.

Lead investors in companies in the upper half of quadrant A, with market values between $20 million and $50 million, are also usually bottom-up, stock-picking small cap money managers. And they are also venturesome, tending to buy performance or price. Managements should cultivate one-to-one relationships with them and seek word-of-mouth support from them. Dominant sponsors may be analysts at major regional brokerage firms. But sponsors at retail/institutional firms also begin to process information at this market value level.

The Clothestime, Inc. (Anaheim, CA) is an example of a company which moved from quadrant A to quadrant B. It is also another clear example of the influence of lead investors in attracting dominant sponsors and the ability of dominant sponsors to attract a popularity flow. The Clothestime was a play on both performance and price. It was a low-cost competitor with a large share in a growth niche of the retailing industry. But its stock price failed to reflect its future growth and profit potential.

The company is an off-price retailer of junior apparel. The Clothestime came public in December 1983 at $11 per share. It closed the year at that same bid price for a one-month initial return of 0 percent. On top of that, its investment banker, Prudential-Bache, did not sponsor the company in the aftermarket for about 10 months.

By March of 1984, the Clothestime's share price drifted down to a low of $7 bid per share, a market value of approximately $35 million. Its shares traded at about $9.125 bid per share at the end of June 1984 and at $9 bid per share by August 1, 1984.

Historical perspective on the average price/performance specifications of the industry and the company are helpful to understand the company's mispricing. According to Value Line, the retail industry averaged 12.42 percent annual sales growth between 1979 and 1984. Industry earnings grew at an average annual rate of 12.66 percent over the same period. And 1984 return on equity was 13.2 percent versus a five-year weighted return on equity of 10.5 percent. Industry composite price per share was 133 percent of industry composite book value per share. A 1 percentage point increase in industry return on equity added 11 percentage points in industry price per share (as a percent of book value per share).

An examination of the price/performance specifications of The Clothestime's peer competitors showed that sales of The Dress Barn, Inc. (from an S & P *Stock Report*) grew at an average annual rate of 37.23 percent between 1982 and 1984. Earnings grew at an average rate of 75.87 percent over the same period. And 1984 return on equity was 28.7 percent versus a five-year weighted average return on equity of 34.82 percent. Average 1984 share price was 343 percent of book value per share. A 1 percentage point move in the company's return on equity in 1984 added almost 12 percentage points in share price (as a percent of book value per share).

According to an S & P *Stock Report*, sales of Charming Shoppes Inc. grew at an average rate of 23.97 percent per year between 1982 and 1984. Earnings grew at an average annual rate of 19.93 percent over the same period. And 1984 return on equity was 26.6 percent versus a five-year weighted average return on equity of 29.18 percent. Average 1984 share price was 446 percent of book value per share. A 1 percentage point move in return on equity in 1984 added about 16.75 percentage points to the company's price per share (as a percent of book value per share).

Sales of Deb Shops, Inc. grew at an average annual rate of 31.53 percent between 1982 and 1984 (according to S & P). Earnings grew at an average rate of 51.47 percent per year over the same time period. And 1984 return on equity was

39.7 percent versus a four-year weighted average return on equity of 33.12 percent. Average 1984 share price was 548 percent of book value per share. A 1 percentage point increase in the company's return on equity in 1984 contributed 13.8 percentage points to share price (as a percent of book value per share).

Finally, sales of The Limited, Inc. grew at an average annual rate of 62.83 percent between 1982 and 1984. Earnings grew at an average annual rate of 67.66 percent between 1980 and 1984. And 1984 return on equity was 44.8 percent versus a five-year weighted average return on equity of 23.8 percent. Average 1984 share price was 654 percent of book value per share. A 1 percentage point increase in the company's return on equity added about 14.6 percentage points in share price (as a percent of book value per share).

Against this backdrop, sales of The Clothestime, Inc. grew 39.9 percent in 1982, 74.6 percent in 1983 and 48.7 percent in 1984, a 53.7 percent compound annual growth rate in sales since 1981. Earnings rose 86.5 percent in 1982, 193.8 percent in 1983 and 113.4 percent in 1984, a 127 percent compound annual growth rate since 1981. The company reported returns on average equity of 27.6 percent in 1982, 52.5 percent in 1983 and 52.6 percent in 1984 (an average annual rate of 44.23 percent). Average 1984 share price was 1,368 percent of book value per share. A 1 percentage point increase in the company's return on equity contributed 26 percentage points to its share price (as a percent of book value per share).

Two money managers who had taken down The Clothestime stock on the deal were the company's lead investors. They also became the company's dominant sponsors. Cumberland Associates (New York, NY), manager of about $350 million in equity assets and Andron Cechettini & Associates (Lafayette, CA), manager of about $80 million, wielded their influence. Starting in August 1984, they put the pressure of investor demand on The Clothestime's underwriter to sponsor its corporate finance client on a research basis.

The company's shares began to run in August 1984. They reached a high of $13.25 bid per share around September 10 and closed for the month at $11.75 bid. By October 1984, the company's investment banker assumed its sponsorship role and issued its first research report. The Clothestime's stock traded in a narrow range until the end of November. It closed the year of 1984 at $9.25 bid per share, a one-year capital loss of 15.9 percent. Meanwhile, earnings per share rose from $.09 in 1983 to $.20 in 1984.

Popularity flow pushed the stock up in January 1985. It started to run and was trading above $12 bid per share by mid-February. About this time, Montgomery Securities, a retail/institutional brokerage firm initiated research coverage and recommended purchase of the company's shares. Furman Selz Mager Dietz & Birney, another retail/institutional firm, also became active. The stock hovered in the $11 to $12 bid per share range until April 3 when it started to make a major move. Popularity flow drove the stock up to $19 bid per share by May 22.

At that time, Alex. Brown & Sons, a retail/institutional brokerage firm, became a dominant sponsor and initiated research coverage of the company. The firm's industry specialist securities analyst recommended purchase of the company's shares. The firm hosted The Clothestime's management at a presentation to about 280 portfolio managers at one of the firm's investment conferences. Investor response was enthusiastic. The company's shares closed at $20.25 bid per share on May 31 and $24.25 bid on June 30. They traded to a high of $27.50 bid by July 18 and were split 3-for-2 on August 16.

In September 1985, Oppenheimer & Co., a national institutional firm, placed the company on its Recommended List. The company's shares proceeded to trade to a high of $27.75 bid per share by November 11 ($41.625 per share on a pre-split basis). The stock closed at $23.50 bid per share ($35.50 pre-split) at the end of 1985, a virtual quadrupling from the previous year-end. The Clothestime's market capitalization had risen to about $160 million. Earnings rose to $.24 in 1985, headed for $.71 in 1986.

Assuming the same market threshold parameters mentioned earlier, popularity flow for companies in the upper half of quadrant A, with market values between about $20 million and $50 million, comes from money managers who manage equity assets of about $150 million or less, whose average portfolio position is about 1 percent or less of total assets, and whose average maximum ownership of an issuer's outstanding securities is 3 percent. They maintain minimum market capitalization thresholds of $50 million and can invest in these companies. Those who manage about $300 million, whose average portfolio position is about half of 1 percent (0.005) or less of total assets and whose average maximum ownership limit is 3 percent, also maintain minimum market capitalization thresholds of $50 million or less.

Companies in quadrant B fall into two categories: those with market capitalizations between $50 million and $100 million and those with market values between $100 million and $250 million. There are two sorts of companies in quadrant B: those which are closely held and those which are widely held. Closely held companies in this quadrant usually have both a sponsorship problem and a liquidity problem. Commission potential is low and trading cost is high. They lack dominant sponsors and dominant market-makers. Lead investors are passive value buyers.

Widely held companies in quadrant B with growing shares in growing product/markets and attractive reinvestment opportunities move up another information processing notch. Lead investors in companies in the first category above are active and aggressive. They tend to remain bottom-up stock pickers who tend to buy either performance or price. And brackets expand to include national wirehouse firms and special situations analysts at national institutional firms.

Lead investors in companies in the second category above are active and aggressive or passive and cautious. Both tend to use bottom up strategies. The first buys low yield, above market betas and performance. The second buys high yield, below market betas and price.

These companies' valuation networks also expand. Popularity flow stems from money managers who manage around $300 million or less in equity assets, whose average portfolio position is about 1 percent or less of total assets and whose average maximum ownership limit is 3 percent of an issuer's outstanding securities. Within these parameters, they maintain minimum market capitalization thresholds of $100 million or less. Those who manage about $600 million, whose average portfolio postion is about half of 1 percent (0.005) or less of total equity assets and whose average maximum ownership limit is 3 percent also maintain minimum market capitalization thresholds of $100 million or less. As before, market capitalization thresholds vary with changes in parameters.

Sources of dominant sponsorship become traditional for widely-held companies in the second category. In addition to research coverage from major regional brokerage firms and retail/institutional firms, industry specialist analysts at national wirehouse firms and national institutional firms can begin to profit by researching and recommending these companies' securities. Coverage may originate with firms in any of the top three brackets. Lower bracket firms tend to relinquish their roles as primary information processors. As these companies continue to expand their equity bases, securities analysts begin to attract a popularity flow from managers of large pools of equity assets. Competition for companies' returns begins to intensify. This heightens pricing efficiency in their shares.

Between $100 million and $250 million in market value in quadrant B, the universe of potential investors enlarges. Money managers who manage equity assets of about $750 million or less, whose average portfolio position is about 1 percent or less of total assets and whose average maximum ownership limit is 3 percent of an issuer's outstanding securities maintain minimum market capitalization thresholds of $250 million or less. Those who manage about $1.5 billion, whose average portfolio position is about half of 1 percent or less of total equity assets and whose average maximum ownership limit is 3 percent also maintain minimum market capitalization thresholds of $250 million or less. Again market capitalization thresholds vary with changes in the three parameters.

Companies in quadrant C with high share prices and large floats usually have few sponsorship problems. Lead investors may be active and aggressive or passive and defensive. The first buys low yield, large capitalization, high beta performance issues. The latter buys high yield, large capitalization, low beta issues on price. They use top-down or bottom-up strategies to hunt for value. Above $250 million in market value, brokerage economics essentially opens all doors to sponsorship competition for commissions. At the same time, portfolio

economics essentially eliminates all entry barriers to ownership. National institutional firms and national wirehouse firms provide the most extensive research
coverage. Competition for commission dollars becomes very aggressive.

Companies in quadrant D with low share prices but large floats can develop
sponsorship problems, as discussed earlier. Lead investors are active and aggressive and yield and beta are largely immaterial. They buy on price and profit on
price change. They want organizational or ownership restructuring. The first are
more long-term owners who perceive value-enhancing competitiveness in existing markets (i.e., Chrysler). The second are short-term traders who perceive
value-creating opportunities in battles for corporate control (i.e., Gillette).

According to March 31, 1986 *Business Week*, 231 companies had market
values between $322 million and $500 million. And 769 other companies had
market capitalizations in excess of $500 million. These companies are obviously
the most heavily capitalized. Their shares are most widely held by institutional
investors (43 percent on average) and can be most easily traded.

The information environment surrounding companies in quadrants C and D is
usually semi-strong. Share prices adjust quickly to new information as it becomes available. But an ironic problem arises for dominant sponsors. At this
market value level, opportunities to exploit pricing inefficiencies in the shares of
large capitalization companies are relatively small. But the competition among
securities analysts to identify inefficiencies is significant. The biggest opportunities to exploit pricing inefficiencies are in the shares of small capitalization
companies. But the competition to identify them is least. The paradox presents
an excess returns opportunity to lead investors.

Most analysts perceived to be influential among top tier investing institutions
cannot compete to discover potential excess returns in the shares of emerging
companies. They cannot get paid adequately to do so. Therefore, excess returns
in the shares of small capitalization companies may persist as evidenced in the
results of stock selection strategies mentioned in Chapter 2. But that means that
pricing inefficiency may also persist, until a lead investor(s) triggers the demand-
creating cycle. Ultimately, executives must correct pricing inefficiency by recognizing and using lead investors and by identifying and using dominant sponsors.
Management holds the key to the fair value of their companies' equity.

CHRONOLOGY OF MARKET SPONSORSHIP

Valuation networks exist for all public companies, regardless of market
capitalization. And, as mentioned earlier, within the network, a bracket structure
of dominant sponsors of equities with certain investment characteristics "speaks
to" a tier structure of buyers of those equities. The popularity flow might be
equated to a "clientele" effect for information.

The revaluation of National Medical Care, Inc. (Waltham, MA) from August
1982 to September 1983 shows clearly how changes in market capitalization

bring changes in sponsorship which bring changes in ownership. The chronology of its revaluation offers insight into what managements of small capitalization companies may expect as they translate economic value into market value.

The company is the largest provider of outpatient kidney dialysis services in the United States. It was listed on the New York Stock Exchange until going private in a leveraged buyout in 1984. It was not an emerging company. But a significant drop in market value from November 1980 to June 1982 moved the company from quadrant C to quadrant D and brought it into the market capitalization range of an emerging company.

At their high in 1981, the shares of National Medical Care (NMC) traded at $25.875 per share. With close to 18 million shares outstanding, its market value was about $470 million. At the time, the shares traded at about 433 percent of book value per share. Its 1980 return on equity was 25.8 percent versus a five-year weighted average return on equity of 20.36 percent. A 1 percentage point gain in ROE added 16.8 percentage points in market value (as a percent of book value). The company was widely followed on a research basis and its shares were widely owned by investing institutions. Mutual funds alone owned almost 14 percent of the company's equity.

Regulatory problems developed in 1981. The Health and Human Services Department of the U.S. government initiated plans to reduce the reimbursement rate per dialysis treatment for the company's services. Management terminated contact with Wall Street in order to lobby Washington. The company's share price dropped to a low of $5.50 per share on March 11, 1982 and $5.625 per share on June 14/15, 1982, about 80 percent of book value per share. Its return on equity was about 15.2 percent. A 1 percentage point gain in profitability added only about 5.4 percentage points to share price (as a percentage of book value). Market value dropped to about $100 million. Institutional ownership fell to about 33 percent (mutual fund ownership fell to 2.5 percent) and research coverage disappeared.

The company's lead investor, its largest institutional owner, was Rothschild Asset Management. The money manager firm owned about 1.5 million shares. The firm came by this distinction by default. It had owned the company's shares at about a $20 per share cost basis and had been unable to get out of the position as the stock dropped. Its strategy was to "double up" at lower prices to average down its cost basis.

At $5.675 per share, the company was virtually neglected. Only an investment information service (Standard & Poor's *Stock Reports*), an investment advisory service (Value Line *Investment Survey*) and a local small regional brokerage firm (Adams, Harkness & Hill) provided ongoing research coverage. The company emerged as a turnaround situation. As a low cost provider with a large market share in slow growth market, it was a margin play. Its stock price failed to reflect management's ability to enhance its competitiveness in its existing market by reducing costs and expanding operating margins.

Management resumed Wall Street contact in September 1982. At the time, the company's shares were trading at $7.875 per share. Lead investors came first. Two buy-side institutional securities analysts from Putnam Fund's (Boston, MA) Health Sciences Trust sector fund visited management. Putnam is a top-tier investing institution. Two of its funds bought about 10 percent of the company's outstanding equity. Two principals in a small California-based money management firm also visited. The company's shares closed at $7.75 per share on September 30, 1982 and $8.25 on October 30, for a market value of about $150 million.

Lead investors started the charge but dominant sponsors emerged soon thereafter. In November 1982, newsletter publisher/analysts initiated research coverage of the company. United Business Service (Boston, MA), a fundamentals-oriented money management firm, recommended purchase on November 8 ($8.50 per share). John Magee, Inc. (Boston, MA), a technically-oriented brokerage firm, recommended purchase on about November 12 ($9.375 per share). The *Professional Tape Reader* (Hollywood, FL), another technically-oriented newsletter, also recommended purchase. The combined sponsorship attracted a popularity flow from individual investors, retail producing stockbrokers at small regional brokerage firms and small money managers.

On November 30 ($10.125), Adams, Harkness & Hill issued a positive two-page report. Its perspective was that of a contrarian value buyer (i.e., a turnaround situation). On December 21, 1982 ($9.375), a health care industry specialist securities analyst at Lehman Brothers (New York, NY, precursor to Shearson Lehman Brothers), a national institutional brokerage firm, issued a negative report. It recommended sale of the company's shares because of perception of management's inability to generate consistent profitability. It caused a share volume, not share price, reaction. The company's stock closed the year of 1982 at about $10 per share. Earnings were $1.03 versus $1.09 for the year ($.59 versus $.43 in the second half).

On January 6, 1983 ($10.75 per share) a multi-industry generalist analyst at Interstate Securities Corporation (Charlotte, NC), a major southeastern regional brokerage firm, initiated research coverage with a buy recommendation. The company's transfer sheets clearly showed the effects of the analyst's merchandising efforts. Individual investors and small institutions in the southeast bought several hundreds of thousands of shares.

On January 26, the health care industry specialist analyst at Goldman, Sachs (New York, NY), a national institutional brokerage firm, issued a one-page update report on the company. The firm had followed the company closely, at higher prices, in the past. By the end of January, the company's shares were trading at $12.50 per share, a market capitalization of about $228 million.

In February 1983, a health care industry specialist analyst at Montgomery Securities (San Francisco, CA), a retail/institutional brokerage firm, emerged as the company's dominant sponsor. He reinitiated coverage which had previously been dropped. An internal "buy" memo was circulated to the firm's securities sales force on February 4 ($14.75 per share). A research report was released on February 22, 1983 ($14.125 per share).

The analyst merchandised his research product aggressively and attracted a popularity flow from second-tier institutional buyers. He hosted management in presentations to interested investors. And he tried to leverage his sponsorship of the company into investment banking business for his firm (fee income for him). He advised future financing with his firm as manager of any deal. On a trading basis, the firm developed a franchise in the company's shares.

On March 4 ($15.875 per share), the *Professional Tape Reader* newsletter issued an update. On the basis of the company's technical upward move, it advised readers to put in "stop-loss (sell) orders" with their brokers to lock in trading profits. These orders would be entered on the book of the New York Stock Exchange specialist in NMC's stock. On March 9 ($16.375 per share), a health care industry specialist analyst at Merrill Lynch (New York, NY), a national institutional brokerage firm, reinitiated research coverage which had previously been dropped. Having missed about a triple in the company's stock, the analyst decided not to miss the boat completely. But he did not aggressively merchandise his research product.

On March 10, 1983, NMC shares traded to an interday high of $17.375 per share. Weekly share volume had more than doubled from an average of about 400,000 shares per week in August 1982 to about 900,000 shares per week in March 1983. On March 24 ($15.875 per share), the *Professional Tape Reader* showed the clout of its technical analysis (mentioned in Chapter 8).

Rothschild Asset Management lightened up in the company's stock by selling 600,000 shares in a block trade on March 24 at $15.875 per share. Its cost basis had declined to about $10 per share. The trade at that price triggered the wave of stop-loss sell orders on the specialist's book representing the interests of the readers of the *Professional Tape Reader*. The popularity outflow forced the stock down without interruption to $13 per share on March 30. In six trading days, the stock lost more than 18 percent in market value (to about $235 million). The company's shares closed at $13.50 per share on March 31.

Between September 1982 and the end of the first calendar quarter of 1983, research coverage of the company had increased and institutional ownership had broadened to about 45 percent from about 33 percent. The highest weekly volume in the company's shares in two years occurred at the start of the second calendar quarter.

On April 13, 1983, a new dominant sponsor emerged. A health care industry specialist analyst at Dean Witter (New York, NY), a national wirehouse brokerage firm, initiated research coverage of the company ($15.125 per share). He issued a 22 page research report recommending purchase and aggressively merchandised the product. He attracted a popularity flow from second-tier institutions and medium-sized investment advisers. NMC shares traded to $16.50 per share by April 22 and closed at $15.75 at the end of the month. They traded to an interday high of $19 per share by May 6, up to about $345 million in market value.

A flurry of update reports appeared at this time: Goldman, Sachs (May 11 at $18.50 per share), Adams, Harkness & Hill (May 13 at $18.375 per share) and Interstate Securities (May 16 at $18.125 per share). On May 16, Laidlaw Adams & Peck (New York, NY), a retail/institutional brokerage firm initiated research coverage. Montgomery Securities issued an update on May 25 ($18.625 per share). The company's shares traded to an interday high of $19.75 on May 26, 1983 and closed at $18.50 per share at the end of May.

NMC's shares closed at $19.625 on May 26, 1983, about 265 percent of book value. With a return on equity now close to 17.1 percent, a 1 percentage point gain in ROE added about 15.6 points to share price (as a percentage of book value). The company's market capitalization had increased by more than $250 million in about nine months. Linked quarterly earnings were $.90 versus $.61. Institutional ownership had increased to about 54 percent from about 45 percent at the end of the first calendar quarter. It increased further to about 57 percent by the end of the third calendar quarter.

On Tuesday, July 5, a rumor surfaced concerning fatalities in one of the company's facilities. The story was that use of contaminated water in the dialysis process had caused patient deaths. Using a network of money managers, the origin of the story was traced to comments made by a competitor on the road show circuit. The effect of the recycled story and investors' uncertainty about the extent of the company's insurance coverage knocked NMC shares from an interday high of $18.625 per share to an interday low of $14.50 per share and a close of $15 per share. The sharp price drop prompted a flurry of telephone calls from reporters at newspapers and trade journals.

On Wednesday, July 6, management requested a trading halt on the New York Stock Exchange to issue a press release to clarify the story. After a delayed opening, the shares traded to an interday high of $17.875, an interday low of $16 per share and closed at $16.

The stock traded in a fairly narrow range through the rest of 1983. It hit a low of $12.75 per share on November 10 and closed for the year at $14 per share. Earnings per share for 1983 increased to $1.26 from $1.03. By the end of the first calendar quarter of 1984, institutional ownership had risen to 75.5 percent.

The company was written up on a research basis in 1984 by Donaldson, Lufkin & Jenrette (May 18), Goldman, Sachs (June 14), and Montgomery Securities (August 2). All expected to be named co-managers of a possible convertible debt financing deal. Donaldson hosted management in a presentation to investors. And portfolio managers at Fidelity Investments, a top tier investing institution, emerged as new value-oriented lead investors in the company's shares. Management made a private presentation to them. Ultimately, the company went private in August 1984 at about $19.25 per share, a market value of about $360 million.

Bull markets never hurt executives' quest to create investor demand for their companies' shares. But to manage the demand-creating cycle effectively, management should understand how sponsorship changes with market capitalization and how ownership changes with sponsorship. That knowledge is essential to managements' use of Wall Street's lead investors and dominant sponsors.

10

Credibility

MATERIALITY AND DISCLOSURE

This book has been based, throughout, on three premises. First, investors' perceptions of risk and expected returns drive share prices. Second, the relative availability of information drives perception. And, third, competition for excess returns drives information. The competition for and availability of only material public information is implicit in these premises. Use of material non-public information, known as inside information, is not only anathema, it is illegal.

The last premise is critical. It is embodied in disclosure rules set forth in Rule 10b-5 promulgated under the Securities and Exchange Act of 1934, as amended. "Issuers must be particularly circumspect about communicating material non-public information to persons other than those with a need to know."[1] The rule pertains directly to management's dealings with securities analysts. Executives have to be careful in what they say to those who sell information.

Possession of inside information, in and of itself, is not considered illegal. Trading on material non-public information is illegal. The second U.S. Circuit Court of Appeals has ruled in the past on a company's liability under Section 10(b)/Rule 10b-5. Three cases of prominence were *State Teachers Retirement Board vs. Fluor Corporation* (1981), *Elkind vs. Liggett & Myers, Inc.* (1980) and *SEC vs. Monarch Fund* (1979).

A precise definition of inside information has always been elusive. The case of *Elkind vs. Liggett Myers, Inc.* yielded a reasonably clear interpretation. The court concluded that management statements do not constitute inside information if they are not "reasonably certain to have a substantial effect on the market price [and if they would not] have been likely to affect the decision of potential buyers and sellers."[2]

The case involved a lack of disclosure by management about an unexpected worsening of business conditions for Liggett & Myers, Inc. in 1972. Securities analysts estimated a 10 percent increase in the company's 1972 earnings. However, management's forecasts called for only a two percent increase. And management, in reviewing analysts' research reports on the company prior to publication, essentially made no comment about the gap in earnings expectations. Rather executives talked in postive terms about the company's new product introductions and market share gains.

Positive first quarter earnings comparisons, year-to-year, for Liggett fueled investors' optimism. Executives did nothing to try to contain that enthusiasm. When they determined that second quarter results would disappoint investors' expectations, they changed their tone with analysts. Executives talked about narrower operating margins. But management made no public disclosure about results for the first half of the company's fiscal year until three weeks after the close of the second quarter.

The courts found that Liggett management's review of analyst reports without comment about the accuracy of their projections "did not amount to its 'entangling' itself sufficiently in the earnings forecasts to make them attributable to itself."[3] The court also concluded that "the information added little to the conventional wisdom that Liggett was experiencing an earnings downturn. The fact that institutional investors who received [from brokerage firm securities analysts] the information [about Liggett's prospects] did not sell any of their holdings was viewed as probative of a lack of materiality."[4]

Materiality has always been subject to interpretation. It is loosely and ambiguously defined as any information which may have a material impact on a company's business prospects. The assumption is that investors would consider such information important to their perception of a company's risk and expected returns prospects. It would affect their expectations and would be germane to their decisions about whether to buy, sell or avoid a company's shares.

In the *Liggett* case, the court also held that certain information was not material, even though it may have been a departure from normalcy. For example, "statements confirming prior public information, a general statement about a division's competitive position and a statement that a preliminary earnings statement would be released in a week"[5] were not considered material. On the other hand, the court claimed that "a statement that there was a good possibility that earnings would be down, coupled with a request to keep the information confidential"[6] would constitute material non-public inside information.

In effect, past rulings and interpretations highlight good bottom-up fundamental securities analysis. Although all analysts work with the same published data, Chapter 8 discussed the fact that the quality of information which they glean from the data may differ substantially. Some analysts ask better questions, perform more thorough checks outside the company and discern changes in operating trends or company fundamentals more clearly and quickly than others. The better analysts, by their analysis, find themselves more in the quadrant of information discovery (knowing what no one else knows) and less in the quadrant of information efficiency (knowing what everyone else knows).

In this regard, past rulings advise executives to be aware of the constant risks of release of material non-public information to savvy analysts.

A skilled analyst with a knowledge of the company and the industry may piece seemingly inconsequential data together with public information into a mosaic which reveals material non-public information. Whenever (corporate) managers and analysts meet elsewhere than in public, there is a risk that analysts will emerge with knowledge of material information which is not publicly available.[7]

How can or should the management of an emerging company talk to analysts? From a legal perspective "companies must structure such communications so as to avoid the possible disclosure of material non-public information, bearing in mind the level of sophistication of securities analysts and the fact that they may draw material conclusions from seemingly innocent statements by management."[8]

Executives should talk in noncommittal terms about a company's fundamentals. They should discuss structural assumptions about sales and earnings growth. And they should speak about earnings in relation to macroeconomic variables and consensus estimates on the industry and peer industry competitors. Management's "if. . .then" statements about future growth and profitability offer a range of possible scenarios for an analyst to consider in constructing an earnings model.

For example, in December 1986 John F. Welch, Jr., chairman of General Electric Co. made the most specific forecast management had ever made. He told a group of about 180 money managers and securities analysts that the company's earnings in 1987 and 1988 would increase by "strong double digits," assuming growth in gross national product of 2 percent to 3 percent and a 4 percent rate of inflation. Ultimately, as discussed in Chapter 6, management may want to make public "good faith" forecasts about their companies' prospects. A voluntary forecast should be corrective and should guide investors' expectations. It should depend on the perceived size of consensus forecast errors. The potential for predictive accuracy should be judged in terms of perceived variance in operating cash flows. Recall that companies with sustainable competitive advantages in their product/markets are most likely to incur low (or at least predictable) earnings volatility.

Many brokerage firm analysts may request that management conduct a prerelease review of research reports to guarantee accuracy and realism. But, as seen in the *Liggett* case, the law believes it is a risky practice. The issue is one of management's avoiding attribution of earnings estimates to itself.

For example, in the *Liggett* case the court warned:

Management must navigate carefully between the 'Scylla' of misleading stockholders and the public by implied approval of reviewed analyses and the 'Charybdis' to tipping material inside information by correcting statements that it knows to be erroneous. A company that undertakes to correct errors in reports presented to it for review may find itself forced to choose between raising no objection to a statement that, because it is contradicted by internal information, may be misleading and making that information public at a time when corporate interests would best be served by confidentiality. Management thus risks sacrificing a measure of its autonomy by engaging in this type of program.[9]

But the court realized the potential for giving a "false impression that all was well without stating any untrue facts [and stated] the misleading character of a statement is not changed by its vagueness or ambiguity. Liability may follow where management intentionally fosters a mistaken belief concerning a material fact, such as its evaluation of the company's progress and earnings prospects in the current year."[10]

Short of replacing analysts' estimates with management's forecasts, a pre-release review of an analysts' material can be conducted on the same basis as other conversations. Reactions and responses must be general and noncommittal. And management can turn analysts' questions back to analysts. Executives should ask: (1) On which valuation model(s) does an analyst rely? (2) What assumptions underlie an analyst's earnings model? (3) Why does the analyst's estimate differ from consensus forecasts? This sort of noncommittal effort helps analysts to fine tune their assumptions for growth and earnings. It should force them to conduct necessary checks to substantiate their estimates relative to consensus estimates. And it avoids managements' estimating or predicting earnings for them.

The risks to and responsibilities of management in dealing with securities analysts seem clear. Material non-public information is not to be made available. The measure of materiality is the extent to which company information affects trading in the company's shares.

As of this writing, the importance of this issue is great. Wall Street is embroiled in the biggest insider trading scandal in its history, both in terms of the number of persons and the dollar value of illegal profits. Those who trade on inside information trade on expectations. One money manager, Ivan Boesky, paid the federal government $100 million dollars to settle its financial claim against him. The number accused of wrongdoing, currently between 10 to 15 persons of a possible 60 (some already serving jail terms), are those primarily engaged in merger and acquisition-related work for law firms and securities firms. Paul Thayer was the only prominent corporate executive to serve time, for insider trading abuses while at LTV Corporation.

The unfortunate scandal has made very clear that information has value. Some may use it for direct personal gain while others may use it for customers' gain. And some may not use it at all. Within that context, talking with institutional (buy-side) analysts, in particular, differs from dealing with brokerage (sell-side) analysts. Neither wants inside information. But buy-side analysts fit more into the third category above because they represent the owners of the equity capital they manage. They are buyers, not sellers, of material public information. Ethics dictate that the information they receive and use is proprietary.

Management should handle brokerage firm (sell-side) analysts, however, at arm's length. Information they receive and use is for sale. Their job is to serve and protect institutions' portfolios. Within the context of public disclosure, they strive to be in the quadrant of discovery, to find information which nobody else knows. They want to be first with information, they want to be right with it, and they want to be paid for it.

In that sense, management's borderline information may contribute to an analyst's mosaic and lead to use of material non-public information. And that information travels quickly from sell-side to buy-side. National institutional and national wirehouse brokerage firms tend to act most quickly. Management can clearly observe the effects. Borderline information may move from material non-public status to material public status with blinding speed. The shift stimulates trading on expectations. The results are usually swiftly reflected in a company's share price and share volume.

Reichold Chemicals, Inc. (White Plains, NY) faced the problem. In June 1985, the company's director of investor relations told three sell-side securities analysts from national institutional brokerage firms that results for the company's second fiscal quarter would be substantially worse than the prior year. Earnings were expected to come in at less than $1 per share versus prior year's earnings of $1.26 per share. This information fell into the category of selective disclosure and into the quadrant of discovery. It was information these analysts knew but nobody else knew.

The sell-side, brokerage firm securities analysts rushed to inform their commission-paying clients. The effect was obvious as Reichold's stock swiftly traded down on the New York Stock Exchange from a record high $43.125 per share to $37.625 per share. The share price drop prompted telephone calls from reporters but management could not explain the drop. The chairman of the company claimed that the quarter's earnings would be less than the prior year but, in keeping with company policy, offered no specific estimate.

Sears Roebuck & Co. (Chicago, IL) faced the opposite situation. On December 5, 1985, the president of the company met with three brokerage firm analysts from a national wirehouse firm. He did not discuss specific plans for the company's future but hinted at the possibility of a major organizational restructuring.

The meeting altered analysts' perceptions of Sears. The company had previously been thought to be conservative and resistant to change. The fact that the company's president talked seriously about shifts in the company's assets led the analysts to conclude that Sears might be on the verge of, and may already have decided upon, major structural improvements. The discussions changed analysts' assumptions about Sears' future growth. And they soon changed investors' expectations of Sears' returns potential. The information fell into the quadrant of analysts' discovery, that which no one else knew.

The next morning, the analysts reported the results of their meeting with Sears' president to their firm's national securities sales force. They also offered an estimate of Sears' restructured value per share, about $63.50 versus a current price of $37.625 per share. Sears became a quick asset play, a restructuring story. The firm's retail brokers sold it to their customers.

The merchandising resulted in aggressive buying of Sears' stock. On Friday, December 6, 1985, Sears's shares ran up one and one-half points in a down market. In six trading sessions, the stock price rose 9.3 percent. That was more than two and one-half times the rise in the Dow Jones Industrial Average over the same period. Sears's market value increased by more than $1.2 billion.

Information which can affect investors' expectations for a company's growth and profitability, positively or negatively, are considered material. They must be publicly disclosed. They generally fall into four categories (mentioned in Chapter 6): investment, financing and operating decisions, and changes in organizational and ownership structure.

For example, significant changes in planned capital expenditures, in investment in research and development, or corporate share repurchase programs must be declared. Introductions or terminations of products or technologies, awards or cancellations of contracts, and entry or exit form product/markets must be released. Changes in capital structure brought on by public offerings security swaps or changes in financial policy as a result of stock splits or stock dividends, called debt securities, special (nonrecurring) earnings, or dividends to shareholders must be announced.

Changes in management (additions or dismissals), events which require SEC filings, spin-offs, sell-offs, joint ventures and liquidations, merger bids or tender offers received or made for the securities of other companies, targeted share repurchases and interfirm equity ownership must be disclosed. Antitakeover amendments such as poison pills, staggered boards or super-majority provisions must also be made public.

The timing of these required disclosures can be most inopportune. For example, Interleaf, Inc. (Cambridge, MA), maker of turnkey systems and computer-aided publishing software, had to cancel an already completed initial public offering because of material information which had to be made public. The company had lost a government contract in which it was a subcontractor. The original issue, successfully offered at $11 per share, was rescinded. Three million shares were offered a week later at $10 per share. The offering price was reduced to reflect uncertainty about future bidding on the govenment contract.

CREDIBILITY

Credibility is a corporate asset. It is synonymous with predictability, consistency and stability. It is also an image conjured at the mention of a company's name. It is perceived to be either intrinsic to or missing from a company's corporate culture and business practices.

As a reflection of this belief and the desire to build an image of credibility, corporate nomenclature has become serious business. Managements believe it has equity value. They became conscious of that link in the "go-go" mutual fund performance years of the early 1970s. After concluding an 18-month bear market cycle in May 1970, the market made a then historic bull run through January 1973. The S & P 500-stock index rose from 62.29 to a high of 120.24, a 93.03 percent increase in 32 months.

At that time, investors bought performance and earnings momentum. They bought the shares of companies with fancy-sounding technology names which oozed dynamic earnings growth potential. They bought names first and wondered later about the credibility or viability of company fundamentals behind the names.

Suffixes became symbolic of explosive growth, or the sound of growth. Corporate names of new issues ended in "-ics," "-ix," "-yne." They seemed to reek of unbridled growth and profitability. They sent "sexy" signals to the market of aggressive youth, talent and unbounded returns potential. Their flavor was "racy." Market values of new issues soared while the market multiples of good-sounding suffixes skyrocketed.

Trends in corporate identity have changed in the 1980s. Managements have tried to send signals which suggest breadth, depth, sophistication, predictability and sustainability. Corporate names now contain titles such as "systems," "technology" and "logistics." Suffixes often end in "-tech." They are intended to present images and shape perceptions of controlled growth and manageable risk through responsible planning systems.

The managements of both emerging and established companies realize the value of image. They understand the effect of a name on perception of fundamentals. They consider it an integral part of overall corporate strategy. As a reflection of that, managements of a record total of 1,382 companies changed their company's names in 1986. Of 579 changed in the first half of the year, 290 were the result of mergers or acquisitions.

One academic study examined 16 different types of name changes for 355 New York Stock Exchange companies that changed their names between 1961 and 1985.[11] It found, on average, that cumulative abnormal positive returns surrounding announcements of name changes (excluding other noise as much as possible) were 2.4 percent, the most significant portion of which occurred 10 days before announcements of name changes in the *Wall Street Journal*. The study also concluded that abnormal returns were most positive for names changed to acronyms, broadened to include the name of a merger partner or truncated. The information asymmetry hypothesis might best be used to explain this market reaction. The study suggested that name changes were part of revised business strategy policy. Announcements of changes signalled commitment to those revisions.

The belief in the strategic use of image becomes most clear when managements of troubled companies try to reshape investors' perception through corporate name changes. For example, management of Massey-Ferguson Ltd. (Toronto, ON) believed its name was perceived to be synonymous with poor performance and consistent losses in the farm equipment industry. Management changed the company's name to Varity Corp. on June 17, 1986. It initiated advertising campaigns under the banner of "A Corporate Renewal and a New Identity." Advertising copy claimed that its outlook and strategic priorities had really changed. The company was profitable again, suggesting that perception of the company's future should change with its name.

Evidence shows that name changes for troubled companies do not always add value, as measured by company total return relative to market return from date of name change. For example, Varity's total return to shareholders dropped 13 percent between the date of its name change and the end of February 1987. That was 31.2 percent worse than the S & P 500. Total return on International Harvester, which changed its name to Navistar on February 20, 1986, also dropped 10.3 percent through February 1987. That was 41.8 percent worse than the S & P 500. On the other hand, total return on U.S. Steel, reborn as USX on July 9, 1986, increased 47.2 percent percent through February 1987. That was 28.4 percent better than the S & P 500. It was also due partly to rising oil prices and a takeover bid by Carl Icahn.

The perception value of name change in mergers and acquisitions is also often strategic to employee motivation and morale. For example, management of the Burroughs Corporation (Detroit, MI) initiated an employee "name that new company" contest after Burroughs bought the Sperry Corporation (New York, NY). Executives believed employees would perceive a new corporate name, totally unassociated with either of the names of its predecessor companies, as a sign of equality, harmony and synergy between the two companies and their employees. Unisys was born on November 25, 1986. It registered an increase in total return of 32.8 percent through February 1987. That was 18.1 percent better than the S & P 500's total return over the same period.

Credibility of management in Wall Street's eyes is a crisis waiting to develop for many emerging companies. Many are founded by young entrepreneurs or executives with highly specialized skills, creative visions or anticipatory luck. While they may believe they demonstrate managerial competence, investors often perceive management inexperience.

Some entrepreneurs try to compensate for their youth by appearing brash, overly agressive and cocky. They may try to act older than they are or to be something (financial managers) that they are not yet. Such behavior makes investors nervous and uncertain about what to expect on an operating basis. Potential unpredictability adds to investors' perceptions of a company's risk relative to alternative investments they might make.

Entrepreneurial management may be fine during early corporate years when high growth/high returns investment opportunities tend to relax the need for professional operating skill. It can disguise operating mistakes. But decelerating growth/moderating returns or changing fundamentals do not forgive operating ineptitude. They demand traditional management style. To protect a company's operating margins and competitive advantage, young entrepreneurs may have to recruit more experienced executives.

For example, Steve Jobs, founder and chairman of Apple Computer (Cupertino, CA), recruited John Scully, head of Pepsico's North American operations, to be president. But a combination of internal turmoil and operating problems, declining profitability on rising sales, created a power struggle. Jobs was forced out of the company. Apple's stock price dropped to a low of $14.25 per share from about $30 per share in 1985. It closed for the year at $22 per share, off $7.125 per share from the previous year's close.

Opportunity often emerges from chaos. For Apple, investors perceived in Scully a greater management focus on value-creating competitive advantages in new product/market niches, such as desktop publishing. Their expectations were rewarded. By the summer of 1986, management had effectively turned the company's operations around. In its second 1986 fiscal quarter for example, revenues increased about 6 percent but profitability increased threefold. Stock price traded up to about $36 per share. The stock closed for the year 1986 at $40.50 per share, up $18.50 points from 1985's close.

Executives in emerging companies must be sensitive to the expectations of potential investors who may be older and more conservative. This is especially true in executives' personal presentation. Personal appearance and manner of speech send signals and shape investors' perceptions of maturity and predictability.

For example, Mitch Kapor, founder of Lotus Development Corporation (Cambridge, MA) was well known for wearing Hawaiian shirts. The appearance supported a well cultivated, laid-back, creative atmosphere at the company. But, in front of professional investors, pinstripes were the order of the day. Conservative attire enhanced his personal credibility, and by extension, that of the company.

CRISES AND MANAGING EXPECTATIONS

Crises test a company's credibility and management's mettle. Gerald Meyers, former chairman of American Motors Corporation, believes there are nine basic types of industrial crises. Most arise from unexpected negative changes in fundamentals.

First, public perception of management can cause a major credibility crisis. Lack of belief in a company and its management may sink to levels of outright distrust. Meyers offers General Public Utilities' involvement with Three Mile Island as an example. Manville Corporation's handling of asbestos is another.

Second, a company's industrial relations and labor problems can kill a company's cost structure. International Harvester, now Navistar, is the prime example. Third, management depth and succession is critical to the issue of management quality and depth. The replacement of Steve Jobs at Apple Computer is an example. Management transition from Harry Gray at United Technologies, Inc. (Hartford, CT) was always a nagging problem for that mature company.

Fourth, management's inability to narrow value spreads or to increase shareholder value to satisfactory levels is implicit in any unwanted tender offer. Outside corporate raiders perceive the need for organizational restructuring. This leads to ownership restructuring. T. Boone Pickens' attempts to purchase Gulf Oil, Phillips Petroleum and Unocal are examples, as are Carl Icahn's efforts to take over TWA and USX.

Fifth, cash-generating problems may arise as market demand moderates or turns negative. Meyers offers the example of the demise of Warner Communications' Atari video game business. Sixth, new product introductions may fail. He cites Procter & Gamble's toxic shock syndrome experience with its Rely Tampons. Seventh, market shifts may drain cash as management fails to adjust discretionary spending to changes in market demand. Meyers claims Eastern Airlines and the old Chrysler Corporation are examples.

Eighth, world politics (systematic risk) can alter customer buying cycles and distort cost structures for an industry or a company. He cites the impact of the OPEC cartel's sharp increase in the price of oil on market demand for smaller, more fuel efficient cars and on operating costs in the airline industry. Ninth, he suggests that regulation or deregulation may increase competition and lower prices. The break-up of AT&T and the creation of People Express Airline are examples.

Investors' expectations can create crises in confidence. For example, company meetings send signals to investors. Executives must manage, control and police investors' expectations which may surge in anticipation of company-specific and/or industry developments.

Minnesota Mining & Manufacturing created a credibility problem for itself when a company official prepared the market for announcement of a supposedly major business transaction for the company. Investors anticipated management's shedding the company's low growth floppy disk and videotape units. In about 20 minutes before trading was halted prior to the announcement, investor demand drove the company's stock price up $7.50 per share (to $139 per share).

But the public disclosure concerned the company's purchase of a dental brace manufacturer from Bristol Myers Co. It was an acquisition perceived by investors to be of minimal importance to the company's fundamentals and returns potential. Investors' reaction was swift and angry. Within six minutes after trading resumed, their selling drove the company's stock price down $8.00 per share.

There are wrong ways and right ways to manage investors' expectations. They either destroy reputation or preserve credibility. Recall from Chapter 8 that changes in consensus expectations, not actual changes themselves, affect share prices. For example, unexpected changes in sales growth rates, prices, costs, competition, or product acceptance during a forecast period can squeeze a company's operating margins. The effects of these unexpected changes must be addressed publicly because they affect consensus expectations.

Informing investors about unexpected changes in a company's competitive environment is paramount. Executives must shape investors' perceptions of what these unexpected changes suggest about their company's competitive position, cash-generating ability, and business risk. Failure or refusal to do so penalizes shareholders and management.

Hospital Corporation of America (Nashville, TN) and Daisy Systems Corp. (Mountain View, CA) are examples of the wrong way for management to manage investors' expectations. IBM (Armonk, NY) is an example of the right way.

HCA, a hospital management company, had been considered a classic growth company. Since the late 1960s, the company had consistently gained market share through acquisitions. It had recorded consistent gains in profitability in the range of or greater than 20 percent per year. Between 1975 and 1983, the company's stock price had risen more than 30 times.

But on October 1, 1985, HCA executives forecasted flat earnings for fisal 1986. In and of itself, the announcement was disappointing. But the manner in which it was made shook Wall Street's confidence in the company and analysts' confidence in management.

Before October 1, the company's shares had been rated 1, a buy, by many brokerage firm analysts. Consensus earnings estimates centered around $4 per share for 1986 and $4.75 per share for 1987. And, as recently as five days before the October 1 announcement, management of the company had offered assurances that its results for the third fiscal quarter would be up and that estimates of $4 per share for the year were reasonable.

But right on the heels of assurance, management voluntarily revised its earnings forecast for the year. Management reported that the company's patient admission trends had declined, costs of its in-house administered health insurance programs had increased and that its recently acquired hospitals had recorded unexpected losses. The operating margin squeeze and earnings revision announcement were a major surprise to investors.

The company's shares had traded earlier in 1985 to a high of $52.25 per share. At the time of the announcement, they were trading at $38 per share. On October 2, 1985, share price dropped $7.75 to $31.25 per share. By October 7, 1985, the company's share price had dropped to a 52-week low of $28.125 per share. It was a drop in market value of about $829.5 million in one week. The intra-industry information transfer effect was powerful. The four major publicly traded hospital management companies, as a whole, lost more than $1.5 billion in market value. By June 1986, HCA shares were trading at about $38 per share.

Daisy Systems Corp. competes in the computer-aided engineering and design industry. Management made the mistake of trying to avoid disclosure of weakening fundamentals to analysts. For its fiscal year ended September 30, 1985, the company reported revenues of $122.6 million and earnings of $1.22 per share. For its first fiscal quarter of 1986, the company reported earnings per share of $.35 per share versus $.31 per share in the same period in 1985. Fundamentals seemed intact.

Credibility problems began for management in a January 22, 1986 meeting with securities analysts in San Francisco. Executives initially painted a bright picture of continued growth. But analysts were skeptical for two reasons. An accounting change for research and development costs had added $.06 per share to first quarter's reported $.35 per share. And officers and directors (insiders) had sold stock in October and November 1985 after the company's fourth quarter earnings had been reported.

Heavy questioning of Daisy's executives finally elicited their response that linked quarter revenue comparisons would be weak. Revenues in the second fiscal quarter, ending March 31, 1986, were expected to decline from the previous quarter, ended December 31.

Investors wasted no time in penalizing the company. In two days, half of Daisy Systems' 17.3 million shares traded. Its share price fell more than 20 percent from about $22.50 bid per share over the counter to $19 bid per share. Its shares had traded as high as $37.50 bid per share in 1985. They had closed for the year of 1985 at $29.50 bid per share and had traded above $26 bid per share as recently as January 17, 1986. The company's share price closed for the year of 1986 at $8.375 bid per share, off $21.125 for the year.

Investors believe IBM handles credibility challenges well. For example, on April 11, 1985, the company reported its first quarterly decline in profitability in more than three years. Its shares rose $1.25 to $127 per share because the announcement was simply not a surprise to investors. During the quarter, the company's management had talked about worsening trends. A strong dollar and order delays were expected to slow quarterly earnings growth.

On Wednesday June 12, 1985, IBM disclosed more bad news. Declining growth in corporate productivity and capital spending and weak market demand for IBM's mid-range computers were blamed for a 10 percent decrease in expected unit shipments. Profit in the company's first nine months was expected to come in below that of the prior year. The announcement confirmed previous discussion of expected weakness.

The company's shares had traded down at $138 per share in February 1985. A day before the announcement was made, the stock fell from $127.625 per share to $126 per share. On the day of the company's meeting with analysts, the shares dropped $5.25 points. They dropped another $2.125 points, to $118.625 per share, the day after the meeting. They rebounded $2.50 points on the next trading day, to $121.125 per share, to close the week with a $6.25 point loss. The Dow Jones Industrial Average, in sympathy, lost 15.46 points, closing at 1,300.96.

The company's share price had fallen about 17 points since February. But most observers believed the company had avoided the steep downward gaps in pricing which other computer issues, such as Data General Corporation and Wang Laboratories, had suffered. For example, on February 12, 1985, Data General reported that profitability for its fiscal quarter, ended March 31, would come in significantly below Wall Street's consensus estimates. The company's share price dropped $14.125 points per share, to $58.75 per share.

Professional investors usually have high regard for IBM management's consistency, predictability and guidance in shaping investors' perceptions of the company's operating trends and earnings potential. They think the company's executives are credible and skillful in managing investors' expectations and in orchestrating the company's public disclosures. As a result, market reaction to unexpected surprises or disappointments seems relatively gentle. Such perceived management concern seems to preserve executives' credibility and to deepen shareholders' loyalty to the company.

The credibility lesson is straightforward. Consistency should prevail in good and bad times. Investors pay up for predictability of earnings and stability of returns. But they penalize heavily for surprises because they destroy expected returns. Management credibility is an unsystematic risk factor. At the same time, it is a company's passbook to market sponsorship and a ticket to market value and market multiples.

Chapter 2 showed that dispersion in analysts' estimates lowers stock prices, and Chapter 8 revealed that changes in consensus expectations also affect share prices. Investors punish or reward companies for the information content of negative or positive unexpected announcements. What does this mean for managements of emerging companies? The sustainability of these companies' competitive advantage and cash-generating ability may be unclear. How do their executives preserve credibility while trying to discuss the future?

Managements of these companies must try to minimize the unexpected. They must talk to their stock, monitor investors' perceptions and closely apprise lead investors and dominant sponsors of unexpected changes in fundamentals as they develop. Executives can also couch discussions of management expectations in terms of consensus for their industry or peers. Ultimately, predictable earnings growth and stable returns narrow estimation risk. But these cash flow communications efforts help to enhance management credibility, to reduce information deficiency and to smooth returns.

CONCLUDING REMARKS

Creating investor demand is a marketing function, though rooted deeply in finance and strategy. Its goal is to translate internally created economic value into externally realized market value. Its objectives are market sponsorship, information and pricing efficiency, market value and liquidity.

The process requires that managements shape investors' perceptions of their cash-generating and value-creating abilities. Those managements which invest at the widest capital spreads for the longest periods potentially create the most economic value. Those which generate the highest sales growth rates at the widest operating spreads for the longest periods realize the most actual economic value. Ultimately, sustainable competitive advantages in positive net present value investment opportunities create the most long-term value.

Creating economic value is one matter. Realizing market value is another. Translating economic value into market value requires that managements use Wall Street to affect the market's pricing mechanism. It necessitates an understanding of the equity valuation process. Executives must think as buyers of their stock, in terms of excess returns potential relative to alternative investments of equal risk. That perspective enables them to understand what their company's stock price implies about investors' returns expectations. It also enables them to learn how their shares are valued, and to identify precise reasons for market misperceptions and mispricings. With that understanding, they can create shareholder wealth for shareholders by correcting market misperceptions. Or they can transfer wealth to shareholders by capitalizing on market mispricings.

Translating value also requires an understanding of the demand-creating cycle. Executives must define the investment characteristics of their equity product and understand who buys equities with those returns-generating features. They must recognize and use lead investors. They must identify and use dominant sponsors. And they must be aware of how popularity flow into their stock changes with market capitalization and sponsorship. Ultimately, executives must manage the cycle to reduce information and trading costs in their shares.

I end this book as I began it, with the notion of economic value creation expressed by Professor Fruhan. Profitability is the key to value. Managements of those companies which have it should flaunt it; those which do not have it should try very hard to get it, and those which cannot get it from their current capital and business strategies should get out of those strategies.

Executives who understand the equity valuation process know how to communicate value to Wall Street. They know how to use Wall Street to create investor demand. That knowledge is the key to shareholders' realized returns.

Notes

PREFACE

1. O'Flaherty, J. S. *Going Public: The Entrepreneur's Guide.* (New York: John Wiley & Sons, 1984).

2. Fruhan, W. E., Jr. "How Fast Should Your Company Grow," *Harvard Business Review* (January-February 1984): 84-93.

CHAPTER 1

1. Salpukas, A. "Philip Morris Chairman Studies Several Options," *New York Times* (September 30, 1985), p. 1D.

2. Donnelly, B. "Investors Looking for 'Neglected' Stocks Shouldn't Rule Out Big Issues, Studies Say," *Wall Street Journal* (January 28, 1987), p. 31.

3. Arbel, A. *How to Beat the Market with Generic Stocks.* (New York: Morrow, 1986).

4. Brealey R., and S. Myers. *Principles of Corporate Finance*, 2d ed. (New York: McGraw-Hill, 1984).

5. Fruhan, W. E., Jr. "How Fast Should Your Company Grow?" *Harvard Business Review* (January-February 1984): 89.

6. Arbel, A. "Generic Stocks: An Old Product in a New Package," *Journal of Portfolio Management* (Summer 1985): 4-13.

7. Murphy, K. "Corporate Performance and Managerial Remuneration," *Journal of Accounting and Economics* (April 1985): 11-42.

8. Coughlan, A. T., and R. M. Schmidt. "Executive Compensation, Management Turnover, and Firm Performance," *Journal of Accounting and Economics* (April 1985):43-66.

9. Benston, G. J. "The Self-Serving Management Hypothesis," *Journal of Accounting and Economics* (April 1985):67-84.

10. Brickley, J. A., S. Bhagat, and R. C. Lease. "The Impact of Long-Range Managerial Compensation Plans on Shareholder Wealth," *Journal of Accounting and Economics* (April 1985): 115-29.

11. Lambert, R. A., and D. F. Larcker. "Golden Parachutes, Executive Decision-Making, and Shareholder Wealth," *Journal of Accounting and Economics* (April 1985):179-203.

12. Tehranian, H., and J. F. Waegelein. "Market Reaction to Short-Term Executive Compensation Plan Adoption," *Journal of Accounting and Economics* (April 1985):131-44.

13. Furtado, E. P. H., and M. S. Rozeff. "The Wealth Effects of Company Initiated Management Changes," *Journal of Financial Economics* (March 1987): 147-60.

CHAPTER 2

1. Beaver, W. *Financial Reporting: An Accounting Revolution.* (Englewood Cliffs, NJ: Prentice Hall, 1981): 143.

2. Fruhan, W. E., Jr. *Financial Strategy: Studies in the Creation, Transfer, and Destruction of Shareholder Value.* (Homewood, IL: Richard D. Irwin, 1979): 12-13. Fruhan expresses the ratio of economic value to book value as a function of capital spread, size of reinvestment opportunities (fraction of anticipated after-tax profit), and perceived duration of those reinvestment opportunities:
[(1 plus return on equity times reinvestment rate) divided by (1 plus the cost of equity capital)] compounded over a forecast period

plus

[(return on equity times 1 minus reinvestment rate) divided by (the cost of equity capital minus return on equity times reinvestment rate) times (1) minus the result compounded over a forecast period of (1 plus return on equity times reinvestment rate divided by 1 plus the cost of equity capital)].

3. Rappaport, A. *Creating Shareholder Value.* (New York: The Free Press, 1986): 72-73.
Rappaport's formula for incremental threshold (break-even) operating margin (on incremental sales) at which operating profit equals the cost of capital (investors' minimum required returns) is:
[(incremental fixed plus working capital investment rate times cost of capital) divided by (1 plus cost of capital times 1 minus income tax rate)].
Calculation of threshold (break-even) operating margin on total sales is:
[prior period operating profit plus (incremental threshold margin times incremental sales)] divided by [prior period sales plus incremental sales].

4. Gitman, L. J., and V. A. Mercurio. "Cost of Capital Techniques Used by Major U.S. Firms: Survey and Analysis of Fortune's 1000," *Financial Management* (Winter 1982): 21-29.

5. Sharpe, W. F. "Capital Asset Prices: A Theory of Market Equilibrium Under Conditions of Risk," *Journal of Finance* (September 1964): 425-44.

6. Lintner, J. "The Valuation of Risk Assets and the Selection of Risky Investments in Stock Portfolios and Capital Budgets," *Journal of Finance* (December 1965): 587-614.

7. Jesup, P. F., and R. B. Upson. *Return in Over-the-Counter Markets.* (Minneapolis: University of Minnesota Press, 1973).

8. Hamada, R. S. "The Effects of the Firm's Capital Structure on the Systematic Risk of Common Stocks," *Journal of Finance* (May 1972): 435-52.

9. Lev, B. "On the Association Between Leverage and Risk," *Journal of Financial and Quantitative Analysis* (September 1974): 627-42.

10. Mullins, D. W., Jr. "Does the Capital Asset Pricing Model Work," *Harvard Business Review* (January-February 1982): 105-14.

11. Ross, S. A. "The Arbitrage Theory of Capital Asset Pricing," *Journal of Economic Theory* (December 1976): 341-60.

12. Bower, D. H., R. S. Bower, and D. E. Logue. "A Primer on Arbitrage Pricing Theory," *Midland Corporate Finance Journal* (Fall 1984): 31-39.

13. King, B. F. "Market and Industry Factors" *Journal of Business* (January 1966): 139-91.

14. Sorensen, E. H., and T. Burke. "Portfolio Returns from Active Industry Group Rotation," *Financial Analysts Journal* (September-October 1986): 43-69.

15. Farrell, J. L., Jr. "Homogeneous Stock Groupings," *Financial Analysts Journal* (May-June 1975): 58.

16. Ibid., p. 50.

17. Ibid.

18. Ibid.

19. Martin, J. D., and R. C. Klemkosky. "The Effect of Homogeneous Stock Groupings on Portfolio Risk," *The Journal of Business* (July 1976): 339.

20. Ibid., p. 342.

21. Farrell, p. 58.

22. Fisher L., and J. Lorie. "Some Studies of Variability of Returns on Investment in Common Stocks," *Journal of Business* (April 1970): 99-134.

23. Estep, T. "Manager Style and the Source of Equity Returns," *Journal of Portfolio Management* (Winter 1987): 4-10.

24. Sharpe, W. F. "Factors in New York Stock Exchange Security Returns, 1931-1979," *The Journal of Portfolio Management* (Summer 1982): 5-19.

25. Ibbotson, R. G., and R. A. Sinquefield. "Stocks, Bonds, Bills and Inflation: 60 Years of Historical Returns 12/31/25 - 12/31/85," (Chevy Chase, MD: CDA Investment Technologies, 1985).

26. Gale, B. T., and B. Branch. "Cash flow Analysis: More Important Than Ever," *Harvard Business Review* (July-August 1981): 131-35.

27. Fruhan, W. E., Jr. *Financial Strategy*: 24-55.

28. Rappaport, A. *Creating*: 29-31.

29. Ibid., pp. 9-10.

30. Branch, B., and B. T. Gale. "Linking Corporate Stock Price Performance To Strategy Formulation," *The Journal Of Business Strategy* (Summer 1983): 40-50.

31. Hawkins, D. F., and W. J. Campbell, *Equity Valuation: Models, Analysis and Implications* (New York: Financial Executives Research Foundation, 1978).

32. Miller, M., and F. Modigliani. "The Cost of Capital, Corporation Finance and the Theory of Investment." *The American Economic Review* (June 1958): 261-97.

362 Notes

33. Rappaport, p. 252.

34. Sorensen, E. H., and D.A. Williamson. "Some Evidence on the Value of Dividend Discount Models," *Financial Analysts Journal* (November-December 1985): 60-69.

35. Hawkins, D. F. *Equity Valuation*: 195.

36. The equation for a two-phase dividend discount model comprises two terms (a three-phase model has three terms, etc.). The first is the present value of dividends during a forecast period of above-average growth. The second is the dividend in the last year of above-average growth times the dividend growth rate discounted to the present. Using words instead of symbols to express the equation as constructed by Professor Rappaport (see footnote 38):

Share price equals (net income) times (the dividend payout rate in the forecast period of above-average growth) times (1 + the company's sales growth rate compounded over the same period) divided by (1 + the company's cost of equity capital compounded over the same period)

plus

(dividends in the last year of above-average growth) times (1 + the company's sales growth rate in subsequent period of normal growth) divided by (the company's cost of equity capital minus its sales growth rate in the subsequent period) times (1 + the company's cost of equity capital compounded over the forecast number of years of above-average growth).

37. Molodovsky, N., C. May, and S. Chottiner. "Common Stock Valuation: Theory and Tables," *Financial Analysts Journal* (March-April 1965): 104-23.

38. Rappaport, A. "The Affordable Dividend Approach to Equity Valuation," *Financial Analysts Journal* (July-August 1986): 52-58.

Rappaport's equation for a two-phase dividend discount model also comprises two terms. The first is essentially the same as mentioned in footnote 36 above. The second is the affordable dividend in the first year of a company's transition to normal growth (dividend payout rate adjusted for the cash consequences of changes in the company's sales growth rate) discounted to the present.

A company's affordable dividend payout rate equals [(1 − the company's sales growth rate) times (the per dollar of sales increase in both its working capital and fixed capital less depreciation)] divided by [(1 + the company's sales growth rate) times (its pretax earnings-to-sales ratio) times (1 − its cash income tax rate) times (1 + its target debt/equity ratio)].

A company's share price equals [(net income) times (the affordable dividend payout rate in the forecast period of above-average growth) times (1 + the company's sales growth rate compounded over the same period)] divided by [(1 + the company's cost of equity capital compounded over the same period)]

plus

[(net income in the last year of above-average growth) times (1 + the company's sales growth rate in the period of normal growth) times (the affordable dividend payout rate in the first year after transition to normal growth)] divided by [(the company's cost of equity capital minus its normal sales growth rate) times (1 + the company's cost of equity capital) compounded over the forecast number of years of above-average growth)].

Solving for affordable dividend payout ratio, [(a company's sales growth rate in its period of above-average growth minus its sales growth rate in its period of normal growth) divided by (1 + its above-average sales growth rate + its normal sales growth rate + its above-average sales growth rate times its normal sales growth rate)],

times

[(a company's per sales dollar increase in its working capital + fixed capital less depreciation) divided by (1 − the company's cash income tax rate) times (1 + its target debt/equity ratio) times (its pretax earnings-to-sales ratio)].

39. Piper, T. R., and W. E. Fruhan, Jr. "Is Your Stock Worth Its Market Price," *Harvard Business Review* (May-June 1981): 124-32.

40. Statman, M. "Growth Opportunities vs. Growth Stocks," *The Journal of Portfolio Management* (Spring 1984): 70-74.

41. Oppenheimer, H. R. "A Test of Ben Graham's Stock Selection Criteria," *Financial Analysts Journal* (September-October 1984): 68-74.

42. Donnelly, B. "Recent Market Rally Saw Failure of Proven Stock-Picking Methods," *Wall Street Journal* (September 15, 1987), p. 35.

43. Holt, C. C. "The Influence of Growth Duration on Share Prices," *Journal of Finance* (September 1962): 465-75.

44. "Growth Stock Sampler," *Barron's* (June 2, 1986): 18.

CHAPTER 3

1. Peavy, J. W. III, and D.A. Goodman. "How Inflation, Risk and Corporate Profitability Affect Common Stock Returns," *Financial Analysts Journal* (September-October 1985): 59-65.

2. Smith, C. W., Jr. "Investment Banking and the Capital Acquisition Process," *Journal of Financial Economics* (January/February 1986): 3-29.

3. Titman, S., and B. Trueman. "Information Quality and the Valuation of New Issues," *Journal of Accounting and Economics* (June 1986): 159-172.

4. Carpenter, C. G., and R. H. Strawser. "Displacement of Auditor When Clients Go Public," *Journal of Accountancy* (June 1971): 55-58.

5. Logue, D. "On the pricing of unseasoned equity issues: 1965-1969," *Journal of Financial and Quantitative Analysis* (January 1973): 91-103.

6. Ritter, J. R. "The 'Hot Issue' Market of 1980," *Journal of Business* (April 1984): 215-40.

7. Beatty, R. P., and J. R. Ritter. "Investment Banking, Reputation, and the Underpricing of Initial Public Offerings," *Journal of Financial Economics* (January/February 1986): 213-32.

8. Miller, R. E., and F. K. Reilly. "An Examination of Mispricing, Returns, and Uncertainty for Initial Public Offerings," *Financial Management* (Summer 1987): 33-38.

CHAPTER 4

1. Mullins, D. W., Jr. "Does The Capital Asset Pricing Model Work?" *Harvard Business Review* (January–February 1982): 105-14.

2. Farrell, J. L., Jr. *Guide To Portfolio Management.* (New York: McGraw-Hill, 1983): 128-36.

3. Wilcox, J. W. "The P/B-ROE Valuation Model," *Financial Analysts Journal* (January-February 1984): 58-66.

4. Branch, B., and B. Gale. "Linking Corporate Stock Price Performance to Strategy Formulation," *Journal of Business Strategy* (Summer 1983): 43-44.

5. Ibid., pp. 46-48.

6. Ellis, C. D. "How to Manage Investor Relations," *Financial Analysts Journal* (March-April 1985): 35.

7. Bhagat, S., J.A. Brickley, and R. C. Lease. "Incentive Effects of Stock Purchase Plans," *Journal of Financial Economics* (June 1985): 195-215.

8. Keynes, J. M. *The General Theory of Employment, Interest and Money.* (New York: Harcourt, Brace and Co., 1936): 156

9. Elton, E. J., M. J. Gruber, and M. Gultekin. "Expectations and Share Prices," *Management Science* (September 1981): 975-87.

CHAPTER 5

1. "Companies Feel Underrated By The Street," *Business Week* (February 20, 1984): 14.

2. "General Motors May Be on the Road to Giving Additional Financial Information to Analysts," *Wall Street Journal,* (December 27, 1985), p.31.

3. Ibid., p. 31.

4. Ibid.

5. Ibid.

6. Piper, T. R., and W. E. Fruhan, Jr. "Is Your Stock Worth Its Market Price?" *Harvard Business Review* (May-June 1981): 125-26.

7. Ibid., p. 130.

8. Rappaport, A. *Creating Shareholder Value.* (New York: The Free Press, 1986): 142-43.

9. Arzac, E. R. "Do Your Business Units Create Shareholder Value?" *Harvard Business Review* (January-February 1986): 121-26.

10. Rappaport, A. "The Affordable Dividend Approach to Equity Valuation," *Financial Analysts Journal* (July-August 1986): 52-58.

11. Rappaport, A. *Creating,* p. 148-68.

12. Levitt, T. "Marketing Success Through Differentiation of Anything," *Harvard Business Review* (January-February 1980): 83-91.

13. Seitz, N. "Shareholder Goals, Firm Goals and Firm Financing Decisions," *Financial Management* (Autumn 1982): 20-26.

14. Myers, S. C. "The Search for Optimal Capital Structure," *Revolutions in Corporate Finance* (New York: Basil Blackwell, 1986): 91-99.

15. Scott, D. F., Jr., and D. J. Johnson. "Financial Policies and Practices in Large Corporations," *Financial Management* (Summer 1982): 51-59.

16. Miller, M., and F. Modigliani. "Dividend Policy, Growth and the Valuation of Shares," *Journal of Business* (October 1961): 411-33.

17. Black, F., and M. Scholes. "The Effects of Dividend Yield and Dividend Policy on Common Stock Prices and Returns," *Journal of Financial Economics* (May 1974): 1-22.

18. Brealey, R., and S. Myers. *Principles of Corporate Finance*, 2nd ed. (New York: McGraw-Hill 1984): 348.

19. Rozeff, M. "How Companies Set Their Dividend-Payout Ratios," *Issues in Corporate Finance* (1982): 151-57.

20. Richardson, G., S. E. Sefcik, and R. Thompson. "A Test of Dividend Irrelevance Using Volume Reactions to a Change in Dividend Policy," *Journal of Financial Economics* (December 1986): 313-33.

21. Wertheim & Co., Inc. "The Sources of Earnings Growth" (1978)

22. Ibid., "The Sources of Sales Growth"

23. Wertheim, "Earnings"

24. Ibid.

25. Ibid.

26. Dennis, C. N. "An Investigation into the Effects of Independent Investor Relations Firms on Common Stock Prices," *Journal of Finance* (May 1973): 373-80.

CHAPTER 6

1. Beaver, W. H. "The Information Content of Annual Earnings Announcements," *Empirical Research in Accounting: Selected Studies*, 1968. Supplement to *Journal of Accounting Research* (6, 1968): 68-9.

2. Ball, R., and P. Brown. "An Empirical Evaluation of Accounting Income Numbers," *Journal of Accounting Research* (Autumn 1968): 159-78.

3. Bamber. L. S. "The Information Content of Annual Earnings Releases: A Trading Approach," *Journal of Accounting Research* (Spring 1986): 40-56.

4. Beaver, W. H., Clarke, R., and W. F. Wright. "The Association Between Unsystematic Security Returns and the Magnitude of Earnings Forecast Errors," *Journal of Accounting Research* (Autumn 1979): 316-40.

5. Foster, G. "Quarterly Accounting Data: Time Series Properties and Predictive-Ability Results," *Accounting Review* (January 1977): 1-21.

6. Rendleman, R. J., Jr., C. P. Jones, and H. A. Latane. "Empirical Anomalies Based on Unexpected Earnings and the Importance of Risk Adjustments," *Journal of Financial Economics* (November 1982): 269-87.

7. Watts, R. L. "Systematic Abnormal Returns After Quarterly Earnings Announcements," *Journal of Financial Economics* (Summer 1978): 139.

8. Bamber, L. S. "Unexpected Earnings, Firm Size and Trading Volume Around Quarterly Earnings Announcements," *Accounting Review* (July 1987): 510-32.

9. Kross, W., and D. A. Schroeder. "An Empirical Investigation of the Effect of Quarterly Earnings Announcement Timing on Stock Returns," *Journal of Accounting Research* (Spring 1984): 153-76.

10. Penman, S. H. "Abnormal Returns to Investment Strategies Based on the Timing of Earnings Reports," *Journal of Accounting and Economics* (December 1984): 165-83.

11. Foster, G. "Stock Market Reaction to Estimates of Earnings Per Share by Company Officials," *Journal of Accounting Research* (Spring 1973): 25-37.

12. Kaplan. R. S., and R. Roll. "Investor Evaluation of Accounting Information: Some Empirical Evidence," *Journal of Business* (April 1972): 225-57.

13. Grant, E. B. "Market Implications of Differential Amounts of Interim Information," *Journal of Accounting Research* (Spring 1980): 255-67.

14. Firth, M. "The Relative Information Content of the Release of Financial Results Data by Firms," *Journal of Accounting Research* (Autumn 1981): 521-29.

15. McNichols, M., and J. G. Manegold. "The Effect of the Information Environment on the Relationship Between Financial Disclosure and Security Price Variability," *Journal of Accounting and Economics* (April 1983): 49-74.

16. Arbel, A. "Generic Stocks: An Old Product in a New Package," *The Journal of Portfolio Management* (Summer 1985): 4-13.

17. Ibid., p. 13.

18. Foster, G. "Intra-Industry Information Transfers Associated with Earnings Releases," *Journal of Accounting and Economics* (December 1981): 201-32.

19. Smith, C. W., Jr. "Investment Banking and the Capital Acquisition Process," *Journal of Financial Economics* (January/February 1986): 3-29.

20. Schipper, K., and A. Smith. "A Comparison of Equity Carve-outs and Seasoned Equity Offerings: Share Price Effects and Corporate Restructuring," *Journal of Financial Economics* (January-February 1986): 153-86.

21. Smith, p. 8.

22. Benesh, G. A., A. J. Keown, and J. M. Pinkerton. "An Examination of Market Reaction to Substantial Shifts in Dividend Policy," *Journal of Financial Research* (Summer 1984): 131-41.

23. Divecha, A., and D. Morse. "Market Responses to Dividend Increases and Changes in Payout Ratios," *Journal of Quantitative Analysis* (June 1983): 163-73.

24. Branch, B., and B. Gale. "Linking Corporate Stock Price Performance to Strategy Formulation," *The Journal of Business Strategy* (Summer 1983): 45.

25. Kalay, A., and U. Loewensteim. "The Informational Content of the Timing of Dividend Announcements," *Journal of Financial Economics* (July 1986): 373-88.

26. Fama, E. F., L. Fisher, M. Jensen, and R. Roll. "The Adjustment of Stock Prices to New Information," *International Economic Review* (February 1969): 1-21.

27. Grinblatt, M. S., R. W. Masulis, and S. Titman. "The Valuation Effects of Stock Splits and Stock Dividends," *Journal of Financial Economics* (December 1984): 461-90.

28. Bar-Yosef, S., and L. Brown. "A Re-examination of Stock Splits Using Moving Betas," *Journal of Finance* (September 1977): 1069-80.

29. Copeland, T. "The Evidence Agaisnst Stock Splits," *The Revolution in Corporate Finance* (New York: Basil Blackwell, 1986): 12-16.

30. Murray, D. "Further Evidence on the Liquidity Effects of Stock Splits and Stock Dividends," *The Journal of Financial Research* (Spring 1985): 59-67.

31. Woolridge, J. R., and D. R. Chambers. "Reverse Splits and Shareholder Wealth," *Financial Management* (Autumn 1983): 5-15.

32. McConnell, J. J., and C. J. Muscarella. "Corporate Capital Expenditure Decisions and the Market Value of the Firm," *Journal of Financial Economics* (September 1985): 399-422.

33. Branch, B., and B. Gale, p. 44.

34. Ibid., p. 45.

35. Smith, p. 8.

36. Morse, D. "Wall Street Journal Announcements and the Securities Markets," *Financial Analysts Journal* (March/April 1982): 69-76.

37. Jensen, M. C., and R. S. Ruback. "The Market for Corporate Control: The Scientific Evidence," *Journal of Financial Economics* (April, 1983): 5-50.

38. Ibid.

39. Dodd, P. "Merger Proposals, Management Discretion and Stockholder Wealth," *Journal of Financial Economics* (June, 1980): 105-38.

40. Hite, G. L., and J. E. Owers. "Security Price Reactions Around Corporate Spin-off Announcements," *Journal of Financial Economics* (December 1983): 409-36.

41. Smith, p. 13.

42. Ibid.

43. Ibid.

44. Jensen and Ruback: 38-39.

45. Ibid., pp. 34-35.

46. Jarrell, G. A., and A. B. Poulsen. "Shark Repellents and Poison Pills: Stockholder Protection—From the Good Guys or the Bad Guys?" *Midland Corporate Finance Journal* (Summer 1986): 39-47.

47. Mikkelson, W. H., and R. S. Ruback. "An Empirical Analysis of the Interfirm Equity Investment Process," *Journal of Financial Economics* (December 1985): 523-53.

48. Jensen and Ruback: 28-29.

49. Mikkelson, W. H., and M. M. Partch. "Stock Price Effects and Costs of Secondary Distributions," *Journal of Financial Economics* (14, 1985): 165-94.

50. Scholes, M. "The Market for Securities: Substitution Versus Price Pressure and the Effects of Information on Share Prices," *Journal of Business* (April 1972): 179-211.

CHAPTER 7

1. Timbers, S. "The Non-Efficient Sector Is Not For Institutions," *Journal of Portfolio Management* (Fall 1977): 59.

2. Ibid., p. 61.

3. Ibid.

4. Loeb, T. F. "Trading Cost: The Critical Link Between Investment Information and Results," *Financial Analysts Journal* (May-June 1983): 39-44.

5. Amihud, Y., and H. Mendelson. "Liquidity and Stock Returns," *Financial Analysts Journal* (May-June 1986): 43-48.

6. Arbel, A., S. Carvell, and P. Strebel. "Giraffes, Institutions and Neglected Firms," *Financial Analysts Journal* (May-June 1983): 57-63.

7. Nesbitt, S. "'Hot Money' Can Trip Up Fast Track Advisory Firms," *Pensions and Investment Age* (September 5, 1983): 40.

8. Lueck, T. J. "Can Fidelity Maintain Its Frenzied Growth?" *New York Times* (March 16, 1986): 7F.

9. Reader, A. C. "The Care and Feeding of Buy-Side Analysts," *Financial Analysts Journal* (March/April 1981): 42-51.

10. Groth, J. C., W. G. Lewellen, G. G. Schlarbaum, and R. C. Lease. "An Analysis of Brokerage House Securities Recommendations," *Financial Analysts Journal* (January-February 1979): 32-40.

11. Reilly, F. K., and D. J. Wright. "Block Trading and Aggregate Stock Price Volatility," *Financial Analysts Journal* (March/April 1984): 54-60.

CHAPTER 8

1. Rivel, A. "The Changing Role of the Stockbroker," *The Amex Journal* (December 1982): 1.

2. Givoly, D., and J. Lakonishok. "The Quality of Analysts' Forecasts of Earnings," *Financial Analysts Journal* (September-October 1984): 40-47.

3. Benesh, G. A., and P.P. Peterson. "On the Relation Between Earnings Changes, Analysts' Forecasts and Stock Price Fluctuations," *Financial Analysts Journal* (November-December 1986): 29-39.

4. Givoly, D., and J. Lakonishok. "The Information Content of Financial Analysts' Forecasts of Earnings," *Journal of Accounting and Economics* (December 1979): 165-85.

5. Penman, S. H. "An Empirical Investigation of the Voluntary Disclosure of Corporate Earnings Forecasts," *Journal of Accounting Research* (Spring 1980): 132-60.

6. Waymire, G. "Additional Evidence on the Information Content of Management Earnings Forecasts," *Journal of Accounting Research* (Autumn 1984): 703-18.

7. Patell, J. M. "Corporate Forecasts of Earnings Per Share and Stock Price Behavior: Empirical Tests," *Journal of Accounting Research* (Autumn 1976): 246-76.

8. Elton, E. J., M. J. Gruber, and M. Gultekin. "Expectations and Share Prices," *Management Science* (September 1981): 975-87.

9._____. "Professional Expectations: Accuracy and Diagnosis of Errors," *Journal of Financial and Quantitative Analysis* (December 1984): 351-63.

10. Elton, E. J., M. J. Gruber, and S. M. Koo. "Effect of Quarterly Earnings Announcements on Analysts' Forecasts," *Research in Finance* (6, 1986): 247-59.

11. Ajinkya, B., and M. Gift. "Corporate Managers' Earnings Forecasts and Symmetrical Adjustments of Market Expectations." *Journal of Accounting Research* (Autumn 1984): 425-44.

12. Hassell, J. M., and R. H. Jennings. "Relative Forecast Accuracy and the Timing of Earnings Forecast Announcements," *Accounting Review* (January 1986): 58-75.

13. Dreman, D. *Contrarian Investment Strategy* (New York: Random House, 1979): 144.

14. Penman, S. H. "A Comparison of the Information Content of Insider Trading and Management Earnings Forecasts," *Journal of Financial and Quantitative Analysis* (March 1985): 1-17.

15. Ellis, C. D. "How to Manage Investor Relations," *Financial Analysts Journal* (March-April 1985): 37.

16. Arbel, A., and P. Strebel. "Pay Attention to Neglected Firms," *Journal of Portfolio Management* (Winter 1983): 37-42.

17. Davies, P. L., and M. Canes. "Stock Prices and the Publication of Second-Hand Information," *Journal of Business* (51, 1978): 43-56.

18. Stanley, K. L., W. G. Lewellen, and G. C. Schlarbaum. "Investor Response to Investment Research," *Journal of Portfolio Management* (Summer 1980): 20-27.

19. Black, F. "Yes, Virginia, There is Hope: Tests of the Value Line Ranking System," *Seminar: Center for Research in Security Prices* (University of Chicago, May 1971).

20. Stickel, S. E. "The Effect of Value Line Investment Survey Rank Changes on Common Stock Prices," *Journal of Financial Economics* (March 1985): 121-43.

21. Ellis, p. 38

22. Kleinfield, N. R. "The Many Faces of the Wall Street Analyst," *New York Times* (October 27, 1985): 8F.

23. Chugh, L. C., and J. W. Meador. "The Stock Valuation Process: The Analysts' View," *Financial Analysts Journal* (November-December 1984): 48.

24. Kleinfield, p. 8F.

25. Copeland, T. E., and D. Galai. "Information Effects on the Bid-Ask Spread," *Journal of Finance* (December 1983): 1457-69.

26. Smirlock, M., and L. Starks. "A Further Examination of Stock Price Changes and Transaction Volume," *The Journal of Financial Research* (Fall 1985): 217-25.

27. Verrecchia, R. E. "On the Relationship Between Volume Reaction and Consensus of Investors: Implications for Interpreting Tests of Information Content," *Journal of Accounting Research* (Spring 1981): 271-83.

28. Cooper, S. K., J. C. Groth, and W. E. Avera. "Liquidity, Exchange Listing, and Common Stock Performance," *Journal of Economics and Business* (February 1985): 27.

29. McConnell, J. J., and G. C. Sanger. "A Trading Strategy for New Listings on the NYSE," *Financial Analysts Journal* (January-February 1984): 34-8.

30. _____. "The Puzzle in Post-Listing Common Stock Returns," *Journal of Finance* (March 1987): 119-40.

31. Sanger, G. C., and J.J. McConnell. "Stock Exchange Listings, Firm Value, and Security Market Efficiency: The Impact of NASDAQ," *Journal of Financial and Quantitative Analysis* (March 1986): 1-23.

32. Baker. H. K., and J. Spitzfaden. "The Impact of Exchange Listing on the Cost of Equity Capital," *Financial Review* (September 1982): 128-41.

33. Grammatikos, T., and G. Papaioannou. "Market Reaction to NYSE Listings: Tests of the Marketability Gains Hypothesis," *Journal of Financial Research* (Fall 1986): 215-27.

34. Loeb, T. F. "Trading Cost: The Critical Link Between Investment Information and Results," *Financial Analysts Journal* (May-June 1983): 39-44.

CHAPTER 10

1. Fogelson, J. H. "Disclosure Laws Retain Teeth Despite Recent Court Limitations," *The National Law Journal* (February 22, 1982): 30.

2. Ibid.

3. Ibid.

4. Ibid.

5. Ibid.

6. Ibid.

7. Ibid.

8. Ibid.

9. Ibid.

10. Ibid., p. 31.

11. Bulkeley, W. M. "A Firm by Any Other Name Means Likely Rise in Stock, Research Finds," *Wall Street Journal* (July 10, 1987): 22.

Bibliography

BOOKS

American Stock Exchange. *Investor Relations Programs Among Amex Listed Companies*. New York: American Stock Exchange, 1976.

Arbel, A. *How to Beat the Market with Generic Stocks*. (New York: Morrow, 1986).

Beaver, W. H. *Financial Reporting: An Accounting Revolution*. (Englewood Cliffs, NJ: Prentice Hall, 1981).

Birinyi, L., Jr., and L. R. Weber. *Equity Market Data*. (New York: Salomon, 1986).

Brealey, R. A. *An Introduction to Risk and Return from Common Stocks*. (Cambridge, MA: M. I. T. Press, 1983).

Brealey, R., and S. Myers. *Principles of Corporate Finance*. (New York: McGraw-Hill, 1981).

———. *Principles of Corporate Finance*, 2d ed. (New York: McGraw-Hill, 1984).

Dreman, D. *Contrarian Investment Strategy*. (New York: Random House, 1979).

Farrell, J. L., Jr. *Guide to Portfolio Management*. (New York: McGraw-Hill, 1983).

Foster, G. *Financial Statement Analysis*. (Englewood Cliffs, NJ: Prentice-Hall, 1978).

Fruhan, W. E., Jr. *Financial Strategy: Studies in the Creation, Transfer, and Destruction of Shareholder Value*. (Homewood, IL: Richard D. Irwin, 1979).

Graham, B., D. Dodd, S. Cottle, and C. Tatham. *Security Analysis*, 4th ed. (New York: McGraw-Hill, 1962).

Greenwich Associates, Inc. *Institutional Equity Services 1986: Flash Report*. (Greenwich, CT: Greenwich Associates, 1986).

Hawkins, D. F., and W. J. Campbell. *Equity Valuation: Models, Analysis and Implications*. (New York: Financial Executives Research Foundation, 1978).

Ibbotson, R. G., and R. A. Sinquefield. *Stocks, Bonds, Bills and Inflation*. (Charlottesville, VA: Financial Analysts Research Foundation, 1977).

———. *Stocks Bonds, Bills and Inflation: 60 Years of Historical Returns 12/31/25 -12/31/85*. (Silver Spring, MD: CDA Investment Technologies, 1986).

371

Jesup, P. F., and R. B. Upson. *Return in Over-the-Counter Markets*. (Minneapolis: University of Minnesota Press, 1973).

Keynes, J. M. *The General Theory of Employment, Interest and Money*. (New York: Harcourt, Brace and Co., 1936).

Lorie, J. H., P. Dodd, and M. H. Kimpton. *The Stock Market: Theories and Evidence*. Sd ed. (Homewood, IL: Dow Jones–Irwin, 1985).

National Association of Securities Dealers, Inc. *1986 Fact Book*. (Washington, DC, 1986).

New York Stock Exchange. *Shareownership 1985*. (New York: 1986).

O'Flaherty, Joseph S. *Going Public: The Entrepreneur's Guide*. (New York: John Wiley & Sons, 1984).

Porter, M. E. *Competitive Strategy*. (New York: Free Press, 1980).

————. *Competitive Advantage*. (New York: Free Press, 1985).

Donaldson, Lufkin & Jenrette Securities. *Market Perspective*. (New York: Pershing Division, September, 1985).

Prospectus. *Fidelity's Growth Funds*. (Boston: Fidelity Distributors Corporation, 1986.)

Prospectus. *Fidelity Select Portfolios*. (Boston: Fidelity Distributors Corporation, 1985).

Rappaport, A. *Creating Shareholder Value*. (New York: The Free Press, 1986).

Stern, J., ed. *The Revolution in Corporate Finance*. (New York: Basil Blackwell, 1986).

Technimetrics, Inc. *1986 Target Cities Report*. (New York: 1986).

Technimetrics, Inc. *ANAMAIL Data Base Distribution*. (New York: 1986).

Williams, J. B. *The Theory of Investment Value*. (Cambridge, MA: Harvard University Press, 1938).

MONOGRAPHS

"The Art of Forecasting." New York: Wertheim & Co., Inc., 1981.

"The Sources of Earnings Growth." New York: Wertheim & Co., Inc., 1978.

"The Sources of Sales Growth." New York: Wertheim & Co., Inc.

JOURNALS

"The After-IPO-Market-Maker Blues," *Venture* (May 1985): 144.

Ajinkya, B., and M. Gift. "Corporate Managers' Earnings Forecasts and Symmetrical Adjustments of Market Expectations," *Journal of Accounting Research* (Autumn 1984): 425-44.

Amihud, Y., and H. Mendelson. "Liquidity and Stock Returns," *Financial Analysts Journal* (May-June 1986): 43-48.

Antia, M. J., and R. L. Meyer. "The Growth Optimal Capital Structure: Manager Versus Shareholder Objectives," *Journal of Financial Research* (Fall 1984): 259-67.

Arbel, A. "Generic Stocks: An Old Product in a New Package," *Journal of Portfolio Management* (Summer 1985): 4-13.

Arbel, A., S. Carvell, and P. Strebel. "Giraffes, Institutions and Neglected Firms," *Financial Analysts Journal* (May-June 1983): 57-63.

Arbel, A., and P. Strebel. "Pay Attention to Neglected Firms," *Journal of Portfolio Management* (Winter 1983): 37-42.

Arzac, E. R. "Do Your Business Units Create Shareholder Value," *Harvard Business Review* (January-February 1986): 121-26.

Baker. H. K., and J. Spitzfaden. "The Impact of Exchange Listing on the Cost of Equity Capital," *Financial Review* (September 1982): 128-41.

Ball, R., and P. Brown. "An Empirical Evaluation of Accounting Income Numbers," *Journal of Accounting Research* (Autumn 1968): 159-78.

Bamber, L. S. "The Information Content of Annual Earnings Releases: A Trading Volume Approach, " *Journal of Accounting Research* (Spring 1986): 40-56.

———. "Unexpected Earnings, Firm Size, and Trading Volume Around Quarterly Earnings Announcements," *Accounting Review* (July 1987): 510-32.

Bar-Yosef, S., and L. Brown. "A Re-examination of Stock Splits Using Moving Betas," *Journal of Finance* (September 1977): 1069-80.

Beatty, R. P., and J. R. Ritter. "Investment Banking, Reputation, and the Underpricing of Initial Public Offerings," *Journal of Financial Economics* (January/February 1986): 213-32.

Beaver, W. H. "The Information Content of Annual Earnings Announcements," *Empirical Research in Accounting: Selected Studies*, 1968. Supplement to *Journal of Accounting Research* (Autumn 1979): 316-40.

Beaver, W. H., R. Clarke, and W. F. Wright. "The Association Between Unsystematic Security Returns and the Magnitude of Earnings Forecast Errors," *Journal of Accounting and Economics* (Autumn 1979): 316-40.

Benesh, G. A., A. J. Keown, and J. M. Pinkerton. "An Examination of Market Reaction to Substantial Shifts in Dividend Policy," *Journal of Financial Research* (Summer 1984): 131-41.

Benesh, G. A., and P.P. Peterson. "On the Relation Between Earnings Changes, Analysts' Forecasts and Stock Price Fluctuations," *Financial Analysts Journal* (November-December 1986): 29-39.

Benston, G. J. "The Self-Serving Management Hypothesis," *Journal of Accounting and Economics* (April 1985): 67-84.

Bernstein, L. A., and J. G. Siegel. "The Concept of Earnings Quality," *Financial Analysts Journal* (July-August 1979): 46-49.

Bernstein, P. L. "Liquidity, Stock Markets, and Market Makers," *Financial Management* (Summer 1987): 54-62.

Bhagat, S., J. A. Brickley, and R. C. Lease. "Incentive Effects of Stock Purchase Plans," *Journal of Financial Economics* (June 1985): 195-215.

Black, F. "Yes, Virginia, There is Hope: Tests of the Value Line Ranking System," *Seminar: Center for Research in Security Prices* (University of Chicago, May 1971).

———. "Noise," *Journal of Finance* (July 1986): 529-43.

Black, F., and M. Scholes. "The Effects of Dividend Yield and Dividend Policy on Common Stock Prices and Returns," *Journal of Financial Economics* (May 1974): 1-22.

Bower, D. H., R. S. Bower, and D. E. Logue. "A Primer on Arbitrage Pricing Theory," *Midland Corporate Finance Journal* (Fall 1984): 31-39.

Branch, B., and B. Gale. "Linking Corporate Stock Price Performance To Strategy Formulation," *Journal of Business Strategy* (Summer 1983): 40-50.

Brick, I. E., and D. G. Weaver. "A Comparison of Capital Budgeting Techniques in Identifying Profitable Investments," *Financial Management* (Winter 1984): 29-39.

Brickley. J. A. "Shareholder Wealth, Information Signalling and the Specially Designated Dividend," *Journal of Financial Economics* (August 1983): 187-209.

Brickley, J. A., S. Bhagat, and R. C. Lease. "The Impact of Long-Range Managerial Compensation Plans on Shareholder Wealth," *Journal of Accounting and Economics* (April 1985): 115-29.

Bruno, A. V., J. K. Leidecker, and C. G. Torgimson. "Sizing Up Your Company's Takeover Vulnerability," *Mergers & Acquisitions* (Summer 1985): 42-49.

Carpenter, C. G., and R. Strawser. "Displacement of Auditor When Clients Go Public," *Journal of Accountancy* (June 1971): 55-58.

Carvell, S., and P. Strebel. "A New Beta Incorporating Analysts' Forecasts," *Journal of Portfolio Management* (Fall 1984): 81-85.

Casey, C. J., and N. J. Bartczak. "Cash Flow—It's Not the Bottom Line," *Harvard Business Review* (July-August 1984): 61-66.

Chen, N., R. Roll, and S. A. Ross. "Economic Factors and the Stock Market," *Journal of Business* (July 1986): 383-402.

Chugh, L. C., and J. W. Meador. "Break the Barrier Between You and Your Analyst," *Financial Executive* (September 1984): 16-21.

———. "The Stock Valuation Process: The Analysts' View," *Financial Analysts Journal* (November-December 1984): 41-48.

Clayman, M. "In Search of Excellence: The Investor's Viewpoint," *Financial Analysts Journal* (May-June 1987): 54-63.

Collins, W., W. Hopwood, and J. McKeown. "The Predictability of Interim Earnings over Alternative Quarters," *Journal of Accounting Research* (Autumn 1984): 467-79.

Contrarious. "Indexing: The Anatomy of the S&P 500," *Personal Investing* (March 26, 1986): 47-48.

Contrarious. "Beneath the Surface of the Stock Market," *Personal Investing* (April 9, 1986): 56.

Contrarious. "The Trend Toward Mutual Funds," *Personal Investing* (April 23, 1986): 63-64.

Cooper, S. K., J. C. Groth, and W. E. Avera. "Liquidity, Exchange Listing, and Common Stock Performance," *Journal of Economics and Business* (February 1985): 21-33.

Copeland, T. "The Evidence Against Stock Splits," *The Revolution in Corporate Finance*. (New York: Basil Blackwell, 1986): 12-16.

Copeland, T. E., and D. Galai. "Information Effects on the Bid-Ask Spread," *Journal of Finance* (December 1983): 1457-69.

Coughlan, A. T., and R. M. Schmidt. "Executive Compensation, Management Turnover, and Firm Performance," *Journal of Accounting and Economics* (April 1985): 43-66.

Davies , P. L., and M. Canes. "Stock Prices and the Publication of Second-Hand Information," *Journal of Business* (51, 1978): 43-56.

Dennis, C. N. "An Investigation into the Effects of Independent Investor Relations Firms on Common Stock Prices," *Journal of Finance* (May 1973): 373-80.

Dielman, T. E., and H. R. Oppenheimer. "An Examination of Investor Behavior during Periods of Large Dividend Changes," *Journal of Financial and Quantitative Analysis* (June 1984): 197-216.

Divecha, A., and D. Morse. "Market Responses to Dividend Increases and Changes in Payout Ratios," *Journal of Quantitative Analysis* (June 1983): 163-73.

Dodd, P., N. Dopuch, R. Holthausen, and P. Leftwich. "Qualified Audit Opinions and Stock Prices," *Journal of Accounting and Economics* (April 1984): 3-38.

Dodd, P., and R. Ruback. "Tender Offers and Stockholder Returns," *Journal of Financial Economics* (December 1977): 351-73.

Dodd, P. "Merger Proposals, Management Discretion and Stockholder Wealth," *Journal of Financial Economics* (June 1980): 105-37.

Dopuch, N., R. W. Holthausen, and R. W. Leftwich. "Abnormal Stock Returns Associated with Media Disclosures of 'Subject to' Qualified Audit Opinions," *Journal of Accounting and Economics* (June 1986): 93-117.

Dowen, R. J., and W. S. Bauman. "A Fundamental Multifactor Asset Pricing Model," *Financial Analysts Journal* (July-August 1986): 45-51.

Eades, K. M., P. J. Hess, and E. H. Kim. "Market Rationality and Dividend Announcements," *Journal of Financial Economics* (December 1985): 581-604.

Ellis, C. D. "How To Manage Investor Relations," *Financial Analysts Journal* (March-April 1985): 34-41.

———. "The Loser's Game," *Financial Analysts Journal* (July-August 1975): 250-55.

Elton, E. J., and M. J. Gruber. "Estimating the Dependence Structure of Share Prices Implications for Portfolio Selection," *Journal of Finance* (December 1973): 1203-32.

Elton, E. J., M. J. Gruber, and M. Gultekin. "Expectations and Share Prices," *Management Science* (September 1981): 975-87.

———. "Professional Expectations: Accuracy and Diagnosis of Errors," *Journal of Financial and Quantitative Analysis* (December 1984): 351-63.

Elton, E. J., M. J. Gruber, and S. M. Koo. "Effect of Quarterly Earnings Announcements on Analysts' Forecasts," *Research in Finance* (6, 1986): 247-59.

Estep, T. "Manager Style and the Sources of Equity Returns," *Journal of Portfolio Management* (Winter 1987): 4-10.

Fama, E. F., L. Fisher, M. Jensen, and R. Roll. "The Adjustment of Stock Prices to New Information," *International Economic Review* (February 1969): 1-21.

Fama, E. F., and J. D. MacBeth. "Risk, Return and Equilibrium: Empirical Tests," *Journal of Political Economy* (May-June 1973): 607-36.

Farrell, J. L., Jr. "Analyzing Covariation of Returns to Determine Homogeneous Stock Groupings," *Journal of Business* (April 1974): 186-207.

_____. "Homogeneous Stock Groupings," *Financial Analysts Journal* (May-June 1975): 50-62.

"Firms Urged to Buy Street Name List," *Investor Relations Update* (January 1986): 9.

Firth, M. "The Relative Information Content of the Release of Financial Results Data by Firms," *Journal of Accounting Research* (Autumn 1981): 521-29.

Fisher L., and J. Lorie. "Some Studies of Variability of Returns on Investment in Common Stocks," *Journal of Business* (April 1970): 99-134.

"Five Types of Institutional Analysts Profiled," *Investor Relations Update* (May, 1986): 4.

Fogler, R.H. "Common Sense on CAPM, APT and Correlated Residuals," *Journal of Portfolio Management* (September 1982): 20-28.

Foster, G. "Stock Market Reaction to Estimates of Earnings Per Share by Company Officials," *Journal of Accounting Research* (Spring 1973): 25-37.

_____. "Quarterly Accounting Data: Time-Series Properties and Predictive Ability Results," *Accounting Review* (January 1977): 1-21.

_____. "Intra-Industry Information Transfers Associated with Earnings Releases," *Journal of Accounting and Economics* (December 1981): 201-32.

Fruhan, W. E., Jr. "How Fast Should Your Company Grow," *Harvard Business Review* (January-February 1984): 84-93.

Fuller, R. J., and H. S. Kerr. "Estimating the Divisional Cost of Capital: An Analysis of the Pure-Play Technique," *Journal of Finance* (December 1981).

Gale, B. T., and B. Branch. "Cash Flow Analysis: More Important Than Ever," *Harvard Business Review* (July-August 1981): 131-35.

Givoly, D., and J. Lakonishok. "The Information Content of Financial Analysts' Forecasts of Earnings," *Journal of Accounting and Economics* (December 1979): 165-85.

_____. "The Quality of Analysts' Forecasts of Earnings," *Financial Analysts Journal* (September-October 1984): 40-47.

Gordon, M., and E. Shapiro. "Capital Equipment Analysis: The Required Rate of Profit," *Management Science* (October 1952): 102-10.

Grammatikos, T., and G. Papaioannou. "Market Reaction to NYSE Listings: Tests of the Marketability Gains Hypothesis," *Journal of Financial Research* (Fall 1986): 215-27.

Grant, E. B. "Market Implications of Differential Amounts of Interim Information," *Journal of Accounting Research* (Spring 1980): 255-67.

Gray, E. R., and L. R. Smeltzer. "SMR Forum: Corporate Image An Integral Part of Strategy, " *Sloan Management Review* (Summer 1985): 73-78.

Grinblatt, M. S., R. W. Masulis, and S. Titman. "The Valuation Effects of Stock Splits and Stock Dividends," *Journal of Financial Economics* (December 1984): 461-90.

Grossman, S. J., and R. J. Shiller. "The Determinants of the Variability of Stock Market Prices," *American Economic Review* (May 1981): 222-27.

Groth, J. C. "Security-Relative Information Market Efficiency: Some Empirical Evidence, " *Journal of Financial and Quantitative Analysis* (September 1979): 573-93.

Groth, J. C., and D. R. Fraser. "Analysts' Following and the Efficiency of the Information Environment Across Securities, "*Working Paper* (1979).

Groth, J. C., and J. D. Martin. "Impact of Firm Size on Capital Market Efficiency, " *Journal of Economics and Business* (Winter 1980-1981): 166-71.

Hagerman, R. L., M. E. Zmijewski, and P. Shah. "The Association Between The Magnitude of Quarterly Earnings Forecast Errors and Risk-Adjusted Stock Returns," *Journal of Accounting Research* (Autumn 1984): 526-40.

Hamada, R. S. "The Effects of the Firm's Capital Structure on the Systematic Risk of Common Stocks," *Journal of Finance* (May 1972): 435-52.

Harrington, D. R. "Stock Price, Beta, and Strategic Planning," *Harvard Business Review* (May-June 1983).

———. "Whose Beta Is Best," *Financial Analysts Journal* (July-August 1983): 67-73.

Hassell, J. M., and R. H. Jennings. "Relative Forecast Accuracy and the Timing of Earnings Forecast Announcements," *Accounting Review* (January 1986): 58-75.

Hawkins, E. H., S. C. Chamberlin, and W. E. Daniel. "Earnings Expectations and Security Prices," *Financial Analysts Journal* (September-October 1984): 24-38.

"Hell Hath No Fury Like a Surprised Stock Analyst," *Business Week* (January 21, 1985): 98.

Hite, G. L., and J. E. Owers. "Security Price Reactions Around Corporate Spin-off Announcements," *Journal of Financial Economics* (December 1983): 409-36.

Holt, C. C. "The Influence of Growth Duration on Share Prices," *Journal of Finance* (September 1962): 465-75.

Ibbotson, R. G. "Price Performance of Common Stock New Issues," *Journal of Financial Economics* (September 1975): 235-72.

"Institutional Brokers Are Key Target," *Investor Relations Update* (January, 1986): 11.

Jarrell, G. A., and A. B. Poulsen. "Shark Repellents and Poison Pills: Stockholder Protection—From the Good Guys or the Bad Guys," *Midland Corporate Finance Journal* (Summer 1986): 39-47.

Jensen, M. C., and W. H. Meckling. "Theory of the Firm: Managerial Behavior, Agency Costs and Ownership Structure," *Journal of Financial Economics* (October 1976): 305-60.

Jensen, M. C., and R. S. Ruback. "The Market for Corporate Control: The Scientific Evidence," *Journal of Financial Economics* (April 1983): 5-50.

Jones, C. P., R. J. Rendleman, and H. A. Latane. "Stock Returns and SUEs During the 1970's," *Journal of Portfolio Management* (Winter 1984): 18-22.

Kalay, A., and U. Loewenstein. "Predictable Events and Excess Returns," *Journal of Financial Economics* (September 1985): 423-49.

———. "The Informational Content of the Timing of Dividend Announcements," *Journal of Financial Economics* (July 1986): 373-88.

Kaplan, R. S., and R. Roll. "Investor Evaluation of Accounting Information: Some Empirical Evidence," *Journal of Business* (April 1972): 225-57.

Keim, D. B. "The CAPM and Equity Return Regularities," *Financial Analysts Journal* (May-June 1986): 19-34.

Kellogg, R. L. "Accounting Activities, Security Prices and Class Action Lawsuits," *Journal of Accounting and Economics* (December 1984): 185-204.

Kennedy, R. E., and M. H. Wilson. "Are Investor Relations Programs Giving Analysts What They Need?," *Financial Analysts Journal* (March-April 1980): 63-69.

Kiger, J. "An Empirical Investigation of NYSE Volume and Price Reactions to the Announcements of Quarterly Earnings," *Journal of Accounting Research* (Spring 1972): 113-28.

King, B. F. "Market and Industry Factors in Stock Price Behavior,"*Journal of Business* (January 1966): 139-90.

Kross, W., and D. A. Schroeder. "An Empirical Investigation of the Effect of Quarterly Earnings Announcement Timing on Stock Returns," *Journal of Accounting Research* (Spring 1984): 153-76.

Lakonishok, J., and S. Smidt. "Trading Bargains in Small Firms at Year-End," *Journal of Portfolio Management* (Spring 1986): 24-29.

Lambert, R. A., and D. F. Larcker. "Golden Parchutes, Executive Decision-Making, and Shareholder Wealth," *Journal of Accounting and Economics* (April 1985): 179-203.

Levitt, T. "Marketing Success Through Differentiation of Anything," *Harvard Business Review* (January-February 1980): 83-91.

Lev, B. "On the Association Between Leverage and Risk," *Journal of Financial and Quantitative Analysis* (September 1974): 627-42.

Linn, S. C., and J. J. McConnell. "An Empirical Investigation of the Impact of 'Anti-takeover' Amendments on Common Stock Prices," *Journal of Financial Economics* (April 1983): 361-99.

Lintner, J. "The Valuation of Risk Assets and the Selection of Risky Investments in Stock Portfolios and Capital Budgets," *Journal of Finance* (December 1965): 587-614.

Loeb, T. F. "Trading Cost: The Critical Link Between Investment Information and Results," *Financial Analysts Journal* (May-June 1983): 39-44.

Logue, D. "On the pricing of unseasoned equity issues: 1965-1969," *Journal of Financial and Quantitative Analysis* (January 1973): 91-103.

Malkiel, B. G., and J. G. Cragg. "Expectations and the Structure of Share Prices," *American Economic Review* (60, 1970): 601-17.

"Managers of America's Wealth," *Pensions & Investment Age* (May 6, 1985).

Markowitz, H. "Portfolio Selection," *Journal of Finance* (March 1952): 77-91.

Martin, J. D., and R. C. Klemkosky. "The Effect of Homogeneous Stock Grouping on Portfolio Risk," *Journal of Business* (July 1976): 339-49.

Masulis, R. W. "The Effects of Capital Structure Changes on Security Prices: A Study of Exchange Offers," *Journal of Financial Economics* (June 1980): 139-78.

McConnell, J. J., and C. J. Muscarella. "Corporate Capital Expenditure Decisions and the Market Value of the Firm," *Journal of Financial Economics* (September 1985): 399-422.

McConnell, J. J., and G.C. Sanger. "A Trading Strategy for New Listings on the NYSE," *Financial Analysts Journal* (January-February 1984): 34-38.

———. "The Puzzle in Post-Listing Common Stock Returns," *Journal of Finance* (March 1987): 119-40.

McNichols, M., and J. G. Manegold. "The Effect of the Information Environment on the Relationship Between Financial Disclosure and Security Price Variability," *Journal of Accounting and Economics* (April 1983): 49-74.

Mikkelson, W. H., and M. M. Partch. "Stock Price Effects and Costs of Secondary Distributions," *Journal of Financial Economics* (14, 1985): 165-94.

Mikkelson, W. H., and R. S. Ruback. "An Empirical Analysis of the Interfirm Equity Investment Process," *Journal of Financial Economics* (December 1985): 523-53.

Miller, M. H., and F. Modigliani. "The Cost of Capital, Corporation Finance and the Theory of Investment," *American Economic Review* (June 1958): 261-97.

———. "Dividend Policy, Growth and The Valuation of Shares," *Journal of Business* (October 1961): 411-33.

Miller, R. E., and F. K. Reilly. "An Examination of Mispricing, Returns, and Uncertainty for Initial Public Offerings," *Financial Management* (Summer 1987): 33-38.

Molodovsky, N., C. May, and S. Chottiner. "Common Stock Valuation: Theory and Tables," *Financial Analysts Journal* (March-April 1965): 104-23.

Morse, D. "Price and Trading Volume Reaction Surrounding Earnings Announcements: A Closer Examination," *Journal of Accounting Research* (Autumn 1981): 374-83.

———. "Wall Street Journal Announcements and the Securities Markets," *Financial Analysts Journal* (March/April 1982): 69-76.

Mullins, D. W., Jr. "Does the Capital Asset Pricing Model Work?" *Harvard Business Review* (January-February 1982): 105-14.

Murphy, K. J. "Corporate Performance and Managerial Remuneration," *Journal of Accounting and Economics* (April 1985): 11-42.

Murray, D. "Further Evidence on the Liquidity Effects of Stock Splits and Stock Dividends," *Journal of Financial Research* (Spring 1985): 59-67.

Myers, S. C., and N. S. Majluf. "Corporate Financing and Investment Decisions When Firms Have Information That Investors Do Not Have," *Journal of Financial Economics* (June 1984): 187-221.

Myers, S. C. "The Search for Optimal Capital Structure," *Revolutions in Corporate Finance* (New York: Basil Blackwell, 1986): 91-99.

Niederhoffer, V., and P. J. Regan. "Earnings Changes, Analysts' Forecasts, and Stock Prices," *Financial Analysts Journal* (May-June 1972): 65-71.

Offer, A. R., and A. J. Thalor. "A Theory of Stock Price Responses to Alternative Corporate Cash Disbursement Methods: Stock Repurchases and Dividends," *Journal of Finance* (June 1987): 365-94.

Oppenheimer, H. R. "A Test of Ben Graham's Stock Selection Criteria," *Financial Analysts Journal* (September-October 1984): 68-74.

———. "Ben Graham's Net Current Asset Values: A Performance Update," *Financial Analysts Journal* (November-December 1986): 40-47.

Patell, J. M. "Corporate Forecasts of Earnings Per Share and Stock Price Behavior: Empirical Tests," *Journal of Accounting Research* (Autumn 1976): 246-76.

Peavy, J. W. III, and D. A. Goodman. "How Inflation, Risk and Corporate Profitability Affect Common Stock Returns," *Financial Analysts Journal* (September-October 1985): 59-65.

Peavy, J. W. III, and J. A. Scott. "A Closer Look at Stock-for-Debt Swaps," *Financial Analysts Journal* (May-June 1985): 44-50.

Penman, S. H. "An Empirical Investigation of the Voluntary Disclosure of Corporate Earnings Forecasts," *Journal of Accounting Research* (Spring 1980): 132-60.

_____. "Abnormal Returns to Investment Strategies Based on the Timing of Earnings Reports," *Journal of Accounting and Economics* (December 1984): 165-83.

_____. "A Comparison of the Information Content of Insider Trading and Management Earnings Forecasts," *Journal of Financial and Quantitative Analysis* (March 1985): 1-17.

_____. "The Distribution of Earnings News Over Time and Seasonalities in Aggregate Stock Returns," *Journal of Financial Economics* (June 1987): 199-228.

Phelan, J. J., Jr. "1985 National Shareownership Study." Speech to Securities Industry Association (December 4, 1985).

Piper T. R., and W. E. Fruhan, Jr. "Is Your Stock Worth Its Market Price," *Harvard Business Review* (May-June 1981): 124-32.

Posner, B. G. "Back to Basics," *Inc.* (February 1986): 81-87.

"Profiles of European Markets," *Investor Relations Update* (February, 1985): 4-5.

Pruitt, S. W., and L. J. Gitman. "Capital Budgeting Forecast Biases: Evidence from the Fortune 500," *Financial Management* (Spring 1987): 46-51.

Rappaport, A. "Strategic Analysis for More Profitable Acquisitions," *Harvard Business Review* (July-August 1979): 99-110.

_____. "The Affordable Dividend Approach to Equity Valuation," *Financial Analysts Journal* (July-August 1986): 52-58.

Rea, J. B. "Remembering Benjamin Graham—Teacher and Friend," *Journal of Portfolio Management* (Summer 1977): 66-72.

Reader, A. C. "The Care and Feeding of Buy-Side Analysts," *Financial Analysts Journal* (March–April 1981): 42-51.

"Regional Firms Growing in Size, Quality," *Investor Relations Update* (July/August, 1985): 5.

Reilly, F. K. "Institutions on Trial: Not Guilty," *Journal of Portfolio Management* (Winter 1977): 5-10.

Reilly, F. K., and J. M. Wachowicz, Jr. "How Institutional Trading Reduces Market Volatility," *Journal of Portfolio Management* (Winter 1979): 11-7.

Reilly, F. K., and D. J. Wright. "Block Trading and Aggregate Stock Price Volatility," *Financial Analysts Journal* (March/April 1984): 54-60.

Rendleman, R. J., Jr., C. P. Jones, and H. A. Latane. "Empirical Anomalies Based on Unexpected Earnings and the Importance of Risk Adjustments," *Journal of Financial Economics* (November 1982): 269-87.

Richardson, G., S. E. Sefcik, and R. Thompson. "A Test of Dividend Irrelevance Using Volume Reactions to a Change in Dividend Policy," *Journal of Financial Economics* (December 1986): 313-33.

Ritter, J. R. "The 'Hot Issue' Market of 1980," *Journal of Business* (April 1984): 215-40.

Roll, R., and S. A. Ross. "An Empirical Investigation of the Arbitrage Pricing Theory." *Journal of Finance* (December 1980): 1073-103.

———. "The Arbitrage Pricing Theory Approach to Strategic Portfolio Planning." *Financial Analysts Journal* (May-June 1986): 14-26.

Rosenberg, B., and J. Guy. "Prediction of Beta from Investment Fundamentals," *Financial Analysts Journal* (May-June 1976): 3-15.

Ross, S. A. "The Arbitrage Theory of Capital Asset Pricing," *Journal of Economic Theory* (December 1976): 341-60.

Rozeff, M. "How Companies Set Their Dividend-Payout Ratios," *Issues in Corporate Finance* (1982): 151-57.

Ruhnka, J., and J. W. Bagby. "Disclosure: Damned If You Do, Damned If You Don't," *Harvard Business Review* (September-October 1986): 34-43.

Ruland, W. "The Accuracy of Forecasts by Managements and by Financial Analysts," *Accounting Review* (April 1978): 439-47.

Sanger, G. C. and J.J. McConnell. "Stock Exchange Listings, Firm Value, and Security Market Efficiency: The Impact of NASDAQ," *Journal of Financial and Quantitative Analysis* (March 1986): 1-23.

Schaefer, J. M. "Introducing SIA's Investor Activity Report," *Trends: Securities Industry Association* (July 31, 1985).

Schipper, K., and A. Smith. "A Comparison of Equity Carve-outs and Seasoned Equity Offerings: Share Price Effects and Corporate Restructuring," *Journal of Financial Economics* (January-February 1986): 153-86.

Schipper, K., and R. Thompson. "The Impact of Merger-Related Regulations on the Shareholders of Acquiring Firms," *Journal of Accounting Research* (Spring 1983): 184-221.

Scholes, M. "The Market for Securities: Substitution versus Price Pressure and the Effects of Information on Share Prices," *Journal of Business* (April 1972): 179-211.

Scott, D. F., Jr., and D. J. Johnson. "Financial Policies and Practices in Large Corporations," *Financial Management* (Summer 1982): 51-9.

Seitz, N. "Shareholder Goals, Firm Goals and Firm Financing Decisions," *Financial Management* (Autumn 1982): 20-26.

Sharpe, W. F. "Capital Asset Prices: A Theory of Market Equilibrium Under Conditions of Risk," *Journal of Finance* (September 1964): 425-44.

———. "Some Factors in New York Stock Exchange Security Returns, 1931-1979," *Journal of Portfolio Management* (Summer 1982), pp. 5-19.

———. "Factor Models, CAPMs, and the ABT," *Journal of Portfolio Management* (Fall 1984): 21-24.

Siegel. J. G. "The Quality of Earnings Concept—A Survey," *Financial Analysts Journal* (March-April 1982): 60-68.

Skantz, T. R., and R. Marchesini. "The Effect of Voluntary Corporate Liquidation on Shareholder Wealth," *Journal of Financial Research* (Spring 1987): 65-75.

Smirlock, M., and L. Starks. "A Further Examination of Stock Price Changes and Transaction Volume," *Journal of Financial Research* (Fall 1985): 217-25.

Smith, D. B., and D. R. Nichols. "A Market Test of Investor Reactions to Disagreements," *Journal of Accounting and Economics* (October 1982): 109-20.

Smith, C. W., Jr. "Investment Banking and the Capital Acquisition Process," *Journal of Financial Economics* (January/February 1986): 3-29.

Sorensen, E. H., and T. Burke. "Portfolio Returns from Active Industry Group Rotation," *Financial Analysts Journal* (September-October 1986): 43-69.

Sorensen, E. H., and D.A. Williamson. "Some Evidence on the Value of Dividend Discount Models," *Financial Analysts Journal* (November-December 1985): 60-69.

Stanley, K. L., W. G. Lewellen, and G. C. Schlarbaum, "Investor Response to Investment Research," *Journal of Portfolio Management* (Summer 1980): 20-27.

Statman, M. "Growth Opportunities vs. Growth Stocks," *Journal of Portfolio Management* (Spring 1984): 70-74.

Stern, J. (moderator). "A Discussion of Corporate Financial Communication," *Midland Corporate Finance Journal* (Spring 1984): 40-72.

Stewart, G. B., and D. M. Glassman. "How to Communicate with an Efficient Market," *Midland Corporate Finance Journal* (Spring 1984): 73-79.

Stickel, S. E. "The Effect of Value Line Investment Survey Rank Changes on Common Stock Prices," *Journal of Financial Economics* (March 1985): 121-43.

Sutton, D. P., and T. Post. "The Cost of Going Public," *Venture* (April 1986): 30-40.

Tehranian, H., and J. F. Waegelein. "Market Reaction to Short-Term Executive Compensation Plan Adoption," *Journal of Accounting and Economics* (April 1985): 131-44.

Timbers, S. "The Non-Efficient Sector Is Not For Institutions," *Journal of Portfolio Management* (Fall 1977): 59-64.

Titman, S., and B. Trueman. "Information Quality and the Valuation of New Issues," *Journal of Accounting and Economics* (June 1986): 159-172.

"The Top 1000," *Business Week* (April 18, 1986).

Treynor, J. "What Does It Take To Win The Trading Game," *Financial Analysts Journal* (January-February 1981): 55-60.

————. "The Financial Objective of the Widely-Held Corporation," *Financial Analysts Journal* (March-April 1981): 68-71.

Trueman, B. "Why Do Managers Voluntarily Release Earnings Forecasts," *Journal of Accounting and Economics* (March 1986): 53-71.

Van Horne, J. C. "An Application of the Capital Asset Pricing Model to Divisional Required Returns," *Financial Management* (Spring 1980).

Vermaelen, T. "Common Stock Repurchases and Market Signalling: An Empirical Study," *Journal of Financial Economics* (June 1981): 139-83.

Verrecchia, R. E. "On the Relationship Between Volume Reaction and Consensus of Investors: Implications for Interpreting Tests of Information Content," *Journal of Accounting Research* (Spring 1981): 271-83.

Wagner, W. H. "Piecing the Puzzle of '84 Performance," *Pensions & Investment Age* (March 18, 1985): 36.

Watts, R. L. "Systematic Abnormal Returns After Quarterly Earnings Announcements," *Journal of Financial Economics* (Summer 1978): 127-50.

Waymire, G. "Additional Evidence on the Information Content of Management Earnings Forecasts," *Journal of Accounting Research* (Autumn 1984): 703-18.

———. "Earnings Volatility and Voluntary Management Forecast Disclosure," *Journal of Accounting Research* (Spring 1985): 268-95.

Wilcox, J. W. "The P/B-ROE Valuation Model," *Financial Analysts Journal* (January-February 1984): 58-66.

Woolridge, J. R. "Dividend Changes and Security Prices," *Journal of Finance* (December 1983): 1607-15.

Woolridge, J. R., and D. R. Chambers. "Reverse Splits and Shareholder Wealth," *Financial Management* (Autumn 1983): 5-15.

Zaima, J. K., and D. Hearth. "The Wealth Effects of Voluntary Sell-offs: Implications for Divesting and Acquiring Firms," *Journal of Financial Research* (Fall 1985): 227-36.

Zuccaro, R. "Finding the Whys and the Wherefores Behind Small-Stock Theory," *Pensions & Investment Age* (March 5, 1984), p.32

NEWSPAPERS

Anders, G. "Investment Advisers Beat S & P 500 Index In Magic Year," *Wall Street Journal* (January 2, 1986), p. 4B.

———. "Powerful Trader Relies On Information Net, Timing and a Hot Pace," *Wall Street Journal* (March 3, 1986), p. 1.

———. "Managers Fail To Equal Rise Of Benchmarks In Stocks, Bonds," *Wall Street Journal* (January 2, 1987), p. 4B.

———. "Institutional Holders Irked by 'Poison Pill'," *Wall Street Journal* (March 10, 1987): 6.

Bean, E. "National Healthcare's Ailments Mount," *Wall Street Journal* (September 4, 1987), p. 2.

Boland, J. C. "A Down-to-Earth Look at Travel Stocks," *New York Times* (May 4, 1986), p. 12F.

———. "The Tax Bill Stirs Wall Street's Juices," *New York Times* (June 1, 1986), p. 12F.

Buffett, W. "Capital Sin," *Barron's* (April 7, 1986), p. 13.

Bulkeley, W. M. "A Firm by Any Other Name Means Likely Rise in Stock, Research Finds," *Wall Street Journal* (July 10, 1987), p 22.

Casey, C., and N. J. Bartczak. "Another Look at Cash Flow," *New York Times* (April 8, 1984), p. 3F.

"Companies Feel Underrated By The Street," *Business Week* (February 20, 1984): 14.

Crudele, J. "Allied-Signal's Blurred Image," *New York Times* (August 6, 1986), p. 4D.

———. "Investing to Meet Objectives," *New York Times* (September 14, 1986), p. 16.

DeMaria, L. J. "Finding Winners Among Small Stocks," *New York Times* (January 26, 1986), p. 12F.

Donnelly, B. "Investors Looking for 'Neglected' Stocks Shouldn't Rule Out Big Issues, Studies Say," *Wall Street Journal* (January 28, 1987), p. 31.

Dorfman, D. "The OTC Market Is Booming Again," *Greenwich (CT) Time* (February 16, 1986), p. 1E.

Fogelson, J. H. "Disclosure Laws Retain Teeth Despite Recent Court Limitations," *National Law Journal* (February 22, 1982), p. 30.

Fowler, E. M. "Managers to Handle a Crisis," *New York Times* (January 30, 1985), p. 19D.

Gilman, H. "Singer Co. Plans to Divest Itself of Sewing Line," *Wall Street Journal* (February 19, 1986), p. 12.

Greenhouse, S. "The Folly of Inflating Quarterly Profits," *New York Times* (March 2, 1986), pp. 1F.

"Growth Stock Sampler," *Barron's* (June 2, 1986), p. 18.

Gupta, U. "As Initial Public Stock Offerings Heat Up, Analysts See Pitfalls for the Public," *Wall Street Journal* (July 22, 1986), p. 33.

Jensen, M. C. "How to Detect a Prime Takeover Target," *New York Times* (March 9, 1986), p. 3F.

Johnson, R., and B. Morris. "Food Companies Fight to Display More Food Products on Less Shelf Space," *Wall Street Journal* (April 10, 1986), p. 35.

Kanabayashi, M. "Tokyo Shares: The Money Magnet Grows," *Wall Street Journal* (July 15, 1986), p. 32.

Kleinfield, N. R. "The Many Faces of the Wall Street Analyst," *New York Times* (October 27, 1985), p. 8F.

"Laidlaw Boosts Research, Trading," *Wall Street Letter* (September 9, 1985), p. 5.

Lazo, S. A. "Speaking of Dividends," *Barron's* (March 10, 1986), p. 65.

Levin, D. P. "General Motors May Be on the Road to Giving Additional Financial Information to Analysts," *Wall Street Journal* (December 27, 1985), p.31.

Lohr, S. "A Lure to Go Public in Britain," *New York Times* (May 16, 1986), p. 1D.

Lueck, T. J. "Can Fidelity Maintain Its Frenzied Growth?" *New York Times* (March 16, 1986), p. 6F.

Monroe, A. "Just Like Film Stars, Wall Streeters Battle to Get Top Billing," *Wall Street Journal* (January 15, 1986), p. 1.

Nesbitt, S. "'Hot Money' Can Trip Up Fast Track Advisory Firms," *Pensions and Investment Age* (September 5, 1983): 40.

Rivel, A. "The Changing Role of the Stockbroker," *Amex Journal* (December 1972): 1.

Robb, G. A. "Updated Study of Dual Stocks," *New York Times* (July 17, 1987), p. 4D.

Rosett, C. "Chicago School Bets on Inefficiency," *New York Times* (December 11, 1983), p. 10F.

Salpukas, A. "Philip Morris Chairman Studies Several Options," *New York Times* (September 30, 1985), p. 1D.

Sandler, L. "Henley's Huge Initial Offering Casts Shadow on Stock's Future, Some Money Managers Say," *Wall Street Journal* (May 21, 1986), p. 63.

Sebastian, P. "Many Small Investors Quit Picking Stocks, Shift to Mutual Funds," *Wall Street Journal* (February 7, 1986), p. 1.

Sesit, M. R. "U.S. Institutions Find Buying Foreign Stocks Can Be Very Profitable," *Wall Street Journal* (June 3, 1986), p. 1.

Silk, L. "Recovering from the Era of Shocks," *New York Times* (January 8, 1984), p. 1F.

———. "The Confident Stock Market," *New York Times* (March 6, 1987), p. 2D.

Slater, K. "Stellar Results Can Reverse Fast When Mutual Funds Stress Risks," *Wall Street Journal* (December 30, 1985), p. 15.

Smith, R. "IBM Posts Rise Of 23% in Profit For 4th Quarter," *Wall Street Journal* (January 20, 1986), p. 2.

"Two Founders Quit at Entre Computer," *New York Times* (June 23, 1986), p. 2D.

Vartan, V. G. "I.B.M. Stock Still Favored," *New York Times* (June 17, 1985), p. 6D.

_____. "Hospital Corp., 'Fallen Angel'," *New York Times* (October 24, 1985), p. 10D.

_____. "G.M. May Lag Behind Rivals," *New York Times* (December 31, 1985), p. 6D.

_____. "Dividend Rise Candidates," *New York Times* (January 29, 1986), p. 6D.

_____. "Many Eyes on Microsoft," *New York Times* (February 11, 1986), p. 10D.

_____. "Stock-Splitting Surge Is Seen," *New York Times* (March 6, 1986), p. 8D.

_____. "Morgan Stanley's Stock Soars to Big Premium," *New York Times* (March 22, 1986), p. 35.

_____. "Institutions Tilt To Data Stocks," *New York Times* (May 30, 1986), p. 6D.

_____. "Stock Buying by Foreigners," *New York Times* (June 26, 1986), p. 8D.

_____. "I.B.M.'s Stock Losing Luster," *New York Times* (July 16, 1986), p. 6D.

Wallace, A. "The Herd Moves to Growth Stocks," *New York Times* (April 13, 1986), p. 10F.

Wallace, A. C. "The Wisdom of a Limited Stock Portfolio," *New York Times* (March 2, 1986), 12F.

Watkins, L. M. "Coleco's New Toys Aren't Expected to Provide Success of Firm's Cabbage Patch Dolls Line," *Wall Street Journal* (June 23, 1986), p. 43.

Wayne, L. "A Look at New Corporate Tactics to Bolster the Value of Shares," *New York Times* (February 26, 1984), p. 6-7F.

Weiner, S. "Sears's Diversification Effort Isn't Paying Off," *Wall Street Journal* (April 22, 1986), p. 6.

Wessel, D. "Partial Spinoffs Offer Investors a Chance To Get in on a Real Winner—or Real Flop," *Wall Street Journal* (July 17, 1986), p. 27.

Yoshihashi, P. "What Suitors Saw in Alamito," *New York Times* (April 10, 1986), p. 1D.

Index

About the Author

RICHARD M. ALTMAN is the Director of Altman & Co., an equity valuation training and strategy firm. Prior to this, he was the director of Investor Marketing Services at a national financial communications firm, and manager of Investor Relations/Financial Communications for two New York Stock Exchange companies. The stock price of the first quintupled. The stock price of the second quadrupled. He was also involved in institutional securities sales for Goldman, Sachs & Co. He has written articles for *The Boston Globe, New England Business*, the *Harvard Business School Bulletin*, and *Investment Decisions*, and he developed and taught the first course in business/financial journalism at Boston University's College of Communication.

ISBN 0-89930-173-8

EAN

90000>

9 780899 301730

HARDCOVER BARCODE